The Encyclopedia of
Gemstones
and Minerals

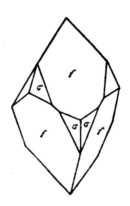

The Encyclopedia of
Gemstones and Minerals

Martin Holden

Consulting Editor
E. A. Mathez, Ph.D.
Associate Curator of Petrology
American Museum of Natural History
New York, New York

Principal Photography by
The British Museum (Natural History)

With line drawings from
Viktor Goldschmidt's Atlas der Krystallformen

Facts On File
New York • Oxford

A FRIEDMAN GROUP BOOK

Copyright © 1991 by Michael Friedman Publishing Group, Inc.

Facts On File, Inc.   Facts On File, Limited
460 Park Avenue South   Collins Street
New York, New York 10016   Oxford OX4 1XJ
USA   United Kingdom

Library of Congress Cataloging-in-Publication Data

Holden, Martin.
   The encyclopedia of gemstones and minerals / Martin Holden; consulting editor, E.A. Mathez.
      p.   cm.
   Includes bibliographical references and index.
   IBSN 0-8160-2177-5
   1. Gems—Encyclopedias.   2. Mineralogy—Encyclopedias.   I. Title.
   QE392.H65   1991
   553.8'03—dc20   917782
                                                    CIP

A British CIP Catalogue record for this book is available from the British Library.

Facts On File books are available at special discounts when purchased in bulk quantities for business associations, institutions or sales promotions. Please call our Special Sales Department in New York at 212/683-2244 (dial 800/322-8755 except in NY, AK or HI) or in Oxford at 865/728399.

THE ENCYCLOPEDIA OF GEMSTONES AND MINERALS
was prepared and produced by
Michael Friedman Publishing Group, Inc.
15 West 26th Street
New York, New York 10010

Editor: Nancy Berliner
Art Director: Jeff Batzli
Designer: Jill Feltham
Illustrator: Irena Pomerantzeff
Photography Editor: Christopher C. Bain
Production: Karen L. Greenberg

Color separation by Scantrans Pte Ltd.
Printed and bound in Hong Kong by Leefung-Asco Printers, Ltd.

10 9 8 7 6 5 4 3 2 1

Preface

This encyclopedia is meant to serve a diverse audience. It is appropriate for the non-specialist, particularly high school students and other young readers whose curiosity of nature is just awakening; it can be used to complement courses on earth science or natural history; it may serve as a primary source of information for the beginning or casual collector or merely the erudite; and it will be equally important for the serious collector. For the latter it is not meant to take the place of encyclopedias of technical information but to complement them by emphasizing that which helps to give a sense of knowledge greater than the collection itself.

The wide appeal of this volume arises because minerals are not treated as simply objects to be collected and catalogued but as a means of understanding nature. Minerals tell us something about the earth, so connections are made between minerals, their conditions of formation, and their geologic settings. The geologic context is provided by sections describing specific rock types (e.g., the igneous rocks), environments in which certain minerals occur together (e.g., cavities in basalts), and phenomena that impart to individual minerals geologic significance (e.g., radioactivity and age dating). In addition, minerals illustrate the symmetry of nature, giving us pause to ponder its beauty. The form of minerals reflects an order of the submicroscopic world and poses the question of why atoms fit together as they do. Thus, while avoiding systematic treatment more appropriate for a text, this volume does provide the general crystal-chemical framework. Individual sections include information on mineral compositions and elemental substitutions, and most sections on mineral groups include a description of general structure, which serves to illustrate how minerals of diverse compositions are related. The periodic table of the elements is included for convenient reference. There is also attention devoted to both the current and traditional uses of minerals, emphasizing how society and nature have impinged on each other and our dependency on our physical world. Finally, many readers will find interesting simply the treatment of etymology.

E. A. Mathez, Ph.D.
Associate Curator of Petrology
American Museum of Natural History
New York, New York

Acknowledgments

This book is a result of the combined efforts of the many people who took a genuine interest in its development, editing, and production. Foremost among these was Dr. Edmond Mathez of the American Museum of Natural History, who drew upon his broad knowledge of rock-forming minerals and earth history to expand the scope of the book and eliminate inaccuracies. I am also indebted to Nancy Berliner for her tireless editorial efforts, and for her many insightful comments on the text. Thanks to Jill Feltham's modern design sensibility, the technical and aesthetic aspects of the book have been united in an entirely original way. Christopher Bain and Jeff Batzli of the Michael Friedman Publishing Group made every effort to secure quality illustrations and maintain high production values under difficult circumstances.

Others provided valuable and unique illustrative materials, which helped to make the book far more visually interesting. The unique creative talents of Irina Pomerantzeff brought the original illustrations to life. Dennis Cox of the United States Geological Survey provided unique photographs from his world-wide travels researching mineral resources in the public interest. Also invaluable were Justin Kerr's inimitable photographs of ancient artifacts. Among the other photographers who graciously provided illustrative materials were Wendell E. Wilson, Cal Graeber, and Breck Kent. Nancy Green at the Wood's Hole Oceanographic Institution, and Linda Novak of the USG Corporation were particularly helpful institutional contacts.

ACTINOLITE AND TREMOLITE HAVE THE SAME CHEMICAL FORMULA BUT DIFFER IN THE proportion of iron to magnesium, with tremolite being relatively depleted in iron. Both form similar crystalline aggregates, including the compact variety known as nephrite jade. Each of the two distinct minerals which can be called jade—nephrite and jadeite—had hundreds of spiritual and curative powers assigned to them by the Chinese and the Indians of Mesoamerica, respectively. Only one of these beliefs became widely accepted in Europe, however: the idea that an amulet of jade worn close to the aggrieved organ could protect the wearer from kidney failure. Jade in general was thus referred to as *lapis nephriticus*, Greek for "kidney stone"; when a chemical distinction was finally made between the two varieties of jade, this phrase provided the name nephrite. The name actinolite comes from the Greek word for ray, *actis*—a reference to the radiating habit of its crystals; tremolite is named for the occurrence at Val Tremola in the Swiss Alps.

There are two forms of jade: nephrite, and the massive form of the pyroxene jadeite. Both share the property of extreme toughness, which arises from their compact textures. The structure of nephrite is characterized by a dense felted mass of short fibers, whereas jadeite consists of an aggregate of more equant microscopic grains. Jadeite is the harder of the two jades but nephrite has greater strength, resisting pressures of over 90,000 pounds per square inch (6000 atmospheres) in laboratory tests. This property made nephrite the stone of choice for making tools and weapons in non-metalworking cultures wherever it was found. Nephrite artifacts were made by slowly and arduously abrading the stone into the desired shape. Like many other cultural groups around the world, the native Maori of New Zealand used nephrite for many of the same purposes that metal artifacts fulfilled in contemporaneous Eurasian cultures. Among the variety of spiritual carvings, tools, and weapons fashioned by the Maori was the lethal *mere*—a combination sword and club which rendered them nearly invincible in hand-to-hand combat.

Nephrite was the most highly valued of gems among the Chinese for millennia, and the artisans of the Imperial Court labored to produce the finest and most intricate carvings imaginable. The stone had great spiritual significance for the Chinese, symbolizing the connection between heaven and earth. Ritual objects made from *lao-yu* (jade) included the pierced discs called *pi*, through which priests and nobles spoke to heaven. Iron-poor, light-colored "muttonfat" nephrite was the most prized in antiquity, but each of the many different shades was given its own ritual meaning. The boulders of nephrite used in China were imported by caravan from the Yurung-kash (White Jade) and Kara-kash (Black Jade) Rivers,

actinolite and tremolite

Classification:
inosilicates, amphibole group

Composition:
$Ca_2(Mg,Fe^{+2})_5Si_8O_{22}(OH)_2$
(hydrous calcium magnesium iron silicates)

Crystal System:
monoclinic

Hardness:
5–6

Specific Gravity:
2.98–3.46 increasing with iron content

Left: *Water-worn nephrite cobbles, like this one from the Mur River in Austria, were an important raw material for tool-making in non-metalworking cultures around the world.*
Right: *Characteristically elongate, bladed actinolite crystals in matrix, from Tasa Province, Japan.*

Nephrite boulder carved in China during the 19th century, depicting a scene from the life of Buddha.

which drain the Kunlun Mountains above the remote Khotan Oasis in the Taklamakan Desert. Only in recent years did jadeite (known as *fei-cui-yu*, or "kingfisher jade") find its way from its major source in Burma to the Chinese.

Actinolite and tremolite also occur as discrete crystals, usually elongated and bladed but also short prismatic. These are frequently twinned, and display perfect prismatic cleavage and an uneven fracture. A fibrous variety of tremolite has been mined in the past as a source of asbestos (see *Serpentine*). Actinolite is dark to light green in color, and tremolite may be white, light green, pink, or brown. Both are transparent to translucent with a vitreous luster. The variety nephrite may be cream-colored to dark green or black, depending on its iron content. It has a somewhat greasy luster and a more uniform color than jadeite, which has a vitreous luster and is frequently mottled. Tremolite resembles wollastonite and sillimanite, but unlike the former is not dissolved in hydrochloric acid, and unlike the latter, has two directions of cleavage. Massive serpentine is the most common substitute used to imitate nephrite, but differs in its lower hardness. Less easily detected substitutes include the harder cryptocrystalline aggregates of vesuvianite (known as californite), and green grossularite garnet, both of which differ from nephrite in density.

Actinolite and tremolite are widespread in their distribution, the former occurring in regionally metamorphosed dolomites and the latter in metamorphic rocks of the greenschist facies. Fine crystals of actinolite occur in the Austrian Alps and in several areas of the Italian Alps. The best North American specimens are found in talc near Chester, Vermont, and Wenatchee, Washington. Excellent white crystals of tremolite are found in the eponymous locality at Val Tremola, Switzerland, and at Greiner, Austria. Good specimens are also obtained from several locations in New York State, and in Ontario and Quebec.

Occurrences of nephrite are much more limited. While the ancient deposits continue to be exploited in Chinese Turkestan and along the Arahura, Hokitika, and Taramakau Rivers of New Zealand, the main commercial sources of nephrite today are located in Australia, Alaska, and British Columbia. Smaller deposits occur in California, Wyoming, Germany, Poland, Italy, Zimbabwe, the Soviet Union, Japan, Korea, New Caledonia, and the Cyclops Mountains of New Guinea.

adamite

Classification:
arsenate

Composition:
$Zn_2AsO_4(OH)$ (hydrous zinc arsenate)

Crystal System:
orthorhombic

Hardness:
3.5

Specific Gravity:
4.4

Globular clusters of adamite on limonite matrix from the EZ Mine, Beltana, Flinders Range, South Australia.

ADAMITE IS ONE OF THE MANY COLORFUL SECONDARY MINERALS FOUND IN THE OXIdized upper parts of hydrothermal sulfide veins, along with limonite, calcite, smithsonite, azurite, malachite, and other species. It is named for the

19th century French mineralogist Gilbert Joseph Adam (b. 1795), who first circulated adamite specimens among scholars. Because of its bright color, vitreous luster, and interesting habit, it is one of the most sought-after species for collections.

Adamite crystals are usually elongated and divergent, growing as radial aggregates from a central point, with only their wedge-shaped terminations visible at the surface of the cluster. Variations on this habit include spherical clusters and drusy coatings on matrix. Individual tabular or equidimensional crystals are known, but are very rare. The typical coloration is a vibrant greenish yellow, but green, pink, violet, and colorless specimens are not uncommon. The luster is vitreous to oily, and the streak colorless or very faintly colored. Adamite typically fluoresces lemon-yellow under ultraviolet light. The typical aggregate habits of adamite are sufficient to distinguish it from other species, and its considerable heft is also distinctive.

Probably the best-known source of adamite specimens is Mina Ojuela at Mapimí, in Durango, Mexico, where beautiful, bright, yellow-green adamite clusters are found growing on rust-red slabs of limonite. Magnificent specimens of adamite are also recovered from the mines at Tsumeb, Namibia. Although rarely occurring as outstanding specimens, adamite is found in a number of deposits in California, Nevada, and Utah. The most important European sources are Laurium, Greece; and Cap Garonne, Var, France. Good specimens of adamite are also obtained from Algeria, Australia, Chile, Germany, and Turkey.

THIS PYROXENE IS NAMED FOR THE NORSE GOD OF THE SEA, AEGIR, BECAUSE specimens were first reported from the coast of Norway. The alternate name—acmite—is derived from the Greek *acme*, meaning "point," and refers to the characteristic termination of this mineral's columnar, prismatic crystals. The distinctive sharp termination helps to distinguish aegirine from the otherwise very similar pyroxene augite. The sodium and iron (Fe^{3+}) in aegirine may be replaced by the calcium, magnesium, and iron (Fe^{2+}) characteristic of augite, creating an intermediate species called aegirine–augite. Such crystals are often zoned, with an outer layer of primarily sodic composition surrounding an augite core. These relationships are best observed in polished thin-sections under the microscope.

Aegirine forms translucent green, brown, or nearly black crystals that have a vitreous luster, a pale brown streak, and an imperfect cleavage parallel to the prism faces. Crystals commonly occur as rough grains or fibrous aggregates.

Aegirine is a common constituent of silica-poor, sodium-rich igneous rocks. The nepheline syenites of the Kola Peninsula in the Soviet Union produce very large, well-formed crystals, as do those at Mont Saint Hilare, Quebec, and Narsarssuk Fjord, Greenland. Excellent specimens are found at Magnet Cove, Arkansas, and Libby, Montana, and in the pegmatites and syenites of Norway, where the first specimens were described. Aegirine is also known to crystallize in the sedimentary rocks of the Green River Formation in the Colorado Plateau.

aegirine (acmite)

Classification:
inosilicate, pyroxene group

Composition:
$NaFe^{+3}Si_2O_6$ (sodium iron silicate)

Crystal System:
monoclinic

Hardness:
6–6.5

Specific Gravity:
3.5

This crystal of aegirine from Magnet Cove, Arkansas, illustrates why this species is also called acmite—from the Greek word for "point."

Because the numerous individual crystals which comprise this hematite "iron rose" are structurally related to one another, the aggregate as a whole retains the hexagonal symmetry of the species.

The serrated edges of these arsenopyrite "cockscomb" aggregates are formed by the terminations of several crystals, which began growing outward from the same point.

MOST MINERALS ARE USUALLY FOUND AS AGGREGATES OF MANY SIMILAR CRYSTALS rather than as isolated individuals. This reflects the fact that when the physical and chemical conditions are right for a mineral to begin crystallizing, the odds are great that hundreds or thousands of individual crystals will nucleate at the same time in the immediate area. The characteristic botryoidal masses of malachite or goethite, for example, begin as tufts or druses of tiny individual crystals on a matrix. These crystals grow together gradually in a roughly parallel orientation, with each individual growing only at its tip and at the same rate as its neighbors. The result is a massive, smooth-surfaced crystalline aggregate composed of thousands of parallel fibrous crystals of the same length. When broken, the fibrous texture of such aggregates becomes evident. Oftentimes, such aggregates are banded like trees, reflecting the variations in their growth rates or in the chemistry of the precipitating solutions over the years. There is a plethora of different types of aggregate habits, dictated both by the crystal forms of different minerals and by the geological environments in which they occur. The following terms describe the aggregate habits most commonly encountered.

Arborescent This term refers to a branching growth pattern, resembling the limbs of a tree, and is typical of the native metals copper, gold, and silver.

Bladed Minerals that form aggregates of thin, lath-shaped crystals are said to be bladed. Kyanite is a typical example of this formation.

Botryoidal—Globular—Mammillary—Reniform These are descriptive terms for the slight variations in the external appearance of the fibrous aggregates mentioned in the first paragraph. Botryoidal comes from the Greek term *botrys*, meaning "grape-cluster"; globular from the Latin *globus*, meaning "spherical"; mammillary from the Latin *mammilla*, meaning "breast"; and reniform from the Latin word for kidney, *renes*. These habits are sometimes referred to collectively as colloform, on the belief that they crystallize from colloidal gels.

Cockscomb This term describes clusters of crystals that are slightly offset and arranged in semicircular fans. These aggregates form when several crystals nucleate at nearly the same point, and then grow outward in the same direction in a "piggy-back" fashion. This habit is common in barite, columbite, hemimorphite, autunite, torbernite, and especially marcasite.

Dendritic Like arborescent, dendritic means tree-like. However, dendritic aggregates are more two-dimensional, forming in the close confines of cracks and fissures where crystals can only spread out on one plane. Dendritic aggregates of manganese oxides like pyrolusite are particularly common in many rock types as well as in the variety of chalcedony called moss agate, which commonly contains delicate filaments of other silicates as well.

Divergent—Radiating—Stellate These terms describe clusters of crystals that grow outward from a common point while retaining their euhedral form. Numerous individuals arranged in a star pattern are referred to as stellate. Although similar in appearance to some twin habits, the crystals in divergent and stellate groups are not structurally related.

Drusy A surface covered with a thin layer of small crystals is said to have a drusy coating.

Fibrous This term refers to crystal aggregates of silicates like asbestiform serpentine and amphiboles, which are typically formed under metamorphic conditions. Individual fibers of the asbestos minerals are extremely long, thin, and flexible, and can even be woven into heat-resistant fabrics.

Foliated—Lamellar Aggregates that are composed of many thin, flat crystals are described as foliated, meaning "leaf-like," or lamellar, meaning "platy." This texture is typical of the phyllosilicates, such as micas and chlorite, and occurs in graphite, molybdenite, and other species whose atomic structures are characterized by loosely connected two-dimensional sheets.

Granular This is a very common aggregate habit in which a great many faceless (anhedral) mineral grains occur together in massive form. The individual crystals may range in size from very tiny (fine granular) to relatively large (coarse granular).

Massive—Compact These very general terms refer to granular mineral aggregates. The term compact specifically denotes a material of low porosity.

Plumose This term refers to aggregates of micaceous or acicular crystals which have adopted spreading, plume-like shapes.

Reticulated Rutile and cerussite are two of the best examples of this unusual aggregate habit, in which many slender crystals form open networks of crisscrossing individuals. Because the individuals are structurally related (although not strictly twins), the angles between the crystals in such reticulated networks tend to remain constant.

Rosettes Rosettes are aggregates formed by several thin, tabular, overlapping crystals, more or less circular in outline, which grow outward in a spiral fashion much like an actual flower. The so-called iron roses of hematite are the best-known example of this habit, but rosettes are also seen in pyrrhotite and a few other species.

Stalactitic Stalactites and stalagmites are pendulous or columnar forms which grow in the same manner as botryoidal masses, and also have a fibrous internal structure. The carbonates aragonite, calcite, malachite, and rhodochrosite commonly form stalactitic aggregates.

Although not twins in the strict sense, these crystals in this reticulated aggregate of rutile (variety sagenite) form constant 60° angles with one another.

ALLANITE HAS A VERY COMPLICATED AND VARIABLE COMPOSITION. THE CALCIUM AND cerium position is commonly occupied by rare earths such as lanthanum or yttrium, or by the radioactive element thorium, which renders the crystals metamict. Allanite is very widespread in small amounts, and is probably a major source of the radioactive radon gas that emanates from the bedrock to pose a significant health threat in some regions. Unlike the phosphate monazite, allanite is not found in sufficient concentrations to be a viable ore mineral, even though it contains rare earth elements of potential interest to industry. Also known as orthite, this species is named for the Scottish mineralogist who first discovered it, Thomas Allan (b. 1777).

Allanite is a common accessory mineral in silica-rich plutonic rocks, such as granites, and in gneisses and other metamorphic rocks where it occurs as shapeless grains surrounded by a distinctive rusty radiation halo. Euhedral tabular, lath-like, or elongate prismatic crystals are found in pegmatites and in some contact metamorphic deposits. Although allanite lacks cleavage, radiation damage makes crystals delicate and notoriously difficult to remove from their matrix intact. The color is dark brown to pitch black, but crystals are commonly coated by yellowish-brown alteration products. Allanite has a very distinctive "pitchy" luster, which ranges from nearly submetallic to resinous and helps to distinguish the species from the rare-earth oxides and monazite.

The best specimens of allanite have come from complex pegmatites enriched in rare earths, as at Falun, Sheppsholm, and Ytterby, Sweden; and Arendal, Norway. North American sources include Madawaska, Ontario;

allanite

Classification:
sorosilicate, epidote group

Composition:
$(Ca,Ce)_2(Fe^{+2},Fe^{+3})(Al_2O)(SiO_4)(Si_2O_7)(OH)$
(calcium, cerium, iron, aluminum silicate)

Crystal System:
monoclinic

Hardness:
5.5–6

Specific Gravity:
3.5–4.2

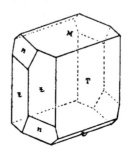

Beringer Hill, Texas; Amelia Court House, Virginia; and numerous locations in New York, New Jersey, California, Arizona, Colorado, and other states. Other notable occurrences include Miask in the Ural Mountains, Greenland, and Madagascar.

amber

Classification:
organic

Composition:
fossilized organic resin containing variable proportions of carbon, hydrogen, and oxygen

Amorphous

Hardness:
1–3

Specific Gravity:
1.05–1.10

AMBER IS THE FOSSILIZED RESIN OF ANCIENT TREES, WHICH FORMS THROUGH THE NATural polymerization of the original organic compounds. The composition, color, and physical properties of amber vary according to its age, the conditions of its burial, and the type of tree that produced the resin. Scientists can determine the genus of the amber-producing tree by studying its composition: Alaskan amber, for instance, is derived from ancient swamp cypress, and Caribbean amber from an acacia-like tree. Amber often encloses perfect fossil casts of leaves, insects, spiders, and other small organisms that were trapped in the resin when it was fresh and sticky. The remains of small animals such as lizards and tree frogs have also been found. Since fossils of such delicate creatures preserved in amber are rarely found elsewhere, amber is a particularly important source of information about life in past ages. Although amber has been found in rocks of Carboniferous to Pleistocene age, most occurs in sediments of Cretaceous and early Tertiary age. The Romans called amber *succinus*, but the modern name comes from the Arabic word *anber,* meaning ambergris. Ambergris is waxy substance which is formed in the intestines of sperm whales and used to make perfumes. Ambergris and amber are unrelated except that both wash up on beaches and are a prize for beachcombers.

The very low specific gravity of amber allows it to float in sea water. For this reason, amber that is liberated from coastal sediments by wave action is commonly found on nearby beaches. (Buoyancy is thus a good test for genuine amber, as most imitations will sink in salt water.) Amber has been collected from the shores of the Baltic Sea for thousands of years. It is found as beads, amulets, and carvings in archaeological sites throughout northern Europe, and was traded as far afield as Asia and the Mediterranean. The pebbles of amber that washed up on the cold shores of the North Sea must have seemed miraculous indeed to the ancients—a distillation of the summer sun itself.

Amber is warm to the touch and readily develops static electricity when rubbed, attracting cloth, hair, or fur. The Greeks called amber *electron*, and it is from this word that the term electricity is derived. Not surprisingly, amber was accorded supernatural powers from earliest times. During the Middle Ages, it even came to be regarded as a cure-all, and concoctions of powdered amber and honey were prescribed for such diverse medical complaints as asthma, gout, and the black plague. Amber pendants were thought to preserve chastity, and were regarded as talismans against the forces of darkness and evil—a tradition which survives in the use of amber for rosary beads. Like the non-fossil tree resins frankincense, myrrh, and copal, amber was used as a fumigant to propitiate the gods or to dispel evil spirits as well as such worldly nuisances such as mosquitos. Ancient seafarers even burned amber on their boats, in the belief that it would drive away sea serpents and other perils of the deep.

The color of amber ranges from colorless through pale yellow, orange, red, and dark brown; whitish, greenish, and bluish variants are also known. Orange, yellow, and brown are the most common colors; other colors are usually caused by the dispersion of light by inclusions or air bubbles. Amber has a resinous luster and is classified according to its translucency. Cloudy or "bastard" amber is opaque; "fatty" amber is translucent; and clear amber is transparent. Clear, well-colored amber is most valuable, particularly if it contains insect fossils. Color variations often reflect the point of origin: Sicilian amber is often dark red or orange, Eastern European amber is brownish yellow, and Burmese amber (usually called Chinese amber) is red or dark brown in color and often heavily crazed (covered with shallow fractures). In the Dominican Republic and a few other places, amber is mined from sedimentary deposits, where it has been concentrated in organic-rich beds with lignite coal.

Copal and other tropical tree resins are commonly substituted for amber. The large "amber" beads seen in much ethnic jewelry are actually made from recent tree resins. "Amberoid" is a reconstructed amber, produced by melting small pieces of amber under pressure; both copal and amberoid are usually opaque. Plastics are widely used to simulate amber as well. The best test for distinguishing amber from plastic is to apply a red-hot needle point to an inconspicuous area of the suspect piece; plastics will emit an acrid, unpleasant odor, while amber and other natural resins will give off a sweet smell. Due to the debunking of amber as a medicine, its relative abundance, and the even greater abundance of cheap imitations, amber is one of the few gems which is both less fashionable and less valuable than it was in times past.

amblygonite

THIS INTERESTING PHOSPHATE IS A COMMON ACCESSORY IN LITHIUM-AND PHOSPHATE-enriched complex pegmatites, but is often overlooked because of its superficial resemblance to the more common surrounding silicate minerals. Amblygonite is a minor ore of lithium, the lightest of the metals. Lithium is used in innumerable specialized alloys and compounds, including lubricants that can endure extreme temperature variations, and a drug that controls manic depression (see *Lepidolite*). When the concentration of hydroxyl (OH) exceeds that of fluorine, the mineral is technically known as montebrasite; many specimens labeled amblygonite are actually montebrasite. The name montebrasite is derived from a source in France, and the name amblygonite from the Greek phrase meaning "blunt angle," a reference to the shallow angle formed by its two best cleavages.

Amblygonite has four cleavages altogether, and is brittle with a conchoidal to uneven fracture. It is usually found as cleavable anhedral masses (sometimes of enormous size) or as rough equant crystals in matrix. Very rarely, well-formed short prismatic crystals with lustrous faces are recovered

Classification:
phosphate

Composition:
$(Li,Na)AlPO_4(F,OH)$
(hydrous lithium aluminum phosphate)

Crystal System:
triclinic

Hardness:
5.5–6

Specific Gravity:
3.08

A euhedral crystal of amblygonite from Divino de Larangeiras, Minas Gerais, Brazil, displaying internal reflections from parallel cleavage planes.

from pegmatite cavities. Amblygonite is either white or a light shade of yellow, green, pink, or blue, with a white streak. Crystals are commonly translucent with a vitreous luster. White amblygonite can be mistaken for quartz or feldspar, but it is softer and much denser. The rare phosphates beryllonite and brazilianite also resemble amblygonite and may be associated with it in pegmatites.

Among the species typically associated with amblygonite in pegmatite dikes are apatite, lepidolite, spodumene, and colored tourmaline. Euhedral crystals are found at many locations in Maine; and enormous masses of amblygonite weighing up to 200 tons have been mined from the pegmatites of the Black Hills of South Dakota. Other important North American occurrences include Pala, California, Taos County, New Mexico, and Yavapai County, Arizona. Transparent yellow amblygonite crystals, which yield attractive gemstones, are mined in Burma and at numerous locations in the Brazilian state of Minas Gerais. Good specimens have also come from Montebras, France, and from sources in Germany, Czechoslovakia, and Sweden.

amphiboles

Anthophyllite: $(Mg,Fe)_7Si_8O_{22}(OH)_2$

Cummingtonite Series
Cummingtonite: $Fe_2Mg_5Si_8O_{22}(OH)_2$
Grunerite: $Fe_7Si_8O_{22}(OH)_2$

Tremolite Series
Tremolite: $Ca_2Mg_5Si_8O_{22}(OH)_2$
Actinolite: $Ca_2(Mg,Fe)_5Si_8O_{22}(OH)_2$

Hornblende: $X_{2-3}Y_5Z_8O_{22}(OH)_2$

Sodium Amphiboles
Riebeckite: $Na_2Fe_2^{+3}Fe_3^{+2}Si_8O_{22}(OH)_2$
Glaucophane: $Na_2Mg_3Al_2Si_8O_{22}(OH)_2$

THE AMPHIBOLES CONSTITUTE ONE OF THE MOST IMPORTANT AND WIDESPREAD GROUPS of rock-forming minerals. The group name comes from the Greek *amphibolos*, meaning "ambiguous," in reference to the difficulty of distinguishing the many varieties represented in this group. This ambiguity is exacerbated by the extensive solid solution which exists between species. They are closely related in crystal form and composition, with the following general formula:

$$W_{0-1}X_{2-3}Y_5Z_8O_{22}(OH,F)_2$$

in which: W = K, Na
X = Mg^{+2}, Mn^{+2}, Fe^{+2}, Ca^{+2}, Na^{+2}, Li^+
Y = Mg^{+2}, Mn^{+2}, Fe^{+2}, Fe^{+3}, Al^{+3}, Ti^{+4}
Z = Si^{+3}, Al^{+3}

The amphibole structure is characterized by cross-linked double chains of Si_4O_{11} groups, which are oriented parallel to the central crystal axis. This structure is outwardly expressed by columnar or fibrous crystal forms. Although most amphiboles crystallize in the monoclinic system, some have orthorhombic symmetry.

The amphiboles are analogous in chemical composition to the pyroxenes, differing in that they contain hydroxyl (OH). They commonly form through the alteration of the primary pyroxenes in igneous rocks during metamorphism, and some species are found only in metamorphic rocks. Conversely, amphiboles can also alter to pyroxenes through dehydration at high temperatures. The generally dark glassy crystals of the two groups can easily be confused, except for their characteristic cleavage patterns. Both display good prismatic cleavage in two directions, but amphibole cleavages intersect at approximately 56° and 124° angles, whereas pyroxene cleavages intersect at nearly 90° angles, producing distinctive blocky fragments. This angular difference results from the fact that the structural chains in the amphiboles are twice as wide as those in the pyroxenes.

As an abundant and widely distributed constituent in igneous and metamorphic rocks, the amphiboles are of great interest to geologists. The most commonly encountered amphibole outside of scientific circles is nephrite jade, the massive variety of actinolite and tremolite. Some species have fibrous varieties, which as a form of asbestos have been used in thermal insulation.

ANALCIME IS WEAKLY PYROELECTRIC, BECOMING SLIGHTLY CHARGED WITH ELECTRICITY when heated or rubbed. For this reason, its name is derived from the Greek phrase *an alkimos*, meaning "not strong." The name could just as easily be a reference to its physical strength, for analcime, though it has no cleavage, is extremely brittle and disintegrates into subconchoidal fragments if handled roughly. Although usually classified among the zeolites, analcime is chemically and structurally related to the feldspathoids.

Crystals are trapezohedrons or cubes modified by trapezohedral faces, and granular aggregates are common. Analcime is transparent to translucent, and may be colorless, white, pink, or yellow with a vitreous luster and a colorless streak. Some analcime crystals are colored red by hematite inclusions. Although its crystals resemble those of leucite and garnet, crystals of the former are commonly embedded in matrix and neither are likely to be found in the same geological environment as analcime.

Analcime occurs primarily with the zeolite minerals and calcite in basalt cavities, although it does occur as a primary mineral in some sodium-rich basalts and in nepheline syenites. Fine crystals come from Table Mountain near Golden, Colorado, the Keweenaw Peninsula of Michigan, and the basalt cavities of northern New Jersey. Large transparent crystals have long been found on the Cyclopean Islands near Sicily, and in the Italian Alps. Other sources of exceptional specimens include Faskrudsfjord, Iceland; Aussig, Czechoslovakia; Flinders Island, Tasmania; Kerguelen Island in the Indian Ocean; and Cape Blomidon, Nova Scotia.

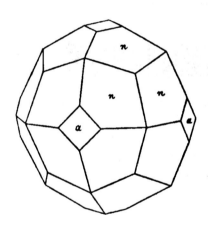

analcime

Classification:
tectosilicate, feldspathoid

Composition:
$NaAlSi_2O_6 \cdot H_2O$
(hydrated sodium aluminum silicate)

Crystal System:
isometric

Hardness:
5–5.5

Specific Gravity:
2.27

Trapezohedrons of analcime from Tabular Mountain, County Antrim, Ireland.

This elongated pseudo-octahedral crystal of anatase on quartz from Bourg d'Oisans, Iseré, France, mimics an isometric crystal form, but actually shows only tetragonal symmetry.

anatase

Classification:
oxide

Composition:
TiO₂ (titanium oxide)

Crystal System:
tetragonal

Hardness:
5.5–6

Specific Gravity:
3.82–3.97

THE NAME ANATASE IS DERIVED FROM THE GREEK WORD *ANATASIS*—"EXTENSION"—because its sharp, dipyramidal crystals are steeper, or "extend beyond," those of true octahedra. Because of these pseudo-octahedral crystals, anatase was once known as octahedrite. Along with rutile and brookite, anatase is one of three polymorphs of TiO₂. The stability range of these polymorphs is not fully understood, but it is apparent that the structure of rutile is the most stable, since it occurs far more commonly than either anatase or brookite and in a variety of geological environments.

Anatase crystals are usually transparent to opaque and may be brownish, deep blue, or black; however, green, yellow, lavender, and dark-red specimens are also encountered. The luster is strongly adamantine to submetallic, and the streak colorless to yellow. Anatase is very brittle, with two perfect cleavages and a subconchoidal fracture. Transparent crystals from the placer deposits of Brazil and South Africa have been fashioned into gems.

Anatase is an uncommon accessory mineral in many types of igneous and metamorphic rocks, and in placer deposits derived from them. However, the finest specimens of anatase occur in fissures in gneiss or schist, in association with quartz, titanite, and adularia, as in the Swiss, Austrian, and Italian Alps. Fine specimens also occur near Dauphine, France, and in Norway. Anatase is found in weathered quartz diorites in the California Coast Ranges, and as excellent blue crystals lining fissures in diorite at Gunnison, Colorado.

andalusite

Classification:
nesosilicate

Composition:
Al₂SiO₅ (aluminum silicate)

Crystal System:
orthorhombic

Hardness:
6.5–7.5

Specific Gravity:
3.13–3.16

ALONG WITH KYANITE AND SILLIMANITE, ANDALUSITE IS ONE OF THE THREE POLYmorphs of Al₂SiO₅, all of which occur primarily in aluminum- and silica-rich metamorphic rocks, such as schists. Which of these three minerals will form in a particular environment depends upon the ambient pressure and temperature at the time of crystallization; changes in the physical environment can cause one of the three polymorphs to alter into another. Generally speaking, andalusite forms at lower pressures than kyanite, and at lower temperatures than sillimanite. Andalusite is a very important source of aluminum silicate for porcelain refractory products such as sparkplugs, which must endure very high temperatures.

Andalusite normally forms simple, stubby prismatic crystals with flat terminations and square cross sections. The faces of such crystals are typically dull, often altering into fine-grained muscovite mica. Well-developed cleavages parallel the prism faces. The typical coloration is dull red, olive drab, or brown, with a white streak. Andalusite formed in pegmatites is commonly pink, due to the substitution of manganese and iron in the place of alu-

minum, and could be confused with opaque rubellite tourmaline but for the lack of cleavage in the latter. An interesting variety called chiastolite (from the Greek *chiastos*, or "X-marked") forms tapering crystals with a distinct cross pattern evident in cross section, due to the selective inclusion of dark carbonaceous impurities during their growth. These crystals were prized as amulets by early Christians, as were the cross-shaped twins of the related species staurolite. The gem gravels of Brazil and Sri Lanka have produced some remarkable transparent crystals, which have revealed another interesting property of this mineral—transparent andalusite displays intense pleochroism. Properly cut stones will appear yellowish green when viewed perpendicular to the prism face, but distinctly reddish when viewed end-on.

As noted, andalusite is characteristic of aluminum-rich regional metamorphic rocks, particularly schists, where it is typically associated with cordierite; it is also an uncommon constituent of granites and granitic pegmatites. Andalusite is a widespread and common mineral, but good specimens are unusual and much sought after. It has been mined at the Champion Sparkplug Mine in the White Mountains of California, in the Black Hills of South Dakota, in Standish, Maine, and elsewhere in the United States. The variety chiastolite is found in Massachusetts, California, and Bimbowrie, South Australia, among other places. Andalusite is named for the Spanish occurrence in the province of Andalucia. Another Spanish occurrence is in the cathedral town of Santiago de Campostela, a destination for Christian pilgrims.

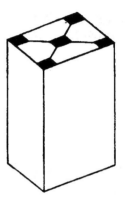

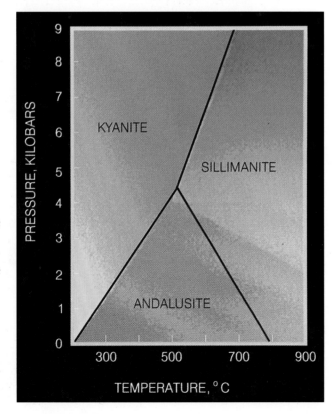

anglesite

Classification:
sulfate

Composition:
PbSO$_4$ (lead sulfate)

Crystal System:
orthorhombic

Hardness:
2.5–3

Specific Gravity:
6.38

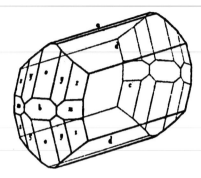

This fine prismatic anglesite crystal from the Linares District in Spain displays the bright luster characteristic of lead-bearing minerals.

THE FIRST SPECIMENS OF THIS MINERAL TO BE DESCRIBED WERE FOUND IN PARY'S Mine on the Welsh Isle of Anglesey, from which the name is taken. A typical secondary mineral of the oxidized portions of lead–zinc sulfide veins, anglesite forms at the expense of the primary lead sulfide galena. When found in sufficient concentrations, anglesite and other secondary lead minerals, such as cerussite and pyromorphite, may be exploited for their lead content.

Anglesite crystals display a wide variety of habits, from equant to slender and prismatic, and may be elongated in any crystallographic direction. The faces on anglesite crystals may display a bewildering variety of forms, are often curved, and are usually striated. Sharp single crystals and crystal groups are common, as are granular aggregates, stalactitic formations, and alteration crusts surrounding galena. Anglesite is transparent to translucent and usually colorless or white, but may also be pale gray, yellow, green, or blue; it often fluoresces yellow under ultraviolet light. The luster is adamantine to vitreous, and the streak colorless. Anglesite resembles both barite and celestite, but differs in its occurrence and striking adamantine luster. Unlike cerussite, anglesite crystals are untwinned.

Anglesite is found in association with other secondary lead minerals like cerussite, mimetite, pyromorphite, and wulfenite. Although the oxidized upper levels of most major lead deposits are mined out, good specimens are still produced from a number of sources. Extraordinary crystals as long as 12 cm were once found at the Wheatly Mines of Chester County, Pennsylvania. The Coeur d'Alene District in Idaho has also produced exceptional material, as have the Tintic and Park City districts in Utah and many other locations throughout the western United States. Excellent crystals are found in association with sulfur at Los Lamentos, Chihuahua, Mexico. The Isle of Anglesey still produces fine specimens, as does the Derbyshire region of England, and Leadhills and Wanlockhead, Scotland. Wonderful crystals are found at Sidi-Amorben-Salem, Tunisia; Mibladen, Morocco; and Tsumeb, Namibia. Other notable sources include Broken Hill, New South Wales, Australia; Dundas, Tasmania; and New Zealand, Brazil, Germany, Zaire, and Zambia.

ANHYDRITE IS ONE OF THE MOST IMPORTANT SPECIES IN EVAPORITE DEPOSITS, ALONG with gypsum, halite, and sylvite. Its name is derived from the Greek phrase *an hydros,* meaning "without water," a reference to the lack of water in its crystal structure, when compared with the much more abundant calcium sulfate gypsum. Gypsum often loses its structural water as it is buried by other deposits, altering to anhydrite and losing nearly 40% of its volume in the process. Although primary anhydrite can precipitate from extremely concentrated brines, most ancient calcium sulfate evaporites are composed of such secondary anhydrite. When anhydrite is exposed to circulating groundwater, it may change back into gypsum. The resulting increase in volume produces contorted bedding called enterolithic folds, after their resemblance to convoluted intestines. Anhydrite is sometimes used as a soil conditioner, a source of sulfur for the production of sulfuric acid, and is added to cement to slow the drying process.

Anhydrite is usually seen in massive form, often as nodules or thinly laminated beds. Crystals are usually equant, thick tabular or blunt prismatic, and are quite rare. More common are coarsely crystalline, transparent to translucent cleavable masses. These may be colorless, white, gray, bluish, reddish, brown, or pale violet (depending upon the nature of included impurities), with a grayish-white streak. Anhydrite has three good cleavages which intersect at nearly right angles to produce blocky fragments with pearly luster. This cleavage helps to distinguish anhydrite from calcite, which has a rhombohedral cleavage; gypsum is softer.

In addition to its extensive occurrence in evaporite deposits, anhydrite is also found in hydrothermal veins, basalt cavities, and in minor amounts in other environments. Fine crystals are sometimes found in massive bedded deposits such as those in New Mexico, Texas, Nova Scotia, Poland, and Germany. Good specimens are found in the Homestake gold mine in South Dakota, at the Faraday uranium mine in Bancroft, Ontario, and in an apatite deposit at North Burgess, Ontario. Attractive violet cleavages are found in the New Cornelia pit, Ajo, Arizona; similar material comes from the St. Gotthard region of Switzerland. Sometimes anhydrite occurs with zeolite minerals in basalt cavities, as in northern New Jersey and Massachusetts.

anhydrite

Classification:
sulfate

Composition:
$CaSO_4$ (calcium sulfate)

Crystal System:
orthorhombic

Hardness:
3.5

Specific Gravity:
2.98

A fibrous mass of anhydrite crystals, collected from the Simplon Tunnel in the Alps between Italy and Switzerland.

antimony

Classification:
native element

Composition:
Sb (antimony)

Crystal System:
hexagonal

Hardness:
3–3.5

Specific Gravity:
6.7

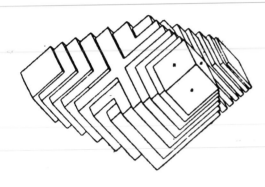

ELEMENTAL ANTIMONY IS OVERSHADOWED BY ITS SULFIDE STIBNITE, WHICH IS FAR more common and the primary source of antimony for industry. Antimony is used for various specialized alloys, such as pewter and alloys used for type metal (for movable print). Because it expands on cooling, rather than contracting and pulling away from its mold, antimony alloys make true castings. In antiquity, antimony, bismuth, and tin were categorized as varieties of lead, which is why Pliny warns in his *Natural History* that stibnite should not be "roasted too much, lest it turn into lead." Many Middle Eastern and Central Asian women still use a mixture of powdered antimony and soot called *kohl* as an eye shadow. The name antimony comes from the Arabic name for stibnite, *al-athmud.*

Antimony rarely forms pseudocubic or tabular crystals; granular or lamellar cleavable masses are more common. It is a brilliant tin-white color, with a brightly reflective metallic luster and a gray streak. Antimony is often coated with a pale-yellow rind of the alteration product valentinite (Sb_2O_3). Antimony is difficult to distinguish from allemontite (AsSb) and arsenic without chemical tests.

Antimony is typically found in hydrothermal veins with allemontite, arsenic, stibnite, and other sulfides, particularly of silver. The crystallization of the sulfide is so favored in most environments that antimony is rarely found in significant concentrations; even so, masses weighing nearly 150 kg have been recovered from mines in Kern County, California. Excellent specimens are found in Sarawak Province, Borneo; at Nuevo Tepache, Sonora, and Arechuybo, Chihuahua, Mexico; Huasco, Chile; and Los Animos, Bolivia. European localities include Sala, Sweden; Andreasberg, Germany; Coimbra, Portugal; Val Cavargna, Italy; and other locations in Bulgaria, Czechoslovakia, England, France, and Sardinia. Antimony is also found in the Ilimaussaq intrusion, Greenland, and at several locations in Australia.

Massive native antimony from Arechuybo, Chihuahua, Mexico.

antlerite and brochantite

Classification:
sulfates

Composition:
antlerite: $Cu_3SO_4(OH)_4$
brochantite: $Cu_4SO_4(OH)_6$
(hydrous copper sulfates)

Crystal Systems:
antlerite: orthorhombic
brochantite: monoclinic

Hardness:
3.5–4

Specific Gravity:
3.9

ANTLERITE AND BROCHANTITE ARE CLOSELY ALLIED COPPER MINERALS WHICH OCCUR IN the oxidation zones of copper deposits in arid regions. They are so similar in composition and physical properties that it is nearly impossible to distinguish between them. Although less common than many other secondary copper minerals, both are abundant enough in some copper deposits (such as Chuquicamata, Chile) to be mined as a copper ores. Both form small, equant, stout prismatic or tabular crystals, but usually occur as druses or masses of fibrous acicular crystals. Both are emerald-green to very dark green, transparent to translucent, and have a vitreous luster and a pale green streak. Antlerite and brochantite can easily be confused with the copper carbonate malachite, but unlike malachite they do not effervesce in hydrochloric acid. Brochantite is named for the French mineralogist A.T.M. Brochant de Villiers, and antlerite for its occurrence at the Antler Mine in Arizona.

Both antlerite and brochantite are found in many of the copper deposits of the western United States, although the upper, oxidized portions of many deposits have been exhausted by mining. Classic sources include the Seven Devils and Alder Creek Districts, Idaho; the mines at Tiger and

Bisbee in Arizona; the Darwin District in California; the Tintic District in Utah; the Blanchard Mine in New Mexico; the Monarch Mine in Colorado; Black Mountain, Nevada; and Kennecott, Alaska. Other significant sources include Coahuila, Mexico; Ain Barbar, Algeria; Tsumeb, Namibia; Soviet Kazakhstan; and the previously mentioned deposit in northern Chile. European localities include Sardinia; Rezbanya, Romania; Piesky, Czechoslovakia; Austria's Rauris Valley; and the Black Forest of Germany.

Top: A druse of tiny brochantite crystals, which grew in an open fissure at Fowey Consols, Tywardreath, Cornwall. Bottom: Antlerite, Chuquicamata, Calama, Antofagasta, Chile.

apatite group

Classification:
phosphate

Composition:
Ca₅(PO₄)₃(F,Cl,OH) (calcium phosphates
with fluorine, chlorine, or hydroxyl)

$Ca_5(PO_4)_3(F,Cl,OH)$

Crystal System:
hexagonal

Hardness:
5

Specific Gravity:
3.1–3.2

Top: *Violet apatite crystals from the Pulsifer
Quarry, Auburn, Maine—widely considered
the world's finest source of apatite crystals.*
Bottom: *Hexagonal, tabular apatite crystal
from the tungsten mines of Panasquiera,
Serra da Estrella, Portugal.*

APATITE IS THE MOST ABUNDANT AND IMPORTANT OF THE PHOSPHATE MINERALS. THE name actually refers to a group of calcium phosphates, in which fluorine, chlorine, and hydroxyl may also act as anions, and carbonate may substitute for the phosphate ion. Although this group is divided into several species on the basis of composition, fluorapatite is by far the most commonly encountered as well-crystallized mineral specimens. Apatite takes its name from the Greek word for deception, *apatos*, because its broad range of colors and crystal shapes creates confusion with other species.

Apatite crystals adopt an amazing array of forms, from delicate acicular shapes to individual tabular crystals weighing hundreds of pounds. Crystals are commonly hexagonal prisms, which may be terminated by flat basal planes, dipyramids, or an elaborate combination of forms. Apatite also occurs as nodular aggregates, granular masses, or botryoidal crusts. Although usually some shade of green or brown, virtually every color is represented in this species, including vibrant canary-yellow, green, indigo blue, violet, and deep purple. The streak is white, and the luster distinctly resinous, verging on oily. Apatite is a very brittle mineral, with a conchoidal fracture and two rather indistinct cleavages. It can usually be distinguished from its many look-a-likes on the basis of hardness. While apatite is hard relative to similar-appearing carbonates, it is softer than most silicate minerals and can be scratched by a knife-blade.

Although apatite is prized by mineral collectors for its beautiful crystals and rich variety of colors, its primary importance lies in being the main repository of phosphorous—one of the basic building blocks of life. The weathering of rocks containing apatite liberates phosphorous into the biosphere, where it is taken up by organisms at the base of the food chain, both in the oceans and on land. Phosphorous is a vital component of all kinds of plant and animal tissues, and innumerable organic compounds such as adenosine triphosphate, the basic source of metabolic energy. In higher organisms, apatite forms the hard parts of bones, teeth, and scales. The remains of these organisms may accumulate in sedimentary basins, where they are even further enriched in phosphorous by bacterial, physical, and chemical processes. Sedimentary phosphate deposits formed in this manner are known as phosphorites, and contain fossils of marine mammal and fish bones, shells, fecal pellets, and other debris preserved as calcium fluorapatite. These fossils are often surrounded or replaced by cryptocrystalline apatite, or collophane. Other phosphorites are formed directly on land from the excrement of seabirds, or *guano*. Such deposits can accumulate to great thickness, providing an extremely lucrative, if somewhat piquant, export for the residents of the remote islands and coastlines where they occur.

Phosphorites are mined for use in agriculture, since phosphorous is vital to the growth of crops and must be constantly replenished. Millions of tons are extracted each year from extensive deposits in Florida, France, Spain, and especially in the Saharan countries of Algeria, Tunisia, Morocco, and Egypt. An enormous phosphorite deposit called the Phosphoria Formation, which formed in a shallow sea during the Permian period, underlies thousands of square kilometers in the Rocky Mountain states. Apatite is used in smaller amounts in the chemical industry in a variety of vital applications, from phosphoric acid to the elemental phosphorus from which matches and flares are made.

Apatite is present as microscopic crystals in most igneous rocks, usually in very small quantities. The exceptions to this rule are unusual formations known as carbonatites—igneous intrusions enriched in a variety of rare minerals which commonly contain mineable concentrations of apatite. Such deposits are mined at Alno, Sweden, and Palabora, South Africa. Another kind of magmatic apatite deposit on the Kola Peninsula provides the Soviet Union with most of its phosphate fertilizer. Unusually rich veins of apatite in gabbric rocks are exploited along the southern coast of Norway. Apatite crystals enclosed in marble are found in the province of Ontario, Canada;

some of these crystals weigh over 200 kg, but are rarely mined for their phosphorous content.

The pegmatites of Brazil and California produce attractive specimens, as do the crystal-lined clefts of the Alps. Perhaps the most striking apatite specimens are the deep-purple crystals from the pegmatites of Mount Apatite, near Auburn, Maine. Apatite frequently occurs as an accessory mineral in various hydrothermal deposits. Large, lustrous green and violet crystals are found in the tungsten mines Panasqueira, Portugal, and large, complex crystals at Potosí, Catavi, and in the tin mines of Llallagua, Bolivia. Commonly seen, but nonetheless remarkable, are the beautifully formed golden-yellow crystals found in the vast open-pit iron mine at Cerro de Mercado, Durango, Mexico. Apatite is found as transparent blue crystals of gem quality in the gem gravels of Mogok, Burma; despite their softness, these are cut into gemstones which display marked pleochroism. The mineral has been synthesized for use in special types of lasers, but there is no danger of encountering artificial apatite gemstones.

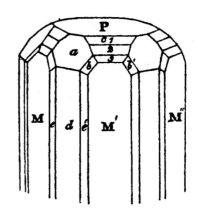

THE NAME APOPHYLLITE WAS COINED FROM THE GREEK WORDS FOR "OFF" AND "LEAF," due to the fact that flakes separate from specimens as they are heated. This exfoliation is due to the loss of water, which is held loosely in the mineral's structure through hydrogen bonding, rather than as integral hydroxyl (OH) ions. Apophyllite differs from all other sheet silicates in that its layers of silica tetrahedra are composed of both four- and eight-fold rings, bound together by ions of calcium, potassium, or fluorine. Apophyllite is actually a group name encompassing the three species fluorapophyllite, hydroxylapophyllite, and natroapophyllite, of which the first variety is by far the most common.

Apophyllite commonly forms fine crystals which may be colorless, white, yellowish, pink, brown, or bluish green, with a strong vitreous to pearly luster. These crystals are usually "pseudocubic," meaning that they form nearly perfect cubes. This resemblance to isometric species can hinder identification. However, apophyllite crystals have striated sides and smooth, lustrous ends, whereas isometric crystals have similar faces all around. Apophyllite is brittle, with an uneven fracture and one perfect cleavage.

Apophyllite usually occurs with the zeolite minerals in cavities formed by gas bubbles in basaltic rocks, and is likely to be found wherever ancient basalt flows are quarried. In North America, good specimens have been found in the basalts of Oregon, northern New Jersey, and Virginia. The region around Poona, India, which lies within the enormous basalt field known as the Deccan Traps, has in the past produced wonderful greenish apophyllite crystals as large as 15 cm on a side. Fine specimens are now being produced from the basalts of Rio Grande do Sul in southern Brazil. Apophyllite sometimes occurs in cavities in granite or gneiss, and has been found in sulfide veins as well. Large drusy coatings of pink or white crystals have been taken from the silver mines of Guanajuato, Mexico, and the copper mines of Michigan have also produced fine specimen.

apophyllite

Classification:
phyllosilicate

Composition:
$KCa_4Si_8O_{20}(F,OH) \cdot 8H_2O$
(hydrated potassium calcium silicate)

Crystal System:
tetragonal

Hardness:
4–5

Specific Gravity:
2.3–2.4

A layer silicate like the micas, apophyllite forms fine crystals like these from Poona, India, in basalt cavities with zeolite minerals.

aragonite

Classification:
carbonate

Composition:
CaCO₃

Crystal System:
orthorhombic

Hardness:
3.5–4

Specific Gravity:
2.95

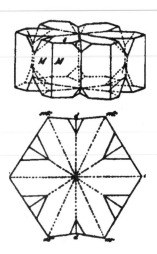

ARAGONITE IS NAMED FOR THE SPANISH PROVINCE OF ARAGON, WHERE WELL-FORMED twins of aragonite are still recovered from sediments around Molina de Aragon. Aragonite forms orthorhombic crystals and, along with the hexagonal form calcite, is one of the polymorphs of calcium carbonate. As in calcite, aragonite is composed of stacked horizontal layers of triangular carbonate ions. In calcite, these layers are in parallel alignment, but aragonite contains alternating layers in which the carbonate ions point in opposing directions. This structure is stable only at higher pressures than normally prevail at the earth's surface, such as in metamorphic rocks. Aragonite tends to alter gradually to calcite over time, and may alter instantly when heated.

However, aragonite does readily form as a product of biological activity, or in special environments where the chemistry and temperature of the ground water favors its development over that of calcite. Many of the marine organisms whose shells and skeletons are formed from calcium carbonate precipitate aragonite for this purpose. The iridescent nacre and pearls which form in many mollusc shells is aragonite, as is the framework of the widespread and important calcareous algae. In the shallow reaches of the Caribbean Sea, the Great Salt Lake and other warm bodies of water, aragonite may be precipitated as tiny pellets called oolites, which accumulate in vast sedimentary deposits. Aragonite also comprises a large part of the sinter deposits which form around springs, especially hot springs. The banded ornamental stone known as travertine or Mexican onyx, which is used for carving architectural details and art objects, is largely composed of aragonite. Aragonite grows in caves as stalactites and stalagmites, and in iron mines as coral-like growths called *flos ferri,* meaning "flowers of iron."

Aragonite crystals usually adopt elongated prismatic or acicular habits, but may be tabular as well. This species readily forms cyclic twins composed of three members, which together resemble a single hexagonal crystal. These twins can be recognized by the presence of prominent sutures in the center of each crystal face (reentrant angles), and opposing striations on the basal faces. Aragonite is transparent to translucent with a glassy luster; colors range from colorless to white, yellow, blue, green, or pink. Aragonite is rarer than calcite, heavier, and harder; it also lacks the perfect rhombohedral cleavage of its polymorph. Both display strong double refraction, however.

Well-formed crystals of aragonite are not abundant, but are sometimes recovered from the upper levels of sulfide deposits, and in cavities in volcanic rocks. In addition to the classic locality in Spain, fine aragonite twins are found in the Sicilian sulfur deposits and in locations in France, Austria, Poland, Czechoslovakia, and Hungary. Tabular aragonite crystals and attractive acicular sprays of tapering "church steeple" crystals have been recovered from the mines of Leadhills, Scotland, as well as Alston Moor, Cleator Moor, and elsewhere in Cumberland, England. Fine twins are found at Lake Arthur, New Mexico, and *flos ferri* in the Organ Mountains of New Mexico and at Bisbee, Arizona.

Left: *Tiny crystals of aragonite often precipitate in warm shallow waters to form sand-sized spherical aggregates called oolites. Along with aragonite fragments from calcareous algae and other marine organisms, oolites collect to form broad carbonate shoals such as these off the coast of Belize, Central America.*
Right: *The common aragonite "church-steeple" habit is exemplified by these crystals from Blackrock quarry, Buckfastleigh, Devon, England.*

ARGENTITE AND ACANTHITE ARE POLYMORPHOUS SULFIDES CONTAINING NEARLY 87% silver, of which they are among the most important ores. Ironically, they are also the only minerals with an entire industry devoted to their elimination—silver sulfide is the tarnish on silver, the bane of housekeepers the world over. Argentite is only stable at temperatures over 179°C, and is replaced pseudomorphically by acanthite at lower temperatures. For this reason, specimens of silver sulfide are always acanthite, although they may display the external crystal form of, and be labeled as argentite. The name argentite comes from the Latin word for silver, *argentum*, and acanthite from the Greek word for thorn, *akantha*—an allusion to its sometimes spiky crystal habit.

Crystals displaying the form of argentite may be cubic, octahedral, or dodecahedral in form, and frequently exhibit penetration twinning. Malformed or skeletal crystals, subhedral aggregates and encrustations are common. Crystals that formed at low temperature as acanthite are prismatic in habit. Both of these soft sulfides are malleable and sectile, and display poor cleavage. Their color is leaden gray with a bright metallic luster, but fresh surfaces tend to blacken eventually; the streak is metallic black. In cubic form, argentite–acanthite could be confused with galena, but lacks its excellent cleavage. Arborescent growths may resemble native silver, but can be distinguished by the rapid blackening of fresh surfaces.

Acanthite and argentite form a part of the so-called supergene enrichment on the top of silver-rich hydrothermal veins, in association with chlorargyrite, native silver, polybasite, stephanite, proustite, and pyrargyrite, among other species. In most parts of the world, these shallow deposits have long been mined-out. The famous Comstock Lode in Virginia City, Nevada, was one such deposit, as were the original silver mines of Guanajuato and Zacatecas, Mexico, although the latter areas still produce excellent specimens from their present workings. Good specimens are also found in Chanarcillo, Chile, and in Bolivia, Peru, and Honduras. Acanthite and argentite are also found in lead and zinc deposits, in association with cerussite and native silver, often as oriented overgrowths on the faces of silver-bearing galena crystals. Excellent specimens have come from Kongsberg, Norway; the Freiberg District and the Harz Mountains of Germany; and Kremnitz and Schemnitz, Czechoslovakia. Other European localities include the sulfide veins of England, Norway, and Sardinia.

argentite and acanthite

Classification:
sulfides

Composition:
Ag_2S (silver sulfide)

Crystal System:
isometric (argentite), monoclinic (acanthite)

Hardness:
2–2.5

Specific Gravity:
7.2

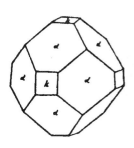

This silver sulfide specimen from Johanngeorgenstadt, Saxony, Germany, originally crystallized as the high-temperature isometric polymorph argentite. On cooling, it underwent internal reorganization to become the monoclinic polymorph acanthite, but retained its original external form.

arsenic

Classification:
native element, metal

Composition:
As (arsenic)

Crystal System:
hexagonal

Hardness:
3.5

Specific Gravity:
5.72

ARSENIC IS AN EXTREMELY POISONOUS ELEMENT, WIDELY USED IN THE PAST IN PIGments, insecticides, and homicidal concoctions. Because it remains indefinitely in the environment without decomposing into nontoxic compounds (as modern synthetic poisons are supposed to do), its use has been banned in most countries. Arsenic is still alloyed with lead to make bird shot, unfortunately compounding the serious lead-poisoning problem in areas of heavy waterfowl hunting. The name comes from the Greek *arsenikon*, a word derived from the Indo-European root meaning "yellow," and was originally applied to the yellow antimony sulfide orpiment. Native arsenic and antimony are very closely related, sharing many physical properties and uses. They often combine to form the hybrid stibarsen (AsSb), which is also known as allemontite for its occurrence in the Mine des Chalanches, near Allemont, France.

Arsenic sometimes forms small, rhombohedral or acicular crystals, but is usually seen as massive aggregates, either granular, reniform, or stalactitic. The color is tin-white, but arsenic tarnishes rapidly in the open air to dark gray; it is opaque, with a submetallic to metallic luster and tin-white streak. The strong odor of garlic emitted by arsenic when heated is its most distinctive feature, but this procedure is not recommended, since the fumes are poisonous.

A pitted mass of native arsenic, Burraton Combe quarry, St. Stephens-by-Saltash, Cornwall.

Arsenic occurs with cobalt, nickel, and silver ores, or with cinnabar and barite in hydrothermal veins. It is also found in dolomites and in the anhydrite cap rock of salt domes. Large masses of arsenic are found on Alder Island, British Columbia; and at Washington Camp, Santa Cruz County, Arizona. Additional sources include the Homestake Mine in South Dakota; the Winnfield Salt Dome in Louisiana; and several California locations. Good specimens are found in the mines of Saxony, Germany; and at Saltash, Cornwall, England; Akadani, Japan; and Copiapo, Chile. Other sources include Czechoslovakia, Italy, France, Romania, Australia, New Zealand, and Borneo.

arsenopyrite

Classification:
sulfide

Composition:
FeAsS (iron arsenic sulfide)

Crystal System:
monoclinic

Hardness:
5.5–6

Specific Gravity:
6.1

ARSENOPYRITE IS THE MOST COMMON OF THE ARSENIC-BEARING MINERALS; ITS NAME is a contraction of the archaic term "arsenical pyrites." It is the primary source of arsenic, which is produced as a by-product of the smelting of arsenopyrite-bearing ores for copper, tin, gold, silver, and cobalt. Substitution of cobalt for iron gives a complete series extending to glaucodot (Co,Fe)AsS. Although the industrial uses of arsenic have diminished in recent years due to its poisonous character, the metallic arsenic derived from arsenopyrite is still used in some specialized alloys (see *Arsenic*). The compound arsenious oxide has diverse applications in glass-making, medicine, preservatives, and pigments, while arsenic sulfide finds use in fireworks and paints.

Crystals of arsenopyrite are common, usually being elongated and prismatic, often with diamond-shaped cross sections and vertical striations. Twinning produces crystals of a pseudo-orthorhombic habit or repeated contact twins similar to marcasite; cruciform twins are also known. Arsenopyrite often occurs as granular masses as well. The color is normally silver or whitish, with a distinctive pinkish cast and metallic luster; the streak is black. Crystals are brittle, with one distinct cleavage and uneven fracture. Its color and streak distinguish arsenopyrite from marcasite, and the strong, garlic-like arsenic odor it gives of when struck or heated is also distinctive.

Arsenopyrite is fairly ubiquitous. It is found in sulfide deposits formed from magmatic segregation in layered igneous intrusions, with tin minerals in some pegmatites, and with gold, silver, and nickel minerals in the high temperature hydrothermal sulfide deposits. Important European deposits include Tavistock, Devonshire, England; Boliden, Sweden; Freiberg and Munzig, Germany; and Sulitjelma, Norway. Very large crystals are found at Llallagua, Bolivia, and attractive druses occur near Hidalgo de Parral, Chihuahua, Mexico. Large quantities are mined at Deloro, Ontario. Although not widespread in the United States, good specimens have been found in Franconia, New Hampshire; Roxbury, Connecticut, and Leadville, Colorado.

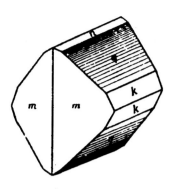

Above: Note the characteristic diamond-shaped cross-sections of these arsenopyrite crystals from Parral, Chihuahua, Mexico.
Left: White fireworks are made with artificial arsenic sulfide.

atacamite

Classification:
halide

Composition:
$Cu_2Cl(OH)_3$ (hydrous copper chloride)

Crystal System:
orthorhombic

Hardness:
3–3.5

Specific Gravity:
3.78

Atacamite crystals such as these from Australia are readily soluble in water and are only found in the most arid environments.

ATACAMITE IS A MINERAL OF THE DESERT, AND IS IN FACT NAMED FOR ONE OF THE most arid regions on earth—the forbidding Atacama Desert of Chile. Although the Atacama lies close to the Pacific Ocean, parts of it have not seen a drop of rain in all recorded history. Only in arid areas does atacamite form large enough concentrations to be mined as an ore of copper; elsewhere, it is dissolved by circulating groundwater. It was originally discovered overlying copper deposits in the Atacama desert, forming deep drifts and dunes of sparkling, bright-green sand.

Atacamite is translucent with vitreous to adamantine luster, and bright emerald-green to nearly black in color. Crystals are commonly slender and prismatic, with wedge-shaped terminations and vertical striations; other habits include tabular and pseudo-octahedral. However, atacamite most often occurs as granular, lamellar, or even fibrous aggregates. This species is difficult to distinguish from antlerite and brochantite without chemical tests, but can be distinguished from malachite by its lack of effervescence in hydrochloric acid.

Atacamite forms primarily through the alteration of copper sulfides near the surface of sulfide deposits in arid regions, and has also been observed to crystallize around volcanic vents. Large concentrations occur in the provinces of Atacama, Antofagasta, and Tarapaca, Chile; and in the Cruz del Sur Mine, Rio Negro Province, Argentina. Beautiful large dark-green crystals are found in the Burra District and elsewhere in South Australia. Numerous North American sources of atacamite include Bisbee and Jerome, Arizona; Tintic, Utah; and Goffs, California. Good specimens have also been obtained from Boléo and El Toro, Baja California, Mexico. Small amounts are found in Cornwall, England; the Bogoslowsk District, Soviet Union; and Austria, Peru, Bolivia, and Namibia.

atomic structure

Opposite page: Periodic table of the chemical elements. The elements shown in blue together comprise the vast bulk of the earth's crust, while those shown in green are also important industrially or as components of common minerals. The elements on the left side of the table have a strong tendency to lose electrons when forming mineral compounds, while those on the right tend to gain or share them—except for the noble gases, which have a stable electron configuration in their outermost shell and do not form compounds.

FROM THE TIME OF THE ANCIENT GREEKS, PHILOSOPHERS AND SCIENTISTS SPECULATED that all matter might be composed of exceedingly small, basic components. These hypothetical building blocks were termed "atoms," from the Greek word *atomos*, meaning indivisible. The structural regularity of crystals led early thinkers to postulate that, in the minerals at least, these minute particles might be arranged in some systematic fashion. By the 18th Century it had become apparent that there were correlations between the chemistry and the physical properties of minerals, but direct evidence of their atomic structure was still lacking.

Not until the early 20th century was this supposition confirmed, when the German physicist Max von Laue and his colleagues irradiated a crystal of copper sulfate with X-rays. This experiment produced an X-ray diffraction pattern on a piece of film placed behind the crystal, graphically representing its orderly lattice of atoms. Shortly afterward, the first crystal-structure analysis of a mineral (halite) was published. This development unleashed a veritable mineral-structure mapping boom, and by the early years of this century it had become possible to outline the general rules whereby the atoms of the various elements combine to form crystals.

NOBLE GASES

CHEMICAL
SYMBOL — Mg 12 — ATOMIC NUMBER
Magnesium — ELEMENT'S NAME

ELEMENTS OF GREATEST
ABUNDANCE IN THE CRUST

OTHER GEOLOGICALLY—
IMPORTANT ELEMENTS

TRANSITION ELEMENTS

* LANTHANIDE
(RARE EARTH) ELEMENTS

* ACTANIDE
ELEMENTS

| H 1 Hydrogen | | | | | | | | | | | | | | | | | | He 2 Helium |

| Li 3 Lithium | Be 4 Beryllium | | | | | | | | | | | B 5 Boron | C 6 Carbon | N 7 Nitrogen | O 8 Oxygen | F 9 Fluorine | Ne 10 Neon |

| Na 11 Sodium | Mg 12 Magnesium | | | | | | | | | | | Al 13 Aluminum | Si 14 Silicon | P 15 Phosphorus | S 16 Sulfur | Cl 17 Chlorine | Ar 18 Argon |

| K 19 Potassium | Ca 20 Calcium | Sc 21 Scandium | Ti 22 Titanium | V 23 Vanadium | Cr 24 Chromium | Mn 25 Manganese | Fe 26 Iron | Co 27 Cobalt | Ni 28 Nickel | Cu 29 Copper | Zn 30 Zinc | Ga 31 Gallium | Ge 32 Germanium | As 33 Arsenic | Se 34 Selenium | Br 35 Bromine | Kr 36 Krypton |

| Rb 37 Rubidium | Sr 38 Strontium | Y 39 Yttrium | Zr 40 Zirconium | Nb 41 Nobelium | Mo 42 Molybdenum | Tc 43 Technetium | Ru 44 Ruthenium | Rh 45 Rhodium | Pd 46 Palladium | Ag 47 Silver | Cd 48 Cadmium | In 49 Indium | Sn 50 Tin | Sb 51 Antimony | Te 52 Tellurium | I 53 Iodine | Xe 54 Xenon |

| Cs 55 Cesium | Ba 56 Barium | La 57–71 Lanthanides* | Hf 72 Hafnium | Ta 73 Tantalum | W 74 Tungsten | Re 75 Rhenium | Os 76 Osmium | Ir 77 Iridium | Pt 78 Platinum | Au 79 Gold | Hg 80 Mercury | Tl 81 Thallium | Pb 82 Lead | Bi 83 Bismuth | Po 84 Polonium | AT 85 Astatine | Rn 86 Radon |

| Fr 87 Francium | Ra 88 Radium | Ac 89–103 Actinides* | | | | | | | | | | | | | | | |

| La 57 Lanthanum | Ce 58 Cerium | Pr 59 Praseodymium | Nd 60 Neodymium | Pm 61 Promethium | Sm 62 Samarium | Eu 63 Europium | Gd 64 Gadolinium | Tb 65 Terbium | Dy 66 Dysprosium | Ho 67 Holmium | Er 68 Erbium | Tm 69 Thulium | Yb 70 Ytterbium | Lu 71 Lutetium |

| Ac 89 Actinium | Th 90 Thorium | Pa 91 Protactinium | U 92 Uranium | Np 93 Neptunium | Pu 94 Plutonium | Am 95 Americium | Cm 96 Curium | Bk 97 Berkelium | Cf 98 Californium | Es 99 Einsteinium | Fm 100 Fermium | Md 101 Mendelevium | No 102 Nobelium | Lw 103 Lawrencium |

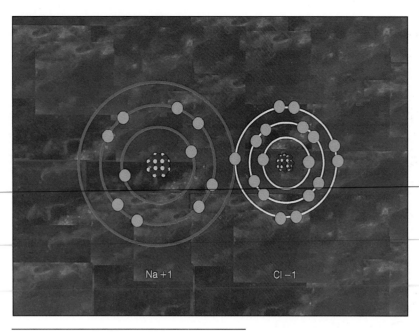

Na +1   Cl −1

Atomic structure of halite, or table salt. In the schematic figure above; a Na^{+1} cation has given up the single electron in its outer shell to form an ionic bond with an anion of Cl^{-1}. Each cation is surrounded by four anions, and visa-versa, in the ionic solid, or crystal, thus formed [opposite page].

Atoms, isotopes and ions Atoms consist of a cloud of negatively charged particles called electrons, which orbit around a relatively small, positively charged nucleus of protons and neutrons. Each of the more than 100 elements in the periodic table (see page 31) has its own unique atomic configuration. The distinctive characteristic of a given element is the number of protons in its nucleus, which never varies, and is expressed as the *atomic number*. The sum of the number of protons and neutrons in the nucleus is the *atomic weight*. Due to the fact that not every atom of the same element has the same number of neutrons, the atomic weight of an element is variable.

Atoms of a single element which have differing atomic weights are called *isotopes*. Carbon, for instance, has an equal number of protons and neutrons in the nucleus of its most common isotope, $_6C^{12}$. (Isotopes are often written with the atomic number before, and the atomic weight after the chemical symbol.) However, carbon also has other naturally occurring isotopes such as $_6C^{14}$, which has two additional neutrons in its atomic nucleus.

Many isotopes are unstable, and through the process of radioactive decay can change into entirely different elements. $_6C^{14}$, for instance, decays at a constant, known rate to become the nitrogen isotope $_7N^{14}$. Scientists use this relationship to find the age of plant and animal fossils, which when living assimilated carbon isotopes according to their relative abundance in the atmosphere. By comparing the ratio of the original $_6C^{14}$ to $_7N^{14}$, they can determine the time that has passed since the organism died.

Electronic Configuration The present notion of atomic structure envisions electrons as orbiting the atomic nucleus in specific orbitals, the geometry of which reflects different energy levels. These orbitals are often referred to as "shells," since they were once thought to form concentric spheres of varying radii around the nucleus. It is now known, however, that electrons occupy both spherical and non-spherical orbitals, interwoven in a complex fashion. Each orbital can hold a limited number of electrons, from two in the innermost shell to as many as thirty-two in others. However, the highest energy orbitals never have more than eight electrons.

The elements are classified on the basis of their electronic structures. Most of the earth's common elements gain or lose one or more electrons in order to assume a stable configuration of eight electrons in their outermost electron shell. These active electrons are called *valence* electrons, and they determine the ways in which the elements combine to form minerals. Sodium, for example, one of the alkali metals on the left side of the periodic table, has eight electrons in its second-highest energy shell, and one lone valence electron in its unstable outer shell. Chlorine, found all the way across the table among the halogen elements, has seven valence electrons, and needs one more to acquire a stable configuration. When a sodium atom relinquishes its extra electron to chlorine, the two are drawn together by the opposing charges generated, forming the mineral halite, or table salt.

Ions are positively or negatively charged atoms or groups of atoms, formed through the gain or loss of one or more electrons. An atom that has lost electrons becomes a positively charged ion, or *cation*, while one that has gained electrons becomes a negatively charged ion, or *anion*. Ions are written with a plus or minus symbol denoting their charge, and a number indicating how many electrons they have lost or gained. For instance, Fe^{+2} is a cation which, having lost two electrons, carries a positive charge of +2. A particular element can form more than one type of ion. Iron, for instance, commonly occurs as trivalent Fe^{+3} cations as well. An element retains its identity despite these changes, because the number of protons in its nucleus remains the same. Complex ions are those that consist of two or more atoms of different elements, such as the carbonate ion CO_3^{-2}.

Atomic Bonds There are only a few basic types of atomic bonds that hold together the various elements in minerals. Since some minerals may contain several different elements with different valence requirements, more than one bond type may be present within a single crystal. Furthermore, the distinctions between the following bond types are sometimes blurred, so the definitions should be taken with a grain of halite.

Ionic bonds predominate in most minerals, except for the native elements and sulfides. For ionic bonds to form, atoms must become ionized, losing or gaining electrons and acquiring an electromagnetic charge. Halite, mentioned earlier, is an example of an ionically bonded mineral. Since the attractive forces are exerted in all directions, each cation of sodium in a salt crystal is surrounded by six anions of chlorine, and vice versa. Thus, the crystal can be thought of as being composed of interlocking octahedral units, with an anion at each of the six corners and a cation in the middle.

Because of this constant relationship between ions, salt is said to be octahedrally *coordinated*, and is given a coordination number of six. Different coordination numbers may correspond to other geometric forms, including the four-cornered silicon tetrahedra of the silicate minerals. Coordination numbers generally reflect the relative size of the ions: the larger the ion, the more opposing-charge ions are needed to surround it. Anions are generally much larger than cations, and tend to take up most of the space in a crystal. Ions do not need exactly opposing charges to form ionic bonds. For instance, two Fe^{+3} ions combine with three O^{-2} ions to form the basic unit of the iron oxide hematite, Fe_2O_3.

Covalent bonds develop between atoms that share their valence electrons with other atoms in order to acquire a stable configuration, rather than gaining or losing them. While the atoms in ionically bonded crystals form continuous, homogenous networks, those in covalently bonded crystals tend to form distinct charge-sharing molecules of two or more individual atoms. The covalent bond is the strongest of all the atomic bonds, and minerals in which this bond dominates are typically very stable, insoluble, and have high melting points.

Carbon is one element that behaves in this way, never forming ions, but readily sharing its electrons. In a diamond crystal, each carbon atom is surrounded by four others, each of which "shares" its two valence electrons so that all four achieve the stable configuration of eight electrons in their outer shell. The coordination number of carbon in this case is four, and the basic structure is a tetrahedron. The carbon atoms in graphite are also covalently bonded, but instead of forming a network as in diamond, they form flat sheets held together by weak van der Waals' forces.

Van der Waals' forces (also called "residual bonds") are far less strong than either ionic or covalent bonds, but exist between all ions and atoms in solids. These forces are the weak attraction that arises from the electrical polarization of individual atoms. Usually their influence is overshadowed by the stronger bond types, but they are important in holding together certain mineral structures, such as that of the micas, which lack strong bonding in a particular direction. Like the weakest link in a chain, the

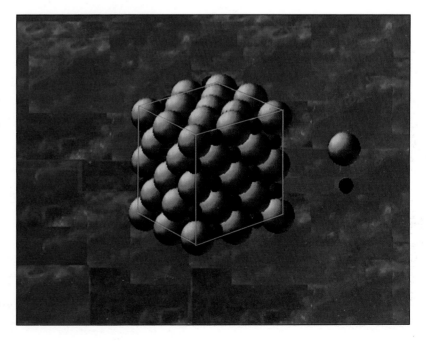

weakest bonds determine the physical properties of a mineral, such as cleavage and hardness.

Metallic bonding is dominant only in the metals, but is also partially expressed in sulfide minerals such as galena. The metallic elements have from one to three valence electrons, which are relinquished as their atoms combine in crystalline form. Thus, crystals of the native metals consist of very closely spaced, positively charged metal atoms, with "free agent" electrons roaming freely between them. The presence of these mobile electrons accounts for the excellent thermal and electrical conductivity of the metals, since the electrons are free to transport energy through the solid metal, be it a cast-iron pan or copper wire. The shiny luster characteristic of the metals and some sulfides arises from the interaction of light with the free electrons, which literally swarm over the surface of the crystal. The malleability and ductility of the metals reflects their simple, uniform structure: when subjected to mechanical stress, the atoms simply shift positions without permanently severing bonds.

augite

Classification:
inosilicate, pyroxene group

Composition:
$(Ca,Na)(Mg,Fe,Al)(Si,Al)_2O_6$
(calcium, sodium, magnesium, iron aluminum silicate)

Crystal System:
monoclinic

Hardness:
5.5–6

Specific Gravity:
3.2–3.52

AUGITE IS THE MOST COMMON PYROXENE AND ONE OF THE MOST UBIQUITOUS ROCK-forming minerals. It is the typical pyroxene of the dark-colored (mafic) igneous rocks, such as basalts, gabbros, and peridotites. Augite also forms in the very high-grade metamorphic rocks such as granulites and eclogites, while other pyroxenes of the diopside-hedenbergite series are typical of lower-grade metamorphic rocks. There is complete solid solution between augite and aegirine, with the $Ca(Mg,Fe^{+2})$ of the former being replaced by Na and Fe^{+3} in the latter. When the same group of ions is replaced by Na and Al, the species is called omphacite. Chromium, manganese, and titanium are typically present in augite in small quantities.

Crystals of augite are commonly short prismatic or columnar. Typical habits include disseminated anhedral crystals, granular masses, and lamellar aggregates called diallage. It is brittle with an uneven fracture, and displays the perfect prismatic cleavage at right angles typical of the pyroxenes. Augite is translucent, and may be dark green, grayish green, brown, or black in color, with a greenish-grey streak. It has a bright, vitreous luster; indeed,

A euhedral crystal of augite in volcanic rock from Sasbach, Kaiserstuhl, Sudbaden, Baden-Wurttenberg, Germany.

its name is derived from the Greek word *augites*, meaning "brightness." Augite and the other pyroxenes are easily distinguished from the amphiboles and other dark-colored silicates by their right-angled cleavage. The closely related pyroxenes diopside and hedenbergite are generally lighter in color than augite, and crystals of aegirine are generally less stubby.

In addition to the geological environments noted above, augite is also found in nepheline syenites and in some carbonatites. Although augite is very common and widespread in its distribution, well-formed crystals are unusual. The lavas of Vesuvius in Italy commonly contain euhedral phenocrysts of augite, and similar crystals are found encased in basalt in many areas, notably at Cedar Butte, Oregon, and the Gold Run Creek area, Colorado. Good crystals are sometimes obtained from the contact metamorphic marbles of St. Lawrence County, New York, and Renfrew County, Ontario. Fine specimens have been obtained from many areas including Val di Fassa in Trentino, Italy, and Czechoslovakia, the Scandinavian countries, Greenland, Namibia, India, and Japan.

AURICHALCITE IS A RELATIVELY RARE MEMBER OF THE HYDROUS CARBONATES, A GROUP which includes the better known species malachite and azurite. Its name is apparently derived from a Greek phrase meaning "mountain copper." This species characteristically forms lustrous, light-blue, tufted aggregates of slender, acicular crystals on limonite matrix. The crystals are generally transparent, with a silky to pearly luster and a light blue-green streak. Aurichalcite is extremely fragile, with one perfect cleavage. Open clusters of acicular crystals distinguish aurichalcite from the compact botryoidal aggregates of the similarly colored zinc carbonate smithsonite.

Aurichalcite occurs in many parts of the world in the oxidation zones of zinc and copper sulfide deposits, particularly those rich in dissolved carbonate. Classic specimens are found at Mina Ojuela, Mapimí, Durango, Mexico, where they are associated with calcite and hemimorphite. Fine specimens of aurichalcite are also found at several locations in the western United States, including Bisbee, the Banner District, and elsewhere in Arizona; Cottonwood Canyon, Utah; Kelly, New Mexico; Wellington, Nevada; and the Darwin District in California. Excellent specimens come from Tsumeb, Namibia, and Mindouli, in the Congo. The most important European localities are Laurium, Greece; Chessy, France; Leadhills, Scotland; and Romania. In an unusual occurrence at the Tin Mountain Mine, Custer County, South Dakota, aurichalcite occurs in a pegmatite in association with cassiterite, columbite, hemimorphite, and smithsonite.

aurichalcite

Classification:
carbonate

Composition:
$(Zn,Cu)_5(CO_3)_2(OH)_6$
(hydrous zinc copper carbonate)

Crystal System:
orthorhombic

Hardness:
1–2

Specific Gravity:
3.96

Divergent sprays of aurichalcite crystals from Sa Duchessa Mine, Domus Novas, Iglesias, Sardinia.

Austinite from Mina Ojuela, Mapimí Durango, Mexico.

austinite and conichalcite

Classification:
arsenate

Composition:
Austinite: CaZn(AsO$_4$)OH
(calcium and zinc arsenate)
Conichalcite: CaCu(AsO$_4$)(OH)
(hydrous calcium copper arsenate)

Crystal System:
orthorhombic

Hardness:
4–4.5

Specific Gravity:
4.13–4.33

THESE COLORFUL COPPER ARSENATES FORM A SOLID-SOLUTION SERIES, WITH SPECIMENS grading toward conichalcite in composition being more common in nature. Austinite is named for the American mineralogist Austin Flint Rogers (b. 1877), while conichalcite derives its name from the Greek phrase meaning *lime copper*—a reference to the calcium and copper in its composition.

Both species typically occur as very tiny equant to prismatic crystals, which in turn form bladed or acicular aggregates, or botryoidal crusts. Austinite may be colorless, yellowish white, or bright green, and has a sub-adamantine luster and a white to pale-green streak. Conichalcite is a vibrant yellowish to emerald green, with a vitreous to resinous luster and green streak. Austinite has good prismatic cleavage in one direction, and conichalcite none; both are very brittle and display an uneven fracture. Adamite may be very similar in appearance, but it has two good cleavages and is both softer and heavier than these species.

Austinite and conichalcite are secondary minerals found in the oxidized portions of hydrothermal copper sulfide veins, where they are typically associated with limonite, adamite, and other secondary species such as the copper arsenates olivenite and libethinite. Good specimens of austinite are found at Gold Hill, Utah; Table Mountain Mine, Arizona; the Cleveland Mine in Washington; Sterling Hill, New Jersey; and Lomitos, Bolivia. Excellent specimens of conichalcite have been obtained from the Tintic District, Utah, and Bisbee, Arizona. Fine specimens of both species occur at the Mina Ojuela, Mapimí, Durango, Mexico; Bou Azzer, Morocco; Tsumeb, Namibia; and the Kamareza Mine, Attica, Greece.

AUTUNITE IS A SOFT, HEAVY, FRAGILE, AND RADIOACTIVE MINERAL. LIKE A PHOSPHO-rescent fungus in the woods, autunite seems vaguely sinister. Although it is now more of a mineralogical curiosity, it was very popular and much sought after by both the Allies and the Axis countries in the final days of the second World War, as the primary source of uranium for atomic weapons. The atomic bombs that destroyed the Japanese cities of Hiroshima and Nagasaki were composed of uranium extracted from autu-nite. Autunite was well-known at that time because of its occurrence with less lethal ores in hydrothermal veins; since World War II, however, the nuclear industry has found several more profitable sources of uranium (see *Carnotite, Uraninite*).

Autunite forms crusts of extremely thin, squarish crystals; divergent, fan-shaped aggregates; and chaotic masses of bladed crystals. It is also common as dull, earthy masses. Lemon-yellow to greenish yellow in color, autunite has a bright vitreous luster and a yellow streak, and fluoresces strongly yellow-green under ultraviolet light. Torbernite, $Cu(UO_2)_2(PO_4)_2 \cdot$ 8-12 H_2O, is isostructural with autunite, and the two are commonly associated. Although very similar in color and morphology to autunite, torbernite is not fluorescent.

Autunite forms as an alteration product of uranium minerals in hydrothermal veins, sedimentary deposits, granitic pegmatites, or simply in hydrothermally altered granites. The finest specimens of this relatively rare species come from the Daybreak Mine near Spokane, Washington, where crusts several inches thick have been recovered. Autunite is also found in the pegmatites of the Black Hills of South Dakota; Grafton Center, New Hampshire; and Spruce Pine, North Carolina. Excellent specimens are found at St. Austell and Redruth, Cornwall, England; Sabugal, Portugal; and Saxony and Autun, France, from whence the name is derived. In Australia, autunite occurs in the Flinders Range and the Rum Jungle area, Northern Territory. Specimens are also obtained from Musonoi, Katanga, Zaire; and from Brazil, Japan, and Iran.

autunite

Classification:
phosphate

Composition:
$Ca(UO_2)_2(PO4)_2 \cdot 10–12 \ H_2O$
(hydrated calcium uranium phosphate)

Crystal System:
tetragonal

Hardness:
2–2.5

Specific Gravity:
3.05–3.2

axinite

Classification:
cyclosilicate

Composition:
$(Ca,Mn,Fe,Mg)_3Al_2(BO_3)(Si_4O_{12})(OH)$
(calcium, manganese, iron, magnesium, aluminum borosilicate)

Crystal System:
triclinic

Hardness:
6.5–7

Specific Gravity:
3.2–3.3

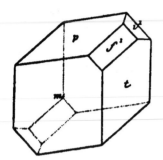

LIKE THE IMPORTANT GEM MINERALS BERYL AND TOURMALINE, AXINITE IS A CYCLOSILI- cate, and is also cut as a gemstone on occasion. Unlike its more common relatives, whose structures consist of regular layers of Si_6O_{18} rings, axinite has a complex structure of Si_4O_{12} rings interspersed amid borate triangles and hydroxyl groups. Axinite is one of the many minerals that have been subdivided into groups of several discrete species on the basis of minor compositional variation. The members of the axinite group are ferroaxinite, magnesioaxinite, manganaxinite, and tinzenite. These species are more alike than different, and are usually referred to collectively as axinite. The name comes from the Greek *axine*, or axe—a reference to the sharp, wedge-shaped crystals.

The color of axinite is usually a distinctive clove-brown, although it may also be yellow, greenish, gray, or black. It is transparent to translucent, vitreous, and the streak is colorless. It has good cleavage in one direction, and the fracture is uneven to conchoidal. Crystals are commonly flattened, tabular, and striated, and have very sharp edges; lamellar, granular, bladed aggregates are common. The distinctive color and the flattened striated crystals are usually sufficient to distinguish axinite from other species.

Axinite forms in a number of different environments, including contact metamorphic rocks, high-temperature hydrothermal veins, veins and fissures in granitic and various metamorphic rocks, and some granitic pegmatites. Large transparent crystals are found near Coarse Gold along California's Feather River. Bright-yellow crystalline druses of manganaxinite occur in the zinc mines of Franklin, Sussex County, New Jersey. Attractive specimens are found in the contact metamorphic rocks of the Jensen Quarry at Crestmore, California. Crystals 5 cm in length are found in the tungsten mines of the Sierra Juarez, northern Baja California. Beautiful specimens are found in fissures in schists at St. Just, Cornwall. Classic specimens are obtained from St. Cristophe, near Bourg d' Oisans, Iseré, France, in association with epidote, quartz, and prehnite. Large, lustrous crystals are culled from the Toroku Mine on the Japanese island of Kyushu.

The sharp angles between faces in this axinite crystal from Bourg d'Oisans, France, suggest why this species is named from the Greek word for axe.

NAMED FOR ITS INTENSE AZURE BLUE COLOR, AZURITE IS FOUND WITH THE CLOSELY related and more abundant copper carbonate malachite in the oxidation zones of sulfide copper deposits. These minerals are formed when copper sulfate is leached from the primary copper ores by oxygenated groundwater, which reacts with carbonate minerals in the surrounding rock. Azurite readily alters to malachite in the presence of water, and pseudomorphs of malachite after azurite crystals are quite common. This change is also seen in some medieval and early Renaissance paintings, where the once vibrant blue skies painted with azurite pigment have changed to a muddy green. Recognizing the drawbacks of azurite pigment, artists eventually switched to a more expensive—but permanent—lazurite pigment, ultramarine.

Azurite often forms extremely complex crystals displaying a variety of modifying forms; basic habits include rhombohedral, equant, stout columnar, tabular, wafer-like or sharp wedge-shaped forms. Massive material occurs as stalactites, botryoidal or spherical aggregates, commonly in interlayered with green malachite. Azurite is brilliant azure blue or deep blue-black in color, sometimes transparent, with a glassy luster. Crystals display conchoidal fracture and three directions of cleavage, and are extremely brittle.

Although found in virtually every hydrothermal copper deposit, large, sharp crystals are rare and sought after. Fine crystal groups are found at numerous locations in the western United States, including Morenci and Bisbee, Arizona; and Magdalena, New Mexico. Excellent specimens are also obtained from Mazapil, Zacatecas and elsewhere in Mexico; Tsumeb, Namibia; Broken Hill, Australia; and the Guang Dong province of China. The finest European specimens come from the copper deposits of Chessy, near Lyon, France; Laurium, Greece; and Sardinia. Fine specimens of azurite also occur in the Ural and Altai Mountains of the Soviet Union.

Excellent sharp crystals of azurite, partially altered to green malachite, from the the world's greatest crystal-producing mineral deposit—Tsumeb, Namibia.

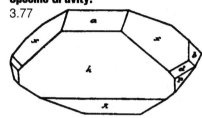

azurite

Classification:
carbonate

Composition:
$Cu_3(CO_3)_2(OH)_2$
(copper hydroxyl carbonate)

Crystal System:
monoclinic

Hardness:
3.5–4

Specific Gravity:
3.77

babingtonite

Classification:
inosilicate, pyroxenoid

Composition:
$Ca_2Fe^{+2}Fe^{+3}Si_5O_{14}(OH)$
(calcium iron silicate)

Crystal System:
triclinic

Hardness:
5.5–6

Specific Gravity:
3.36

A nest of lustrous black babingtonite crystals from Lane's quarry, Westfield, Hampden County, Massachusetts.

BABINGTONITE, NAMED FOR the Irish physician and mineralogist William Babington (b. 1833), is a rare silicate found in basalt cavities with zeolite minerals, quartz, and calcite. Although crystals are small, their greenish to brownish black coloration makes them conspicuous against the background of their light-colored associates. Crystals are short prismatic or platy, with two directions of cleavage and uneven fracture; their luster is vitreous.

In addition to its occurrence in basalt cavities, babingtonite is found in other low-temperature hydrothermal environments, especially fissures in diabase, granites, and gneiss. Good specimens are found in quarries in Passaic County, New Jersey, and in Hampden and Middlesex Counties, Massachusetts. European localities include the iron mines of Haytor, Devonshire, England; Herborn, Germany; San Leone, Sardinia; and Baveno in the Italian Piedmont. Babingtonite is also associated with the zeolites of the Deccan Basalts in India.

barite

Classification:
sulfate

Composition:
$BaSO_4$ (barium sulfate)

Crystal System:
orthorhombic

Hardness:
3–3.5

Specific Gravity:
4.5

BARITE HAS AN UNUSUALLY HIGH SPECIFIC GRAVITY FOR A NONMETALLIC MINERAL, which makes even massive specimens readily identifiable in the field. Miners once believed barite to be a heavy form of gypsum, and cursed it for being hard to shovel and worthless to boot. Not surprisingly, the name is derived from the Greek *barys*, meaning "heavy." The metal barium was first extracted from this mineral in 1901.

Although considered a worthless gangue mineral for hundreds of years, barite has come into its own as an important part of modern industry and medicine. Ninety percent of all barite mined is made into a slurry for use in the drilling of deep oil wells, where natural gas under intense pressure may be encountered. The extra weight of this barium mud helps to keep the explosive gases from bursting out of the drillhole. Barite is also added to concretes that require extra weight, or are to be used as radiation screens. Since barium absorbs radiation and X-rays unusually well, it is widely used in protective shields. Patients undergoing X-ray examination of their digestive tracts are compelled to drink a "barium milk-shake," which, because of its opacity to this kind of radiation, causes their soft tissues to show up better on the X-ray film. Various barium compounds are also used in television tubes, signal flares, fireworks, and tracer bullets. Once an important source of white pigment in the paint industry, barite has largely been replaced by the titanium pigment derived from rutile and ilmenite.

Barite often occurs in beautiful crystals in hydrothermal deposits such as sulfide veins, hot spring deposits, and in various sedimentary rocks. Growing freely in open cavities, these crystals may adopt many complex forms, from tabular to prismatic. Interesting intergrowths of tabular crystals called "desert roses" often form in the sediments of ephemeral lakebeds, like those in the Sahara Desert and the Great Basin. Crystalline aggregates of barite may be stalactitic, lamellar, fibrous, cryptocrystalline or granular; massive granular barite is mined as the main source of barium ore. Barite is brittle, with an uneven fracture and a perfect pinacoidal cleavage. Although it is often brown when first unearthed, due to inclusions of iron minerals, barite crystals tend to turn pale blue on exposure to

Barite crystals from the ancient silver mines of the Brezevé Hory District, Pribram, Czechoslovakia.

light; finely disseminated organic matter or sulfide minerals may give crystals a gray or black hue. Many barite specimens display distinct fluorescence under ultraviolet light, and may also display thermoluminescence or phosphorescence. Barite and the strontium sulfate celestite form a solid-solution series, but most specimens are compositionally close to the end members of the series. These two species are easily confused, but barite is somewhat heavier and far more common. The barium carbonate witherite is a common alteration product of barite.

The United States produces more than one million tons of barite annually, mostly from deposits in the desert ranges of central Nevada. A nearly equal amount is imported from places as far away as Ireland and Peru. At an unusual barite mine near Petersburg in southern Alaska, the ore is drilled, blasted, and removed from a deposit under more than 30m of water. Specimen-quality barite usually does not occur in large sedimentary deposits such as these, but rather as a gangue mineral in hydrothermal ore veins, in association with siderite, fluorite, dolomite, calcite, and various lead, silver, and antimony sulfides. It is a very common and widespread species, and fine specimens have been produced from nearly every nation. The most famous source of barite specimens is the mining regions of Northumberland, Westmoreland, and Cumberland, where beautifully formed crystals up to a meter in length have been recovered. Fine crystals are also found in the mines of Saxony and elsewhere in Germany, as well as in Romania and Czechoslovakia. Among the many important North American localities are Cheshire, Connecticut; Rosiclare, Illinois; and the lead–zinc mines of the Tri-State region, particularly those in Missouri. Remarkable honey-colored crystals are found in sedimentary concretions in the badlands of South Dakota, and good "desert roses" in Oklahoma.

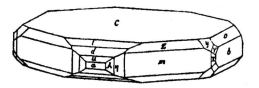

basalts and basalt cavities

Minerals of Basalt Cavities

albite	laumontite
analcime	mesolite
apophyllite	natrolite
babingtonite	pectolite
bornite	phillipsite
calcite	prehnite
chabazite	quartz
chalcopyrite	scolecite
chlorite	stilbite
datolite	thomsonite
harmotome	
hematite	
heulandite	

The rocks exposed in these cliffs above the Columbia River between Oregon and Washington were deposited as flood basalts during the Miocene Epoch. The basalts of the Columbia River Plateau cover more than 200,000 square kilometers, and are a source of many exceptional mineral specimens.

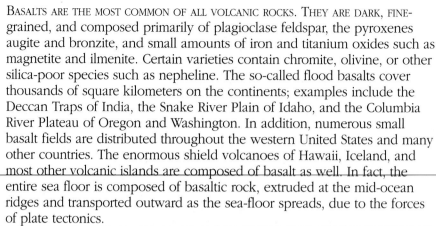

BASALTS ARE THE MOST COMMON OF ALL VOLCANIC ROCKS. THEY ARE DARK, FINE-grained, and composed primarily of plagioclase feldspar, the pyroxenes augite and bronzite, and small amounts of iron and titanium oxides such as magnetite and ilmenite. Certain varieties contain chromite, olivine, or other silica-poor species such as nepheline. The so-called flood basalts cover thousands of square kilometers on the continents; examples include the Deccan Traps of India, the Snake River Plain of Idaho, and the Columbia River Plateau of Oregon and Washington. In addition, numerous small basalt fields are distributed throughout the western United States and many other countries. The enormous shield volcanoes of Hawaii, Iceland, and most other volcanic islands are composed of basalt as well. In fact, the entire sea floor is composed of basaltic rock, extruded at the mid-ocean ridges and transported outward as the sea-floor spreads, due to the forces of plate tectonics.

Some magmas of basaltic composition do not erupt on the earth's surface as basalts, but rather cool more slowly beneath the surface to form the coarser-grained rock types, diabase and gabbro. These rocks are coarser-grained because they cooled slowly, allowing the individual crystals time to grow larger. Diabases are intermediate between gabbro and basalt in grain size, and usually form as horizontal sills or vertical dikes in the relatively confined spaces between other rocks. Although all of these rocks tend to have simple mineralogy, they often undergo some very interesting late-stage hydrothermal mineralization, which takes place in various cavities and fissures.

Gas bubbles that were unable to escape before the basaltic lava hardened into rock are often preserved as cavities, in which a variety of crystals may form from the ion-enriched waters moving gradually through the rock. Since these cavities are commonly elliptical in shape, they are termed amygdaloid—from the Greek word for almond, *amygdaloeides*. Basalts that were deposited underwater, known as pillow basalts, are particularly porous. The characteristic rounded knobs, or "pillows," from which the term is derived were formed as the lava was cooled by the seawater; subsequently, the molten rock inside these knobs leaked out, leaving cavities beneath the cooled shells. In diabase, cavities consist primarily of fault and fracture fissures.

Not all basalt cavities host interesting mineral associations. Some remain completely empty, while others are filled only with crystalline and cryptocrystalline quartz. Concentric layers of chalcedony of varying colors and degrees of translucency commonly form parallel to cavity walls, or as the perfectly straight bands called onyx. Since the layers of onyx are always deposited horizontally, they show which way was "up" when the cavity was filled. Crystalline quartz commonly forms in addition to chalcedony, often as amethyst. Quartz often covers or forms pseudomorphs after species such as aragonite, anhydrite, and glauberite, which tend to form early on and may later be dissolved. Many basaltic cavities have more complex mineralogy, however, and it is in these cavities that the beautiful and delicate crystals of prehnite, pectolite, datolite, and zeolite minerals are formed. There are a number of basalt fields around the world that produce excellent mineral specimens, including the Deccan Traps of India, the Rio Grande Do Sul region of Brazil, and the Columbia River Plateau in Oregon and Washington. Important sources of secondary basalt cavity species occur in smaller basalt fields and diabase sills in Germany, France, Scotland, Ireland, Iceland, Nova Scotia, and the northeastern United States.

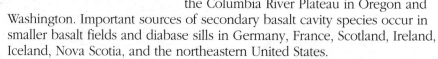

IN THE WINTER OF 1907, IN CALIFORNIA'S SAN BENITO COUNTY, TWO PROSPECTORS were camping in a wooded glade in the Diablo Range above the mercury-mining town of New Idria. Waiting in their bedrolls for the morning chill to subside, they were surprised to see the sun reflected by "thousands of blue gems" glinting on the slope above their camp. They thought that they had discovered sapphires, but an examination by mineralogists at the University of California showed the gems to be a new mineral, which was promptly named for its place of discovery.

San Benito County is the only locality where benitoite has ever been found in place. Its discovery in 1907 was particularly gratifying to crystallographers, who soon realized that benitoite was the sole example of the ditrigonal-dipyramidal class of the hexagonal crystal system—which had been purely hypothetical until that point. Unlike the common cyclosilicates beryl, cordierite and tourmaline, whose structures are based upon circular rings of six SiO_4 tetrahedra, the unique structure of benitoite is based upon three tetrahedra linked together to form a triangular group. Two other equally rare minerals share this structure with benitoite, and together they form the benitoite group of orphan silicates. Bazirite, $BaZrSi_3O_9$, is found only on Rockall Island, Inverness-shire, Scotland; pabstite, $Ba(Sn,Ti)Si_3O_9$, was found only in a limestone quarry in Santa Cruz, California, now the site of a housing development.

Benitoite forms flattened triangular crystals of 5 cm or less in size. They are normally pale to deep, sapphire blue with a vitreous luster, and are often cloudy due to inclusions of glaucophane. Other colors include pinkish, purple, white, or colorless, often occupying zones within a single crystal. Short-wave radiation produces a bluish fluorescence. Transparent crystals have been cut into beautiful gems, which are generally under five carats in weight and *very* expensive.

Benitoite has been found in brecciated serpentine at the Dallas Gem Mine and one other location near the headwaters of the San Benito River. Crystals are usually nestled in white natrolite, in association with prismatic black crystals of neptunite, and the rare honey-colored barium-titanium mineral joaquinite. This deposit now appears to be depleted, however, and the dust from numerous abandoned asbestos mines in the area makes the air hazardous to breathe and prospecting inadvisable. Tiny grains of benitoite have been found by scientists examining sand grains under the microscope, in places as far afield as Belgium and Texas, suggesting that another source of specimens may eventually be discovered.

benitoite

Classification:
cyclosilicate

Composition:
$BaTiSi_3O_9$ (barium titanium silicate)

Crystal System:
hexagonal

Hardness:
6–6.5

Specific Gravity:
3.64–3.68

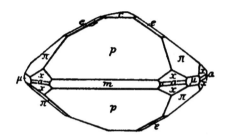

Benitoite crystals in a matrix of white natrolite, with a brilliant-cut benitoite gem from the Dallas Gem Mine, San Benito County, California.

Classification:
cyclosilicate $Be_3Al_2Si_6O_{18}$
(beryllium aluminum silicate)

Crystal System:
hexagonal

Hardness:
7.5–8

Specific Gravity:
2.63–2.80

BERYL IS ONE OF THE MOST INTERESTING AND ECONOMICALLY IMPORTANT OF ALL MINerals, and is remarkably diverse in its varieties and occurrences—even though common beryl has been found in single crystals weighing as much as 100 tons, the rare and precious emeralds can be as valuable as diamonds. The great variation seen among the beryl varieties is due their structure of stacked layers of Si_6O_{18} rings. The central holes in these rings are all aligned, forming open channels which can accomodate all sorts of extra molecules and ions (Cs, K, H_2O, Rb, etc.), which in turn affect the physical characteristics of their host. The name comes from the Greek *beryllos*, a term probably derived from the Sanskrit word for "cat's eye" (chrysoberyl).

Common beryl is of great importance as the primary ore of beryllium, a metal essential to technological applications ranging from nuclear reactors to rocket fuel to neon signs. It is also essential to the strong, light alloys and composites used in the aerospace industry, as well as more common applications such as bicycle parts and fishing rods. Ironically, virtually all commercial beryl is mined from relatively small and widely dispersed pegmatite deposits. In Brazil, the world's primary source of commercial beryl, miners in small, isolated workings still separate the beryl from gangue minerals by hand. Concentrations of the secondary beryllium mineral bertrandite, $Be_4Si_2O_7(OH)_2$, currently provide a large part of the United States supply, but such deposits are rare.

As varied as the modern uses of beryllium are, beryl itself was an important part of everyday life in the past, when belief in its healing and divinatory powers was widespread. Greek physicians used water in which a beryl crystal had been soaked to treat kidney and bladder stones, and sailors carried aquamarines to ensure the good graces of Poseidon. Beryl came to be seen as a symbol of purity in the Middle Ages, and doctors used it as a remedy for gas and to relieve asthma and liver problems. Equally effective in preventative medicine, beryl was thought to provide protection against malicious threats such as poisoning, and to prevent disputes—including marital discord.

The varieties of beryl described below show a remarkable range of colors, from the rich green of emerald to aquamarine blue, golden yellow, peach, and even red. While the rarer gem varieties are transparent, common beryl is generally an opaque, milky green. All beryl varieties form excellent crystals, usually in the form of a simple hexagonal prism with flat, pinacoidal terminations, although terminations including combinations of hexagonal or dihexagonal pyramids are also common. Cleavage is indistinct, and crystal faces are often subject to etching by corrosive fluids. Beryl crystals may resemble those of apatite or tourmaline, but the former is much softer, and the latter generally striated. Euclase, $BeAlSiO_4(OH)$, a rare species which sometimes forms gemmy blue crystals, can be distinguished from beryl on the basis of its perfect cleavage.

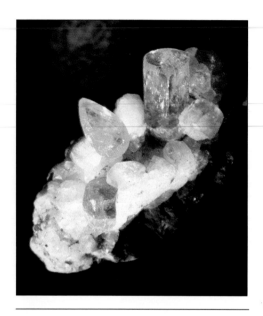

Left: Emerald crystals on calcite from Columbia, and a cut stone from the Ekaterinburg region of the Ural Mountains in the Soviet Union. **Right:** *A slender columnar prism of aquamarine and an aquamarine gemstone from a pegmatite on Mt. Antero, Chaffee County, Colorado.*

Aquamarine The name aquamarine is taken directly from the Latin term *aqua marina,* or "sea water," and refers to blue-green to deep blue beryls colored by traces of iron. In ancient times, truly sea-green stones were most prized, but now any hint of green causes the price of a stone to plummet. Unlike most precious stones, aquamarine sometimes forms very large crystals; stones as large as 200 pounds have been discovered in Brazilian pegmatites. Important aquamarine-producing pegmatites occur in the states of Minas Gerais, Bahia, and Espirito Santo, Brazil. The island of Madagascar is another important producer, as are Namibia, Zambia, and Mozambique. Fine aquamarines are also found in the Ural Mountains and elsewhere in the Soviet Union.

Blue topaz, glass, and synthetic blue spinel are commonly used to imitate aquamarine. Unlike these substitutes, however, true aquamarine is pleochroic, showing a deeper color when viewed in one direction than in another. Drab greenish beryls are often heated until they take on the color of aquamarine, and this is considered an acceptable practice by most gemologists.

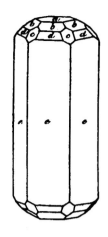

Emerald Beryl displays a wide range of greenish hues, due to the presence of various transition metals in trace amounts, but only the bright green stones colored by chromium have traditionally been considered emeralds. This began to change in the 1960s, when vibrantly colored deep-green vanadium-bearing beryls were discovered at Salininha, Brazil; more recently, similar emeralds from Africa have come on the market. After the initial controversy, the vanadian beryls were accepted as emeralds, although chromian emeralds are still thought to have finer color.

Despite having once been considered a symbol of purity, emeralds tend to contain a great deal of extraneous matter not accounted for in the chemical formula. Almost all emerald crystals display numerous fractures and inclusions of gasses and liquids, which are readily apparent in cut stones. These inclusions may contain microscopic crystals of pyrite, calcite, or mica, or even bits of organic matter. The source of an emerald gemstone can sometimes be approximated from a study of its inclusions: Columbian stones, for instance, are characterized by "three-phase" inclusions containing water, a gas bubble, and a tiny salt crystal.

Colombia is the world's primary source of fine emeralds, although Brazil produces a greater quantity. There are several emerald deposits in the country, of which Chivor and Muzo in the mountains north of Bogota are the most important. These mines were first worked by the native peoples of the area, who traded the stones to other groups as far away as Mexico. When the Spanish conquistadors invaded the region in the 16th century, they pillaged great troves of emeralds and sent them back to Europe. The stones were merely a novelty in Europe, but the Spanish were able to sell them at great profit to the Islamic rulers of the Mughal and Ottoman Empires, who saw in the green stones a vision of the gardens of Paradise. The Spanish colonials forced the local Indians to work as slaves in the emerald mines under such odious conditions that the Pope and the King of Spain eventually had to intercede.

Unlike emeralds from most other localities, the chromium-colored Columbian stones may form euhedral crystals, which grow in small calcite and plagioclase feldspar veins dissecting calcareous shales. The mines are worked both by underground tunnelling and by terracing, and the mine tailings are collected and washed in the rivers below by thousands of independent miners called *guaqueros*, who sell their meager gleanings on the black market. Although a greater volume of emeralds is produced by Brazil than by Columbia, the quality and value of the vanadium-colored stones is much lower. Several mines are located in Goias state, the largest of which is near Santa Teresinha. Similar deposits in Zambia and Zimbabwe together produce about twenty percent of the world's emerald supply.

In most of its occurrences worldwide, emerald forms in hydrothermally altered mica schists. Emeralds were first mined from such deposits over 3500 years ago by the ancient Egyptians, in Sikait-Zebara region near the Red Sea. Stones from these mines can be seen in ancient jewelry found in Egyptian tombs, but the mines now appear to be exhausted. The Romans apparently mined emeralds in the Austrian alps, where stones are sometimes still discovered. In 1830 emeralds were discovered by a charcoal-burner collecting wood along the Takovaya River in the Ural Mountains of

Simple hexagonal prism of the rare red beryl bixbite on rhyolite matrix, from the Wah Wah Mountains, Utah.

Russia. The Takovaya Mines remain an important source of large—though rarely euhedral—emeralds, as well as chrysoberyl. Smaller emerald deposits are mined in Afghanistan, Pakistan, Australia, Madagascar, South Africa, Tanzania, and North Carolina (see *Spodumene*).

In 1935 Carroll Chatham synthesized emeralds in a simulated hydrothermal environment in his San Francisco laboratory. Several months are required for the crystals to grow in this process, and the resulting stones are distinguishable from their natural counterparts only on the basis of their inclusions. Several other concerns currently produce emeralds, using both chromium and vanadium for color.

Other Varieties One of the most beautiful and unusual types of beryl is morganite, which was named for the famous New York tycoon and gem fancier John Pierpont Morgan. It is a warm peach-colored beryl which occurs as short prismatic or tabular crystals in pegmatites, along with aquamarine, tourmaline, and topaz. Morganite contains the relatively rare elements cesium and lithium, which give it a higher specific gravity than other beryls. Its distinctive color is due to trace amounts of the metal manganese. Relatively uncommon, morganite occurs in Minas Gerais, Brazil; Namibia; Madagascar; and San Diego County, California.

Golden beryl is the name commonly applied to golden-yellow stones. Heliodor, from the Greek phrase meaning "gift of the sun," is the name commonly applied to yellowish-green beryl. The colors of these varieties are apparently caused by natural radiation, and they display a distinctive blue luminescence under ultraviolet light. Both are relatively common, occurring in Brazil, Namibia, Madagascar, the United States and elsewhere. Colorless beryl is known as goshenite, after the town of Goshen, Massachusetts.

A very interesting and rare variety of beryl was discovered in the Wah Wah Mountains of Utah in 1974. This beryl is an intense ruby-red color and occurs as euhedral crystals in the silica-rich volcanic rock rhyolite. It is usually called *bixbite*, and should not be confused with the unrelated oxide *bixbyite* which occurs in the same environment.

betafite

Classification:
oxide

Composition:
$(Ca,Na,U)_2(Ti,Nb,Ta)_2O_6(OH)$
(hydrous uranium titanium niobium oxide)

Crystal System:
isometric

Hardness:
4–5.5

Specific Gravity:
3.7–5.0

This betafite crystal from the Silver Crater Mine, Hastings County, Ontario, displays nearly equal development of the cubic and octahedral forms.

THIS IMPORTANT SOURCE OF THORIUM, URANIUM, NIOBIUM, AND RARE EARTHS IS ALSO one of the most commonly collected of the rare pegmatite minerals. It is prized not for its color, which is black or brown when not coated with greenish or yellow alteration products—but for its well-formed crystals, which may weigh several kilograms. These take the form of octahedra or dodecahedra, often modified by other isometric forms, and frequently distorted by the "flattening" of a pair of opposing faces. Although sometimes translucent with a vitreous luster, betafite is commonly opaque and earthy when metamict. It is radioactive, and displays good conchoidal fracture and no cleavage.

Betafite is a common accessory in granitic pegmatites rich in rare earth elements, and in contact metamorphic marbles bordering such pegmatites. Common associates include fergusonite, zircon, columbite–tantalite, biotite, euxinite, allanite, thorite, and beryl. Very sharp crystals over 7 cm in diameter are found with zircon in the Silver Crater Mine, near Bancroft, Ontario. Smaller specimens are found in pegmatites throughout the western United States, including the Pidlite pegmatite near Mora, New Mexico, and the Brown Derby Mine in Gunnison County, Colorado. The classic betafite localities, however, are the complex pegmatites of the Malagasy Republic, Madagascar, where single crystals larger than 100 kg have been found; the species is named for a locality near Betafo. Other sources include Norway, Brazil, Spain, Pakistan, India, Peru, Manchuria, and the Soviet Union.

BIOTITE AND PHLOGOPITE ARE THE TWO COMMON DARK-COLORED MICAS. IT IS USEFUL to discuss them together since they are so similar in appearance and have complementary virtues: biotite is by far more common, but euhedral crystals of phlogopite are more often seen in collections. The two micas also tend to occur in very different geological environments: biotite in silica-rich metamorphic and igneous rocks, and phlogopite in contact metamorphic and silica-and-iron-poor igneous rocks.

Phlogopite, like the white mica muscovite, is prized as an electrical insulator, an application for which iron-rich conductive biotite is unsuitable. However, a humble alteration product of biotite has great commercial importance. Vermiculite is a micaceous mineral which forms as biotite loses its K content and absorbs large amounts of interstitial water. When vermiculite is heated, this water flashes into steam, causing the crystal to expand up to thirty times in volume. The resulting material is very porous and lightweight, and an excellent insulator for both heat and sound. It is also used in fireproofing and as a soil amendment in agriculture. The name of this mineral is derived from the Latin *vermiculare,* "to breed worms," a reference to the way the crystals expand into worm-like shapes when heated. Biotite itself is named in honor of Jean Baptiste Biot (b. 1774), a French physician who studied the micas.

The crystals of biotite and phlogopite usually form as foliated masses or disseminated flakes in rock matrix, or as thin elongated plates; biotite crystals form particularly long ribbon-like plates in granitic pegmatites. Biotite occasionally forms small, squat hexagonal prisms in some intrusive and extrusive igneous rocks. Phlogopite often forms large, euhedral prismatic

biotite and phlogopite

Classification:
phyllosilicates, mica group

Composition:
biotite: $K(Mg,Fe)_3(Al,Fe)Si_3O_{10}(OH,F)_2$
(potassium, magnesium
hydroxyl aluminosilicates)
phlogopite: $KMg_3AlSi_3O_{10}(OH,F)_2$

Crystal System:
monoclinic

Hardness:
2–3, harder parallel to cleavage

Specific Gravity:
biotite: 2.8–3.4, increasing with iron content
phlogopite: 2.76–2.9

Cluster of tabular biotite crystals from Tory Hill, Haliburton County, Ontario.

The lustrous cleavage surface on this phlogopite crystal from Templeton Township, Quebec, shows deformation due to metamorphic stress.

crystals, which may taper at the ends and assume triangular cross sections. Both minerals have the excellent basal cleavage typical of the mica group.

Biotite is dark brown, dark green, or black, with a vitreous to submetallic luster. Phlogopite is usually red-brown or dark yellow-brown, but may also be greenish, white, or even colorless. Its name comes from the Greek, *phlogopos*, or "fire-like," because of the distinctive coppery sheen which most specimens display. Oriented inclusions of rutile commonly cause phlogopite to display asterism in the form of a six- or twelve-sided star. Both species are translucent, or transparent in very thin sheets, and have a colorless streak. The best way to distinguish between these species is on the basis of geological environment. Also, euhedral crystals with a coppery glint suggest phlogopite, while very dark color is indicative of biotite.

Phlogopite occurs primarily in contact metamorphic marbles, as an accessory in many mafic igneous rocks, and in some unusual magnesium-rich pegmatites. Biotite is one of the most important rock-forming minerals, constituting a major part of many granitic rocks (including granitic pegmatites), and siliceous metamorphic rocks such as the gneisses and schists. There are few particularly noteworthy sources of biotite specimens, although many pegmatite districts produce interesting and sometimes very large crystals of this extremely common mineral. Remarkable phlogopite specimens, however, are found in many locations around the world. Perhaps the most famous of these are the well-formed hexagonal prisms from the Grenville marbles and associated pegmatites in Quebec and Ontario. The largest mica crystal ever seen was mined from the Lacy Mine in Ontario; it weighed 90 tons and was nearly 4 x 10 m in size. Good phlogopite crystals are also found in similar deposits across the border in New York State. Fine specimens are obtained from the zinc mines at Franklin, New Jersey, and from Fresno County, California. Excellent crystals are also found in Sri Lanka and at Fort Dauphin in the Malagasy Republic.

bismuth

Classification:
element, semimetal

Composition:
Bi (bismuth)

Crystal System:
hexagonal

Hardness:
2–2.5

Specific Gravity:
9.8

THE NAME BISMUTH IS DERIVED EITHER FROM THE ANCIENT GERMAN *WISMUTH*, meaning "mining claim in a meadow"; or from a Greek phrase meaning "lead-white." The former etymology is more whimsical, but the latter does make sense. Bismuth was considered a nuisance to ancient metallurgists, because it made bronze brittle when mistakenly alloyed with copper in the place of tin. German miners learned to recognize bismuth at an early date, however, since it was an indication of silver ore. Bismuth compounds are used in medicine to treat gastric disorders, most notably in the familiar, bright pink over-the-counter antacid. Metallic bismuth expands on cooling like the related semimetal arsenic, and is thus used in certain specialized alloys. Alloys of bismuth with lead, tin, and cadmium have low melting points and are used as fire plugs in automatic fire-sprinklers and electric fuses. Elemental bismuth is as stable as any of its compounds, and being relatively common, is thus the chief source of industrial bismuth. It often contains traces of sulfur, tellurium, arsenic, and antimony.

Crystals are rare and usually subhedral; granular or lamellar masses, or dendritic and skeletal aggregates being the norm. Bismuth is silver-white with a pink cast, and often tarnished with an iridescent film; its luster is metallic and its streak silver-white. It is sectile but not malleable, and one of its three cleavages is excellent and easily developed. Bismuth is distinguished from other semimetals by its pronounced cleavage, pink hue, and faint twinning striations.

Bismuth is found in hydrothermal veins associated with nickel, cobalt, silver, tin, and uranium minerals, and in some pegmatites and placers. The most important industrial deposits occur at several places in Bolivia, including Sorata, near La Paz. Excellent specimens come from the Cobalt District, Ontario, and the pitchblende deposits of the Great Bear Lake, Northwest

Territories. Fine specimens are also obtained from the pegmatites of Kingsgate, New South Wales, Australia; the Black Hills of South Dakota; and San Diego County, California. Important sulfide vein deposits include the El Carmen Mine, Durango, Mexico; and the mines of the Erzgebirge in Germany. Additional deposits are located in Cornwall, England; Kongsberg, Norway; and many other places around the world.

THIS RARE MINERAL IS SEEN MORE OFTEN THAN ONE WOULD SUSPECT FROM ITS LIMITED distribution, because collectors prize its lustrous, black cubic crystals. These may be highly modified, and commonly form penetration twins. Crystals are never more than 1–2 cm on edge, and display faint cleavage and sub-conchoidal fracture. The black crystals are opaque, with a brilliant metallic luster and a black streak.

Bixbyite is named for the Utah mineral collector Maynard Bixby, and was first found in the Thomas and Wah Wah Mountains, Juab County, Utah. Here it forms in cavities in the siliceous volcanic rock rhyolite, in association with topaz, hematite, garnet, and the equally rare red beryl bixbite. Other occurrences include Saddle Mountain, Pinal County, Arizona; San Luis Potosí, Mexico; and localities in Argentina, India, South Africa, Spain, and Sweden.

Perfect cubic crystal of bixbyite on rhyolite matrix, from the Thomas Range, Juab County, Utah.

bixbyite

Classification:
oxide

Composition:
$(Mn,Fe)_2O_3$ (manganese iron oxide)

Crystal System:
isometric

Hardness:
6–6.5

Specific Gravity:
4.95

boléite

Classification:
halide

Composition:
$Pb_{26}Ag_9Cu_{24}Cl_{62}(OH)_{48}$
(hydrated lead copper chloride)

Crystal System:
isometric

Hardness:
3–3.5

Specific Gravity:
5.05

BOLÉITE AND ITS RELATIVES CUMENGITE (WHICH LACKS THE SILVER COMPONENT) AND tetragonal pseudoboléite, $Pb_5Cu_4Cl_{10}(OH)_8$, are exceedingly rare and highly prized by collectors. Mother Nature seems to have designed boléite with her tongue firmly in cheek: although crystals may look like perfect cubes, they are actually twins of three interpenetrant individuals; twinning also results in pseudo-octahedral or pseudododecahedral forms. To further complicate matters, cumengite forms oriented pseudo-octahedral overgrowths on boléite crystals, and pseudoboléite grows as short, square prisms emerging from each face.

Boléite and cumengite are translucent with vitreous luster, and an unmistakable deep indigo blue color. The streak of boléite is light blue-green, and that of cumengite is sky-blue. Boléite is named for the premier locality—the copper mines at Boléo, near the French colonial town of Santa Rosalia on the Gulf side of Baja California; and cumengite is named for the French mining engineer Edouard Cumenge (b. 1828).

Boléite and cumengite occur as loose crystals or masses in residual clays in the leached zone of certain copper sulfide deposits. The source at Boléo in Baja California has provided the best specimens, including cubes that may be as large as 2 cm on a side. Boléite has also been found at several Arizona copper deposits, including the Mammoth–St. Anthony Mine in Pinal County, the Apache Mine in Gila County, and the Rowley Mine in Maricopa County. Other localities include the copper mines in Challacollo and Huantajaya, Chile; Broken Hill, New South Wales, Australia; the Anarak region of Iran; and the Ruhr District of Germany. Cumengite occurs by itself in the cliffs near Falmouth, Cornwall.

Pseudocubic boleite crystals (left), and a crystal of cumengite (right) from Boléo, near Santa Rosalia, Baja California, Mexico.

boracite

Classification:
borate

Composition:
$Mg_3B_7O_{13}Cl$ (magnesium chloroborate)

Crystal System:
orthorhombic

Hardness:
7–7.5

Specific Gravity:
2.95

BORACITE IS A RARE AND UNUSUAL BORATE MINERAL WHICH, UNLIKE THE MORE COMMON hydrated borates, usually occurs in evaporite deposits of marine origin. Crystals are generally found as isolated rough-surfaced cubes, dodecahedra, pseudo-octahedra, or cubo-octahedra of 2 cm or less in size. These are transparent to translucent; and may be colorless, white, gray, yellow, or pale to dark green or blue-green, with a vitreous luster. Boracite crystals are pyroelectric, becoming electrically charged when rubbed or heated. The name of this species is an allusion to the boron in its composition.

Boracite is typically found in association with anhydrite, gypsum, halite, and carnallite, but unfortunately, specimens in matrix are rare. The finest boracite specimens have traditionally come from the evaporite deposits of Germany. Particularly good crystals are found with sylvite and carnallite in the potash mines of the Hanover and Srassfurt Districts. Fine crystals are found on the margins of the Inowroclaw salt

Dodecahedral crystals of boracite from the salt mines of Germany's Hanover District.

dome in Poland, at Luneville, France, and in Yorkshire, England. Boracite is also found in Louisiana's Choctaw salt dome, where it forms part of the insoluble residue left over from the salt purification process. In California, boracite has been found at Otis in San Bernardino County.

THIS IMPORTANT MINERAL CLASS INCLUDES OVER 100 SPECIES, EACH OF WHICH CONtains boron as the primary anion. The basic building block of the borates is the triangular borate ion, BO_3^{-3}; but because this ion is close to the upper stability limit for its coordination number of three, tetrahedral, four-coordinated BO_4 ions are also common. These basic borate ions combine to form complex groups, and like the silica tetrahedra in the silicate minerals, can form elaborate frameworks and infinite chains and sheets. A structure consisting solely of borate triangles, similar to the quartz structure of silica tetrahedra, is possible but very unstable, and thus does not occur in nature as a crystalline mineral. Material of this composition readily forms an amorphous glass, however, which is used in optics and other industrial applications that require lightweight glass plates and lenses even more transparent than their silica counterparts.

The most familiar borates are the hydrated borates, of which the most common are borax, kernite, colemanite, and ulexite. These species are found in deposits precipitated from brines in the ephemeral lakes of the western United States, Australia, Central Asia, and other arid regions over the last few million years. They form colorless or white crystals and crystalline aggregates within the the soft lakebed sediments, and white crusts or efflorescences on the lakebeds above. Due to the rather loose structure of borate and other ions linked together between layers of unstable water molecules, the hydrated borates are soft, prone to dehydration, and extremely soluble in water. For this reason, great care must be taken to prevent specimens from disintegrating after removal from the earth.

The less commonly encountered anhydrous and hydroxyl-halogen borates are much more durable. Tight clusters of borate ions without interstitial water make these minerals very hard and stable. Examples include boracite, hambergite, and the rare species sinhalite ($MgAlBO_4$), which was known only as gem-quality pebbles from the gem-bearing gravels of Sri Lanka, before finally being discovered *in situ* in skarn deposits.

The borates are the primary commercial source of the element borax, one of the most useful natural substances. Borax is derived from the mineral of the same name as well as the other hydrated borates, and is used in metallurgy and in cleaning and pharmaceutical products (see *Borax*). The borates also provide elemental boron, which used to harden steel, to absorb stray neutrons in nuclear reactors, and to make a variety of artificial compounds. Among the many industrial boron compounds are boron carbide and boron nitride, synthetic abrasives second only to diamond in hardness and widely used in drill bits and other tools. Other boron compounds are added to gasoline to improve the performance of high-compression engines, and in fuels for missiles and airplanes. Synthetic boron fibers are becoming increasingly important as components of flexible and durable industrial materials, including insulation and textiles.

Lath-like crystals of the rare hydrated borate hambergite $Be_2BO_3(OH,F)$, which is found only in pegmatites. These crystals are from Anjanabonoina, Malagasy Republic.

Borax crystals, partially altered to powdery white tincalconite, from the Jennifer mine, Kramer District, Kern County, California.

borax

Classification:
borate

Composition:
$Na_2B_4O_5(OH)_4 \cdot 8H_2O$
(hydrated sodium borate)

Crystal System:
monoclinic

Hardness:
2–2.5

Density:
1.7

THE MINERAL BORAX IS THE PRINCIPAL SOURCE OF INDUSTRIAL BORAX AND OF THE element boron, which is used to make a variety of compounds. This mineral, which gets its name from the Arabic word for white, *buraq*, is one of the most useful of all natural substances. Because molten borax is able to dissolve many otherwise insoluble metallic oxides, one of its first uses was as a flux to aid in metal working. The antiseptic and detergent properties of borax make it a vital component of cleaning and pharmaceutical products, such as detergents, medicines, disinfectants and cosmetics. Fibers of borax glass are widely used in textiles and insulation as well. Elemental boron is used in a wide variety of compounds, from nonferrous alloys to rocket fuels (see *Borates*).

During medieval times, borax was transported to Europe by caravan from China and Tibet, which were the only known sources of the mineral. In the early 19th century, a method was found for precipitating sassolite (H_3BO_3) from the mineral-rich vapors of natural geysers in Tuscany, Italy. The commercial product borax was easily made from this precipitate, and Tuscany soon became the world's chief source. In 1857, a San Francisco doctor searching for medicinal springs in northern California discovered borax in the sediments of a shallow lakebed, and soon Borax Lake had become the world's pre-eminent source of this mineral. Several years later, enormous reserves of borax and other borate minerals, including kernite and ulexite, were found in the dry lakebeds of the Mojave Desert. Today, the open-pit mine at Boron in Kern County, California provides the bulk of the world supply, although the largest known deposits are in the Kirka region of Turkey.

Borax forms stubby prismatic or tabular crystals, usually clustered in blocky groups on massive borax, like buildings tumbled together in the wake of an earthquake. Borax is usually colorless or white, but may also be yellowish, bluish, or greenish; it is transparent to translucent with vitreous to earthy luster and a white streak. It is very brittle, with one perfect cleavage and conchoidal fracture. Borax is easily soluble in water, and can be distinguished by its astringency and faint sweet taste when touched to the tongue. Unless given a protective coating, borax quickly loses half of its water content after being removed from the ground, altering to the powdery, opaque mineral tincalconite.

Borax is found in the evaporite deposits derived from the waters of saline lakes in arid regions, and in some hot spring deposits. Layers up to 3 m in thickness are mined in the Boron Open Pit in Kern County,

California; borax is also extracted from Searles Lake in San Bernardino County and other depressions throughout the Great Basin region. Borax Lake in northern California produces fine large crystals seen in many museums. Borax deposits are also found in the Salta Province of Argentina, and in India, Kashmir, Turkey, Iran, Tibet, and Soviet Central Asia. The deposit at Lop Nor in China's Taklamakan Desert, located on the ancient Silk Road caravan route, is now a nuclear test site.

BORNITE, NAMED FOR THE AUSTRIAN MINERALOGIST IGNAZ VON BORN (B. 1742), IS one of the most important ores of copper and is certainly among the more colorful. Its colorful nickname—"peacock ore"—is a reference to the intense multicolored (but primarily purple) iridescence that is developed on fracture surfaces on exposure. There is extensive solid solution between the copper sulfides bornite, covellite, and chalcopyrite at high temperatures. On cooling, the individual species separate, or "exsolve," forming massive aggregates.

Bornite crystals formed at temperatures above 228°C display isometric symmetry, while those formed at lower temperature, including the bulk of bornite ores, are tetragonal. Although nearly always massive, bornite is seen in pseudocubic, -octahedral, or -dodecahedral crystals with curved or rough faces. Less tarnished specimens are bronze-colored with metallic luster, and the streak is light gray to black. Bornite is best distinguished from other sulfides by its striking iridescence, but is usually associated intimately with covellite and chalcocite, to which it easily alters.

Although sometimes found in pegmatites and basalt cavities, economic concentrations of bornite are restricted to the oxidation zones of copper deposits, where it is associated with the usual colorful cast of secondary species. Bornite is also found in some layered igneous intrusions, where it forms from the alteration of primary sulfide chalcopyrite. Bornite itself is easily altered, and crystals are often replaced by covellite or secondary chalcopyrite. Good crystals have been collected in the mines of Redruth, Cornwall, England; and Tsumeb, Namibia. Fine crystals are also found at Butte, Montana, and Bristol, Connecticut. Massive bornite is found in virtually every oxidized copper deposit the world over.

bornite

Classification:
sulfide

Composition:
Cu_5FeS_4 (copper iron sulfide)

Crystal System:
isometric and tetragonal

Hardness:
3

Specific Gravity:
5.06–5.08

Unusual columnar aggregates of bornite crystals from the Carn Brea Mine, Illogan, Cornwall.

bournonite

Classification:
sulfide (sulfosalt)

Composition:
$CuPbSbS_3$ (lead copper antimony sulfide)

Crystal System:
orthorhombic

Hardness:
2.5–3

Specific Gravity:
5.8–5.9

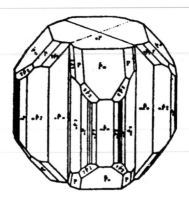

BOURNONITE, NAMED FOR THE FRENCH MINERALOGIST COUNT JACQUES LOUIS DE Bournon (b. 1751) is an important ore of lead, copper, and antimony. It is also prized by collectors for its interesting crystals. These are commonly stubby prisms which form fourling twins of a characteristic flattened, radiating "cogwheel" shape. More often, however, bournonite occurs as massive granular aggregates. Bournonite is brittle, with a subconchoidal to uneven fracture, and three distinct cleavages. It is steel-gray to iron-black in color, with a metallic luster and gray-black streak.

Perhaps the most abundant of the sulfosalts, bournonite occurs in medium-temperature hydrothermal veins in association with stibnite, chalcocite, galena, tetrahedrite, chalcopyrite, siderite, and quartz. The best specimens are the lustrous cogwheel twins from the Wheal Boys Mine, Endellion, and from Liskeard, Cornwall, England. Excellent crystals are also found at Andreasberg, in the Harz Mountains, and Willroth, Germany; Kapnik, Romania; and at Pribram, Czechoslovakia. Very large crystals are found at Machacamarca, Bolivia, and Park City, Utah. Very attractive small, untwinned crystals on tetrahedrite come from Concepción del Oro, Zacatecas, Mexico.

Classic "cogwheel" twins of bournonite from the Herodsfoot Mine, Lanreath, Liskeard, Cornwall.

brookite

Classification:
oxide

Composition:
TiO_2 (titanium oxide)

Crystal System:
orthorhombic

Hardness:
5.5–6

Specific Gravity:
4.1

BROOKITE, NAMED FOR THE ENGLISH MINERALOGIST HENRY JAMES BROOKE (B. 1771), is the rarest of the three polymorphs of titanium oxide, the others being anatase and rutile. The structure of brookite is characterized by octahedra of TiO_4, each of which share three edges. In rutile, similar octahedra share only two edges, and this structure seems to be stable under the widest range of conditions, since rutile is the most common of the polymorphs. Although potentially an ore of titanium, brookite has never been found in sufficient concentration to be commercially exploited.

Crystals of brookite take a variety of forms, from tabular to prismatic, pseudohexagonal or pyramidal, and are commonly striated. They are transparent to translucent, and brown to black in color, with an adamantine to submetallic luster and a yellow or grayish-brown streak.

Brookite is most commonly found in Alpine vugs, the crystal-lined fissures which occur in gneisses and schists in the Alps and other mountainous regions. Brookite also occurs as an accessory in some igneous rocks and contact metamorphic deposits, and as a detrital mineral in sedimentary rocks. The best specimens are found in the Alps—at Bourg d'Oisans, France; in the Binnatal and St. Gotthard regions of Switzerland; near Salzburg, Austria; and in the Val d'Ossola and elsewhere in Italy. Sharp, black, lustrous crystals of varied habit are found in the contact metamorphic deposits of Magnet Cove, Arkansas, and Mont St. Hilare, Quebec.

Flattened crystals of brookite from near Tremadoc, Gwynedd, Wales.

BRUCITE, NAMED FOR THE EARLY NEW YORK MINERALOGIST ARCHIBALD BRUCE, IS AN important ore of magnesium (see *Magnesite*). This light metallic element is very important in the manufacture of light alloys, and in pyrotechnics, to which it provides an intense white light; various magnesium compounds are vital to medicine and the photographic and chemical industries. Brucite has a very simple, sheet-like structure consisting of two layers of closely packed hydroxyl (OH) ions, between which the magnesium ions are nestled in octahedral coordination. Since the magnesium and hydroxyl ions satisfy each others charge requirements, the structural sheets of brucite are held together only by Van der Waals' forces, as in the sheet silicates.

Brucite is usually found as foliated or finely granular masses, or very rarely as broad, tabular hexagonal crystals. Perfect cleavage produces flexible but inelastic sheets. The color of brucite ranges from colorless through green, blue, and pinkish; the manganese-bearing variety may be yellow, brown, or reddish. Brucite is transparent or translucent, with pearly or waxy luster and a white streak. It most closely resembles gypsum, from which it can be distinguished by its easy solubility in dilute acid. At high temperatures, hydroxyl is driven off and brucite converts to periclase (MgO).

Brucite is characteristic of low-grade metamorphic rocks such as serpentinites and chloritic or dolomitic schists, in which it forms by alteration of primary manganese minerals. Commonly associated species include aragonite, calcite, chrysotile asbestos, and talc. It is also found in contact metamorphic dolomites and low-temperature hydrothermal veins. The finest specimens are crystals that may be 15 cm in length, found in the past in the Wood's and Low's chromite mines, Lancaster County, Pennsylvania; and pale-blue specimens from the Tilly Foster Iron Mine, Brewster, New York. Brucite is common in the serpentinites of the California Coast Ranges in the Asbestos and Thetford Mines, Quebec; and at Bancroft, Ontario. Other sources include Hoboken, New Jersey; the asbestos mines at Bajenov in the Soviet Union; the Shetland Islands of Scotland; England; Sweden; Italy; Austria; and Turkey.

brucite

Classification:
hydroxide

Composition:
$Mg(OH)_2$ (magnesium hydroxide)

Crystal System:
hexagonal (rhombohedral)

Hardness:
2.5

Specific Gravity:
2.39

Massive brucite from the Tilly Foster Mine, Brewster, New York.

calcite

Classification:
carbonate

Composition:
$CaCO_3$ (calcium carbonate)

Crystal System:
hexagonal (rhombohedral)

Hardness:
3

Specific Gravity:
2.6–2.8

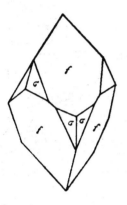

ALTHOUGH EXTREMELY COMMON IN NATURE, CALCITE IS ONE OF THE MOST FASCINATING minerals; it occurs in such a wide variety of forms that some mineral collectors specialize in this one species alone. The name comes from *chalix*, the Greek word for lime. The production of lime was one of the first uses found for calcite. When heated to a certain temperature, calcite loses CO_2 and decomposes into lime, CaO, which is then mixed with water to make slaked lime or cement, $Ca(OH)_2$. As it dries, cement absorbs CO_2 and gives off water, solidifying as reconstituted $CaCO_3$. At first, cement was used primarily as mortar to hold stones in place. The Romans discovered that burning volcanic ash with the calcite would produce a much more durable cement, and they pioneered the construction of entire buildings from this material. After the fall of Rome, cement was little used as a structural material, but by the early 19th century English engineers were mixing clay with slaked lime to build lighthouses, bridges and tunnels. Now there are all kinds of elaborate recipies for producing cements with just the right strength, weight and drying time for every concievable use, and the "artificial stone" continues to spread across the landscape.

Calcite has perfect rhombohedral cleavage, and the transparent cleavage fragments thus produced exhibit the property of double refraction. Because the light entering a calcite crystal is broken into two separate rays, images observed through the parallel faces of a cleavage fragment appear doubled. This property remained an interesting novelty until it was adapted for the construction of lenses for light-polarizing microscopes, which are indispensable to the study of rocks and minerals. This property also made calcite lenses ideal for the sights used by bombardiers, and large quantities of clear calcite were mined for this purpose during the Second World War. Now, the advent of "smart bombs" has made it unnecessary for military personnel to actually *see* what they are destroying.

Calcite often forms excellent crystals, sometimes of enormous size. Hundreds of combinations of crystal forms have been observed in calcite, more than in any other mineral species. Among the more common crystals are the tapering scalenohedral-prismatic forms, blocky rhombohedral shapes, and tabular forms with dominant basal faces. Calcite forms nearly every possible kind of twin, including

The elaborate coral formations of this Caribbean reef are colonies of millions of tiny coral polyps, which draw calcium carbonate from seawater to form their calcite skeletons.
Opposite page: *Classic scalenohedral or "dogtooth" calcite crystals from the Pallaflat Mine, Biggrigg, Egremont, Cumbria.*

polysynthetic twins and heart-shaped contact twins. "Sand calcite" crystals that have grown *in situ* in sediments retain a distinct crystal form, even though they may contain up to 65% sand by volume. Common aggregate habits of calcite include the chatoyant, fibrous satin spar, stalactitic cave onyx, and the fine to coarsely crystalline form typical of the metamorphic rock marble.

Pure calcium carbonate is usually colorless and transparent, or translucent and white, but inclusions of extraneous material can give calcite a wide range of colors. Inclusions of hematite commonly cause a reddish hue; other variations are yellow, brown, pink, violet, blue, and green. The luster is vitreous to greasy, and the streak white. The best way to recognize calcite is by its perfect cleavage, which always yields perfect, sharp rhombohedra. Its vigorous reaction with cold, dilute hydrochloric acid distinguishes calcite from dolomite, siderite and other carbonates whose reactions are more mild. Calcite is the calcium end-member of a solid-solution series with the manganese carbonate rhodochrosite.

Calcite is a very common mineral, occurring in extremely large amounts as the primary constituent of the sedimentary rock limestone, and its more coarsely crystalline, metamorphic counterpart, marble. Limestone is formed from sediments composed of the skeletons of marine animals, such as the corals and the planktonic *foraminifera*, and plants, such as the calcareous algae and the planktonic *coccolithophorids*.

The corals and calcareous algae form enormous accumulations in warm shallow seas, while the planktonic material can accumulate on the ocean floor in deposits of remarkable purity, free from contamination by other sediments. The microscopic plates of the coccoliths have accumulated in huge amounts since they first evolved in the Mesozoic Era. The light, porous stone formed by these fossils is called chalk—not to be confused with blackboard chalk, which is now made from gypsum. Much of southern England and northern France is underlain by chalk, which makes the Cliffs at Dover white and the wines of Chablis "flinty." Although the original form of calcium carbonate may actually be aragonite or magnesium-rich calcite, geological processes gradually turn it into calcite or dolomite after burial.

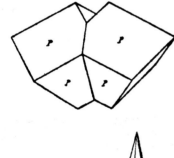

These marine plants and animals may play an important part in controlling the climate of the earth. As they precipitate their skeletons of calcium carbonate, they draw dissolved carbon dioxide (CO_2) out of the seawater. The ocean is then able to absorb more heat-trapping CO_2 from the atmosphere, and thus help to control the "greenhouse effect." If marine organisms did not precipitate shells of $CaCO_3$, this so-called drawdown would not occur, and the addition of CO_2 to the atmosphere from volcanic and other sources would cause the earth's surface temperature to rise to unbearable levels.

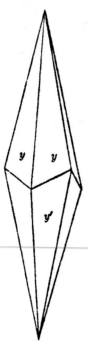

Calcite occurs in virtually every other rock type as well, although it is uncommon in most igneous rocks. Notable exceptions are the carbonatites, magmatic rocks composed primarily of either calcite or dolomite. The origin of carbonatites was highly controversial, until the actual molten magma was observed in the carbonatite volcano Ol Doinyo Lengai near Mt. Kilimanjaro in the East African Rift. Calcite is so common in fine specimens that only a few important localities are worth mentioning. The most exceptional sources in North America are the Tri-State mining district of Missouri, Kansas, and Oklahoma; the lead-zinc deposits of Wisconsin and Illinois; and the Elmwood mine in Smith County, Tennessee. Marvelous crystals in every possible form have been found in the mines of Cornwall, Cumberland, Durham, and Lancashire, England. Large cleavage fragments of perfectly transparent calcite are known as "Iceland spar," after the famous basalt-cavity deposit at Eskifjord, Iceland.

THIS STRANGE AND BEAUTI-
ful mineral grows in rich,
green carpets of tiny
prismatic crystals on
matrix in the upper, oxi-
dized zones of lead-cop-
per sulfide veins, incor-
porating nearly every
type of ion available in
its environment. The
crystals are usually of
microscopic size, form-
ing divergent groups or
massive aggregates;
however, some may
reach 1.25 cm in length
and display lustrous, striated faces. Crystals are
transparent to translu-
cent, and their color
ranges from dark green
to blue, with a vitreous
to resinous luster and a
bluish- or greenish-white
streak.

The best specimens
have come from Arizona,
particularly the large, blue clusters from the Mammoth Mine, Tiger, Arizona.
Caledonite is found in many other lead-copper sulfide deposits in the western United States, including the the Wonder Prospect at Darwin in Inyo
County, where it is associated with linarite. Other countries from which fine
caledonite specimens are obtained include Canada, Chile, England, France,
Germany, Namibia, Sardinia—and, of course, Scotland, from whose ancient
name *Caledonia* this mineral's name is derived.

Classification:
sulfate
Composition:
$CU_2Pb_5(SO_4)_3CO_3(OH)_6$
(copper-lead hydroxyl carbonate sulfate)
Crystal System:
orthorhombic
Hardness:
2.5–3
Specific Gravity:
5.76

Crust of caledonite from Tsumeb, Namibia.

CALOMEL IS ALSO KNOWN AS "HORN MERCURY" OR SIMPLY MERCUROUS CHLORIDE. IT
was a common household drug for centuries, taken as a cathartic (purga-
tive). Modern applications of mercury chloride include insect and fungus
control in agriculture.

The name apparently
comes from the Greek
phrase *kalon meli*,
meaning "fair honey"—
an allusion to its sweet
taste (do not taste
calomel however, as it
contains mercury). This
property is also reflected
in its Latin name,
Mercuris dulcis, or
"sweet mercury."

An alternative deriva-
tion of this species is
often given, based on
the Greek phrase *kalos
melas*, meaning "beauti-
ful black"—supposedly a

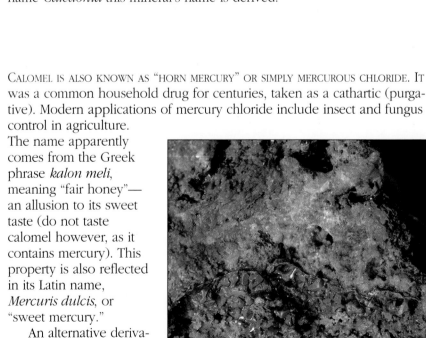

calomel

Classification:
halide
Composition:
HgCl (mercury chloride)
Crystal System:
tetragonal
Hardness:
1.5
Specific Gravity:
7.16

*Cluster of calomel crystals from San Onofre,
Plateros, Zacatecas, Mexico.*

reference to the tendency of this otherwise white-to-yellowish-gray species to darken on exposure to natural light. Calomel is transparent to translucent, with an adamantine luster; exposure to ultraviolet light produces a dark-red fluorescence. Crystals are often complex, usually tabular, but also equant, prismatic, or pyramidal. Massive earthy crusts are more common, however.

Calomel is an uncommon secondary mercury mineral which forms at the expense of native mercury, cinnabar, and other primary species in the oxidized portions of hydrothermal mercury deposits. Good crystals are found in the Terlingua District, Texas; in the Denio District, Oregon; in the Sunflower District, Arizona; and near Jackport, Arkansas. Calomel is also found in the mercury deposits of California's Coast Ranges in San Mateo and Napa Counties. Other sources include Zacatecas and Queretaro, Mexico; Gvassington Moor, Yorkshire, England; and locations in France, Germany, and Spain.

carbonates

ALTHOUGH MOST OF THE SEVENTY SPECIES OF CARBONATES ARE UNCOMMON TO RARE, much of the earth's surface is covered with rocks composed almost exclusively of the two most important species, calcite and dolomite. The prevalence of these minerals is due to the fact that marine organisms like algae, plankton, and coral cause carbonate minerals to precipitate from seawater. When these plants and animals die, their carbonate skeletons collect to form sediments which may eventually turn into carbonate rocks like limestone, dolostone, or marble. The carbonate anion (CO_3^{-2}) consists of one carbon atom bonded to three oxygen atoms, and forms the basic structural unit which determines the symmetry of carbonate crystals.

The most commonly encountered carbonates belong to one of three basic groups: the *calcite, aragonite,* and *dolomite* groups. The calcite group is characterized by the combination of a small metal cation with the carbonate anion, and includes the similar species calcite, $CaCO_3$, magnesite, $MgCO_3$, siderite, $FeCO_3$, rhodochrosite, $MnCO_3$, and smithsonite, $ZnCO_3$. The aragonite group includes those species characterized by single, large metal cations, including witherite, $BaCO_3$, strontianite, $SrCO_3$, and cerrusite, $PbCO_3$. Although aragonite, $CaCO_3$, shares the same chemical composition

Fine prismatic crystals of the rare secondary lead carbonate phosgenite, $Pb_2(CO_3)Cl_2$, from Matlock, Derbyshire. Phosgenite crystallizes from saline hydrothermal fluids in which galena has been dissolved.

as calcite, its structure is of this type. The dolomite group includes dolomite, $CaMg(CO_3)_2$, and ankerite, $Ca(Fe,Mg)(CO_3)_2$, which contain two metal cations associated with the carbonate anion in alternating layers. The only other commonly encountered carbonates are the colorful hydrous copper carbonates azurite, $Cu_3(CO_3)_2(OH)_2$, and malachite, $Cu_2CO_3(OH)_2$.

The carbonates display a remarkable variety of crystal forms and habits, but the group as a whole shares a number of distinct characteristics. Many common carbonates dissolve easily in acids, with the release of carbon dioxide, resulting in mild to vigorous effervescence. Carbonate minerals are soft, with hardnesses between 3 and 5, and tend to break readily along characteristic cleavage planes. Most carbonates are white or colorless, although many of the species found in hydrothermal ore deposits (like azurite, rhodochrosite, and smithsonite) can be brightly colored indeed, due to the presence of metal ions such as copper and manganese.

CARNALLITE, NAMED FOR THE PRUSSIAN MINING ENGINEER RUDOLPH VON CARNALL (b. 1804), is a very important source of potassium, which is essential as a fertilizer and vital to the the chemical and pharmaceutical industries (see *Sylvite*). Like other evaporite minerals, carnallite forms extensive beds of granular material. Interesting pseudohexagonal crystals are sometimes produced from the mines, but they tend to absorb water and disintegrate on exposure. The crystals are colorless and transparent, or red due to hematite inclusions, and display a vitreous or greasy luster. Carnallite is further distinguished by its strong fluorescence; solubility in water; and bitter, salty taste.

A late-forming component of evaporite deposits, carnallite is found in association with other halides like sylvite and halite (salt). It is mined along with these minerals from extensive deposits in west Texas and southern New Mexico; Stassfurt, Germany; and the Ukraine. Other notable deposits occur in Iran, Mali, China, Tunisia, and Spain.

carnallite

Classification:
halide

Composition:
$KMgCl_3 \cdot 6H_2O$
(hydrated potassium magnesium chloride)

Crystal System:
orthorhombic

Hardness:
2.5

Specific Gravity:
1.6

Carnallite grains from the salt mines of Stassfurt, Magdeburg, Germany.

Left: In the event of thermonuclear war, the multiple nuclear warheads in the cone of this intercontinental ballistic missile are designed to rain destruction over a vast area of the earth's surface. The plutonium in these warheads is made using enriched uranium from carnotite.
Right: Massive, earthy carnotite from the canyonlands of southern Utah.

carnotite

Classification:
vanadate

Composition:
$K_2(UO_2)_2(VO_4)_2 \cdot 3H_2O$
(hydrated potassium uranium vanadate)

Crystal System:
monoclinic

Hardness:
unknown—soft

Specific Gravity:
4.95

CARNOTITE, NAMED FOR THE FRENCH CHEMIST AND ENGINEER MARIE-ADOLF CARNOT (b. 1839), is one of the most important ores of uranium and a significant source of vanadium as well. It is extremely radioactive, and for this reason should not be included in one's mineral collection, despite its attractive canary-yellow color. Microscopic crystals of carnotite are very rare, and it usually occurs as opaque, earthy, or powdery aggregates. The Indians of the American Southwest apparently used this soft yellow mineral for adornment and war paint, but a later generation of Americans found an even more war-like application: carnotite was the main source of the uranium enriched to make fissionable uranium for the Cold War arms race.

Extensive reserves of carnotite are located in the Triassic and Jurassic sandstones of the Colorado Plateau region of the American Southwest. For a brief period in the 1920s, carnotite was mined in small quantities to produce radium for luminescent watch dials. The advent of the arms race, however, turned this dangerous substance into the focus of a national frenzy. During the "uranium rush" after the Second World War, amateur prospectors probed every canyon in the Colorado Plateau with Geiger counters, even flying across vast stretches of desert dangling scintillometers from small aircraft. Production peaked at the height of the Cold War in the mid-1950s, when the United States Government was paying a guaranteed price for large quantities of "yellow cake" (processed carnotite), to produce its enormous hydrogen bombs and other nuclear devices. New sources of fissionable material have since been found, although carnotite continues to be mined on the Navajo Indian Reservation in Arizona and New Mexico, at great expense to the health of the local population.

Sandstones derived from the weathering of igneous rocks often contain appreciable quantities of primary uranium minerals like allanite and uraninite, in the form of small grains. Over the millennia, oxygenated groundwater flowing through these porous formations dissolves these grains, gradually transports the uranium and other elements and ions through the rock. The uranium minerals in such orebodies from a "rolling front," dissolving on the upstream side and reprecipitating at the leading edge. Thus, over the millennia, the deposit moves imperceptibly through the porous rock. Since many of these sandstone formations represent ancient streambeds or river channels, the orebodies are restricted to a relatively small area. Organic matter in the sediments influences the precipitation of carnotite and other minerals;

one giant log over 30m long and 1m in diameter was once found to be petrified with carnotite, and was worth nearly a quarter-million dollars to its lucky discoverers. Although primarily known for producing uranium and vanadium from carnotite and other minerals, copper, molybdenum, selenium, and silver have also been mined from such deposits.

In the United States, carnotite also occurs in Wyoming and South Dakota, and in Carbon County, Pennsylvania. Extensive deposits are found in the Ferghana Basin of Soviet Turkestan, and in South Australia. In Africa, carnotite is mined at Katanga, Zaire; Mounana, Gabon; and at El Borouj and Louis Genil, Morocco.

KASSITEROS IS THE GREEK WORD FOR TIN, AND CASSITERITE IS THE MOST IMPORTANT ore of this metal. Around six thousand years ago, it was discovered that tin and copper could be alloyed to produce a relatively strong metal, called bronze (see *Copper*). This discovery is one of the developments that facilitated the technological, commercial, and political advances that catapulted human culture out of the Stone Age. Around three thousand years ago, the Phoenicians began importing large quantities of tin into the Mediterranean region from islands to the north, then called the Cassiterides. It is now known that these ancient seafarers sailed nearly 2000 km north to the British Isles, trading for tin with the Celtic miners of Cornwall. These deposits were later exploited by the Romans, and remained an important source of tin into the present century.

Cassiterite is still the primary ore of tin, but the metal itself is becoming less important than it was in ancient times, or even in the recent past. Although the terms "tin can" and "tin foil" are still in use, these products are now likely to contain no tin at all. Tin was used to make household foil because of its great malleability, which allows it to be made into very thin sheets; now, however, it has been replaced by the relatively abundant, strong and light metal aluminum in foils. "Tin" cans are actually steel, with an electroplating of tin or tin-lead alloy to protect them from rusting. The introduction of less expensive, lead-free containers of aluminum, paper, and plastic has resulted in a decline in tin-plating. Pewter is an alloy consisting primarily of tin, with variable amounts of lead, antimony, bismuth, copper, and zinc. It was used as early as Roman times, and was the main material for tableware in England and much of Europe from the Middle Ages through the eighteenth century. Pewter fell out of fashion as the use of other metals and of china became more widespread, and as the toxic

cassiterite

Classification:
oxide

Composition:
SnO_2 (tin oxide)

Crystal System:
tetragonal

Hardness:
6–7

Specific gravity:
6.8–7.1

Left: *Lustrous aggregate of cassiterite crystals from Panasqueira Mine, Serra da Estrella, Portugal.* **Right:** *The casting of bronze, the versatile alloy of copper and tin, was already a highly developed art when this 25-cm-tall Greek statue of Zeus was sculpted in the fourth century BC.*

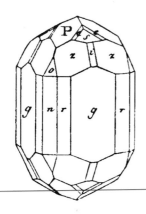

properties of lead began to be understood. One lead–tin alloy that retains its importance is solder, which is primarily used to secure electrical connections in electronics.

Cassiterite has the same structure as rutile, and like rutile forms lustrous, stubby prismatic crystals of complex habit, often in elbow-shaped twins. It is most commonly seen, however, as tough, concentrically banded, botryoidal masses known as "wood tin." This massive material is brown, and crystals are black and translucent (transparent on thin edges), with an adamantine luster and a white streak. Cassiterite can be distinguished from most other heavy black minerals by its translucency.

The tin deposits of Cornwall were formed through a process called greisenization, in which granitic rocks are invaded and altered by fluorine- and boron-rich hydrothermal fluids at medium-to-high temperatures. This process converts the granite to a mixture of quartz, kaolin clay, lepidolite, fluorite, tourmaline, and topaz. Ore minerals, such as cassiterite, molybdenite, rutile, and wolframite, tend to occur in discrete veins in the altered granite. Such deposits were once mined in the Bohemia region of Czechoslovakia and Saxony, Germany. Today, the only important vein deposits of cassiterite are those in Bolivia, including the Araca, Llallagua, and Ouro districts, where crystals as large as 8 cm in diameter have been recovered.

Cassiterite forms in a variety of other geological environments as well, including contact metamorphic deposits, pegmatites, and rhyolites. Fine crystals occur in the pegmatites of New England, Southern California, the Black Hills of South Dakota, and elsewhere; and wood–tin aggregates are found in vast rhyolite fields of northern Mexico and New Mexico. Since cassiterite is hard, tough, and heavy, it easily weathers out of the primary deposits to collect in placers, and the largest deposits occur in river and beach placers where cassiterite has been accumulating over millennia. The ancient tin miners, lacking explosives or mechanical mining equipment, secured all of their ore from placer deposits. Great quantities of cassiterite are recovered from "tin belts" in the Andes of South America, Southwest Africa, Western Australia and Tasmania, and Southeast Asia. The placers of the Malay Peninsula, Thailand, and Sumatra supply the bulk of the world's tin needs.

celestite

Classification:
sulfate

Composition:
$SrSO_4$ (strontium sulfate)

Crystal System:
orthorhombic

Hardness:
3–3.5

Specific Gravity:
3.95–3.97

THE LATIN WORD *COELESTIS*, OR "HEAVENLY" PROVIDES THE NAME OF THIS PALE BLUE mineral. Celestite is the most important ore of strontium, which is used to produce the crimson flame in tracer bullets, flares, and fireworks. It is also used in refining sugar from sugar beets, and in the manufacture of batteries, paint, rubber, glass, porcelain, and depilatories—chemical hair-removal products. Strontium has similar properties to barium, and thus celestite finds similar uses to barite as a radiation absorber in the nuclear industry.

There is complete solid-solution series between barite and celestite, and a limited series between anhydrite and celestite.

Celestite crystals are sometimes tabular but more often prismatic, generally resembling barite in morphology.

Bladed crystals of celestite from Clay Center, Ohio.

Frequently, celestite occurs as massive, radiating or granular crystalline aggregates, or as concretions with terminated crystals pointing inward. In addition to its nominal sky-blue color, celestite may be white, colorless, yellowish, reddish, greenish, or brownish. It is a very fragile mineral, with perfect basal cleavage. Celestite can be distinguished from barite by its lower density.

Celestite is most abundant in carbonate rocks and evaporate deposits. The sulfur mines of Agrigento in Sicily produce excellent specimens in association with gypsum, aragonite, and sulfur. It is also found in hydrothermal sulfide veins and basalt cavities. Some of the finest specimens have been recovered from pegmatite deposits, such as those in Czechoslovakia and Madagascar. Exceptional crystals 75 cm in length are found at Put-in Bay and other sites around Lake Erie. Large deposits of massive celestite are exploited in Gloucestershire, England, the Soviet Union, and Tunisia.

cerussite

THE NAME OF THIS SPECIES COMES FROM THE LATIN *CERUSSA*, OR "WHITE LEAD," AND is an important ore of that metal (see *Galena*). Cerussite is renowned for its variety of crystal habits. Single crystals may be tabular or prismatic, but cerussite is usually twinned in the form of pseudohexagonal "sixlings" of three intersecting individuals, with deep reentrant angles. Another common habit is the "jackstraw" aggregate, which consists of numerous reticulated crystals intersecting at 60° angles. These aggregates may form symmetrical, dendritic groups resembling a Christmas tree, or open frameworks like an arbor lattice.

Cerussite is usually transparent or translucent and colorless to white, although it may be colored blue, green, or black by inclusions; the streak is colorless to white. This species is distinguished by its strong luster, which ranges from adamantine to submetallic. Occasionally, specimens of cerussite will fluoresce yellow under long-wave ultraviolet light. Cerussite resembles the much rarer lead carbonate phosgenite, $PbCOCl_2$, and, to a lesser extent, the sulfate anglesite. It can be distinguished from these species most readily by its distinctive growth habits.

Cerussite is a secondary mineral which precipitates from carbonated hydrothermal fluids in which other lead minerals, such as galena, have been dissolved. It is most often found in the enriched portions of lead-zinc hydrothermal replacement deposits and in other sulfide deposits, in association with secondary minerals such as anglesite, smithsonite, pyromorphite, and goethite. Particularly beautiful crystals, including snowflake-like jackstraw aggregates, occur at Tsumeb, Namibia; Broken Hill, New South Wales, Australia; Dundas, Tasmania; Mt. Te Aroha, New Zealand; and the Toussit Mine, Oujda, Morocco. Among the many North American deposits that produce fine specimens are the Mammoth Mine in Pinal County, Arizona; Idaho's Coeur d'Alene District, the Organ Mountains of New Mexico; Phoenixville, Pennsylvania; and Leadville, Colorado. Important European sources include Lanarkshire, Scotland; Monte Poni and Monte Veccio, Sardinia; and numerous other localities in Germany and eastern Europe.

Classification:
carbonate

Composition:
$PbCO_3$ (lead carbonate)

Crystal System:
orthorhombic

Hardness
3–3.5

Specific Gravity:
6.55

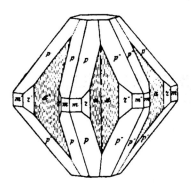

Classic cerusite sixling twin from the Pentire Glaze Mine, St. Minver Highlands, Cornwall.

chabazite

Classification:
tectosilicate, zeolite group

Composition:
$Ca_2Al_2Si_4O_{12} \cdot 6H_2O$
(hydrated calcium aluminum silicate)

Crystal System:
hexagonal rhombohedral

Hardness:
4–5

Specific Gravity:
2.05–2.16

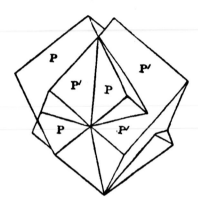

CHABAZITE IS NAMED FOR *CHABAZIOS*, ONE OF A SCORE OF STONES CELEBRATED BY THE ancient Greek poet Orpheus in his *Lithica*. Orpheus believed that all things possess a soul, including the minerals, and that the essence of God was the formative power embodied in natural things. This notion reflects the tradition of animism, common to many indigenous peoples around the world.

Chabazite has a very loose atomic structure, in which large open spaces between silica tetrahedra are connected to one another by channels approximately 3.9 angstroms in diameter (one millimeter equals ten million angstroms). Since these channels allow molecules of lesser diameter to pass right through the crystal while trapping larger ones, chabazite can be used as a "molecular sieve" to separate and purify certain mixed gasses and liquids. Although most zeolites used for this purpose are manufactured synthetically, natural chabazite is still mined for commercial use.

This common zeolite mineral usually occurs as simple, pseudocubic, rhombohedral crystals, which often form penetration twins. Usually translucent and colorless or white, chabazite may also be yellowish, pinkish, greenish, or reddish, with a vitreous luster and a white streak. It displays rhombohedral cleavage, but not as well-developed as that of calcite and dolomite; chabazite is further distinguished from these carbonates by its hardness and lack of effervescence in dilute hydrochloric acid.

Chabazite is found primarily in basalt cavities associated with other zeolites, as well as in fractures in metamorphic rocks. Beautiful flesh-red crystals, locally known as *acadialite,* are found in the basalts of Nova Scotia (home of the French Acadians). Excellent specimens come from the basalts of Ireland's Giant's Causeway, the Faeroe Islands, Iceland, and the Isle of Skye in Scotland. Other European localities include Aussig, Czechoslovakia; Oberstein, Germany; and Seiser Alp in Italy. Good specimens have also been found in the Columbia River Plateau near Ritter Hot Springs and Goble, Oregon, and in the diabase sills near Patterson, New Jersey. Chabazite is found down under near Melbourne, Australia, and along the west coast of Tasmania.

Pseudocubic crystals of chabazite from the basalt cavities of Oberstein, Birkenfeld, Rheinland-Pfalz, Germany.

MANY PEOPLE ARE FAMILIAR WITH CHALCANTHITE IN ITS SYNTHETIC FORM; HIGH school chemistry teachers often demonstrate the wonders of crystallization to students by precipitating large vivid blue crystals of this copper sulfate from solution, in their classrooms or laboratories. Mineral forgers often affix such synthetic chalcanthite crystals to rock matrix, offering them to unwitting collectors as natural specimens. The medieval name for chalcanthite—"blue vitriol"—could equally well describe the response of the collector who has just discovered such a forgery.

Unfortunately, chalcanthite does better in captivity than in the wild: since it dissolves so easily, natural crystals are rare. These crystals are usually thick and tabular or short and prismatic; they may also be found as curved, parallel aggregates known as *ram's horns*. Most commonly, chalcanthite occurs in massive or stalactitic aggregates, or fibrous veins. The most distinctive characteristic of this mineral is its intense color, which ranges from pale sky-blue to deep blue, sometimes tinted with green. Crystals are transparent to translucent, with vitreous to resinous luster and a colorless streak. Specimens tend to disintegrate in humid climates; and they may give off water when heated.

Chalcanthite is a secondary mineral found in the oxidized zone of copper-sulfide-bearing hydrothermal deposits, in association with other hydrated copper and iron sulfates. Crystals sometimes form on the timbers of old mines. It is mined as an ore of copper at Chuquicamata and other places in Chile. Many of the copper deposits in Arizona, California, Colorado, Nevada, and New Mexico produce interesting specimens as well.

chalcanthite

Classification:
sulfate

Composition:
$CuSO_4 \cdot 5H_2O$ (hydrated copper sulfate)

Crystal System:
triclinic

Hardness:
2.5

Specific Gravity:
2.28

Massive chalcanthite from San Rafael, Bolivia.

chalcocite

Classification:
sulfide

Composition:
Cu₂S (copper sulfide)

Crystal System:
orthorhombic

Hardness:
2.5–3

Specific Gravity:
5.5–5.8

Classic pseudohexagonal twins of chalcocite from St Ives, Consols, Cornwall.

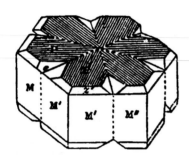

CHALCOCITE IS ONE OF THE MOST important copper ores and is named from the Greek word for that metal, *chalkos*. Although sometimes forming as a primary mineral, economically important concentrations of chalcocite are always secondary. Copper deposits are often "enriched" by secondary chalcocite in the following manner. As oxidizing waters percolate downward through a sulfide deposit, primary copper minerals are dissolved, and the copper is transported downward in the form of soluble sulfates. At the water table, these solutions enter a reducing (low-oxygen) environment, and the copper is precipitated in thick layers (called "blankets") of chalcocite. Some of the world's richest copper deposits were formed in this way, including the deposits at Bisbee, Miami, and Morenci, Arizona; Butte, Montana; and Spain's Rio Tinto. Chalcocite is also one of the most important ore minerals in the enormous low-grade porphyry-copper deposits which now supply most of the world's copper.

Although chalcocite forms striated, prismatic, or tabular single crystals, the most common crystalline form is pseudohexagonal prismatic twins. Most material is massive and granular, however. Crystals may be black with a metallic luster, but massive chalcocite is usually dull gray in color, with greenish alteration. The streak is dark gray to black. Chalcocite is brittle, with conchoidal fracture, and is slightly sectile as well.

Primary chalcocite is disseminated throughout hydrothermal sulfide deposits, in association with bornite, chalcopyrite, enargite, and pyrite. Most specimens are examples of secondary material, however, which has been reprecipitated along with typical secondary copper minerals like covellite, cuprite, malachite, and azurite. Chalcocite is mined in many places in the western United States, including Alaska, Arizona, Utah, Montana, Nevada, and New Mexico. Excellent specimens are recovered from the mines at Butte, Montana, and from a deposit near Bristol, Connecticut. The classic European source is Cornwall, England, from which magnificent pseudohexagonal crystals are obtained; other European sources include the Soviet Union, Czechoslovakia, Sardinia, Spain, and many places in Germany. Important African sources are Tsumeb and Messina in Namibia, and the South African Transvaal. Fine specimens also come from Chile, Peru, Mexico, and Australia.

chalcopyrite

Classification:
sulfide

Composition:
CuFeS₂ (copper sulfide)

Crystal System:
tetragonal

Hardness:
3.5–4

Specific Gravity:
4.2

CHALCOPYRITE MEANS "COPPER PYRITE," *CHALKOS* BEING THE GREEK WORD FOR "COPper," and *pyrite* the general term for metallic minerals that produce sparks when struck. This common species is the most important ore of copper, providing about 80% of the world supply (see *Copper*). Small amounts of gold and silver may substitute for copper in the chalcopyrite structure, and in many places these metals are produced as a by-product of copper mining. Chalcopyrite is also the primary source of copper for the many beautiful and interesting secondary copper minerals found in the enriched zones of hydrothermal sulfide veins, including azurite, cuprite, covellite, and malachite.

Chalcopyrite forms curious double-wedge-shaped (disphenoidal) crystals, which resemble tetrahedrons; aggregates of parallel individuals are common. Usually, however, chalcopyrite occurs in massive form, either granular or botryoidal. The color is dark or brassy yellow, with an iridescent tarnish on broken surfaces. Chalcopyrite has a very strong metallic luster on fresh surfaces, and a greenish-black streak. Like pyrite, chalcopyrite is known as "fools gold" because of its yellow color and bright luster, but it is easily distinguished from gold by its brittleness. Chalcopyrite is distinguished from pyrite by its streak, color, and hardness—it can be scratched by a steel knife-blade, while pyrite cannot.

Chalcopyrite is extremely common and widespread, occurring in many different geological environments. The most economically important of these have been the hydrothermal sulfide vein and replacement deposits. Of increasing importance are the enormous low-grade porphyry-copper deposits, which form through the alteration of primary copper-rich igneous bodies. Another type of magmatic copper deposit in which chalcopyrite is the primary ore mineral is the layered igneous intrusions, such as the one at Sudbury, Ontario, where the associated species include pyrrhotite and pentlandite. Other locations that produce specimens of this common species include Ducktown, Tennessee, and elsewhere in the Tri-State district; Butte, Montana; Bingham, Utah; and many other copper deposits in the western United States. Important European localities include Cornwall, England; Falun, Sweden; Rio Tinto, Spain; Schemnitz, Czechoslovakia; and Freiburg, Germany. Chalcopyrite specimens are also obtained from Zaire, Chile, Peru, Australia, New Guinea, Japan, Cyprus, and the Soviet Union, to name just a few of the many countries in which it is found.

These raw copper ingots were cast in the form of anodes at the smelter at the Ajo copper mine in Arizona. At a refinery, they will be dissolved in an elecrolytic solution, through which the copper ions will pass to accrete onto a copper cathode as the pure metal. Impurities dropping to the bottom of the vat will then be further processed for gold, silver, platinum and other valuable metals. (Dennis Cox, United States Geological Survey.)

These disphenoidal crystals of chalcopyrite from the Robinson Mine in Treece, Kansas, resemble isometric tetrahedra but actually show tetragonal symmetry.

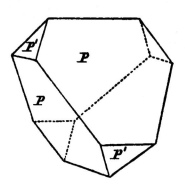

The medieval scholar Albertus Magnus noted that the best ore of silver is "found in the earth as a soft, thick mush," like this specimen of chlorargyrite from Mercedes del Nudo, Tres Puntos, Chile.

chlorargyrite (cerargyrite)

Classification:
halide

Composition:
AgCl (silver chloride)

Crystal System:
isometric

Hardness:
2.5

Specific Gravity:
5.56

SCATTERED THROUGHOUT THE FORLORN DESERT RANGES OF THE WEST ARE SEVERAL crumbling ghost towns, all with the same enigmatic name: Chloride. The chloride so dear to the miner's hearts was chlorargyrite, a secondary silver mineral that occurs in rich but limited concentrations on the surface of silver-bearing sulfide deposits. "Chloride" formed a veneer of rich ore over many a marginal deposit, through a process called supergene enrichment, whereby metals are leached out of the rock by hydrothermal fluids and redeposited in localized concentrations. Prospectors searched out these rich deposits, and boomtowns would spring up almost overnight where they were discovered. When these were mined out, the towns folded up and the miners moved on to pursue deeper diggings. The name reflects the mineral's chlorine and silver content, *argentum* being the Latin word for "silver."

Crystals of this species are cubic, sometimes modified by other isometric forms, but most material is massive, either encrusting, or stalactitic. Chlorargyrite is transparent to translucent, colorless when fresh, but turns gray to brown on exposure; the luster is resinous or adamantine and the streak is white. Chlorargyrite is sectile and ductile, and has no cleavage; the lack of cleavage helps to distinguish chlorargyrite from the mercury chloride calomel, which displays cubic cleavage.

Chlorargyrite is found in the upper regions of hydrothermal sulfide veins, in association with acanthite, stephanite, and calcite. This was one of the main silver ores of Nevada's famous Comstock Lode; large amounts were also mined at Treasure Hill, Nevada. Euhedral specimens occur in the Silver City District, Owyhee County, Idaho. Chlorargyrite is common in the Andean silver deposits of Bolivia, Peru, and Chile. In Europe, it is found in England, France, Italy, and Spain, and in the mines of Saxony and the Harz Mountains of Germany. Large concentrations are found at Broken Hill, New South Wales, Australia.

Cleavages of chlorite—specifically the variety of clinochlore called penninite—from Val Di Vizze, Italy.

THE VARIOUS SPECIES OF THE CHLORITE GROUP ARE COMMON IN ALL KINDS OF GE-
ological environments, but often go unnoticed due to their typically drab
camouflage coloration and usually massive habits. Well-crystallized chlorites
cleave easily into flexible sheets, like the micas, and share many properties
of the clay minerals as well. The general formula above is divided into two
parts, which represent the two structural units that are repeated in alternating layers in chlorite. Curiously, these two units essentially mimic the composition and structure of the phyllosilicate talc and the hydroxide brucite.
Nine separate species have been identified within this group, but geologists
usually refer to all of the chlorite group minerals collectively as "chlorite."
Aluminum, chromium, lithium, nickel, or manganese substitute for magnesium or iron to varying degrees in these species, giving the chlorite group a
wide range of physical properties. Many chlorite species are further divided
into varieties; clinochlore, for example, has seven varieties, ranging from
average-looking dull-green types to the vibrant crimson of kämmererite.

Generally, chlorite minerals are translucent to transparent, and some
shade of dark green, blue-green, olive-green, or bright green; thus the
name, which comes from the Greek, *chloros*, meaning "green." In addition
to the red variety mentioned, yellow, brown, and white chlorites are also
known. The streak is colorless; the luster is vitreous, but pearly on the
cleavage planes. Crystals are usually tabular hexagonal prisms, like the
micas, splitting easily and often along the one perfect basal cleavage. The
chlorite minerals are most abundant as massive, foliated aggregates, as
scaly crusts and coatings, or as earthy masses. Chlorite is harder than talc,
and unlike the micas, cleavage plates do not rebound elastically when bent.

The chlorite minerals are generally formed through the alteration of
pyroxene, amphibole, biotite, garnet, and other silicate minerals containing
iron, aluminum, and magnesium, and commonly comprise a large proportion of siliceous metamorphic rocks such as schists. Along with actinolite,
albite, and epidote, chlorite is an essential component of the abundant
greenschist facies metamorphic rocks, which form when rocks are subjected to temperatures in the range of 300°C–500°C at fairly low pressures.
Euhedral chlorite crystals are more common in contact metamorphic environments and hydrothermal deposits, however. Kämmererite, the much
sought after violet variety of clinochlore, occurs with chromite in serpentinites in Brome and Richmond Counties, Quebec; at Low's Mine and
Wood's Chrome Mine, Lancaster County, Pennsylvania; and in Turkey.

chlorite group

Classification:
phyllosilicates

Composition:
$(Mg,Fe)_3(Si,Al)_4O_{10}(OH)_2$•$(Mg,Fe)_3(OH)_6$
(magnesium–iron hydroxyl aluminum
silicates)

Crystal System:
monoclinic and triclinic (pseudohexagonal)

Hardness:
2–2.5

Specific Gravity:
2.6–3.3, increasing with iron

Good specimens of clinochlore are found in Renfrew County, Ontario; and at the Tilly Foster Iron Mine near Brewster, New York. Excellent green crystals are found in contact metamorphic deposits of the Ala Valley, in the Italian Piedmont. Fine chlorite crystals are common in the Alps, at Zermatt, Switzerland; in the Austrian Zillertal; and near Trentino, Italy.

Twinned, dipyramidal crystal of the rare chromian variety of clinochlore called kämmererite, from the Kop Krom Mine, Askale, Turkey.

chromite

Classification:
oxide, spinel group

Composition:
$FeCr_2O_4$ (iron chromium oxide)

Crystal System:
isometric

Hardness:
5.5

Specific Gravity:
4.5–4.8

CHROMITE IS A MEMBER OF THE SPINEL GROUP OF OXIDES, AND IS ISOMORPHOUS WITH both spinel and magnetite. It forms a solid-solution series with magnesiochromite, $MgCr_2O_4$, and other members of the spinel group. This species is the main ore for chromium, a metal vital for leather tanning, various pigments, and especially for the production of alloys such as stainless steel. Its most familiar use, however, is in the protective and decorative electroplating of other more easily corroded metals. Lots of shiny "chrome" once symbolized America's love affair with the automobile, but the huge hulks of chrome-plated iron that once graced every suburban driveway have gone the way of the dinosaur.

Chromite forms small octahedral crystals, but is usually seen as disseminated anhedral grains or granular masses. The fracture is even and regular, but cleavage is absent. It is black and opaque, with submetallic to pitchy luster and a brown streak. Chromite can be distinguished from spinel by its more metallic luster, and from magnetite by its much weaker magnetism.

Chromite concentrations occur in two types of deposits, the layered igneous intrusions and ophiolite complexes. The layered intrusions consist of layers of various igneous rock types, often enriched in vanadium, platinum group elements, and titanium as well as chromium. In the layered intrusions, chromite is concentrated in layers known as chromitites. Important deposits of this type include the Stillwater Complex in Montana, the Great Dyke of Zimbabwe, and the Bushveld Complex of South Africa. Chromite is also found in lense-shaped bodies in ophiolite complexes, which are essentially slices of the sea floor, consisting of layers of basalts,

Spherical blebs of chromite in serpentine, from Verkhne-Tagil, Verkhotune District, in the Ural Mountains, USSR.

gabbros, and various ultramafic rocks. Such deposits are exposed on the continents in certain tectonically active regions like California, the Mediterranean region, and the Western Pacific, where they have been thrust up on to the continental crust. Chromite is widespread in small concentrations in the ophiolites of California's Coast Ranges, from Santa Barbara County northward into Oregon and Washington. Large deposits are mined in Turkey, the Philippines, New Caledonia, the Baltic countries, India, Canada, and Cuba.

Commonly associated minerals are pyroxenes, magnetite, and pyrrhotite. The original peridotite or other mafic rock in which grains of chromite formed may have subsequently been altered to serpentine; thus, it is often seen in association with this mineral and with other secondary species such as talc and uvarovite garnet. Grains of chromite may also be concentrated in placer deposits with monazite, rutile, and other heavy minerals. Chromite has also been found in meteorites.

CHRYSOBERYL IS A MINERAL WITH AN IDENTITY PROBLEM—EVEN ITS NAME, WHICH means "golden beryl," is confusing. Until the German geologist A.G. Warner performed the first chemical analysis of chrysoberyl in 1789, it was assumed to be a variety of beryl. The chemical formula suggests that it might be a member of the spinel group of oxides, but its pseudohexagonal crystals do not imply an isometric structure. The difference in structure is due to the small size of the Be^{+2} ions and to the hexagonal packing of oxygen, which gives chrysoberyl a structure more like that of the silicate olivine. The relatively common yellow form of chrysoberyl is a minor gemstone, but much more valuable are the two unusual gem varieties alexandrite and cat's-eye.

Alexandrite was first discovered in 1830 in the emerald mines near Sverdlovsk in the Ural Mountains of Russia, and named for Alexander II, heir apparent to the Russian throne. Russian alexandrite is blue-green in natural light, but indoors under incandescent or candlelight turns a bright purple-red. It is thought that the color shift in alexandrite may be due to the differential absorption of different wavelengths of light by trace amounts of chromium. A similar effect has been observed in some grossular garnets from East Africa. Alexandrite has been synthesized, but it is difficult to manufacture and nearly as expensive as its natural counterpart. Much more commonly seen is a synthetic vanadium-bearing corundum with a blue-grey to lilac color shift, which is widely sold as natural alexandrite.

The other important variety of gem chrysoberyl is cat's-eye, or cymophane, which has been a popular gemstone in the Far East for millennia.

Cat's-eye is a translucent gem which, when cut in rounded cabochon form, exhibits a striking chatoyant effect consisting of a very bright, narrow band of light that moves across the surface of the stone as it is turned. This chatoyancy is due to the presence of innumerable, minute inclusions of rutile, which are oriented in parallel, perpendicular to the "eye." Many other minerals with similar inclusions can be cut into gems which display the cat's-eye effect, including quartz, tourmaline, and even apatite. None, however, has the fine, bright eye of chrysoberyl, which is the only chatoyant stone referred to simply as

chrysoberyl

Classification:
oxide

Composition:
$BeAl_2O_4$ (beryllium aluminum oxide)

Crystal System:
orthorhombic

Hardness:
8.5

Specific Gravity:
3.68–3.78

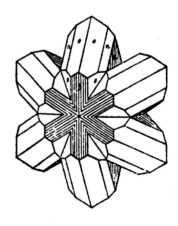

Chrysoberyl cluster from Santa Teresa, Espirito Santo, Brazil, with a large cut stone from the gem gravels of the Ratnapurna District, Sri Lanka.

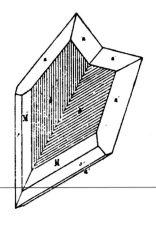

cat's-eye. Composites of the fibrous zeolite ulexite and synthetic sapphire are sometimes used to simulate cat's eye.

Crystals of chrysoberyl are commonly tabular or short prismatic in habit, with lustrous smooth or striated faces and a vitreous luster. Chrysoberyl is usually twinned, either in the form of heart-shaped contact twins or pseudohexagonal sixlings. Three cleavages may be evident, and the fracture is conchoidal to uneven. Chrysoberyl is transparent to translucent, yellow, various shades of green and brown, and of course red under artificial light in the case of alexandrite. The most distinctive characteristic of chrysoberyl is its extreme hardness, which is surpassed only by corundum and diamond.

Chrysoberyl occurs primarily in granite pegmatites, gneisses, mica schists, and dolomitic marbles, and much of the gem material is collected from sedimentary placer deposits. Large crude crystals and aggregates occur in the pegmatites of Custer County, South Dakota, and near Golden, Colorado. Small crystals are found in the pegmatites of Maine and elsewhere in New England, and at Greenfield, New York. The finest crystallized specimens of chrysoberyl are the lustrous twins from Lavra de Hematita and Collatina, Espirito Santo, Brazil; these large sixlings are composed of broadly tabular members which give the groups an almost spherical shape. Cat's-eye is also found in Brazilian placers.

The best specimens of alexandrite are the tabular sixlings from the original localities on the Takowaya and Sanarka Rivers in the Urals, which occur in biotite schist with emerald and phenakite. Alexandrite and cat's-eye are found in the gem gravels of Ceylon and to a lesser extent at Mogok, Burma. Alexandrite from these regions is generally less vividly colored than the Russian material. Fine tabular crystals and twins are found at Lake Alaotra and elsewhere in Madagascar. Notable deposits of this rare species exist in the Swiss and Austrian Alps, Germany, Czechoslovakia, Tanzania, Zaire, and Zimbabwe, among other places.

chrysocolla

Classification:
silicate

Composition:
$(Cu,Al)_2H_2Si_2O_5(OH)_4 \cdot nH_2O$
(hydrous copper aluminum silicate)

Crystal System:
monoclinic

Hardness:
2–4

Specific Gravity:
2.0–2.4

This specimen of chrysocolla is not crystalline, but is covered by a drusy coating of transparent quartz.

ARTIFICIAL PREPARATIONS USED AS a flux in the soldering of gold were referred to by the ancient Greeks as *chrysos kolla*, or "gold glue," and somehow the name came to be applied to this species. Chrysocolla is sometimes used as an ornamental stone, its striking blue-green color often mixed with the rich green of malachite. Both species are rather soft, however, and a more durable alternative is chalcedony with chrysocolla inclusions, which is commonly offered simply as chrysocolla.

This species forms microscopic, acicular crystals, but usually occurs as cryptocrystalline aggregates with a botryoidal morphology and uneven to conchoidal fracture. Also amorphous and earthy. Chrysocolla is translucent, green, blue, or blue-green; sometimes colored brown or black due to impurities. The luster is vitreous to earthy, and the streak white to pale blue or green. Chrysocolla is harder than turquoise, and much softer than chalcedony.

This species is an abundant and widespread secondary mineral, forming in the oxidized zone of hydrothermal copper sulfide deposits in association with azurite, malachite, cuprite, limonite, and native copper. Chrysocolla is particularly abundant in the copper deposits of the western United States, and is also found in Michigan and in Lebanon County, Pennsylvania. Other sources worldwide include Mexico, Chile, England, the Soviet Union, Zambia, Zaire, and Australia.

THE NAME CINNABAR IS APPARENTLY DERIVED FROM THE ANCIENT PERSIAN TERM *zinjifrah*, meaning "dragon's blood"—a reference to its blood-red color and perhaps its potent qualities as well. Cinnabar is the sole ore of mercury, and massive cinnabar actually sweats droplets of mercury—the only metal that is liquid at ordinary temperatures. According to the 13th-century scholar Albertus Magnus, mercury contained the elements Water and Earth in equal parts and, although poisonous to humans, was useful for killing "lice and nits and other things that are produced from filth in the pores. " Mercury found in the native state was called "live-" or "quick silver," since it flows and jiggles in the flask without ever evaporating or solidifying. Pliny and others thought that the mercury extracted from cinnabar was a different kind, and named it "water silver," or *hydrargyrum*, from which the chemical symbol for mercury (Hg) is derived.

A practical use for mercury was discovered at an early date. When added to finely crushed ore, mercury instantly forms an alloy called an *amalgam* with the tiny particles of gold or silver. When this amalgam is heated, the mercury is driven off as vapor, leaving the precious metals behind. The Carthaginians, and later the Romans, developed mercury mines at Almaden in Spain to produce mercury for gold mines in their far-flung provinces. The mines at Almaden are still in operation, and miners there sometime encounter ancient tunnels abandoned nearly two millennia ago.

Unfortunately, mercury is highly poisonous, and miners were subject to chronic degenerative diseases as a result of working with it. Among the symptoms of mercury poisoning is mental instability; since mercury was also used in working felt, hatters often displayed erratic behavior—thus the expression "mad as a hatter" and the Mad Hatter of *Alice in Wonderland*. Mercury is hard to get rid of once it has been introduced into the environment. It is one of the heavy metals which tend to collect in the tissues of animals, becoming more highly concentrated at higher levels

in the food chain and causing a variety of degenerative diseases and birth defects. Thus birds of prey, porpoises, tuna, and humans carry the legacy of hundreds of years of irresponsible industrial waste management.

Mercury amalgamation has been supplanted by other ore-processing techniques in the industrial countries, but continues on a considerable scale in the third world, especially in Brazil. Mercury is still used to prepare chlorine and other chemicals through electrolysis, and in catalysts, drugs, and

cinnabar

Classification:
sulfide

Composition:
HgS (mercury sulfide)

Crystal System:
hexagonal

Hardness:
2–2.5

Specific Gravity:
8.1

Left: *Excellent interpenetrating twins of cinnabar on quartz with dolomite, from the Wan-Shan-Ch'ang Cinnabar Mine, near Tung Jen in Guizhou Province, China.* **Right:** *The only metal that is liquid at room temperatures, mercury is essential to a wide variety of household applications, from thermostats to thermometers. However, mercury is highly toxic, and great care must be taken with its disposal.*

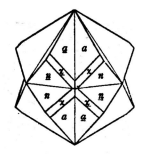

agriculture. Its combination of metallic properties and liquidity make mercury ideal for use in switches (such as home thermostats), barometers, thermometers, and a plethora of scientific instruments. Mercury lamps are made by passing an electrical current through mercury vapor sealed in a closed tube, producing a blue-green light which extends into the ultraviolet end of the spectrum.

Cinnabar crystals are rare and highly sought after. They are rhombohedral to thick tabular or prismatic, and very often form penetration twins. More typically, cinnabar is found in fine-grained massive aggregates or as incrustations on other minerals. It is brittle to somewhat sectile, with a conchoidal to uneven fracture and perfect cleavage. The most distinctive feature of cinnabar is its intense red color and matching scarlet streak. It is transparent to translucent, with an adamantine or silvery submetallic luster. Realgar is similar in appearance but lacks the silvery adamantine luster and excellent cleavage of cinnabar crystals; cuprite is also similar, but softer. Metacinnabar is a metallic, gray, high-temperature polymorph, which crystallizes in the isometric system as rough-faced tetrahedra.

Cinnabar and native mercury are found in near-surface, low-temperature hydrothermal deposits, disseminated in the fractured country rock in the vicinity of hot springs or recent volcanic rocks. Commonly associated species include calcite, pyrite, stibnite, marcasite, metacinnabar, opal, and quartz. The best cinnabar specimens known are the deep red, transparent, twinned crystals as large as 2.5 cm from mines in China's Guizou and Hunan Provinces. The ancient mines at Almaden, Ciudad Real, Spain, still produce fine sharp crystals over 1 cm in size. Fine crystals are found at Charcas, San Luis Potosí, Mexico; and on Mount Avala, near Belgrade, Yugoslavia. Locations in the United States include the Cahill Mine, Humboldt County, Nevada; and New Almaden, San Mateo County, and New Idria, San Benito County, California.

clay minerals

Classification:
phyllosilicates

Composition:
kaolinite: $Al_4Si_4O_{10}(OH)_8$
illite:
$(K,H_3O)(Al,Mg,Fe)_2(Si,Al)_4O_{10}[(OH)_2,H_2O]$
montmorillonite:
$(Na,Ca)_{0.3}(Al,Mg)_2Si_4O_{10}(OH)_2 \cdot nH_2O$
(hydrous silicates of aluminum, magnesium and iron)

Crystal System:
monoclinic

Hardness:
1–2

Specific Gravity:
2–3

Kaolinite clay pseudomorph after feldspar, from North Goonbarrow, Bugle, St Austell, Cornwall. Many such specimens have been "faked" through the years, but the relict feldspar cleavage evident in this specimen shows it to be authentic.

AN IMPORTANT PART OF our everyday life, the clay minerals go virtually unnoticed and unappreciated. Like all books and magazines illustrated with photographs, the pages of this book are composed nearly one third of clay, since the addition of clay to paper makes pages bright, smooth, and chemically inert. The bricks from which your house or apartment may be constructed are clay, as are many of the things inside, from your cups and plates to the litter in Kitty's box. The clays used in these and a host of other applications are not merely raw sediment dug from the earth at random, but minerals with distinct properties, found in limited amounts in particular geological environments.

The clays are a rather loosely defined group of finely crystalline or amorphous hydrous sheet silicates, generally formed through the alteration of primary silicate minerals. Their general structure is characterized by silicon and aluminum ions in tetrahedral coordination with oxygen, combined with aluminum, iron, magnesium, lithium, chromium, manganese, and other ions (in various combinations) in octahedral coordination with the same oxygen ions. These structures are arranged in layers (or sheets), and since the net charge of each layer is negative, cations of various elements including calcium, sodium, and potassium are nestled between the layers. These layers are held together by very weak (van der Waals') forces, and in the presence of water they open up like an accordion file to accommodate the water molecules. The mixture known as bentonite, for instance, expands in volume eight times when hydrated.

This property permits the individual clay layers to glide readily over one another, and gives clays their characteristic plasticity. Human beings long ago discovered that clays could be molded into useful or pleasing shapes, which would retain their form when dried. The basic structure of clay remains unchanged when sun-dried, and wetting can restore its plasticity. However, it was eventually discovered that baking clay in a red hot fire would make the artifact impervious to water. This is because the structure of the clay has been permanently altered into a substance called *metakaolin*, which, while retaining a sheet structure, no longer accepts foreign molecules. If the clay is fired until it is white-hot (at a temperature over 1000°C) the sheet structure collapses altogether, producing an even more durable ceramic called *stoneware*. At much higher temperatures, the clay begins to lose its crystallinity, forming a very hard, glassy, and completely nonporous ceramic called *porcelain*.

Dozens of distinct clay species are recognized, each differing slightly in composition or structure, but three main groups can be distinguished. The clay minerals of the *kaolinite group* are the simplest in composition, and are the primary type used in ceramics. They generally form from the breakdown of feldspars; large kaolinite deposits form from the weathering of

The discovery that clay could be fashioned into useful and durable wares was one of the major advances of the late Stone Age. Potters have been shaping clay on wheels such as this for over 6000 years.

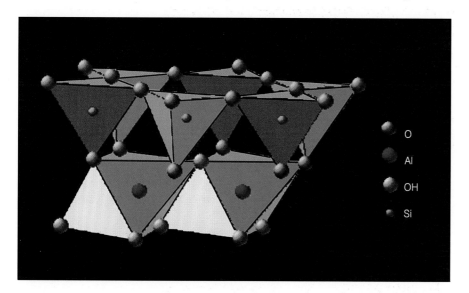

All of the phyllosilicates have structures based on sheets of SiO_4 tetrahedra. In kaolinite, these sheets are bonded to another layer composed of octahedra, in which an aluminum ion is bonded to four hydroxl and two oxygen ions. These simple two-layer sheets are loosely bonded to others by weak van der Waal's forces; the characteristic plasticity of clay results from the ease with which these sheets slide over one another.

O
Al
OH
Si

granites and other feldspar-rich rocks. The name comes from the Chinese word for high ridge, *kauling,* which is the name of a locality in China where kaolinite was mined for porcelain. In Cornwall, England, flotation is used to separate kaolin from the grains of quartz in decomposed granite. In Georgia, kaolinite is mined from relatively pure beds, which formed as kaolin naturally separated during erosion of rotten granites settled into shallow lagoons.

The clays of the *montmorillonite* group, named for an occurrence in France, form through the alteration of volcanic glass and associated silicate minerals in volcanic ash beds. Since they represent a point in time (a volcanic eruption), these beds are very useful to geologists and archaeologists interested in dating strata. Some such ash-fall deposits form a readily identifiable time horizon, extending across thousands of square kilometers, and through all kinds of sediments. Commercially, these clays are called bentonite, and are used extensively in the oil-well-drilling process, to add viscosity to the water in the well. Because of its absorbent qualities, bentonite is also used in the purification of petroleum and edible oils. Bentonite was known as *fuller's earth* in the past, when it was widely used by the fabric workers called "fullers" to draw excess oils and impurities from wool. An alternate name for the montmorillonite group is the *smectite* group, derived from the Latin word for cleansing, *smecticus.*

The third major group of clay minerals is the *illite group*, named for the state of Illinois. These clays are the most important volumetrically, forming a large part of the mudstones, shales and other sedimentary rocks. Illites are intermediate in structure and composition between muscovite mica and the clay montmorillonite. Unusually pure deposits of illite are mined near Eldorado, in Saskatchewan, Canada.

Clays are very common and are mined in many parts of the world, although particularly pure deposits are at premium. The clays seldom make dramatic specimens. Exceptions are pseudomorphs of clay after silicate crystals, such as the commonly seen replacements of tourmaline and spodumene crystals in pegmatites. Only kaolinite is seen in crystals, which may form hexagonal platelets up to 2 mm in size. The clays are transparent to translucent as individual crystals, but generally occur as opaque earthy aggregates. They are generally white in color, but may be yellowish, brownish, reddish, bluish, or even lavender, depending on the presence of impurities or metal ions such as manganese, chromium, or lithium. Clays are easily recognized as soft, light earthy aggregates that become plastic when wet, but distinguishing between the different groups is practically impossible for the non-specialist.

cleavage

The micas are sheet silicates with very weak bonds between layers, resulting in the perfect cleavage demonstrated here.

THE TERM CLEAVAGE REFERS TO THE CHARACTERISTIC, *REGULAR* BREAKAGE PATTERNS displayed by crystalline minerals; other patterns of breakage fall under the rubric of *fracture.* Cleavage occurs along definite planar surfaces, which are determined by the internal atomic structure of a mineral. In some instances, cleavage results from the variation in the bond strengths in different crystallographic directions. In graphite, for example, a strong covalent bond holds the atoms of carbon together in sheets, but the sheets themselves are connected only by weak van der Waals' forces. Thus, while graphite has no cleavage at all *through* its layers, excellent cleavage exists *between* them. In minerals with only one bond type, cleavage can occur along planes defined by the widest gaps between atoms. The strong symmetrical bonds in all directions that connect the silicon and oxygen atoms in quartz, on the other hand, give this species very poor cleavage.

Like the external morphology of crystals, cleavage is related to the symmetry of the basic unit cell. For this reason, cleavages can be described in terms of crystal forms, such as octahedral, cubic, pinacoidal (basal), and so on. Calcite, for instance, has hundreds of crystal habits, yet always cleaves into simple rhombohedra—the shape of its unit cell. Easily developed cleavage which results in flat planes is referred to as "perfect cleavage," while less well-defined cleavages are termed "imperfect" or "poor."

The number and orientation of cleavage planes varies widely between the different mineral species, reflecting the diversity of their internal structures. Many common minerals are easily identified through their characteristic cleavage patterns. Cubic crystals of halite, for instance, cleave easily into perfect cubes, while similarly-shaped crystals of fluorite form octahedra. The pyroxenes and amphiboles, two important rock-forming silicate groups that often look very similar, are easily distinguished by the different angles between their cleavages.

Parting is a type of planar breakage that occurs in some minerals. It is not a true cleavage, as breakage occurs only along planes of weakness not directly related to a mineral's internal structure. Parting occurs between members of twins (even where twinning is not otherwise apparent), and in crystals that have undergone strain in a metamorphic environment. While partings are limited to specific areas of weakness, there is an almost infinite number of parallel cleavages in any crystal, extending down to the smallest structural units.

COBALTITE IS NAMED for the *kobold*, a mischievous underground spirit of old Germany, whose capacity to frustrate was evoked by the difficulty involved in smelting silver ores that contained cobalt. Due to its chemical similarity to cobalt, iron is typically present in cobaltite in concentrations up to 10%. In addition, a solid-solution series exists between cobaltite and gersdorffite (NiAsS), although specimens

cobaltite

Classification:
sulfide

Composition:
(Co,Fe)AsS (cobalt arsenic sulfide)

Crystal System:
orthorhombic

Hardness:
5.5

Specific Gravity:
6.3

Pseudocubic cobaltite crystals in quartz, from Española, Sudbury, Ontario.

of intermediate composition are rare. The metal cobalt is used in several specialized alloys, and cobalt oxide is mixed with other compounds to make smalt, the vibrant blue pigment used in glass-making and ceramic glazes. Cobalt chloride is a wonderful invisible ink, turning blue and legible when heated, then disappearing again! Sheep that are fed cobalt supplements produce better wool, and are more resistant to certain diseases.

The kobold's sense of humor is also apparent in the symmetry of this mineral, which was long thought to belong to the isometric system because of its pseudoisometric cubes, octahedra, and pyritohedra. Cobaltite crystals are commonly striated in different directions on adjacent faces, in the manner of pyrite. This species occurs predominantly in massive granular, steel-gray aggregates with a violet-to-purple tinge, metallic luster, and grayish-black streak. Crystals display perfect pseudocubic cleavage and uneven fracture.

Cobaltite is usually disseminated in metamorphic rocks, or in high-temperature hydrothermal veins in association with other cobalt and nickel sulfides. Specimens have been found in Lemhi County, Idaho, and Boulder

City, Colorado, and at numerous locations in the Sierra Nevada of California. Sharp crystals as large as 3 cm in size occur at Hakansbo, Tunaberg, and Riddarhytten, Sweden. Fine octahedral and cubic crystals have been recovered from the Columbus Mine near Cobalt, Ontario. Excellent specimens are also found in contact metamorphic rocks near Bimbowrie, Australia. The largest commercial producer of cobaltite is Zaire, where it occurs in association with copper ores.

colemanite

Classification:
borate

Composition:
$CaB_3O_4(OH)_3 \cdot H_2O$
(hydrated calcium borate)

Crystal System:
monoclinic

Hardness:
4–4.5

Specific Gravity:
2.4

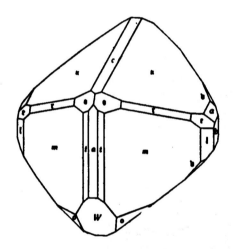

COLMANITE IS ONE OF THE PRIMARY ORES OF BORON, WHICH IS INDISPENSABLE TO THE chemical and pharmaceutical industries, and serves as an ingredient in high-stress alloys, glass, paint, and rocket fuel, among other uses (see *Borax*). It is named for William Coleman, an early entrepreneur in the borax business in California's Death Valley. For forty years following its discovery in 1882, colemanite was the main source of borax, before the kernite and borax deposits in the lakebeds of the Mojave Desert were discovered.

Perhaps the most aesthetically appealing of the borates, colemanite forms sharp dipyramidal or prismatic crystals with complex terminations. Crystals are clear if not tinted yellow or red by impurities, and have a vitreous luster. Colmanite is also found as granular, massive cleavable aggregates, and as crystal-lined geodes.

Colmanite is an evaporite mineral which forms in the intermontane basins of the western United States, Central Asia, and other arid regions. Most specimens come from the vast open pit at Boron, California. There are other deposits throughout the Mojave Desert, and in the Muddy Mountains and White Basin of Nevada. Commercial deposits are exploited at Eskisahir, Turkey; Kazakhstan in the Soviet Union; and Jujuy Province, Argentina.

Before the discovery of colemanite crystals at Ryan, in the Amargosa Range above Death Valley, California (pictured here), efflorescences of ulexite plucked from nearby dry lakes provided the world's main source of borax.

COLUMBITE AND TANTALITE ARE (RESPECTIVELY) THE NIOBIUM AND TANTALUM END MEMbers of a solid-solution series. These have been further broken down into the discrete species ferrotantalite, manganotantalite, ferrocolumbite, manganocolumbite, and *magno*columbite—the latter being a magnesium-rich species found only in pegmatites that dissect bodies of dolomite rock in the remote Pamir Range of central Asia. These distinctions are only heard in the laboratory, however, and "columbite–tantalite" remains the most useful term.

These minerals are the primary ores of niobium and tantalum. Niobium (once called *columbium*) was first isolated from a specimen of columbite from America, and named for its country of origin. Tantalite was named for Tantalus, whose mythic trials chemists sympathized with when they were unable to dissolve the mineral for analysis (apparently 19th century chemists were well-versed in the classics). Niobium is required for the manufacture of stainless steel, and for alloys that retain their strength at high speeds and temperatures, as in jet engines and other aerospace applications. Tantalum is extremely resistant to chemical corrosion, and thus finds use in medicine (scalpels, skull plates, sutures, etc.) and in various apparatus for the chemical industry. Both metals and several compounds derived from them find use in specialized electronic applications.

Crystals of columbite and tantalite typically occur as euhedral individuals or parallel aggregates, embedded in a matrix of quartz and feldspar. They are typically prismatic, stubby or tabular, striated, and often form heart-shaped twins. The color ranges from black in columbite to brownish-black in tantalite; both are opaque with submetallic luster and a black to dark-red streak. Tantalite often displays reddish internal reflections. One good cleavage is in evidence, but it is not as well-developed as the cleavage of the similar-appearing species wolframite, which is also heftier. Another similar species is fergusonite ($YNbO_4$), which has a different crystal morphology and is much less common.

Columbite and tantalite are common in granitic pegmatites, especially the complex ones rich in lithium, phosphate, and rare earths, and are also concentrated in some placer deposits. Single crystals exceeding 100 kg in weight are known, but most pegmatites contain an abundance of small crystals. Typical associates include quartz, feldspar, muscovite, lepidolite, cassiterite, and microlite. Mineable concentrations occur in Western Australia, Mozambique, Madagascar, Brazil, Norway, and the Soviet Union. Notable North American occurrences include the pegmatite districts of Maine, Connecticut, Virginia, North Carolina, Colorado, South Dakota, New Mexico, and California.

columbite–tantalite series

Classification:
oxides

Composition:
$(Fe,Mn)(Nb,Ta)_2O_6$
(iron manganese niobium tantalum oxides)

Crystal System:
orthorhombic

Hardness:
6

Specific Gravity:
5.2–7.9, increasing with tantalum content

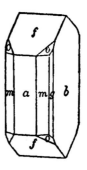

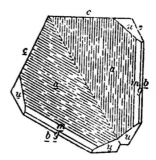

Left: *Columbite crystal in pegmatite matrix, from Standish, Maine.* **Right:** *Columbite-tantalite crystals in situ in a cavity in a Brazilian pegmatite.*

copper

Classification:
native element

Composition:
Cu

Crystal System:
isometric

Hardness:
2.5–3

Specific Gravity:
8.94

Copper has a bright color and luster, is very malleable, and is much more common in its native form than other metals. For these reasons copper was favored by many indigenous peoples for ornaments of all kinds.

LIKE GOLD AND SILVER, COPPER IS MALLEABLE AND FAIRLY CONSPICUOUS IN ITS NATIVE state, and thus was discovered and worked by humans beings at an early date. Among the oldest worked copper objects are some short tubes discovered at the Catal Huyuk site in Turkey, which were probably attached to the fringes of a skirt seven thousand years ago. The technique of working native copper by hammering and bending it into the desired shape was used by pre-industrial peoples into the nineteenth century. North American Indians and Eskimos worked with lumps of pure copper, fashioning them into fish hooks, knives, arrowheads, and sometimes highly artistic ceremonial objects such as embossed breastplates. The Indians of the Pacific Northwest used their "coppers" as symbols of wealth, one such copper slab being worth several thousand blankets. Indians of the Lake Superior region mined native copper from shallow workings on Isle Royale and the Keweenaw Peninsula, in what is now Michigan. The objects they fashioned from this copper were traded far and wide, and have been found in archaeological sites throughout North America. The source of the copper is easily identified through analysis, since native copper is naturally alloyed with different proportions of other metals or semi-metals, depending on its source. The Great Lakes copper, for instance, contains appreciable silver but is otherwise pure, while copper from Mexico is usually laden with arsenic and other impurities.

It was eventually discovered that hammered copper objects are made much stronger through repeated heating, or annealing, and it is likely that this technological development led directly to the casting of the molten metal. Copper was being cast in the Middle East as early as five thousand years ago, ushering in the minor industrial revolution of the Chalcolithic Era, or "copper stone age"—the bridge between the Neolithic (Late Stone Age) and the Bronze Age. Casting probably evolved independently in Asia, and at a much later date in South America. It is thought that the casting of native metals preceded the actual smelting of ores. Imagine the impact of the discovery that the "precious" metal copper could be won from such abundant ores as malachite! The next major metallurgical innovation was the invention of the alloy of copper and tin called bronze, which is much stronger than copper alone. Armies equipped with bronze swords and bronze armor, like that of Alexander the Great, "forged" the great empires of the ancient world.

Today, iron is the most important metal in human culture, but copper runs a close second. Because of its high electrical conductivity and great ductility (which allows it to be drawn into fine wires), copper is widely used in the electrical and electronics industries. Copper is also used in roofing, water pipes, and a host of other special applications. It remains an important alloy, combined with tin to make bronze, with zinc to make brass, and with gold and silver in jewelry. Most of the copper produced today comes from compounds such as copper sulfides and carbonates, but nearly all copper deposits contain at least a small amount of the native metal.

Copper crystals are usually octahedral, cubic, dodecahedral, or combinations of these forms; however, crystals are rarely seen as isolated individuals. Native copper usually occurs as aggregates of many flattened or otherwise distorted crystals, in arborescent or wiry structures squeezed into fissures and crevices. Copper is sectile, malleable, and ductile, with a hackly fracture. Fresh surfaces are a pale rose-red with a strong metallic luster, tarnishing rapidly to the familiar copper-red color, and then to a penny-brown. Blackish or greenish crusts may also develop in the presence of sulfur or carbonate ions. Copper is opaque, but can be drawn into extremely thin foils which transmit a greenish light. The streak is shiny, pale red.

Copper is widespread in limited amounts as a secondary mineral in hydrothermal sulfide veins, where it may form as fine crystals in the oxidation zone along with azurite, malachite, cuprite, and various sulfides. Important deposits of this type include Ajo and Bisbee, Arizona; Santa Rita, New Mexico, and many other locations in the western United States. In

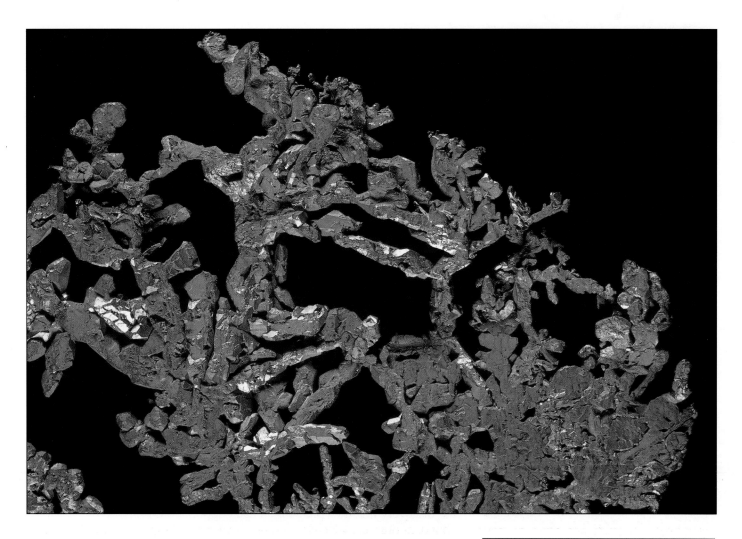

Europe, interesting copper specimens are obtained from sulfide veins in Cornwall, England, and in Scotland, Germany, Italy, and the Soviet Union. The island of Cyprus is the eastern Mediterranean was one of the most important sources of copper in ancient times. The name copper is derived from the Greek name for Cyprus, *Kyprios*. Other important locations of this type are found in Mexico, Bolivia, Chile, and Tsumeb, Namibia.

The most impressive occurrences of native copper are primary, however. Copper is sometimes associated with basic igneous rocks such as basalts. The copper may form in cavities in these rocks, or in the interstices of nearby sedimentary rocks. Usually such deposits are very limited in extent, but in two places in the world such deposits of native copper are extensive enough to be mined. One is at Corocoro, Bolivia, where native copper is found finely disseminated in sandstone, sometimes forming highly unusual pseudomorphs after aragonite. The other, and far more important deposit is on the Keweenaw Peninsula in Lake Superior.

The Algonquin Indians presented the French explorer Champlain with a large chunk of solid copper in 1608, but it was almost 250 years later that the Indians' copper deposits were finally located on Michigan's Keweenaw Peninsula. Over the following century the 200-mile-long series of ancient conglomerates and lava flows experienced the first mining boom in the United States, and became its first great copper-producing district. Hydrothermal solutions rising from the lava flows had precipitated native copper and some native silver in the pore spaces of the conglomerates, cementing the sediments and sometimes even replacing the pebbles and cobbles. Most of this copper was disseminated throughout the sediments, but some of the masses of native copper were so large that they had to be sawed into small pieces by hand before they could be removed from the mines. The largest single mass of native copper found in the mines of the Keweenaw Peninsula weighed 520 tons.

Dendritic aggregate of native copper from Cornwall, England.

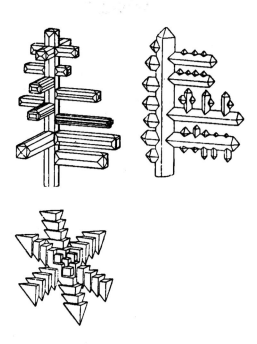

coral

Classification:
organic gemstone

Composition:
CaCO₃, with variable amounts of organic material

Hardness:
2.5–4

Specific Gravity:
2.4–2.7

CORAL IS THE FRAMEWORK, OR "SKELETON," OF A COLONY OF MARINE ANIMALS OF THE phylum Cnidaria. The individual coral animals, or polyps, precipitate calcium carbonate, $CaCO_3$, from the surrounding seawater, gradually building up an arborescent structure. Coral and pearls are unique among gemstones in that they are a renewable resource. Coral, however, is not cultivated, but collected in the wild from a limited environment, with the result that it is disappearing in much of its former range. Thus, coral may have the dubious honor of being the first gemstone to actually become extinct.

Coral has been prized by cultures around the world since the paleolithic era, and was traded thousands of miles away from its coastal sources by early peoples. Although it is attractive enough as an ornamental material, the reasons for its popularity are undoubtedly related to the fact that it comes from the sea. Other gemstones are just that—*stones*, while coral is the remains of a delicate and beautiful living organism that flourished deep beneath the waves. As did other groups throughout Asia, Africa, and Mesoamerica, the ancient Romans believed strongly in the curative powers of coral. Like a mood ring, red coral was thought to change color according to the wearer's health. The art of coral-carving remained undeveloped in ancient Rome, however, since the magical powers of coral were thought to be effective only as long as it remained in its natural form. Like other red stones, coral was thought to provide protection in battle in medieval times; coral amulets were also regarded as effective protection for children and to aid women in childbirth.

Coral occurs throughout the world in shallow tropical and subtropical waters, although some varieties grow at much greater depths. The most important sources are Asia and the Mediterranean Sea, especially along the coasts of North Africa and Italy. The coral that grows here is *Corallum rubrum,* which provides red, pink, and white material. Closely related varieties of coral are native to the waters of the Red Sea, East Asia and the Indo-Pacific. The distantly related *Heliopora* of the Pacific provides the porous blue coral, which is not as durable and does not take as high a high polish as red coral. Members of the genus *Gorgonia,* and several other genera provide the interesting black coral, which is not calcareous, but tough and proteinaceous like horn. Black coral is much more common, and less valuable than the other varieties.

Left: This Nicaraguan craftsman is polishing sections of black coral, an inexpensive but attractive variety. *Right:* Skeleton of a Corallium rubrum colony, and coral cabochons from the Mediterranean region. Note the pits and grooves in the colony, and the distinctive texture of the polished coral.

Most corals exhibit distinctive organic structures including such as concentric banding, which help to distinguish coral from common imitations such as opaque glass, plastic, and cemented calcite. Coral can also be identified on the basis of its hardness, and the fact that it effervesces in dilute acid. A sophisticated synthetic coral has recently come on the market, and one can only hope that there will be as much care given to nurturing living coral as there is to simulating dead coral.

THIS MINERAL IS NOT OFTEN SEEN IN COLLECTIONS, OWING TO ITS RARITY IN SHARP crystals; it is usually enclosed in matrix. Like beryl, cordierite has a silicate ring structure characterized by long, open channels; these typically contain variable quantities of water, calcium, sodium, and potassium. Cordierite is one of the most conspicuously pleochroic of minerals, often changing in color from yellow or gray to violet-blue when viewed from different angles. The name honors the French geologist Pierre Louis Cordier (b. 1777); an alternate name, *dichroite* (meaning "two colors") describes its pleochroism. The violet-colored gem variety of cordierite is commonly referred to as iolite, from the Greek *ion,* meaning "violet."

Cordierite is transparent to translucent; pale to dark blue, violet, gray, brown, or black in color; and has a vitreous luster and a colorless streak. It has a poor cleavage in one direction and subconchoidal fracture. Cordierite may form short prismatic crystals with rectangular cross sections, but it usually occurs as shapeless blebs in the enclosing rock or as massive aggregates. When not identifiable by its color and marked dichroism, cordierite can easily be confused with quartz. Corundum is also similar in appearance, but much harder.

Cordierite is generally found in aluminum-rich metamorphic rocks. It is associated with quartz, andalusite, sillimanite, and biotite in gneisses and other regional metamorphic rocks; and with corundum and spinel in contact metamorphic rocks. It is also found in some andesites, granites, and pegmatites. Massive cordierite occurs in several places in Connecticut, New York, and New Hampshire; in several western states; and in the Yellowknife District of the Northwest Territories. Massive material, and rarely crystals, is also found Antarctica, Australia, England, Finland, India, Norway, Germany, Madagascar, Japan, Brazil, and Greenland.

cordierite

Classification:
cyclosilicate

Composition:
$(Mg,Fe)_2Al_4Si_5O_{18} \cdot nH_2O$
(magnesium–iron–aluminum silicate)

Crystal System:
orthorhombic

Hardness:
7–7.5

Specific Gravity:
2.53–2.78

Massive cordierite, variety iolite, from near Antsirabe, Malagasy Republic.

corundum

Classification:
oxide

Composition:
Al_2O_3 (aluminum oxide)

Crystal system:
hexagonal

Hardness:
9

Specific gravity:
4

THE NATIVE LAPIDARIES OF INDIA AND SRI LANKA ONCE CONSIDERED THE BRILLIANT red rubies and multicolored sapphires that they polished to be the "ripe" and "unripe" versions of the same stone. They reasoned that the two must be related, because both shared the same great hardness. Their contemporaries in Europe, however, divided gems on the basis of color. Rubies, garnets, and spinels were considered together under the rubric *carbunculus,* meaning "ember," while *sapphire* referred to a number of blue stones. The name corundum is probably derived from the Sanskrit *kuruvinda,* via the Tamil (native Sri Lankan) name for ruby, *kuruntam.* The name ruby comes from the Latin word for red, *ruber,* while sapphire originated as *sanipriya,* which in Sanskrit means "dear to the planet Saturn." Sapphires were thought to intercede on their owners behalf with Saturn, whose astrological influence was otherwise generally unfavorable.

Corundum is classified with hematite and ilmenite on the basis of its structure, which is characterized by close hexagonal packing of oxygen. The bonding of oxygen and aluminum in this structure give corundum its great hardness, which is exceeded only by diamond, as well as a higher specific gravity than most nonmetallic minerals. These two factors in combination account for the prevalence of corundum in sedimentary placer deposits, from which virtually all of the gem material is secured.

Corundum has been mined as an abrasive material for millennia, in the form of *emery* , a black, magnetic rock composed of magnetite and corundum. The lapidaries of ancient Greece and Egypt used emery mined on the Agean island of Naxos and on the coast of Asia Minor to cut and polish gemstones, and some of these ancient mines are still in use today. However, it was discovered in the 19th century that emery was composed of two minerals, one of which had negligible abrasive qualities, and its use declined in favor of pure corundum from uncontaminated deposits. Early in the present century, a technique was developed for producing large quantities of artificial corundum from the common aluminum ore bauxite (see *Diaspore*). This

A ruby crystal and cut stones from Burma, with the black aggregate of corundum and magnetite called emery.

development ended the mining of pure corundum, but emery is still used to make grinding wheels for lapidaries, machinists and opticians.

Corundum crystals commonly take the form of six-sided, tapering hexagonal dipyramids, typically striated barrel-shaped, and sometimes exhibiting rhombohedral faces. Ruby crystals in particular may take a tabular form. Although corundum has no cleavage, pervasive polysynthetic twinning commonly produces cubic or prismatic parting. During the gradual crystallization of either rubies or sapphires, excess titanium impurities may exsolve as slender, acicular crystals of rutile, which become aligned at 60° angles according to the crystal's hexagonal symmetry. This gives rise to asterism, in which light is reflected from the rutile inclusions in the form of a six-rayed star. Star sapphires are more common than star rubies.

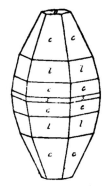

Pure corundum is colorless, and the substitution of certain transition elements for aluminum is responsible for the intense coloration of the gem varieties. Chromium is responsible for the color of ruby, while iron, titanium and other elements cause the coloration of sapphires. The term ruby is used only for deep-red gem corundum, and all other color variants are referred to as sapphires. Sapphires may be pink, green, yellow, violet, or colorless, but the most sought-after hue is bright cornflower blue.

In medieval Europe, sapphires inherited the therapeutic effects which lapis lazuli and other blue stones were traditionally thought to bestow on the eyes, and owners of the stones enjoyed a good business in treating the afflicted. Star sapphires have traditionally been considered good protection against the Evil Eye and general misfortune; they were called "victory stones" in medieval Europe, and carried into battle. In both Europe and Asia, rubies were thought to have the same influence in averting physical harm that was ascribed to garnets and other red stones.

Corundum is widely distributed in small amounts in rocks which are relatively poor in silica and rich in aluminum, including igneous rocks like syenites, and metamorphic rocks like marbles, mica schists, gniesses, and granulites. Rubies are confined the metamorphic environments, where they occur in association with zircon and spinel; sapphires are also found in mafic igneous rocks and with feldspars in pegmatites. Although rubies and sapphires are often found together in placer deposits, the best examples of each variety come from different locations.

The finest rubies are found in the region around Mogok, Burma. These stones display the deep red "pigeon blood" color which is most prized. Some stones are found in the marble which underlies this region, but most gem material is obtained from the placer deposits which have been accumulating for millennia in the streambeds. A much greater quantity of rubies is produced from similar deposits north of Bangkok, Thailand, but these are rarely of the same quality; deposits near Batdambang, Cambodia, also produce fine stones. Rubies are mined in many African countries, including Kenya, Tanzania, and South Africa, as well as in Brazil and China.

The placers of Sri Lanka are the premier source of high-quality sapphires, which occur in association with rubies and other gem minerals such as garnet, spinel, topaz, tourmaline, and zircon in the Ratnapura and Rakwana districts. Three quarters of the world's sapphires are produced from a broad area of Queensland, Australia, where the stones have been weathered from basalt to collect in the sediments. Although the quantity of these stones is great, their quality is generally poor. Small but very colorful sapphires are found in the gravels of the Missouri River, and in a narrow dike of igneous rock called *lamprophyre* at Yogo Gulch, Montana. Sapphires are also found in most of the localities listed above for ruby; perhaps the finest being the cornflower blue stones from Cambodia.

Euhedral crystals of common corundum and large quantities of massive material occur in nepheline syenites at Bancroft and Craigmont, Ontario, and in metamorphic rocks throughout the Appalachian Mountains region. Crystals as large as 170 kg have been found in Madagascar, and very large crystals also occur in some South African pegmatites. Emery, in addition to

A 19th century sapphire and diamond brooch. In medieval times it was widely believed that diseases of the eyes could be cured by touching them with sapphires.

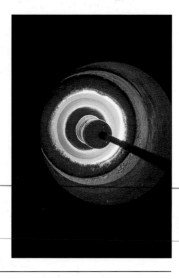

the Mediterranean occurrences noted above, occurs near Chester, Massachusetts, and Peekskill, New York.

One of the first successful attempts at manufacturing gemstones came at the turn of the century, when the French chemist Auguste Verneuil synthesized corundum from powdered aluminum oxide. This powder, with impurities added to create the desired color, is fused to form liquid droplets in an extremely hot flame of 2050° C. This molten material then drips down to crystallize as an elongate cylinder called a *boule*, which can be cut into stones. In 1947, the Linde Company in the United States produced the first synthetic star rubies and star sapphires, by introducing excess titanium into the mix and imitating the natural process of rutile exsolution on cooling.

Synthetic corundum is identical with the natural mineral in all its chemical and physical properties, but unlike natural gems, is generally flawless. Such stones are quite inexpensive, in contrast to natural rubies (for example) which typically cost more per carat than diamonds. The demand for natural gems, despite their expense and the availability of excellent substitutes, highlights the fact that aesthetic beauty is not the sole attraction of gemstones. Indeed, natural gems are fascinating in large part because of the *absence* of human influence.

A boule of synthetic ruby being created using the Verneuil Process. Gemstones cut from this artificial crystal will be almost identical to natural rubies.

covellite

Classification:
sulfide

Composition:
CuS (copper sulfide)

Crystal System:
hexagonal

Hardness:
1.5–2

Specific Gravity:
4.6–4.7

ALSO KNOWN AS INDIGO COPPER FOR ITS DEEP BLUE COLOR, THIS MINERAL IS NAMED for the Italian mineralogist Niccolo Covelli (b. 1790), who collected specimens from Mt. Vesuvius. Unlike most simple sulfides, covellite is not a primary mineral but occurs as an alteration product of chalcopyrite, chalcocite, bornite, enargite, and other primary copper sulfides. Relatively common in its foliated massive form, crystallized specimens are rare and highly valued. Crystals occur as subparallel aggregates of thin, tabular, hexagonal plates, with broad basal pinacoid faces displaying curious hexagonal striations. Covellite is a distinctive deep indigo-blue, with a purple iridescence; it is opaque, with a submetallic luster and and a metallic gray streak. Somewhat sectile and flexible, covellite has an uneven fracture and one easy, perfect cleavage. The distinctive color and well-developed cleavage distinguish covellite from other copper sulfides. Its characteristic aggregates of extremely thin crystals are also unique.

Covellite occurs in the enriched portions of hydrothermal copper sulfide veins, and is commonly intergrown with bornite, chalcopyrite, chalcocite, enargite, and pyrite. Common throughout the western United States, the finest specimens being the box-works of thin crystals 3 cm or more in diameter from Butte, Silver Bow County, Montana. Large masses occur in the La Sal District of Utah, and at the Kennecott Mine, in Alaska's Copper River District. Excellent crystallized specimens are found in the Calabona Mine, Alghero, Sardinia; at Bor, Yugoslavia; Tsumeb, Namibia; and numerous other locations worldwide.

Broad plates of covellite from the famous Leonard Mine, Butte, Montana—once one of the most important crystal-producing mines in the world.

cristobalite

Classification:
tectosilicate, silica group

Composition:
SiO_2 (silicon dioxide)

Crystal System:
high–cristobalite: isometric
low–cristobalite: tetragonal

Hardness:
7

Specific Gravity:
2.3

CRISTOBALITE IS THE HIGHEST TEMPERATURE FORM OF THE THREE IMPORTANT POLY-morphs of SiO_2, the others of which are quartz and tridymite. It initially crystallizes in the isometric system as high cristobalite, which is only stable at temperatures above 1470°C, converting to low cristobalite at normal surface temperatures. Low cristobalite has the most open and symmetrical structure of all the silca polymorphs. Although this structure is technically unstable at surface temperatures, all three polymorphs can and do coexist in nature, as considerable time and energy are required to transform the high-temperature polymorphs into the stable quartz structure.

Cristobalite usually occurs as spherical cryptocrystalline aggregates, in the interior of small cavities in felsic igneous rocks such as andesites, rhyolites, and obsidian, sometimes associated with yellow fayalite (olivine). Since cristobalite often forms an important part of the groundmass of these rocks as well, it can be considered a common mineral, if an inconspicuous one. Spherulites of cristobalite in obsidian are commonly seen from Inyo County, California, the San Juan Range of Colorado, and elsewhere in the western United States. Cristobalite has been found as pseudo-octahedral or pseudocubic crystals under 4 mm in greatest dimension, at the type locality in the andesites of Cerro San Cristobal, Mexico.

Tiny crystalline aggregates of cristobalite in volcanic rock, from Lakabnaus, Reydarfjordur, Iceland.

crocoite

Classification:
chromate

Composition:
$PbCrO_4$ (lead chromate)

Crystal System:
monoclinic

Hardness:
2.5–3

Specific Gravity:
5.9–6.1

THE GREEK WORD FOR "SAFFRON," *KROKOS*, PROVIDED THE NAME OF THIS DEEP orange-red mineral, and indeed, its color is identical to that of the saffron crocus' precious stigma. The first crystals of this mineral were found at Beresovsk, near Sverdlovsk in the Ural Mountains of the Soviet Union, and from these the element chromium was first isolated in 1797 (see *Chromite*). Crocoite is isostructural with the chemically unrelated rare-earth phosphate monazite, $CePO_4$. Although too rare to be valuable as an ore of chromium, crocoite is highly prized by mineral collectors for its striking crystals.

Equant octahedral and acute rhombohedral crystals of crocoite are known, but the typical habit is elongated striated prisms and acicular needles, often bunched in parallel alignment or haphazardly jumbled together in "jackstraw" aggregates. The largest crystals may reach a length of more than 10 cm. Crocite is translucent, with a greasy adamantine luster and a lambent yellowish red color, like the dying embers of a campfire. It is an extremely delicate mineral, with three cleavages, conchoidal to uneven fracture, and an orange-yellow streak. Handle with care.

The crystallization of this rare mineral is made possible only in environments where lead-bearing sulfide veins are hosted by chrome-bearing country rocks. These unusual geological conditions make crocoite a rare species, and specimens are accordingly expensive. Common associates include cerrusite, wulfenite, and vanadinite. The only place where crocoite has ever been found in abundance is the famous, but now apparently depleted occurrence in the Dundas District in Tasmania, Australia. Most of the finest specimens seen in collections and museums are from this locality. From its discovery in the 1880s through the 1920s, great wagon-loads of crocoite were hauled from the mines at Dundas to be smelted for their lead content—a thought that horrifies collectors today. The smaller but geologically similar deposits—in the Urals; at Rezbanya, Romania; and at Congonhas do Campo and Goyabeira in the state of Minas Gerais, Brazil—also seem to be depleted. North American occurrences include the Vulture District, Nevada; the El Dorado Mine in Riverside County, and the Darwin Mines in Inyo County, California.

Crocoite crystals in a fissure of limonite gossan, from the classic locality at Dundas, Tasmania.

cryolite

Composition:
Na$_3$(AlF$_6$) (sodium aluminum fluoride)

Crystal System:
monoclinic

Hardness:
2.5–3

Specific Gravity:
2.95

Parallel aggregate of cryolite crystals from Ivigtut, Arsukfjord, Greenland.

THE NAME CRYOLITE IS derived from the Greek word *kyros*, meaning "frost," an appropriate designation for a species that is almost identical in appearance to ice and which is found in the arctic wastes of Greenland. It has some importance as a clouding agent in the glass and enamel industry, but is most important as a flux in the electrolytic production of aluminum. The melting point of raw aluminum oxide is above 2000°C, but with the addition of cryolite it drops to little more than 1000°C. Since the demand for cryolite can no longer be met by natural sources, it is synthetically produced from fluorite today.

Cryolite is usually found in massive coarsely crystalline aggregates, rarely as good crystals of pseudocubic form. Crystals are usually colorless, and cloudy masses of cryolite are snow-white, reddish, gray, or black. It has a glassy luster and a very low refractive index, almost identical to that of water; when placed in water, a crystal of cryolite will seem to disappear. At a temperature of just over 560°C, monoclinic cryolite alters to cubic symmetry. Clear crystals of cryolite were formed at low temperatures and are monoclinic in symmetry, while the more common cloudy masses have undergone structural modification above this temperature.

Cryolite is almost always pegmatitic in origin, the transparent crystals having formed in fractures in the massive material. The only commercially important deposit for this useful fluorine mineral was at Ivigtut, on the Arsukfjord, in South Greenland, which has been worked since about 1850. Mining was halted in 1962 due to the depletion of the deposit. Specimens are obtained from pegmatites in El Paso County, Colorado, and in a carbonatite in Fremont County. Euhedral crystals up to 1 cm in size are found in the Francon Quarry, near Montreal, Quebec. Small amounts are obtained from Sallent, Huesca Province, Spain, and Miask in the Ural Mountains of the Soviet Union.

crystal systems and crystal symmetry

THE SYMMETRY OF CRYSTALS IS ONE OF THE MOST INTRIGUING ASPECTS OF MINERALS. Regardless of environmental conditions or the presence of impurities, the angle between any two corresponding faces will be the same in every crystal of a particular type—even though individual crystals and their faces may vary greatly in size and shape. This relationship was first proven in 1669 by Nicolaus Steno, working with crystals of quartz. Although symmetry is most apparent in the regular arrangement of crystal faces, it of course reflects the basic structure of a mineral on the atomic level. In the first century A.D., Pliny the Elder suggested that the regular hexagonal crystals of quartz must be composed of a framework of six-sided "bricks." In 1784, the French naturalist René Hauy observed that calcite crystals always break into perfect little rhombohedral fragments, whatever their external shape, and formulated the concept of "integral molcules." Today we call the smallest grouping of atoms which exhibits the basic symmetry of a mineral the *unit cell*.

On the basis of its crystal symmetry, any mineral can be placed into one of thirty-two *crystal classes*, which are in turn grouped into six basic *crystal systems*. These systems are defined according to a set of imaginary axes, which intersect at the center of an ideal crystal; the basic symmetry of the system is determined by the length of these axes and by the angles at which they intersect. Although a crystal system may embrace hundreds of possible forms, each preserves the relationships described by the basic model.

Crystals display three basic kinds of symmetry: plane symmetry, axial symmetry, and symmetry about a center. A crystal is said to have plane symmetry if a "mirror plane" passing through its center divides it into two identical halves. Many organisms, including human beings, display this type of symmetry. Symmetry about an axis is characterized by the repetition of identical faces as a crystal is rotated around a particular axis. Such symmetry can be described as a twofold, threefold, fourfold, etc., depending on how many times these faces are repeated in one 360° rotation. Symmetry about a center characterizes crystals in which each face has a counterpart parallel to it on the opposite side of the crystal.

A crystal may display more than one plane, axis or center of symmetry, and may in fact have several of these in combination. Simple isometric forms such as the cube and octahedron, for instance, have nine axes of rotation and nine planes of symmetry, in addition to a center of symmetry. At the other end of the spectrum is the pedial class of the triclinic system, which has no symmetry whatsoever. The various crystal systems are discussed below in order of decreasing symmetry.

The Isometric System Crystals of this system (also called the cubic system) derive their high degree of symmetry from three mutually perpendicular axes of identical length. This geometry results in forms which are equidimensional, or "equant" in appearance, covered with many similar faces—thus the name of this system, which comes from the Greek phrase meaning "equal measure." There are fifteen basic forms in the isometric system, including the tetrahedron, which has four faces; the cube, with six faces; the octahedron, with eight faces; and the dodecahedron and pyritohedron, both with twelve faces. More unusual forms include the trapezohedron, with twenty-four faces and the hexoctahedron, with forty-eight faces.

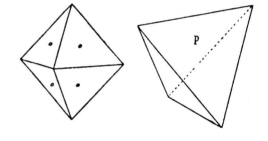

The identification of many isometric minerals is facilitated by their tendency to crystallize in one particular crystal form. The oxides of the spinel group, for instance, tend to form simple octahedra, while the garnets typically crystallize as dodecahedra. Other species, such as fluorite, often display a combination of crystal forms. The greater the number of different forms present in combination, the more individual faces a crystal has, and the more "rounded" it will appear.

The Hexagonal System The crystals of this system are characterized by three axes of equal length, which intersect at angles of 120° and all lie in the same plane. Perpendicular to this plane is another axis of indeterminate length, called the *c axis*. A typical hexagonal form is the six-sided prism, either elongate, as in tourmaline, or squat and tabular, as in apatite. Doubling of this form results in twelve-sided, dihexagonal prisms. Such forms are typically truncated by parallel pinacoidal (also called basal) planes, by pyramids or dipyramids, or by combinations of these forms.

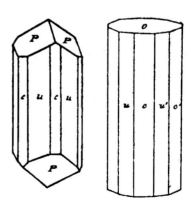

Crystals of the trigonal and rhombohedral classes of the hexagonal system display only three-fold symmetry, and are sometimes classed separately in the "rhombohedral system." Like other hexagonal crystals, rhombohedral forms have three axes of equal length, plus a fourth of varying length. In this case, however, the three similar axes do not lie in the same plane. The basic forms of this group include the simple rhombohedron, the trapezohedron, and the scalenohedron, typical of calcite. These forms often occur in combination with more symmetrical hexagonal forms, as in quartz crystals, which often consist of a hexagonal prism is terminated by one or more rhombohedra.

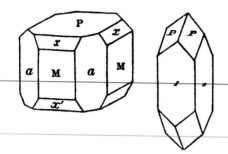

The Tetragonal System As in the isometric system, tetragonal crystals have three mutually perpendicular axes, but in this case only two are of equal length. Like hexagonal crystals, the basic forms here include prisms and pyramids, but in this case the symmetry is only four-fold—thus the name of the system, which means "four-sided." Doubled versions of these forms result in eight-sided, ditetragonal forms with eight similar faces. Tetragonal versions of the trapezehedron and scalenohedron also exist, as does an elongated version of the tetrahedron called the tetragonal disphenoid, sometimes seen in chalcopyrite. Other common tetragonal minerals include rutile and zircon.

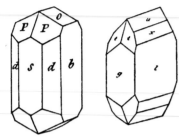

The Orthorhombic System Orthorhombic crystals are similar to those of the tetragonal system in that they have three mutually-perpendicular axes, but in this case the axes are all of different lengths, resulting in two-fold symmetry at best. Simple combinations of prismatic, pinacoidal and pyramidal forms result in stout, blocky crystals, such as those of columbite, olivine and topaz. Extreme development in one crystallographic direction or another results in platy or tabular forms, such as barite, or elongate forms as seen in stibnite and sillimanite.

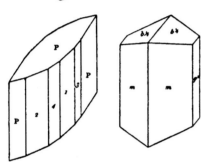

The Monoclinic System The monoclinic ("single inclination") system is named for the way in which it differs from the orthorhombic system. Although both are characterized by three axes of differing length, in monoclinic forms only two axes are perpendicular, while one makes an angle with the others. This results in crystals which are similar to those of the orthorhombic system, but slightly askew. Prism faces are typically parallel to the eccentric axis, with pinacoidal or pyramidal faces parallel to the two mutually perpendicular axes. The elongate prisms of gypsum with their sharply angled, parallel terminations are an example of this morphology.

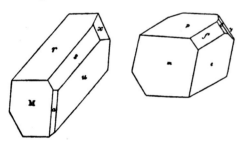

The Triclinic System The name of this system means "three inclinations," reflecting asymmetrical geometry of its forms. Triclinic crystals have three axes of differing lengths, none of which are perpendicular to the others. The only regular forms recognizable in triclinic crystals are the two parallel faces of the pinacoid, and the pedion—a face with no symmetrical relationship to any other. The most important triclinic species are the feldspars of the plagioclase series. Sharp, angular forms, such as the distinctive, wedge-shaped crystals of axinite are common in this system.

cuprite

Classification:
oxide

Composition:
Cu_2O (copper oxide)

Crystal System:
isometric

Hardness
3.5–4

Specific Gravity
6.14

CUPRITE IS A SECONDARY COPPER ORE WHICH OFTEN FORMS VERY ATTRACTIVE TRANSparent red crystals, earning it the miners' name "ruby copper." Its scientific name comes from the Latin *cuprum*, or copper, reflecting its composition. Crystals are usually cubic, octahedral, or dodecahedral in shape, with the dominant isometric form typically being modified by one or more of the others in a variety of interesting ways. A hair-like variety called "plush copper," or chalcotrichite, forms delicate, felted mats and masses. Cuprite commonly occurs in granular aggregates as well, often mixed with earthy limonite. Pseudomorphs of malachite after cuprite are fairly common, particularly from the classic locality at Chessy, near Lyon, France. The color of cuprite crystals is carmine red; massive specimens are typically dark red or red-brown. The luster is adamantine to slightly metallic, due to its high refractive index, which exceeds that of diamond.

Cuprite is found in the oxidation zone of hydrothermal sulfide veins, in association with other secondary species such as native copper, chalcocite, antlerite, limonite, and the copper carbonates. It is an economically important copper ore in some localities. Important sources include Tsumeb and the Onganja Mine in Namibia, and locations in Zaire, Japan, Australia, Mexico, Bolivia, and Chile. In addition to the Chessy occurrence, European sources include Germany, Hungary, and Cornwall, England. Handsome crystals come from mines in Pennsylvania and Tennessee; Bisbee, Clifton, and Morenci, Arizona; and numerous other locations throughout the western United States.

Twinned cuprite crystals amid a druse of smaller crystals from the West Phoenix Mine, Linkinhorne, Cornwall.

danburite

Classification:
tectosilicate

Composition:
$CaB_2Si_2O_8$ (calcium borosilicate)

Crystal System:
orthorhombic

Hardness:
7

Specific Gravity:
2.97–3.02

DANBURITE IS NAMED FOR AN OLD SOURCE IN THE CITY OF DANBURY, CONNECTICUT. An unusual mineral which occurs in small amounts in a variety of different geological environments, danburite is easily mistaken for the much more common topaz. Like topaz, it forms stout prismatic crystals with wedge-shaped terminations. These are usually clear or white, but may also be pinkish, yellow, green, or brown. Danburite has one indistinct cleavage, conchoidal fracture, a vitreous to greasy luster, and a colorless streak. Topaz is harder than danburite, and is also distinguished by its prominent basal cleavage.

At the Danbury locality and at Russell, St. Lawrence County, New York, danburite is associated with feldspar in contact metamorphic dolomites. Fine specimens are found in the crystal-lined vugs in the metamorphic rocks of the Alps, particularly at Piz Valacha, near Uri, Switzerland. Large crystals to 8 cm occur in the hydrothermal sulfide veins of Charcas, San Luis Potosí, Mexico. Even larger danburite crystals, associated with green tourmaline, have recently been recovered from an unusual pegmatite near La Huerta, northern Baja California. Transparent yellow crystals have been recovered from the gem gravels around Mogok, Burma, and cut into fine gems. Danburite is also found on the Japanese island of Kyushu; on Mt. Bity and elsewhere in Madagascar; and in the Soviet Union.

Danburite from Mina la Bufa, Charcas, San Luis Potosi, Mexico.

DATOLITE IS AN UNCOMMON MINERAL, BUT STILL THE MOST ABUNDANT MEMBER OF the gadolinite group, named for a rare beryllium rare-earth silicate. Its structure consists of stacked layers of SiO_4 and $B(O,OH)_4$ tetrahedra, bonded together by calcium ions. Despite this orderly, layered arrangement, datolite has no cleavage to speak of. Although it has been used as a source of boron, it is not an important ore. Datolite's name is derived from the Greek *dateisthai*, "to divide," since its coarser-grained aggregates tend to crumble easily.

Crystals are usually complex, typically forming blunt wedges with a bewildering variety of faces scattered across matrix. Datolite is also found in the granular aggregates, and rarely in compact, porcelanous nodules. It is colorless, white, greenish, yellowish, or pinkish, and transparent to translucent, with a vitreous luster and a colorless streak.

Datolite is found in basalt cavities with zeolites, apophyllite, prehnite, quartz, and calcite, as well as in fissures in granites, gneisses, serpentines, and in some hydrothermal veins. Excellent crystals as large as 7 cm on edge are found in basalt at Lane Quarry, near Westfield, Massachusetts. Good specimens are also found in northern New Jersey, in parts of Connecticut, and at several sites in California. Fine crystals occur in the silver veins of Guanajuato, Mexico; at Andreasberg, Harz, Germany; and at Arendal, Norway. The unusual porcelaneous nodules are found with copper in the basalts of the Keweenaw Peninsula, Michigan; these have been cut into interesting cabochons containing flecks of native copper.

datolite

Classification:
nesosilicate

Composition:
$CaBSiO_4(OH)$
(hydrous calcium borosilicate)

Crystal System:
monoclinic

Hardness:
5–5.5

Specific Gravity:
2.8–3

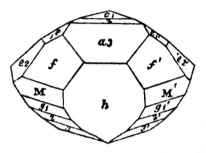

Datolite crystals on matrix from Saltaria-Schlucht, Seisser-Alpe, Tyrol, Austria.

descloizite and mottramite

Classification:
vanadates

Composition:
$(Zn,Cu)Pb(VO_4)(OH)$
(hydrous zinc and/or copper lead vanadates)

Crystal System:
orthorhombic

Hardness:
3.5

Specific Gravity:
5.8–6.3

Plumose crystalline aggregate of descloizite from Berg Aukas, Grootfontein, Namibia.

THESE TWO SPECIES FORM A SOLID-SOLUTION SERIES, OF WHICH DESCLOIZITE IS THE zinc-rich and mottramite the copper-rich end member. Both are rare, but important ores of vanadium nonetheless. Descloizite's tongue-twisting name honors the French mineralogist Alfred Louis Oliver Legrand des Cloizeaux (b. 1817), while mottramite is named for the English locality of Mottram St. Andrews, Cheshire.

Both species commonly form crusts of small plumose crystal aggregates, or botryoidal masses; on rare occasions they may occur as discrete, flattened pseudo-octahedral crystals. Descloizite is reddish brown to black, becoming greenish as the composition approaches that of mottramite. Both are transparent or translucent with a greasy luster, and have streaks ranging from red-brown to greenish brown.

Descloizite and mottramite are found in the alteration zone of lead, zinc, and copper sulfide veins, associated with vanadinite, cerussite, wulfenite, and pyromorphite. By far the best specimens have come from Namibia, particularly Grootfontien and Tsumeb in the Otavi District. Other African sources include Mouana, Gabon; Broken Hill, Zaire; and Algeria, Tunisia, and Zimbabwe. In addition to the Cheshire locality, European sources are mines in Cap Garrone, France; Germany, particularly the Clara Mine in the Black Forest; and Austria and Italy. Good specimens are found in many parts of the western United States as well, particularly at the Silver Queen Mine, Galena, South Dakota; and the Mammoth Mine, Tiger, Arizona. Other sources include Argentina, Bolivia, Brazil, Mexico, and Iran.

diamond

Classification:
native element

Composition:
C (carbon)

Crystal system:
isometric

Hardness:
10

Specific Gravity:
3.51

EVEN IN ANTIQUITY DIAMOND WAS KNOWN AS THE HARDEST SUBSTANCE ON EARTH, which is why the Greeks called it *adamas*, meaning "the invincible." Diamond has the most compact and strongly bonded structure of the four known polymorphs of carbon, and this accounts for its remarkable hardness. Graphite is the most common polymorph of carbon, and is formed under most geological conditions; the other two polymorphs, *chaoite* and *lonsdaleite*, are extremely rare and occur only in meteorites.

The first diamonds seen in Europe were rare uncut crystals from placer deposits near Golconda, India. Although prized for their hardness in ancient times, these rough stones were valued less than pearls or most other colored stones. During the Middle Ages diamonds became increasingly popular, particularly as talismans intended to give the bearer supernatural powers. Naturally, diamond was associated with strength and invincibility in the medieval imagination. A diamond was thought to make its wearer invulnerable in battle; to foster courage; and to protect against against poisons, scurvy, gout, arthritis, and other maladies.

Diamonds have now displaced all colored stones, except the best quality rubies and emeralds, as the most valuable of gemstones. Three quarters of the world's diamond production is used in industrial applications, particularly grinding wheels and drill bits. More than 10,000 kg of natural diamonds, and a similar quantity of synthetic diamonds, are produced each year.

Diamonds form at depths greater than 150 km in the earth's mantle, at temperatures greater than 1000°C, and under pressures greater than 50,000 times that at the surface. They are brought to the earth's surface by kimberlites, gas-rich magmas which originate deep within the mantle and erupt explosively through fissures called diamond pipes, or diatremes. Kimberlite is very complex in composition, containing fragments of a variety of mantle rocks, including the ultramafic igneous rocks in which diamonds are thought to originally form. These rocks are called lheuzolites and eclogites, and also contain olivine, pyrope garnet, and pyroxenes.

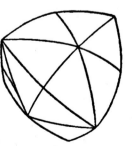

Above: Diamond crystals in fancy colors displaying a variety of forms.
Left: Diamond crystals from Zaire, showing a variety of isometric forms, etching and twinning, and cut gem.

Diamond crystals take the form of octahedrons, dodecahedrons, and cubes, with the first two shapes being by far the more common. Combinations of these forms are also very common, and in diamonds from the Congo and a few other regions, each form is equally developed. Crystal faces often show rounded faces and surface structures acquired during growth, as well as surface marks from subsequent pitting and etching. Twinning is very common in diamonds and sometimes presents difficulties in cleaving and cutting. Twinned crystals usually have triangular flattened forms. Diamond crystals and aggregates that display irregular or radial growth and which are gray to black in color due to graphite inclusions, are known as either bort or carbonado and are used in industrial applications. Diamond is brittle, with a perfect cleavage parallel to the octahedral faces and conchoidal fracture. Bort and carbonado are extremely tough, twins less so, and single crystals even less.

Diamond crystals are mostly colorless, with only slight tints of yellow, brown, or green; nitrogen is thought to be responsible for the slight yellowish tint of many diamonds. Brightly colored diamonds are extremely rare; known as "fancy" diamonds, they command much higher prices than even the cleanest colorless stones. Common fancy colors include golden-yellow, orange-yellow, coffee-brown, green, blue, red, and pink. These colors are caused by the substitution of other elements in the diamond structure, or slight perturbations in the structure itself. Canary-yellow, cognac-brown, and dark-brown diamonds are colored by iron, the rare blue diamonds by boron; and the pinkish-red ones by manganese. The artificial bombardment of diamonds with electrons or neutrons can cause color change as well. Electron bombardment can give colorless stones a blue tint, while neutron bombardment can impart a green color—which, in turn, can be changed to yellow or brown with heat treatment. Diamonds range from full trans-

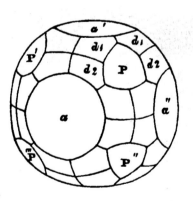

The "Big Hole" at Kimberley, South Africa. Between its discovery in 1872 and abandonment in 1914, over 25,000,000 tons of kimberlite rock were excavated from this deposit, yielding over 14,000,000 carats of diamonds.

parency to translucent and opaque. The striking diamond luster is caused by its high refractive index; the play of colors, or "fire," is due to its strong dispersion. These properties are best displayed in a brilliant cut gemstone, which is the most common diamond cut. Some diamonds may fluoresce pale blue, green, yellow, or more rarely, red.

In 1953, an industrial process for producing diamond from graphite was discovered, employing temperatures in excess of 1400°C and pressures of 50,000–60,000 atm. Diamonds formed in this process are small, and are suitable only for industrial purposes. Larger diamonds have been synthesized, however—some over 1 carat in size and often displaying beautiful colors, but the process is prohibitively expensive. Other synthetic gemstones are commonly substituted for diamond, however. These include strontium titanate (fabulite), synthetic rutile (titania), yttrium aluminum garnet (YAG), gadolinium gallium garnet, and zirconium oxide (cubic zirconia). Each is a passable imitation of diamond, and both YAG and cubic zirconia are excellent.

The first diamond deposits known were the placers located east of the Deccan Highlands in India, in the area of Golconda. Among the many famous diamonds found there is the blue Hope Diamond, and the Kohinoor, or "Mountain of Light." India remained the world's premier source of diamonds until the discovery of placer deposits in Brazil in 1721. These diamonds may have been weathered from kimberlites in Africa, prior to the breakup of Africa and South America by the forces of plate tectonics during the late Mesozoic Era. Crystals embedded in ancient conglomerates, and the alluvium derived from their erosion, are still found in a number of Brazilian states and in neighboring parts of Venezuela and Guyana. Brazil remained the world's primary source of diamonds until 1866, when a little boy was found playing with a 21-carat stone on the banks of the Orange River in South Africa.

Numerous placer deposits were soon discovered in the region, and in 1869 the discovery of a 50-carat stone in a dry wash led to the discovery of the first kimberlite, near Jagersfontien, South Africa. Over 700 kimberlites have been discovered in South Africa, and these have produced many remarkable stones, including the largest diamond ever found—the fist-sized, 3106-carat Cullinan Diamond, unearthed in 1905 at the Premier Mine near Pretoria. Diamond pipes are also mined in Botswana, Tanzania, and Zaire, and vast beach placers are worked along the desert coast of Namibia. Individual miners working the streams of Ghana, Liberia, and Sierra Leone produce a surprisingly large quantity of Africa's diamonds.

In the early 19th century, diamonds were discovered in placer deposits near the Ural Mountains of Russia, and after World War II, kimberlites were found north of Lake Baikal in Siberia. The largest diamond yet found there is the Star of Yakutia, weighing 232 carats. In 1985, mining commenced on a diamond-bearing kimberlite near Lake Argyle in Western Australia, and now the Argyle Mine produces nearly one third of the world's diamond supply. Diamonds have been found in placer deposits at various locations in North America, including the Appalachian Mountains, California, and the glacial moraines around the Great Lakes region. Kimberlites have been found in the Colorado Rockies and at Murfreesboro, Pike County, Arkansas, where crystals weighing up to 40 carats have been discovered.

DIASPORE IS A CONSTITUENT OF TWO ECONOMICALLY IMPORTANT MINERAL AGGRE-gates: the natural abrasive emery (see *Corundum*), and bauxite, the primary ore of aluminum. Bauxite is composed of diaspore, its polymorph boemite, and gibbsite, $Al(OH)_3$, any one of which may predominate. This massive material forms through the weathering of aluminum-rich rocks in tropical and subtropical regions, occurring as earthy or pisolitic ("pea-like") aggregates. Although aluminum is by far the most abundant metal in the earth's crust, a method for commercially producing the metal from its ores was not developed until 1886. Since then, its properties of low density and great strength have made aluminum a vital industrial metal of innumerable uses. Bauxite is also used to produce synthetic Al_2O_3 abrasive and refractories. Of the three components of bauxite, only diaspore is regularly seen in crystalline form. The name, from the Greek *diaspora*, or "scattering," reflects this mineral's habit of *decrepitating*, or bursting apart when heated.

Although usually occurring in massive form, diaspore sometimes forms thin tabular or acicular crystals, occasionally as pseudohexagonal twins. The color ranges from white to yellowish, pink, gray, or green; the manganese-rich variety mangandiaspore is rose to dark red. It is transparent to subtranslucent with a vitreous to pearly luster and a white streak. Diaspore is very delicate, with three directions of cleavage, one perfect. This cleavage, plus its hardness and tendency to decrepitate, serve to distinguish diaspore from axinite.

Diaspore is very widespread and commonly occurs with corundum, chlorite, magnetite, and spinel in marbles and schists, or with gibbsite as a constituent of some bauxites and aluminum-rich clays. Diaspore bladed crystals to 7 cm in length are found in cavities in emery at Chester, Massachusetts, and on the Greek island of Naxos. Good specimens are also found in New Hampshire, Pennsylvania, and at the Champion Sparkplug Mine in California's White Mountains. The red variety mangandiaspore is found in South Africa's Postmasburg District.

diaspore

Classification:
hydroxide

Composition:
AlO(OH) (aluminum hydroxide)

Crystal System:
orthorhombic

Hardness:
6.5–7

Specific Gravity:
3.3–3.5

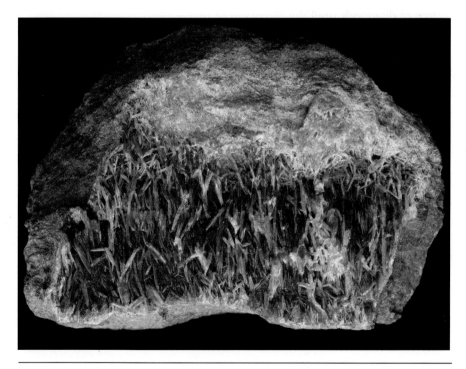

Acicular diaspore crystals in emery from Chester, Massachusetts.

diopside

Classification:
pyroxene group

Composition:
$MgCaSi_2O_6$ (calcium magnesium silicate)

Crystal System:
monoclinic

Hardness:
5.5–6.5

Specific Gravity:
3.22–3.28

Stubby prisms of diopside from Nordmark, Varmland, Sweden.

DIOPSIDE FORMS A SOLID-SOLUTION SERIES WITH THE CALCIUM IRON PYROXENE hedenbergite, $CaFeSi_2O_6$, as well as with the calcium-iron-manganese pyroxene *johannsenite*, $Ca(Mn,Fe^{+2})Si2O6$. An important rock-forming mineral, diopside is more often encountered in euhedral crystals than other pyroxenes. The name is from the Greek phrase meaning "two views," in reference to the two-fold monoclinic symmetry it exhibits. Transparent crystals of diopside, and chatoyant material displaying cat's-eye or star patterns, are sometimes fashioned into gemstones.

Crystals of diopside are commonly short prisms with blunt wedge-shaped terminations, and lamellar or granular aggregates are common. Diopside is transparent to translucent, with a vitreous or dull luster. The color is usually some shade of grayish green, but colorless, white, brown, or greenish black are also common ; the streak is white or grayish. Gem material may be blue or rose colored. Diopside displays good cleavage in two directions, at nearly right angles— like all members of the pyroxene group. Epidote and olivine are similar in appearance, but are each a different, distinctive shade of green, and lack the distinctive cleavage of diopside.

Diopside is a very common and widespread mineral, forming in calcium-rich metamorphic and igneous rocks, including some mafic and ultramafic igneous rocks, and in carbonatites with calcite or dolomite. In igneous rocks, diopside usually contains some iron and aluminum, grading into the compositional range of augite, which is far more common in these environments. Most diopside specimens come from contact metamorphic bodies, where diopside forms from the reaction between dolomite and quartz, occurring in association with grossular garnet, wollastonite, and phlogopite. Excellent specimens crystals to 15 cm in length are found in the marbles of Haliburton County, Ontario; Sherbrooke County, Quebec; and St. Lawrence County, New York. Fine transparent crystals are found in the Ala Valley and elsewhere in northern Italy, at Nordmark, Sweden, and in many other locations.

dioptase

Classification:
cyclosilicate

Composition:
$CuSiO_2(OH)_2$ (hydrous copper silicate)

Crystal System:
hexagonal (rhombohedral)

Hardness:
5

Specific Gravity:
3.28–3.53

WHEN DISCOVERED IN THE LATE 18TH CENTURY IN CENTRAL ASIA, THIS UNUSUAL COPPER silicate was at first thought to be emerald because of its brilliant emerald-green color. Although it is relatively soft, dioptase has been fashioned into small, beautiful gems. The name comes from the Greek *diopteia*, meaning "to see through"—a reference to the fact that minute internal cleavage fractures are usually visible within the crystals.

Dioptase crystals usually occur as short columnar prisms terminated with rhombohedral faces, rarely exceeding one-half inch in length. They are transparent to translucent with a vitreous to greasy luster and a blue-green streak. In addition to the typical green color, dioptase may be deep blue-green or even turquoise-blue. The distinctive color and hardness of dioptase distinguish it from all other species in its geological environment.

Dioptase forms at a late stage of hydrothermal alteration, in the oxidation zones of copper deposits. Characteristic associates include chrysocolla, brochantite, malachite, azurite, and other secondary copper minerals. The classic source is Altyn-Tube, near Tashkent, in the Kirgiz Republic of the Soviet Union, where exceptional crystals are found perched on white lime-stone matrix. Most specimens currently come from Africa, particularly from Tsumeb and Guchab, Namibia; additional sources are the Katanga District in Zaire, and Mindouli and other locations in the Congo. Fine specimens have been obtained from the Nishapur region of Iran; and from Copiapo in the Atacama Desert and other locations in Chile. Outstanding specimens are rare from American sources, which include the Soda Lake Mountains of California, and the Mammoth-St. Anthony mines in Tiger as well as other locations in Arizona.

Druse of dioptase crystals from Tsumeb, Grootfontein, Namibia.

dolomite and ankerite

Classification:
carbonates

Composition:
dolomite: $CaMg(CO_3)_2$
(calcium magnesium carbonate)
ankerite: $Ca(Fe,Mg)(CO_3)_2$
(calcium iron magnesium carbonate)

Crystal System:
hexagonal (rhombohedral)

Hardness:
3.5–4

Specific Gravity:
2.85 (dolomite)
2.97 (ankerite)

DOLOMITE AND ANKERITE FORM A SOLID-SOLUTION SERIES, AND THOUGH THE FORMER is far more common than the latter, they are similar in appearance and crystal form and are often confused with one another. Magnesium often substitutes for calcium in calcite ($CaCO_3$), but dolomite differs in that magnesium and calcium each have their own structural sites. The dolomite structure is characterized by alternating layers, each composed entirely of either calcium, magnesium, or carbonate ions. Ankerite has a similar structure, except that some of the magnesium sites are filled by iron; if less than 20% of the sites are so filled, the mineral is considered merely a *ferroan* (iron-rich) dolomite. Manganese commonly substitutes for magnesium in both species. Dolomite is named for the French mineralogist Deodat de Dolomieu (b. 1750), and ankerite for the Austrian mineralogist Matthias J. Anker (b. 1772).

The typical crystal form of both dolomite and ankerite is the rhombohedron, a shape which resembles a box that is leaning over to one side. Crystals characteristically display a saddle-shaped modification of this form, in which the sagging rhombohedron also appears to have been sat upon. Dolomite crystals may also be tabular or octahedral, or in the form of a prism terminated by a rhombohedron. Both species display perfect, easy cleavage and subchonchoidal fracture. Common colors include gray, white, yellow, brown, and pink; both species are transparent to translucent, with a pearly to vitreous luster and a white streak. The saddle-shaped crystals help to distinguish these species from other carbonates. Both are much less responsive to the acid test than is calcite.

Along with calcite, dolomite is the major constituent of carbonate rocks. Dolomitic sedimentary rocks are called dolostones, to distinguish them from the calcitic limestones; metamorphosed dolostones are referred to as is dolomites, and are similarly analogous to marble. Dolomite also forms as a hydrothermal mineral in fissures in serpentines and other magnesium-rich rocks, and in ore deposits. Fine dolomite crystals are found in the Tri-State lead-zinc deposits of Oklahoma, Missouri, and Kansas; Guanajuato, Mexico, and in similar deposits throughout North America. Good specimens are also found in Cornwall, England, and at many locations in Italy and Germany.

Ankerite is usually precipitated from carbonate-rich solutions derived from the dissolution of siderite, $FeCO_3$, in hydrothermal veins. It is a common gangue mineral at the Antwerp iron mine in Jefferson County, New York; at the Homestake gold mine in Lead, South Dakota; in the Tintic District in Utah; and the Coeur d'Alene region of Idaho. European sources include Lancashire, England; Erzberg, Austria; France; and many parts of Eastern Europe.

Left: *Curved rhombohedra of dolomite from St. Catherine's quarry, Welland County, Ontario.*
Right: *Ankerite crystals on quartz from Morro Velho, Minas Gerais, Brazil.*

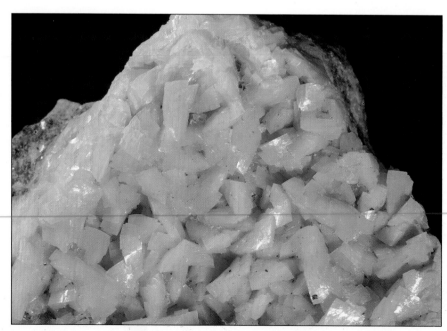

ALTHOUGH RELATIVELY UNCOMMON, ENARGITE IS A VERY IMPORTANT ORE MINERAL, containing nearly 50% copper and appreciable arsenic as well. Additionally, most enargite specimens contain some iron and zinc, and antimony may substitute for as much as 6% of the arsenic component. The name comes from the Greek *enargos*, meaning "distinct," an allusion to the perfect prismatic cleavage which is developed in nearly every specimen.

Enargite forms unmistakable prismatic or tabular crystals with vertical striations, usually lens-shaped in cross section. Twins, including cyclic sixlings, are common, as are lamellar aggregates and granular masses. Three directions of prismatic cleavage are developed, one of which is perfect. Enargite is gray to black in color, with a dark gray streak, and is opaque with a metallic luster, turning dull when coated by chalcocite. The ever-present cleavage surfaces are usually sufficient to distinguished enargite from other dark sulfides and sulfosalts.

Enargite forms in medium-temperature hydrothermal veins, in association with quartz and copper sulfides, or in low-temperature replacement deposits with galena and sphalerite. Excellent specimens are found at Butte, Montana; Bingham, Utah; the Tri-State District in Arkansas and Missouri, and the silver mines of Colorado's San Juan Mountains. Fine specimens come from a number of South American deposits, including Chuquicamata, Chile; Morococha and Cerro de Pasco, Peru; and La Paz, Bolivia. Enargite is also found on the Philippine island of Luzon; at Tsumeb, Namibia; Bor, Yugoslavia; Sardinia; and numerous other European locations.

enargite

Classification:
sulfosalt

Composition:
Cu_3AsS_4 (copper sulfosalt)

Crystal System:
orthorhombic

Hardness:
3

Specific Gravity:
4.45

Enargite crystals from the Leonard Mine, Butte, Montana.

enstatite and hypersthene

Classification:
inosilicates, pyroxene group

Composition:
enstatite: $MgSiO_3$
hypersthene: $(Mg,Fe) SiO_3$
(magnesium or magnesium-iron silicates)

Crystal System:
orthorhombic

Hardness:
5.5

Density:
3.2–3.4

Top: Cleavage fragment of hypersthene from Paistijarvi, Heinola, Finland.
Bottom: Grains of enstatite in granulite rock from Webster, Jackson County, North Carolina.

ENSTATITE AND HYPERSTHENE ARE VERY IMPORTANT ROCK-FORMING MINERALS, referred to by geologists as the *orthopyroxenes* because of their orthorhombic symmetry. Enstatite and hypersthene form a complete solid-solution series, with iron substituting for as much as 90% of the magnesium, although most hypersthene specimens contain the two elements in equal proportions. A pure iron end member called orthoferrosilite, $FeSiO_3$, is very rarely observed in nature, since its components are more stable in the form of olivine (fayalite) and SiO_2. The name enstatite comes from the Greek word meaning "opponent," in honor of its resistant, refractory properties. The name hypersthene is derived from the phrase meaning "very strong," an allusion to its being harder than the similar-appearing amphibole hornblende.

These pyroxenes very rarely form distinct, stubby, prismatic crystals; they usually occur as fibrous or lamellar masses. Enstatite can be colorless, yellowish green, gray, olive, or brown, becoming darker with increasing iron content. Crystals are translucent with vitreous luster; *bronzite* is a name applied to an intermediate member with a distinctive submetallic luster. Distinguished from the amphiboles by their nearly right-angled pyroxene cleavage.

Unlike most pyroxenes, pure enstatite is probably more abundant in metamorphic than in igneous rocks, because most magmas contain too much iron to allow its formation. It is most abundant in high-grade metamorphic rocks such as granulites, where it forms through the dehydration of magnesian amphiboles such as anthophyllite. Bronzite and hypersthene, however, are common constituents of various mafic and ultramafic plutonic and volcanic rocks, including gabbros and peridotites. It is also found in both stony and metallic meteorites. Good crystals have been found in the Tilly Foster Mine in Brewster, New York, in the California Coast ranges, and at many other widely distributed locations.

WHEN A HARD, GREEN, GLASSY MINERAL IS ENCOUNTERED IN THE FIELD, CHANCES are very good that it is epidote. Although most important in low-grade metamorphic environments, this mineral is found in almost all types of rock, very frequently as well-developed crystals. Epidote is the iron-rich end member of a solid-solution series with the somewhat less-common species clinozoisite, which resembles epidote in everything but color; the epidote group also contains the rare earth mineral allanite. This group is characterized by the presence of Si_2O_7 groups, which are essentially two silica tetrahedra sharing one of their oxygens. The structure of the epidote group minerals consists of these groups and regular silica tetrahedra strung out along chains of interconnected aluminum groups, along with ions of calcium, iron, or whatever else fits. It is these long chains which give the epidote group minerals their characteristic elongate habits. The name *epidote* comes from the Greek word meaning "increase," apparently in reference to its slightly asymmetrical crystal shape. Clinozoisite means "monoclinic polymorph of zoisite," but zoisite should really have the derivative title, since its structure appears to be a twin-like repetition of the epidote structure.

epidote and clinozoisite

Classification:
sorosilicates, epidote group

Composition:
epidote: $Ca_2(Al,Fe)Al_2O(SiO_4)(Si_2O_7)(OH)$
clinozoisite: $Ca_2Al_3O(SiO_4)(Si_2O_7)(OH)$
(hydrous calcium iron aluminum silicate)

Crystal System:
monoclinic

Hardness:
6–7

Specific Gravity:
3.25–3.45

Prismatic epidote crystals from the classic Alpine source at Knappenwand, Untersulzbachthal, near Salzburg, Austria.

Epidote group crystals are typically prismatic, tabular or bladed, and often display deeply striated faces. Epidote and clinozoisite commonly occur as granular masses or as aggregates of fine, intermeshed crystals in veins and fracture fillings. The color of the former is usually a distinctive, deep pistachio-green, but ranges from yellowish green to brownish to nearly black. Clinozoisite is typically a much lighter green, or gray. Both are transparent to nearly opaque, with a bright vitreous luster and a colorless streak. Epidote may be confused with green tourmaline in pegmatites.

Epidote is a primary mineral in felsic igneous rocks containing calcium, and may form large crystals in some granitic pegmatites. However, it is most common in regional metamorphic rocks of the greenschist facies, where it forms through the alteration of iron-, calcium-, and aluminum-rich primary silicate minerals. Epidote is also very common in contact metamorphic rocks, and in fissures in all kinds of rocks from which the necessary ions can be leached. Since epidote is so common, only a few of the classic sources are listed. Among the most sought-after specimens are the slender, perfectly terminated crystals from Untersulzbachtal, Austria; equally famous specimens come from contact metamorphic deposits on Prince of Wales Island, Alaska. Fine crystals are found in the pegmatites of northern Baja California, and in the marbles of the Crestmore Quarry, Riverside, California. European localities include Bourg d'Oisans, France; Arendal, Norway; and the Ala Valley of northern Italy.

erythrite and annabergite

Classification:
arsenates

Composition:
erythrite: $Co_3(AsO_4)_2 \cdot 8H_2O$
annabergite: $Ni_3(AsO_4)_2 \cdot 8H_2O$
(hydrated arsenate, cobalt, and nickel)

Crystal system:
monoclinic

Hardness:
1.5–2.5

Specific Gravity:
3.18 (erythrite),
3.07 (annabergite)

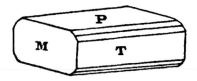

Radiating acicular erythrite crystals from Schneeberg, Germany.

ERYTHRITE AND ANNABERGITE ARE COLORFUL AND CONSPICUOUS MINERALS WHICH HAVE long been an important prospecting guide for miners in search of cobalt and nickel deposits. The name of the former is derived from the Greek *erythros*, or "red," in honor of its characteristic deep purplish-red color; the latter takes its name from the the German mining town of Annaberg. These minerals form a complete solid-solution series, and the composition of any specimen within the series can be approximated from its color. As its nickel content increases, erythrite loses its color to become pinkish or colorless, while annabergite is pale green, becoming vibrant greenish yellow in highly nickeliferous specimens. While erythrite crystals as much as 10 cm in length have been found, the crystals of annabergite are always quite small, and form acicular or leafy aggregates, earthy coatings, or thin films. Erythrite and annabergite have perfect cleavage, easily separating into thin, flexible, sectile sections with vitreous to pearly luster.

Erythrite and annabergite form in the oxidation zones of hydrothermal cobalt-nickel deposits, through alteration of primary cobalt-nickel minerals such as skutterudite and cobaltite. The classic producer of erythrite specimens is the mining region of Schneeberg, Saxony; now, however, the finest specimens are found at Bou Azzer, Morocco, which produces particularly large and beautiful crystal clusters. Other important sources include the Blackbird District, Lemhi County, Idaho; Mina Sara Alicia near Alamos, Sonora, Mexico; and the Cobalt District of Ontario.

evaporites

Evaporite Minerals

anhydrite	colemanite
aragonite	glauberite
boracite	gypsum
borax	halite
calcite	hanksite
carnallite	howlite
celestite	kernite

A VARIETY OF MINERAL SPECIES FORM THROUGH PRECIPITATION FROM CONCENTRATED brines, accumulating in sedimentary deposits called evaporites. While some evaporites may represent the actual evaporation of entire inland seas, it is far more likely that thick evaporite deposits are formed through the gradual settling of precipitates from saturated bodies of water over thousands of years. Such seas are located in basins such as the Mediterranean, where the influx of fresh water is limited, and the evaporation rates high. This is how the enormous deposits of halite (salt), gypsum, and other minerals known as "saline giants" are thought to have formed. Such deposits underlie large areas of Eastern Europe, Michigan, the Gulf of Mexico, and other regions.

Smaller evaporites are formed from the continuous influx of mineralized surface and ground waters to inland lakes with high rates of evaporation. The latter are characteristic of desert regions with high mountains and nearly flat valley floors, typical of the western United States, Asia Minor, and Central Asia. Instead of thick layers of halite and gypsum, such deposits contain an unusual abundance of borate minerals.

The Dead Sea between Israel and Jordan is a classic evaporite environment: the influx of fresh water barely keeps pace with the rate of evaporation. Here halite—the first compound to precipitate in most evaporite sequences—crystallizes on the surface of an artificial embayment.

THE FELDSPARS ARE ONE OF THE MOST IMPORTANT GROUPS OF ROCK-FORMING MINER-als. They are the major constituents of many igneous and metamorphic rock types, and together constitute approximately 60% of the earth's crust. Although the feldspars do not survive weathering as well as quartz, and are less important in the clastic sedimentary rocks, their alteration products are well-represented in abundant mudstones and shales. On weathering, the feldspars generally alter into clay minerals, which form an important group in their own right, both commercially and as an important part of soils. The feldspars are economically important as raw materials for the manufacture of ceramics, such as porcelain and tiles, and special types of glass. Feldspar is also used in scouring powders, since its hardness is lower than the steel and enamel of household surfaces. Some transparent or chatoyant feldspars are used as semiprecious stones, and other colorful feldspathic rocks are used in buildings and monuments. Since feldspar is so commonly turned up in plowed fields overlying igneous rocks, the name of this group comes from the Germanic term *feldt spat,* or "field spar" (*spar* being the general term for minerals with prominent cleavage).

The feldspars are aluminosilicates whose structure is based on a three-dimensional array of AlO_4 and SiO_4 tetrahedra, arranged in four-member rings linked by shared oxygen atoms. Large spaces between the tetrahedra are occupied by cations of (primarily) sodium (Na), potassium (K), and calcium (Ca). These cations are not strongly bonded to the oxygen in the Si-Al rings, and as a result, the feldspars display two prominent and easily developed cleavages. The general chemical formula of the feldspars can be written as $X(Si,Al)_4O_8$, with the cation X being Ca^{+2} or Ba^{+2} in the alkaline earth feldspars, or Na^+ or K^+ for the alkali feldspars. A complete range of compositions is observed between the sodium- and calcium-rich feldspars, and is known as the plagioclase series. The sodium- and potassium-rich feldspars do not form a solid-solution series; species of intermediate composition that form at high temperatures exsolve on cooling to form perthite crystals—finely intergrown mixtures of two distinct species.

The most common of the alkali feldspars are the potassium feldspars (or potash feldspars, or simply K-spars), a series of polymorphs of $KAlSi_3O_8$; these may contain appreciable amounts of sodium in the potassium site. The two main polymorphs are microcline, which is triclinic in symmetry, and orthoclase, which is monoclinic. The plagioclase solid-solution series is divided arbitrarily into species according to the relative proportions of sodium and calcium they contain, with albite ($NaAlSi_3O_8$) as the sodium-rich end member, and anorthite ($CaAl_2Si_2O_8$) the calcic one. The plagioclase feldspars are generally slightly harder than the potassium feldspars, because the sodium–oxygen and the calcium–oxygen bonds are shorter and stronger than the potassium-oxygen bonds. There are other feldspars which do not fit exactly into the orthoclase-albite-anorthite scheme. A barium- to potassium-rich series called the hyalophanes exists between orthoclase and the barium-rich end member celsian ($BaAl_2Si_2O_8$). Another odd feldspar is the ammonium-rich species buddingtonite ($NH_4AlSi_3O_8$), found in certain ammonia-bearing hydrothermal deposits.

Under ideal circumstances, all feldspars would be colorless and transparent; in the real world, however, this is not the case. Most feldspars are rendered translucent to opaque due to innumerable internal reflections arising from polysynthetic twin planes, exsolution interfaces, and cleavage surfaces. The feldspars commonly contain foreign materials which lend them color; the pinks, browns and brick-red color commonly seen in feldspars results from finely dispersed flakes of hematite. Iron (and titanium) oxides may also lend a dark color to the plagioclases, although this can also be caused by external radiation, as with smoky quartz. Rare blues and greens, including the striking amazonite variety of microcline, result from the presence of lead and water in the cation site. In addition, feldspars commonly display pervasive alteration to clay minerals.

No other group of minerals has more frequent and varied twinning habits. Feldspar twins fall into three main types. Both potassium and plagioclase feldspars display growth twins, which may be contact or interpenetrant twins (Baveno, Carlsbad, Manebach, etc.), or polysynthetic.

The triclinic feldspars are characterized by two main types of polysynthetic twinning, the albite and pericline habits. Both kinds of result in lamellae from 1 mm to submicroscopic width, plainly evident from the fine striations on cleavage planes that mark the reentrant gaps between individual members. The second main kind of twinning is through inversion or transformation. Microcline, for example, is characterized by a peculiar tweed-like pattern that results from albite and pericline twins, oriented at right angles to each-other, which formed as the crystal changed from monoclinic to triclinic symmetry during cooling. The third common kind of twinning in feldspars is polysynthetic twinning imposed by external forces, such as mechanical stress on the surrounding rock.

Three-point diagram indicating the compositional relationships between the feldspars. The apices of the triangle represent the end members of solid-solution series, with species of intermediate composition lying in between. The potassium feldspars orthoclase and microcline fall within the compositional range of sanidine on this diagram.

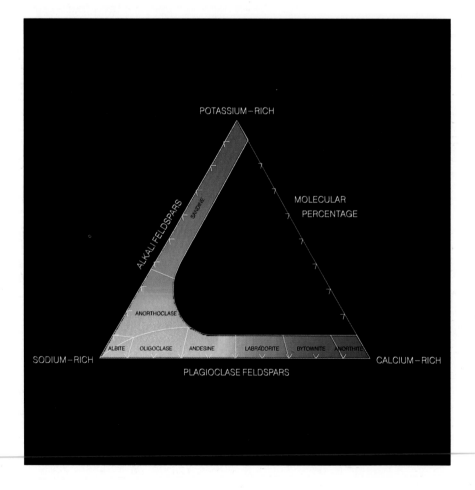

THIS RELATIVELY UNCOMMON GROUP OF ROCK-FORMING MINERALS CONSISTS OF ALU-minosilicates of sodium, potassium, or calcium. The feldspathoids are chemically similar to the feldspars, but generally contain about two thirds the amount of silica. Accordingly, they form in rocks that are too depleted of silica to form feldspars, and contain more alkali elements and aluminum than can be accommodated by feldspars. Feldspathoids may be found in the same rock as feldspars, but never with quartz.

Like the feldspars, the feldspathoids are tectosilicates, their structure characterized by the three-dimensional framework of AlO_4 and SiO_4 tetra-hedra. They differ in that their framework contains large interstices which can accommodate both the large alkali ions (K has the largest atomic radius of any element) and others such as chlorine (sodalite), carbonate (cancri-nite), sulfate, sulfur, and chlorine (lazurite).

Most of the feldspathoids are restricted to igneous rocks. The most common feldspathoid is nepheline, which forms extensive bodies of the plu-tonic igneous rock nepheline syenite, from magmas depleted in silica. Lazurite is the only feldspathoid not formed in igneous rocks; it is found in contact metamorphic marbles where it occurs as massive blue aggregates with calcite and pyrite called lapis lazuli. The lithium-bearing feldspathoid petalite is found in pegmatites.

Cancrinite, $Na_6CaCO_3(AlSiO_4)_6 \bullet 2H_2O$ from Litchfield, Maine. This rare feldspathoid is formed through the alteration of nepheline in the presence of CO_2-rich fluids.

fluorite

Classification:
halide

Composition:
CaF₂ (calcium fluoride)

Crystal System:
isometric

Hardness:
4

Specific Gravity:
3.18

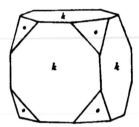

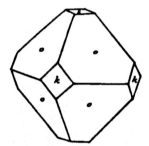

THE ELEMENT FLUORINE IS A PALE YELLOW, POISONOUS AND CORROSIVE GAS AT ORDINARY temperatures. Fortunately, fluorine does not occur naturally in its unpleasant native form, but always in combination with other elements. The most common fluorine-bearing mineral is fluorite, which is also the only commercial source of fluorine. In commerce and mining, fluorite goes by the old mining term fluorspar. The ancient Greeks and Romans prized fluorite for its variety of delicate colors, translucency, and ease of carving, and made lovely goblets, vases, and reliefs from large crystalline masses. The American Indians also carved effigies and beads from fluorite.

Since fluorite often occurs in association with metallic ore minerals in sulfide deposits, it is no surprise that it was discovered at an early date to be an indispensable aid to smelting. When added to the ore prior to smelting, fluorite acts as a flux—facilitating the melting process and helping to draw sulfur and phosphorous out of the molten metal and into the slag on top; it also helps to make the slag fluid, so that it can be easily drawn off. For these reasons, it takes its name from the Latin word *fluere*, "to flow." Fluorite is primarily used in the production of iron and steel; over 10 kg of the mineral are necessary per ton of metal produced, depending on the nature of the ore.

Another major use of fluorite is in the production of hydrofluoric acid, used in the refining of aluminum from its ores. Hydrofluoric acid is also used to produce fluorocarbons, organic compounds used in refrigeration, solvents, pharmaceuticals, and formerly, in aerosol sprays. The use of fluorine compounds (chlorofluorocarbons) in aerosol sprays is being discontinued because of the danger these compounds pose to the protective layer of ozone in the earth's upper atmosphere.

Fluorite has hundreds of other highly specialized uses. Crystalline fluorite is used to make prisms in various scientific instruments, added to glass to make optical lenses, and used to make the opaque glazes for household appliances. Large amounts of sodium fluoride are added to drinking water and toothpaste to fortify the teeth and reduce the incidence of tooth decay. So extensive are the uses of fluorine and its various compounds that the world's reserves of fluorite are expected to be exhausted by the beginning of the next millennia. Fortunately, there are enormous low-grade reserves of fluorine in phosphorite deposits, in the form of calcium fluorapatite (see *Apatite*).

Crystals of fluorite are very common. Simple cubes, sometimes modified by other isometric forms, are the predominant habit, but octahedra and dodecahedra also occur. Interpenetrant twins are fairly common. The crystal faces are generally smooth, cubes more so than octahedra. Fluorite has very easy and perfect octahedral cleavage—the large loose octahedra seen for sale everywhere are cobbed by hand from cubic crystals. Natural and artificial octahedra can be distinguished by the smooth but undulating texture of the cleavage faces on the latter, caused by internal imperfections. The fracture is subchonchoidal to splintery. Crystals of fluorite are usually seen in clusters of similar individuals; other habits include granular, botryoidal, and even fibrous.

Few minerals can match fluorite for variety of color. Crystals are transparent to translucent, colorless, purple, violet, blue, green, yellow, orange, brown, red, or nearly black, with a vitreous luster. In general, octahedral crystals tend to be light-colored, and cubic crystals darker. The various colors are caused by a variety of impurities, including hydrocarbons. Some crystals display zones of different colors or shades, parallel to the crystal faces. Under ultraviolet light, fluorite fluoresces blue, white, pale violet, or reddish; the term fluorescence is in fact derived from this species. Different fluorite specimens luminesce under different conditions, depending on the impurities they contain. Some varieties display thermoluminescence, emitting light when heated, while others are triboluminescent and glow when rubbed or struck. Fluorite is characterized by its distinctive crystal shape and octahedral cleavage; massive material can be distinguished from calcite by its greater hardness and unresponsiveness to dilute hydrochloric acid.

Fluorite is a very common and widespread mineral found in a variety of geological environments. The primary source is hydrothermal ore deposits, where it occurs in association with barite, calcite, dolomite, galena, quartz, and sphalerite. It also crystallizes in sedimentary rock cavities, in association with calcite, celestite, dolomite, and gypsum. Fluorite is found in smaller amounts in some Alpine fissures and in pegmatites.

Large fluorite veins mined in southern Illinois provide excellent and sometimes enormous crystal groups. The largest deposits are in Hardin and Pope counties; others are found in adjacent parts of Kentucky. Large yellowish groups of cubic crystals are recovered from the sedimentary limestones of Putnam and Ottawa counties, Ohio. Clusters of lovely blue cubes are found in the Hansonburg District of Socorro County, New Mexico. Green octahedra are associated with rhodochrosite in the Sunnyside Mine, San Juan County, Colorado; large blue cubes are found in pegmatites of the Crystal Peak area, Teller County, Colorado. Fine specimens are found in Hastings County and elsewhere in Ontario.

The English lead mines provide some remarkable fluorite specimens, including the green and purple penetration twins from Weardale, Durham, and the deep blue cubes from the Wheal Mary Mine in Cornwall. Fine specimens are also obtained from Beer Alston, Devonshire, and Alston and Cleator Moors in Cumberland. "Blue John" is the name given to the deep purple or blue granular fluorite from the Blue John Mine in Derbyshire, which is cut into ornamental objects. Other important European sources of fluorite include the German mining districts in the Harz, Saxony, and Bavaria. Much sought after are the pink octahedra found at various locations in the Alps. Large commercial fluorite deposits are exploited in Mongolia, China, Spain, Thailand, South Africa, and the Soviet Union.

Aggregate of fluorite showing multiple generations of growth, from the Minerva No. 2 Mine, Cave-in-Rock, Illinois.

fracture

THE TERM FRACTURE DESCRIBES THE CHARACTERISTICS OF A MINERAL'S BROKEN SURfaces not due to cleavage or parting (see *Cleavage*). Like cleavage, a mineral's fracture is a distinctive physical property and aids in the identification process. The nature of a mineral's fracture is related to the breaking of molecular bonds *across* crystallographic planes rather than *along* them, as in cleavage. The fracture patterns of minerals with similar bond strengths in all directions are probably determined by the distribution of internal crystal defects.

Several useful terms have evolved to describe fracture, and these are used throughout this book. Although imprecise, these terms are intuitive and descriptive. Smooth, curved fracture surfaces like those of broken glass are termed *conchoidal,* which means "shell-shaped." Less-smooth, or interrupted conchoidal fractures are termed *subchonchoidal.* A flat fracture surface which is not a cleavage is termed *even,* or *uneven* if slightly rough; greater roughness is denoted by the term *regular,* and greater roughness still, by the term *irregular.* Jagged, fibrous, or splintery fracture surfaces may be called *hackly,* after the hackles, or stiff hairs, on the ruff of an angry dog. Minerals from which shavings can be cut with a knife blade are termed *sectile*; the native metals display this property, as do graphite, molybdenite, argentite, realgar, and a few other nonmetal species.

Minerals can also be generally described according to the ease with which they break. Minerals that are broken with great difficulty, such as the native metals and aggregates like rhodonite and jade, are said to be *tough.* Most minerals, however, can be described as *brittle,* meaning that they can be broken with ease; those with which even greater care must be taken are simply labeled *very* brittle. *Friable* minerals are those like graphite which tend to disintegrate when rubbed between the fingers.

franklinite

Classification:
oxide, spinel group

Composition:
(Zn,Fe,Mn) (Fe,Mn)$_2$O$_4$
(zinc manganese iron oxide)

Crystal System:
isometric

Hardness:
5.5–6.5

Specific Gravity:
5.1

Octahedra of black franklinite in white calcite, with peach-colored willemite, from Franklin, Sussex County, New Jersey.

THIS RARE MINERAL IS NAMED FOR its primary occurrence at Franklin and Sterling Hill, Ogdensburg, New Jersey, where it was exploited for zinc in the past. When first noticed, franklinite was thought to be magnetite. After its true nature was discovered, and the value of zinc had risen sufficiently, a special furnace was designed which was able to separate the zinc oxide from the iron and manganese residues. These latter were then smelted to form the alloy *spiegeleisen,* which is used in steel-making. Franklinite has since become too rare to be a commercially important ore mineral, and its greatest importance is scientific, as the rarest of the spinel group oxides (see *Spinel*).

Franklinite forms octahedral or dodecahedral crystals with rounded faces and modified edges, generally embedded in marble. It is black with red tints, and has a metallic luster and reddish-brown streak. Franklinite is only weakly magnetic, which distinguishes it from magnetite, but can be further magnetized by heating. Franklinite only occurs in contact metamorphic dolomites, associated with zincite, willemite, magnetite, rhodonite, and garnet. Besides the Ogdensburg deposit, the only other notable sources are Långban, Sweden; and Ocna de Fer, Vasko, and Banat, Romania.

THE HIGH DENSITY, SOFTNESS, AND METALLIC LUSTER OF GALENA (FROM THE GREEK *galene*, "lead ore") made it an obvious choice for early efforts at smelting. At first this was accomplished simply by throwing raw galena into a campfire, where the sulfide was reduced to native lead, to be recovered from the cold ashes in the morning. Lumps of lead produced in this fashion, dating back 5000 years, have been found in archaeological sites. Warriors from the Balearic islands of the Mediterranean were feared throughout the ancient world for their deadly slings laden with lead missiles, produced from local deposits of galena. American pioneers later produced lead for bullets in the same way; Confederate and Union troops battled throughout the Civil War for control of the rich galena deposits of eastern Missouri.

Galena is not only the most important source of lead—it is also one of the main sources of silver, an element that does not even appear in its formula. This is due both to the substitution of silver atoms for those of lead, and to the physical admixture of silver sulfides such as tetrahedrite and acanthite in massive galena. The atomic structure of galena is identical to that of halite, with lead in the sodium position and sulfur in the place of chlorine; similar-appearing species with the same structure include altaite (PbTe) and alabandite (MnS). Galena is easily oxidized in nature, forming the alteration products anglesite ($PbSO_4$) and cerussite ($PbCO_3$).

Lead is a mildly toxic element that causes brain damage upon prolonged exposure. For this reason, the uses of lead are declining somewhat, especially as a paint pigment and an antiknock compound in gasolines. It is still vital to the production of soft alloys such as solder and type metal, and is essential for storage batteries, which constitute its primary use. It is also the preferred material for radiation shields. Lead is made into the compounds litharge, PbO, and minium, Pb_3O_4, which are used to make glass crystal, glazes, and pigments. It is still indispensable in its traditional and intentionally dangerous use, as ammunition.

Galena commonly occurs in beautifully formed crystals, often of large size. These are found mostly as cubes, octahedrons, dodecahedrons, or combinations of these forms, and commonly as twins. The color is a lead gray, sometimes with a faint reddish tint. It has a strong metallic luster, especially on fresh cleavages; crystal faces and massive pieces are usually tarnished and dull.

galena

Classification:
sulfide

Composition:
PbS (lead sulfide)

Crystal System:
isometric

Hardness:
2.5–3

Specific Gravity:
7.58

Left: *Rough cubes of galena from Galena, Cherokee County, Kansas.* ***Right:*** *A miner at the Broken Hill Mine in New South Wales, Australia, drills holes in massive, galena-rich ore, in preparation for blasting.*

Galena has perfect cleavage in three directions, producing cubic fragments; this cleavage and its extraordinary density make galena unmistakable.

Galena is primarily a mineral of hydrothermal sulfide deposits, where it typically occurs in association with the zinc sulfide sphalerite. It is found in lesser quantities in sedimentary and metamorphic environments, as well as in the metamorphic sulfide deposit at Broken Hill in New South Wales, Australia. Sources of galena specimens are very numerous, and a number of American deposits have produced fine specimens. The most notable galena deposit in the United States, and perhaps the world, is the Tri-State mining district, particularly along the Viburnum Trend lead belt of eastern Missouri. Large well-developed crystals on dolomite matrix, with sphalerite and chalcopyrite are found here in great quantity; single crystals may be as large as 25 cm on an edge. In the Coeur d'Alene District of Idaho, galena is mined primarily for its silver content. Among the important European occurrences are those in Freiberg, the Harz Mountains, Westphalia, and Nassau, Germany; Cumberland, Cornwall, and Derbyshire, England; Pribram, Czechoslovakia; Laurium, Greece; Sardinia; and Yugoslavia.

garnet group

Classification:
nesosilicates

Composition:
Almandite $Fe^{2+}_3Al_2(SiO_4)_3$
(iron-aluminum silicate)

Andradite $Ca_3Fe^{3+}_2(SiO_4)_3$
(calcium-iron silicate)

Grossular $Ca_3Al_2(SiO_4)_3$
(calcium-aluminum silicate)

Pyrope $Mg_3Al_2(SiO_4)_3$
(magnesium-aluminum silicate)

Spessartite $Mn_3Al_2(SiO_4)_3$
(Manganese-aluminum silicate)

Uvarovite $Ca_3Cr_2(SiO_4)_3$
(calcium-chromium silicate)

Crystal System:
isometric

Hardness:
6.5–7.5

Specific Gravity:
3.5–4.3

THE GARNET GROUP IS ONE OF THE BEST EXAMPLES OF THE PRINCIPLE OF SOLID SOLUtion, in which a single general formula accommodates a wide range of different chemical compositions. All garnets share the same crystal structure, but with corresponding places in that structure occupied by different ions. Iron, for example, fills the same niche in almandite as magnesium does in pyrope. Since the partial substitution of one element for another is the rule rather than the exception, the formulas at left really represent idealized, pure species seldom found in nature. The garnet group can be divided into two subseries (pyrope-almandite-spessartite, and uvarovite-grossularite-andradite), with solid solution generally occurring only between the three end-members of each. This division is due to the fact that hybrids between the two groups tend to be unstable, and because rocks suitable for their formation are rare.

Garnets are relatively common and often weather out of their host rock as perfect little faceted crystals—no polishing required. They were thus among the earliest stones to attract the attention of humans, and they have been found in graves and shrines throughout Europe, Asia, and the Americas. In antiquity and the Middle Ages garnets were used according to the theory of *similia similibus curantur*, or "like cures like." Thus red garnets were the prescription for any malady associated with redness, such as blood disorders or anger. As a preventative measure, they were thought to confer invulnerability in battle. During the "pacification" of Kashmir in the 1890s, British army surgeons were surprised to find garnet crystals embedded in their patients; it is not known if the hostile Hunzas loaded their ancient flintlocks with garnet bullets for their special powers, or because they had no lead.

Garnet as a gemstone had its heyday in the Victorian era, when other dark "anti-gems" such as pyrite and jet were also popular. Now the most sought-after gem garnets are the rare green variety of andradite called demantoid, and the even rarer green variety of grossular garnet called tsavorite. Garnet is an important industrial mineral as well: its hardness and lack of cleavage (which allow it to be crushed into regular fragments) make it highly suitable as an abrasive material. The most important garnet deposit in the United States is at Gore Mountain in the New York Adirondacks, where almandite is mined for use in sandpaper.

While most isometric minerals crystallize primarily in cubes and octahedra, the garnet structure favors the development of equidimensional, almost spherical shapes such as the twelve-sided dodecahedron and the twenty-four-sided trapezohedron. The generally reddish, round crystals resemble the seeds of a pomegranate, and it is from *granatum* (pomegranate) that the name garnet is derived. Well-formed garnet crystals are common; since the garnet structure is very stable, garnets crystallize easily even in the most high-pressure and temperature igneous and metamorphic environments.

The occurrence of garnet is as varied as its chemical composition and color. Iron-rich garnets are particularly abundant in regional metamorphic rocks such as schists and gneisses, forming at the expense of chlorite as temperatures exceed 500° C. The appearance of garnets in these rocks is thus a useful means of determining their metamorphic grade (see *Metamorphic Rocks*) and even of mapping the boundaries (or isograds) between facies. The calcium-rich garnets usually form as a product of contact metamorphism in crystalline limestones. Garnets also form in all types of igneous rocks, from mantle peridotites to pegmatites. Because of their high density and resistance to chemical and mechanical weathering, garnets are common in placer deposits.

There are at least sixteen distinct species recognized in the garnet group, but most of these are very rare. The six most important garnet species are described below.

Almandite This deep-red iron-aluminum garnet, also called almandine, is one of the more abundant types, and is widespread in such siliceous metamorphic rocks as schist and gneiss. Almandite polished in cabochon form was the main type of carbuncle used in ancient times; the name comes from the Anatolian city of Alabanda, where the stones were polished in antiquity. Although crystals may be well-formed, they are often internally shattered, and tend to fall apart if an attempt is made to remove them from their matrix. Inclusions found in some crystals give rise to aster-ism, which can be seen as four-rayed stars in polished stones.

Almandite crystal in biotite schist from Wrangell, Alaska. The forms are the dodecahedron (diamond-shaped faces) modified by highly reflective trapezohedral faces. Oval almandite gemstone is from Prussia.

Excellent examples of almandite can be obtained from innumerable locations around the world. Among the classic specimens are the euhedral crystals in biotite schist matrix are found near Wrangell, Alaska, and the very large crystals mined near Salida, Colorado. Fine star garnets occur in the gravels of Emerald Creek, Benewah County, Idaho, and transparent gem crystals are obtained from placer deposits at several locations in India and Sri Lanka.

Andradite Named for the Brazilian mineralogist J. B. d'Andrada e Silva (b. 1763), this common calcium-iron garnet displays a wide range of hues, including black (melanite), brown, brownish-red, brownish-green, yellow, and even vibrant emerald green. The green variety is known as *demantoid*, and is the most valuable of all of the garnets. Faceted stones display its high refractive index and dispersion, properties which earned it a name derived from the Dutch word for diamond. While andradite often occurs as euhedral, dodecahedral crystals, demantoid usually is found as massive nodules. Demantoid is easily distinguished from other species and synthetics on microscopic examination, as it almost invariably contains tiny inclusions of fibrous actinolite, which form distinctive divergent sprays called "horsetails."

Andradite is typically formed in calcareous contact metamorphic rocks, although the varieties melanite and demantoid are restricted to serpentines. Demantoid was discovered in the 1860s by gold miners in the stream gravels of

Crystals and gemstone of the demantoid variety of andradite, from Lanzada, Val Malenco, Lombardy, Italy.

the Ural Mountains in the Soviet Union, and later found *in situ* in serpentines along the Bobrovka River. Euhedral crystals of demantoid are found in the serpentines of the Ala Valley, in the Italian Piedmont. Excellent specimens of andradite are found in cavities in marble at Stanley Butte, Graham County, Arizona; and at Franklin and Sterling Hill, New Jersey. Fine crystals of melanite occur in the carbonatite at Magnet Cove, Arkansas; and in altered serpentine in San Benito County, California (see *Benitoite*). Good melanite specimens are also found in the lavas of Vesuvius, and elsewhere in Italy.

Grossularite The name of this garnet is derived from the name of the gooseberry genus, *Grossularia,* since grossularite crystals are often the same limpid green color as gooseberry fruit. Grossularite is a very common species and often occurs as fine crystals, usually simple dodecahedrons. Grossularite has the broadest color range of all the garnets; it may be colorless or white, greenish, yellow, yellow-orange, orange-red, reddish brown, or pink. A great many varietal names have been applied to grossularite gemstones of different colors, including hessonite, hyacinth, and rosalite; some of these names are of great antiquity, and all have been applied to different minerals. In the early 1970s a new variety of grossularite was discovered in the Taita Hills of southern Kenya. Colored an intense emerald green by traces of vanadium, this new variety of grossular was named *tsavorite* after the nearby Tsavo Plains. The supply of this stone is very limited, both by geology and the political climate, so the price remains quite high.

Grossularite occurs primarily in contact metamorphic deposits, in association with diopside, wollastonite, and idocrase. Among the most remarkable specimens of this species are the light-colored large (to 10 cm) crystals from Lake Jaco, Chihuahua, Mexico; similar crystals occur near Xalostoc, Morelos. Other classic localities include Eden Mills, Vermont; Mont St. Hilare, Quebec; and the Ala Valley of Italy, where fine druses of orange crystals are found in association with diopside. Bright green, massive cryptocrystalline grossularite is mined in Transvaal State, north of Pretoria, South Africa, and sold for ornamental purposes as "South African jade."

Pyrope The name of this deep red, orange-red, or purplish garnet comes from the Greek *pyropos,* which means "fire-eyed." Pure pyrope forms at depths greater than 40 km in the earth's mantle, and thus occurs in kimberlites (see *Diamond*) and mantle xenoliths (see *Olivine*). Mixed crystals close to pyrope composition are more widely distributed in mafic igneous

rocks, serpentines, and high-grade metamorphic rocks. Pyrope crystals are unusually durable, and commonly weather out of their host rocks to collect as small rounded grains in placer deposits and beach sands. An orange-red variety intermediate in composition between pyrope and almandite is known as *rhodolite*.

The major source of garnet gems from the Renaissance through the Victorian Era were the "Bohemian" pyrope deposits in the vicinity of Trebenice, Czechoslovakia. In Africa, pyrope is produced as a byproduct of diamond mining. Pyrope occurs in association with ultramafic igneous rocks in Madras, India, New South Wales and Queensland, Australia; and in Arizona, New Mexico, and Utah. Good specimens of the rhodolite variety are obtained from Macon County, North Carolina.

Spessartite This orange-red garnet is named for the Spessart mining district in Bavaria, where it has been found. Gemstones of this unusually-colored garnet are beautiful but little known, since gem-quality spessartite is quite rare. Most gem spessartite is found in granitic pegmatites, as etched masses covered with diamond-shaped pits, but also as fine dodecahedral or trape-zohedral crystals in gem pockets. Good small crystals are also found in cav-ities in rhyolites, and massive spessartite occurs as well in manganese-rich contact metamorphic deposits, with rhodonite and manganese oxides.

Specimens of spessartite are found in all major pegmatite districts, including those of Brazil, Africa, and the Malagasy Republic. However, the

Rough crystals of pyrope from the Kimberley Diamond Mine in South Africa, with a cut stone from Tanzania.

119

*Left: Malformed trapezohedral crystal of spessartite from Tibagy, Brazil, with a cabochon from Mogok, Burma. **Right:** Uvarovite crystals from Saranovskaja, near Bissersk in the Ural Mountains of Russia.*

finest specimens and gem material are obtained from the Rutherford Mine No. 2 pegmatite at Amelia Court House, Virginia, and the pegmatites of the Ramona District, San Diego County, California. Loose pebbles of gem material are obtained from the gem gravels of Sri Lanka. Unusually dark trapezohedral crystals are found in cavities in rhyolite near Ely, Nevada, and at Ruby Mountain, Colorado, in association with topaz.

Uvarovite This vivid green, chromium-rich garnet is named after Count Sergei Uvarov (b. 1786), a Russian nobleman. Uvarovite is relatively rare, and usually occurs as druses of tiny emerald-green crystals in serpentines, in association with chromite. Fine crystal druses are obtained from the many small chromite prospects along the west coast of the United States, particularly near Riddle, Oregon, and in Whatcom County, Washington; also the Red Ledge gold mine, Yuba County. Good specimens are also found in the Thetford Mines, Megantic County, and at Magog, Stanstead County, Quebec. Uvarovite also occurs near Bissersk, in the Ural Mountains of the Soviet Union; at the Kop Krom Mine in Turkey; and in crystals up to 2 cm in size at Outokumpu, Finland. Uvarovite is also found in the Bushveld complex in South Africa (see *Platinum*).

glauberite

Classification:
sulfate

Composition:
$Na_2Ca(SO_4)_2$ (sodium calcium sulfate)

Crystal System:
monoclinic

Hardness:
2.5–3

Specific Gravity:
2.8

GLAUBERITE IS A VERY PLAIN MINERAL MINED FOR THE COMPOUND CALLED GLAUBERS salt, which is used in dying, as a cathartic in medicine, and in solar energy applications. Crystals are tabular, prismatic, or dipyramidal, and sometimes striated or rounded; also as massive aggregates and crusts. The color may be white, yellow, or reddish, with a greasy luster and a white streak. Glauberite is easily altered, and minerals such as quartz and gypsum commonly form pseudomorphs after its crystals.

Glauberite is precipitated from saline solutions in the sediments of ephemeral lakes in arid regions, formed from the exhalation of fumaroles in volcanic rocks, and deposited from hydrothermal fluids in basalt cavities. Good specimens are obtained from the Searles Lake, Borax Lake, and the Salton Sea area, California; the Great Salt Lake of Utah; and Camp Verde, Yavapai County, Arizona. Glauberite is also found in the ancient evaporites of Salzburg, Austria; Russia; and Texas and New Mexico. Sublimated crystals are found in lavas on the islands of Lipari and Vulcano, off the coast of Sicily.

Glauberite crystal from Borax Lake, San Bernardino County, California.

SWORDS MAY BE BEATEN INTO PLOWSHARES AND BACK AGAIN INTO SWORDS, BUT ALL will eventually end up as rust—and rust consists primarily of the mineral goethite. Pyrite, chalcopyrite, magnetite, siderite, and most other iron-rich minerals will alter to goethite over time, since it is the most stable iron compound at the earth's surface. By virtue of sheer volume, goethite is an important iron ore. Its more colorful red and orange earthy forms are called ochre, and have been used since early prehistory to decorate bodies and cave walls. For reasons known only to them, the Neanderthals sometimes covered their dead with ocher before burial. The name honors the German poet and philosopher Johann Wolfgang von Goethe (b. 1749) for his little-known but important contributions to the natural sciences.

Despite all this, goethite is a very unprepossessing mineral. Thin tablets, or prismatic crystals with vertical striations are known, but are very rare. The typical habit of goethite is an amorphous, earthy lump; its common aggregate habits include fibrous botryoidal, stalactitic, concretionary, and oolitic. The color ranges from brown to black, with a silky luster, and brownish-yellow streak. Its perfect cleavage makes it friable, so that it feels soft and greasy. Pseudomorphs of goethite after pyrite and other iron minerals are very common.

Goethite is one of the most ubiquitous mineral species. It is the primary constituent of limonite, which is a catch-all phrase for mixtures of iron oxides and hydroxides which form in virtually all geological environments where iron and oxygen and hydroxyl come together. Limonite forms the gossan or "iron hat" that typically caps sulfide and gold-quartz veins, and great black lumps of "bog ore" in swamps and springs. It is a major component of commercial iron deposits in the Mayani and Moa districts of Cuba, and in France, Germany, Canada, and the Lake Superior region of the United States. Interesting crystallized specimens are found in Colorado; Pribram, Czechoslovakia; and Cornwall, England.

goethite

Classification:
hydroxide

Composition:
FeOOH (iron hydroxide)

Crystal System:
orthorhombic

Hardness:
5–5.5

Specific Gravity:
3.3–4.3,
increasing with decreasing porosity

Fractured botryoidal mass of goethite from the Restormel Iron Mine, Lanlivery and Lostwithiel, Cornwall, showing fibrous internal structure.

gold

Classification:
native element

Composition:
Au (gold) usually 10%–15% silver; natural alloys with higher silver concentrations are called electrum

Crystal System:
isometric

Hardness:
2.5–3

Specific Gravity:
19.297 (pure)

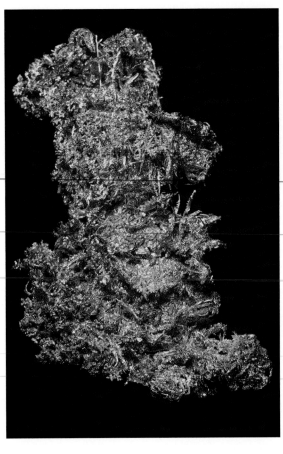

Dendritic crystalline aggregate of gold from the Swauk River Conglomerate, Kittitas County, Washington.

DESPITE ITS RARITY, GOLD was probably the first metal used by ancient peoples. Even the smallest flakes are very conspicuous, and no other metal has a similar combination of aesthetic and physical properties. Humans have been accumulating gold since the Neolithic period, and the actual mining of gold, as opposed to the casual collection of nuggets from streambeds, probably began over 6000 years ago in the Middle East. By the time of the Sumerian culture in Mesopotamia nearly 5000 years ago, artists were crafting elaborate jewelry, chalices, and religious articles from gold. Medieval alchemists postulated that gold was divine, since it alone was incorruptible while all other "baser" metals could be altered chemically. In vain, they labored to wash the worldly taint from base metals such as lead, so that they could be "resurrected" as gold.

Because of its intrinsic and its symbolic value, gold has long been held by nations as a monetary standard and coveted for the power and wealth that it represents. The exploration of distant lands, the waging of wars, and the destruction of civilizations has been done as much for the sake of gold as for any other reason. In the 16th century, the Spanish conquistadors Cortes and Pizarro plundered the Aztec and Inca Empires, respectively, in search for "El Dorado," the mythical city of gold. When this failed to materialize, the conquerors enslaved the natives and worked generations of them to their deaths in the mines. It is estimated that the Spanish conquest of the Americas more than tripled the amount of gold in Europe. Thus, a golden pendant fashioned for a pre-Columbian noble may now be part of an ingot covered with ownership and purity stamps in a vault beneath a bank in Switzerland... or perhaps part of the Voyager spacecraft, slipping out of the solar system at thousands of miles per hour.

Because of its physical properties, gold has long been the metal of choice for jewelers and craftsmen; it can be cast into delicate shapes, carved, easily soldered, drawn readily into wire, and hammered into the thinnest sheets of any metal. These same properties, along with its excellent thermal and electrical conductivity, make gold an important industrial metal as well. Pure gold is too soft for most practical uses, and therefore it is often alloyed with silver, copper, platinum, or nickel. Gold alloyed with silver is slightly lighter in color than pure gold, whereas gold alloyed with copper (red gold) has a reddish color, and gold with nickel is nearly white. The proportions most commonly encountered are 585 parts per thousand (14 karat), 750 ppt (18 karat), and 900 ppt (22 karat); pure gold is 24 karat. The naturally occurring alloy of silver and gold is called electrum.

Gold is rarely seen in distinct crystals, which are mostly rudely shaped and cavernous, or "hoppered." Octahedra are most common, usually flattened to form extremely thin plates, sometimes with triangular surface markings; less common forms are dodecahedrons and cubes. Although crystals are usually very small, single flattened octahedra over 30 cm wide are known. Most specimens form dendritic growths of numerous, subparallel crystals, which have grown in thin crevices in quartz. Complex twinning is typical of dendritic specimens. Gold is highly malleable, sectile, and ductile, and has a hackly fracture; it has a metallic luster and a shining yellow streak. The color of gold is an unmistakable rich yellow, becoming a lighter whitish yellow with increasing silver content. Silver also lowers the specific gravity slightly. The existence of naturally alloyed silver and gold (electrum) is due to the very similar atomic structure of silver and gold, and to their similar atomic radii; atoms of silver can easily occupy sites in the structure of gold. Due to the smaller size of the copper atom, copper is found much less frequently naturally alloyed with gold, despite their similar crystal structures.

As the 12th century scholar Alain de Lille first pointed out, all that glitters is not gold. The brassy-yellow iron sulfide pyrite ("fool's gold"), and the copper-iron sulfide chalcopyrite have been mistaken for gold, but this is indeed foolish. Gold is malleable and can be hammered completely flat, while pyrite and chalcopyrite are brittle and shatter, and have dark streaks. The golden-colored phyllosilicate vermiculite is sometimes mistaken for gold, but only from a distance, as the two share no physical properties whatsoever. Nuggets, thin flakes, and fine gold dust are found in many locations around the world, but well-crystallized specimens are rare; fine crystallized specimens of gold and even water-worn nuggets can be worth several times their "bullion value."

Gold is widespread in very small amounts in many rock types, but the greatest concentrations are found in hydrothermal gold-quartz veins associated with granitic rocks. Although the gold in such deposits may occur as crystallized specimens in cavities, it is usually mixed with the more abundant iron sulfide pyrite, which weathers into a rusty mixture of iron oxides at the surface of the earth. Such iron-stained outcrops are called gossans, and are an important prospecting guide. As these primary deposits are eroded, the gold is washed into streams and rivers to become concentrated in placer deposits as gold dust and nuggets. Such small flakes of gold, spotted in the millrace of Sutters Mill on the south fork of American River led to the "gold rush" California of 1849, the greatest in history. Tens of thousands of miners scoured the streams and rivers draining the Sierra Nevada, removing hundreds of millions of dollars worth of gold over the course of a decade. After the placer deposits began to be exhausted, production shifted to the mines of the Mother Lode, an extensive system of gold-quartz veins that follows the Melones Fault Zone for two hundred miles along the western slope of the mountains. The mines of the Mother Lode country produce excellent crystallized specimens of gold, particularly the Red Ledge and Empire Mines in Nevada County, and from others in El Dorado, Placer, Siskiyou, and Tuolumne counties. Many other rushes have occurred throughout history, in Alaska, Australia, and even now in the rain forests of Brazil.

Other important producers of crystallized gold in North America include the Red Mountain Pass area of San Juan County, and the Breckenridge District, Summit County, Colorado. The Hollinger and Dome mines in Ontario's Porcupine District also produce fine specimens, as do many mines in the states of Chihuahua, Hidalgo, Sonora, and Zacatecas, Mexico. Delicate dendritic growths of pale yellow electrum, usually twinned, are found in the mines of Verespatak, in the Bihar Mountains of Romania. Fine crystals are also obtained from many locations in Australia, including Koolgardie, Western Australia; the Flinders Range, South Australia; and Bendigo and Ballarat, Victoria.

The largest and most important gold deposit in the world is the fossilized placer of Precambrian age discovered in 1886 at Witwatersrand, near Johannesburg, South Africa. Here gold is found in an ancient quartz conglomerate, eroded from a Precambrian mountain range. The gold-bearing rocks occur as vast, flat sheets called reefs, which stretch across hundreds of kilometers and extend to depths of over 4000 m.

Top: Miners must probe the most remote corners of the globe in their search for that elusive metal—gold. At this mine near Wau, in the Highlands of Papua New Guinea, gold is won from veins and breccias in hydrothermally altered volcanic rock. **Bottom:** Gold cacique, or "chieftain" pendant crafted by an artisan of the Tairona culture of Columbia (10th to mid-16th century). The only such pre-Columbian gold artifacts to survive the Spanish conquest were those that had been buried with the dead.

graphite

Classification:
native element

Composition:
C (carbon)

Crystal System:
hexagonal

Hardness:
1–2

Specific Gravity:
2.09–2.23

GRAPHITE IS THE UGLY DUCKLING OF THE CARBON POLYMORPHS, WHICH IN ADDITION to diamond, include two extraterrestrial species found only in meteorites. Unlike its high-pressure cousin diamond, graphite is soft, weak, and sooty in color. Graphite has been used as a pigment for writing and for artistic purposes for millennia; the "lead" in pencils is actually a mixture of graphite and clay. The name comes from the Greek word *graphein,* meaning "to write." Plumbago is another archaic name derived from the Latin word for lead, *plumbum;* in ancient times, both graphite and the lead sulfide galena were used for writing. This mineral has many other uses unrelated its graphic qualities: because of its stability at high temperatures and its good electrical conductivity, it is made into crucibles and electrodes. Most of the graphite mined is powdered for use as the lubricant "graphite grease," applied in places where petroleum lubricants are unsuitable. Even though most commercial graphite is synthesized from coal, natural graphite continues to be mined.

Graphite crystals commonly form thin hexagonal tablets with triangular striations, and foliated, granular, or earthy masses. A perfect cleavage extends in one direction, producing thin, flexible laminae which resemble mica, but are inelastic. It is steel-gray to iron-black in color, with a metallic luster and a gray to black streak. Graphite is sectile and friable, with a greasy feel. Molybdenite is heavier, and has a distinct bluish cast.

Graphite forms through the metamorphism of the organic carbon in sedimentary rocks, and thus forms small flecks in marble and in regional metamorphic rocks such as schist. It can also form through the metamorphism of coal, as in Sonora, Mexico, and Rhode Island. Graphite occurs very rarely as a primary igneous mineral in some pegmatites and nepheline syenites, and in basalts that have assimilated carbonaceous sediments or even flowed over forests. Euhedral crystals occur near Ticonderoga, New York, in hydrothermal veins with quartz, tourmaline, apatite, and titanite; in the marbles at the Sterling Hill Mine at Ogdensburg, Sussex County, New Jersey; and in the schists of Clay County, Alabama. Large commercial deposits are exploited in China, the Soviet Union, the Koreas, India, Mexico, Sri Lanka, and the Malagasy Republic.

Lustrous stellate aggregates of graphite from Buckingham, Labelle County, Quebec.

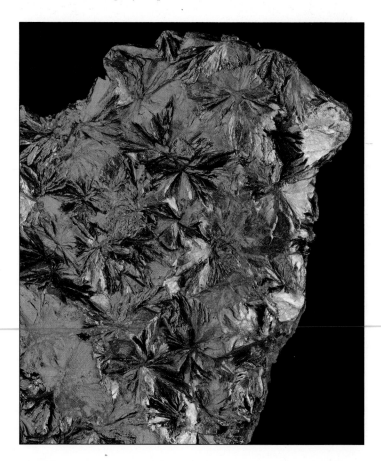

GREENOCKITE IS BOTH RARE AND DIFFICULT TO IDENTIFY, BUT IS PRIZED BY COLLECTORS of microscopic crystals. It typically forms earthy films on zinc minerals such as smithsonite or sphalerite, which may contain trace amounts of cadmium (particularly on the yellow cadmium-rich variety of smithsonite called "turkey-fat" ore). These minerals are the primary sources of cadmium for industry, although secondary greenockite undoubtedly makes a contribution. Cadmium and its sulfide are very poisonous, but find benign uses in medicine, in electronic circuitry and photoelectric cells. Artificial cadmium sulfide is the important pigment "cadmium yellow" used in painting.

Crystals are very small and quite rare, usually forming hemimorphic dipyramids with horizontal striations. Greenockite crystals may resemble those of either polymorph of (Zn,Fe)S, wurtzite or sphalerite. In fact, the largest greenockite crystals found to date (1-cm specimens from the Scottish locality) were originally thought to be sphalerite. The color ranges from yellow through orange to deep red, with a strong adamantine to resinous luster and an orange to red streak.

Greenockite most commonly occurs as an alteration product on cadmium-bearing secondary minerals in hydrothermal sulfide veins. Notable localities include Joplin, Missouri; Marion County, Arkansas; Eureka, Nevada; Mono County, California; and Hanover, New Mexico. Fine specimens are found at Tsumeb, Namibia; in Australia; and in several European countries. Excellent deep-red crystals, sometimes cyclically twinned, are found in the tin veins of Llallagua and Asunta, Bolivia, in association with cassiterite, marcasite, and wavellite. Greenockite is also found in cavities in volcanic rocks, in association with calcite, prehnite, and zeolites. The classic source is in the porphyries of Bishopton, Strathclyde, Scotland; it also occurs in basalt cavities, as in Passaic County, New Jersey. Another type of occurrence is in the unique contact-metamorphic zinc deposit at Franklin, New Jersey.

greenockite

Classification:
sulfide

Composition:
CdS (cadmium sulfide)

Crystal System:
hexagonal

Hardness:
3–3.5

Specific Gravity:
4.82

Greenockite crystal from Bishopton, Strathclyde, Scotland.

gypsum

Classification:
sulfate

Composition:
$CaSO_4 \cdot 2H_2O$ (hydrous calcium sulfate)

Crystal System:
monoclinic

Hardness:
2

Specific Gravity:
2.32

THE FIRST USE OF GYPSUM IN ANCIENT TIMES WAS IN ITS FINE-GRAINED, COMPACT form known as alabaster. All of the ancient cultures of the Mediterranean region carved alabaster into statues, goblets, and artifacts of all kinds, but no group was as enamored of the material as the Etruscans of ancient Tuscany. The Etruscans quarried alabaster near the fortified hill-town of Volterra, trading their handicrafts throughout the ancient world. It was considered *de riguer* for all prominent Etruscans to have an alabaster sarcophagus carved for their mortal remains, with a reclining sculpture of the deceased adorning the lid.

The most important industrial use of gypsum was discovered at an early date as well. When heated to about 200°C, gypsum loses most of its water and forms the semihydrated compound $CaSO_4 \cdot 1/2H_2O$, or plaster. When mixed with water, plaster "sets," forming an interlocking mat of microscopic crystals. Since plaster is not weatherproof, it is used primarily in interiors in the form of drywall, acoustic ceilings, and moldings. "Plaster of Paris" is a high-quality variety used in sculpture and to make delicate castings; it is named for the ancient deposit on Montmartre in Paris. Gypsum is also used in agriculture to loosen up clay-rich soils, as a filler in the paper and textiles industries, and in the production of sulfuric acid.

Smaller gypsum crystals are usually tabular and roughly diamond-shaped. Prismatic crystals are also common, and may reach more than 3 m in length if allowed to grow unimpeded in an open cavity. Intergrowths of platy crystals commonly form rosettes, called "sand roses" or "desert roses," in soft sediments; arborescent growths called helectites often form on the walls of caverns. Twinning is very common in gypsum, either as swallow-tail twins or the similar butterfly twins. Gypsum is  most common in massive form, sometimes fibrous and chatoyant as satin spar, or translucent and finely granular as alabaster. Gypsum is extremely delicate, displaying three directions of cleavage (one perfect) and a splintery fracture; cleavage fragments are slightly flexible, but not elastic. Gypsum crystals are colorless and transparent unless clouded by inclusions, while massive material is translucent and white, if not colored gray, yellowish, reddish, or greenish by inclusions. The luster is vitreous to pearly, and the streak white. The most distinctive characteristic of gypsum is its easy cleavage and softness: it can be easily scratched with the fingernail. Objects carved from alabaster can often be distinguished from marble on the basis of their differing thermal conductivities: alabaster usually feels warm to the touch, while marble feels cool.

Gypsum is precipitated in enormous amounts in evaporite deposits, but not without some difficulty. At water temperatures above 40°C, the precipitation of anhydrite is favored, and in the highly concentrated brines characteristic of evaporites, the formation of anhydrite rather than gypsum occurs at even lower temperatures. In marine evaporites, gypsum is precipitated only at the very beginning of the evaporation process, when salinities are low, and thus typically underlies other evaporite minerals. Many evaporite deposits reflect cyclic changes in salinity over time, and are characterized by thick sequences of anhydrite and gypsum in alternating layers. Anhydrite often alters to gypsum as it absorbs groundwater, expanding over half again in volume. Thus, the original anhydrite beds are warped and folded into serpentine shapes called enterolithic ("intestine-like") folds. Gypsum grains weathered from evaporites form the beautiful dunes of New Mexico's White Sands National Monument.

The large, clear crystals of gypsum seen in museum collections (sometimes called selenite) rarely form in evaporite deposits. Such crystals usually form as secondary minerals in hydrothermal sulfide veins, as sulfate-rich solutions react with calcium from dissolved carbonates. Extraordinary crystals nearly 2 m long were found in such an environment in the "Cave of the Swords" at Naica, Chihuahua, Mexico; crystals over 9 m long were found at the Braden Mine in Chile. More modest, but equally fine specimens are obtained from the sulfur deposits of Sicily and many other locations worldwide.

Alabaster bust of the pharaoh Tutankhamen, taken from his tomb in Egypt's Valley of Kings.

Opposite page: *Massive bedded gypsum being mined in Virginia for use in cement, plaster, drywall, and many other applications. (Courtesy of U. S. Gypsum Corp.)* ***Below:*** *Fish-tail twins of gypsum from the island of Linosa, near Malta in the Mediterranean Sea.*

halides

THE HALIDES ARE COMPOUNDS FORMED BY THE RELATIVELY LARGE ANIONS OF THE halogen elements, fluorine (F), chlorine (Cl), bromine (Br), and iodine (I). When these anions encounter large, oppositely charged cations of sodium, potassium, and other elements, they combine ionically to form very tight crystalline structures of great symmetry. In some halides, such as atacamite, $Cu_2Cl(OH)_3$, the presence of smaller cations makes room for oxygen, water, or hydroxyl (OH). There are at least 85 species of halides, but the bromides and iodides are very rare.

Chlorine is by far the most abundant of the halogen elements, and the chlorides are accordingly the most common of the halides. Halite (NaCl), or table salt, is a chloride mineral which forms vast deposits in sedimentary rocks, and is vital to human nutrition. Halite has a very simple structure (see *Atomic Structure*) in which every anion is surrounded by six neighbors to form an octahedral unit. The halides sylvite (KCl) and chlorargyrite (AgCl) share this structure, as does the sulfide galena (PbS) and the oxide periclase (MgO). Another important halide structure is that of fluorite (CaF_2), in which the fluorine and calcium ions are distributed in the form of a simple cubic unit, with a coordination number of eight. This same structure is shared by the oxides thorianite (ThO_2) and uraninite (UO_2).

Ionic bonding in the halides makes them poor conductors of heat and electricity in the solid state. In solution, however, the halides dissolve into their constituent ions to become excellent electrolytic conductors. A synthetic version of the rare fluoride cryolite (Na_3AlF_6) is used in molten form in the electrolytic preparation of aluminum metal.

Hanksite, $KNa_{22}(SO_4)_9(CO_3)_2Cl$, is a rare and complex halide found in the sediments of Searles Lake, San Bernardino County, and other ephemeral lakes in California.

HALITE (FROM THE GREEK *HALS*, OR "SALT") IS MORE THAN JUST A CONDIMENT—IT IS absolutely essential to human metabolism, and is one of the most vital industrial minerals as well. Among other things, salt allows the body to retain the correct amount of water for the proper functioning of cells and organs, and is essential to the production of digestive fluids. Rock salt was one of the first mineral resources to be mined and traded among humans, and extensive trade routes criss-crossed every continent to connect salt-producing regions with those less well-endowed. The earliest known underground salt workings were developed by the Bronze Age Celts at Hallstatt in Austria. An important use of salt in preindustrial cultures was as a food preservative. Most of the halite currently produced finds use in the chemical industry for the production of the metal sodium and its various compounds, including baking soda, lye (sodium hydroxide), and chlorine compounds like hydrochloric acid. Approximately one fourth is used for cooking and animal feed salt.

As an evaporite mineral, salt forms large deposits of massive granular material, but euhedral crystals do grow in open cavities or in pools of hypersaline water. These are usually simple cubes, rarely displaying octahedral or dodecahedral modifications, but often showing the cavernous faces that result from accelerated growth at the edges (hopper crystals). Salt is usually transparent to translucent, with a vitreous luster, and usually colorless, although iron oxides and other impurities may color it red, yellow, or even blue. Salt is very brittle, has a conchoidal fracture and perfect cubic cleavage, and is highly soluble in water.

Salt is one of the most abundant evaporite minerals, and forms enormous deposits of marine sedimentary origin in many regions of the globe. In a typical evaporite sequence, the least soluble compounds are the first to precipitate: anhydrite, gypsum, then halite, followed by the highly soluble potassium and magnesium salts like sylvite and carnallite. Halite forms nearly 75% of the dissolved minerals in seawater, so it is no surprise that evaporite deposits are dominated by salt layers, which can be hundreds of meters thick. The largest evaporite deposits, formed in great inland seas in past geological epochs, are known as the "saline giants."

Another important source of salt are the salt domes that occur along the Gulf Coast of the United States and in Spain, Germany, and Iran. Since layers of salt are lighter than the overlying sediments, they tends to flow upward through zones of weakness as the sedimentary rocks become compacted, rising in great vertical columns toward the surface. Other chemical sediments such as anhydrite, gypsum, and sulfur are commonly associated with the domes, as are valuable hydrocarbons. In arid regions, a salt column that has reached the surface simply continues to extrude salt across the landscape, since there is not enough rainfall to dissolve it.

Classification:
halide

Composition:
NaCl (sodium chloride)

Crystal System:
isometric

Hardness:
2

Specific Gravity:
2.16

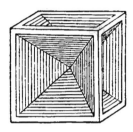

Left: Cubic crystal of halite from Urieliezka, Poland. *Right: Top—In many areas such as the west African country of Mali, salt is a precious commodity to be measured out by the gram. Bottom—Salt is harvested by the ton at saltworks in arid coastal regions, such as this one near Dampier, Western Australia.*

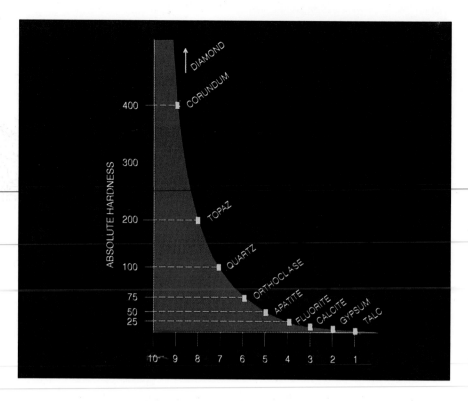

hardness

WHEN A METALLIC MINERAL IS SCRATCHED BY A HARDER OBJECT, THE ATOMS FLOW
outward, leaving a groove. In other minerals, however, atomic bonds are
actually broken, and scratching results in fracturing on a microscopic scale.
The physical property called *hardness* is a measure of a mineral's resistance
to this disruption, and is a useful diagnostic tool for mineral identification.
The mineralogist Friedrich Mohs (b. 1773) devised a simple hardness scale
which is still in use and indicates the *relative,* rather than *absolute* hardness
of the minerals listed (see graph).

With the aid of sophisticated measuring devices, more precise hardness
scales have since been developed primarily for industrial applications,
where it is necessary to know the absolute hardness of an alloy or other
compound. These scales measures a substance's resistance to indentation
(Knoop), abrasion (Pfaff), or grinding (Rosiwall). On these scales, the great
difference between mineral hardnesses beccmes apparent; while the softest
minerals are all very close in hardness, logarithmic increases appear
between quartz, topaz, and corundum. The absolute hardness of diamond
is four times that of corundum.

The prevalence of small atoms and ions tends to promote greater hardness, as does stronger atomic bonding. However, the atomic structure of
minerals is far more important in determining hardness than is chemical
composition, as is shown by the polymorphs diamond and graphite, which
occupy opposite ends of the hardness scale. Diamond has a very uniform,
covalently bonded framework structure which is equally strong in every
direction, while graphite, though also containing covalent bonds, is weak-
ened by the presence of impotent van der Waals' bonds between its structural layers.

Because crystal properties vary with direction, hardness sometimes
varies depending upon where it is measured. An excellent example of this
phenomenon is kyanite, which has a Mohs hardness of 5 parallel to its long
crystallographic axis, but a hardness of 7 across it. Calcite also displays this
property, with a hardness of 3 on all surfaces except the cleavage or crystal
face perpendicular to its long axis, which has a hardness of 2.

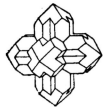

THIS UNUSUAL ZEOLITE IS MADE UNMISTAKABLE BY ITS CRYSTALS, WHICH NEARLY always form cruciform penetration twins, either simple or double ("fourling") twins. The ends of these twins resemble star drill bits. Harmotome may be white, gray, yellow, orange, or brown, and is transparent or translucent with a vitreous luster and white streak. Phillipsite, $KCa(Al_2Si_6O_{16}) \cdot 6H_2O$, is the only mineral with a similar habit.

Harmotome typically crystallizes in basalt cavities with other zeolites, but also in more felsic volcanic rocks, in cavities in gneisses, and low-temperature hydrothermal veins. Specimens are collected near Thomaston Dam, Connecticut; and Glen Riddle, Delaware, and small crystals are found in gneiss near Ossining, New York. Canadian sources include Nisikkatch Lake, Saskatchewan; Rabbit Mountain, Ontario; and Mont St. Hilare, Quebec. Fine twins are also found at Andreasberg, Harz, Germany; at Strontian, Scotland, and in North Wales.

harmotome

Classification:
tectosilicates, zeolite group

Composition:
$Ba(Al_2Si_6O_{16}) \cdot 6H_2O$
(hydrated barium potassium aluminum silicate)

Crystal System:
monoclinic

Hardness:
4.5

Specific Gravity:
2.4–2.5

A RARE MINERAL FORMED UNDER UNLIKELY CONDITIONS, HAUERITE IS AN ECCENTRIC sulfide in a class of prosaic ores. A member of the pyrite group, it is far more uncommon than one would expect from its simple chemistry, only crystallizing in very low-temperature environments. Hauerite forms small octahedral or cubo-octahedral crystals, with perfect cleavage. It is opaque, blackish brown in color, with an adamantine to submetallic luster and a gray-black streak.

Hauerite occurs primarily in evaporite deposits with gypsum, calcite, and native sulfur, crystallizing as a result of the reduction of primary

hauerite

Classification:
sulfide

Composition:
MnS_2 (manganese sulfide)

Crystal System:
isometric

Hardness:
3.5–4.5

Specific Gravity:
3.4

Octahedral crystals of haurite from Raddusa, Catania, Sicily.

evaporite minerals. Classic specimens, including crystals over 2 cm long, are found in the sulfur-bearing clays of Raddusa and Destricello, Sicily. Good specimens also occur at Kalinka and Schemnitz, Czechoslovakia, and in schists around Lake Wakatipu, New Zealand. Hauerite is fairly common in concretions capping the salt domes of Louisiana and Texas, and even in the manganese nodules which develop gradually over the millennia on the sea floor.

hematite

Classification:
oxide

Composition:
Fe_2O_3 (iron oxide)

Crystal System:
hexagonal (rhombohedral)

Hardness:
5–6

Specific Gravity:
5.2–5.3

BECAUSE OF ITS STRIKING RED STREAK, HEMATITE TAKES ITS NAME FROM THE GREEK word *haima,* or "blood"; it is still sometimes referred to as "bloodstone." The ancients often fashioned pendants, beads, and other jewelry from hematite, and must have been impressed when this black, metallic stone produced a blood-red slurry on the grinding wheel. Hematite pendants were worn by warriors to ward off wounds or aid in their healing, and preparations including ground hematite were used to treat a variety of ailments. Since iron is indeed an essential nutrient and a vital component of blood hemoglobin, such concoctions may indeed have been therapeutic. As our primary source of iron ore, hematite is among the most important of all industrial minerals.

Hematite crystals show a rich variety of forms, including thin to thick tabular, pyramidal, rhombohedral, and even prismatic. The most distinctive aggregate forms are botryoidal masses pictured here, and the rosettes of thin tabular plates, known as "iron roses". Massive material may be earthy, granular, or micaceous and brilliantly metallic, in which case it is known as specular hematite. Crystals are opaque and black to steel-gray in color (deep blood-red on very thin edges), with a submetallic to metallic luster and an iridescent tarnish. Massive material is brownish red to bright red, with a dull or earthy luster. Hematite is easily distinguished from massive goethite, ilmenite, and magnetite by its red streak. Hematite often forms pseudomorphs after magnetite crystals, which are known as martite.

Enormous deposits of hematite precipitated from sea water in the distant past, and now form important orebodies in many different parts of the world. All of these deposits were formed before two billion years ago, around the time that oxygen became an important part of the earth's atmosphere. Since iron is readily soluble in seawater in the absence of oxygen, the ancient seas were laden with iron in the same way that modern seawater is salty. In fact, so much iron was dissolved in the oceans that it precipitated out to form the sedimentary hematite deposits that are mined today. These deposits usually contain hematite and chert (see *Quartz*) interbedded in narrow bands, and are referred to as banded iron formations. These deposits can become even more enriched in iron through the dissolution and removal of the silica component by hydrothermal fluids.

Hematite is widely distributed in other geological environments as well, although usually in smaller concentrations. It is an accessory mineral in many igneous and metamorphic rocks (especially contact metamorphic deposits), hydrothermal veins, and volcanic tuffs and ashes. The sedimentary banded iron formations are the most important volumetrically, reaching thicknesses of hundreds of meters in the Lake Superior region and other parts of the world. The large ore deposits at Itibiara, Bahia, Brazil often produce good crystals. Well-formed crystals occur in the Alpine clefts of Switzerland, and in the volcanic rocks of Etna and Vesuvius in Italy and the Madiera Islands. Other localities include Bimbowrie, South Australia; Banat, Romania; and the Island of Elba, Italy.

__Opposite page:__ Banded iron formation at Cerro Bolivar, Venezuela. Weathering of the original finely layered sedimentary chert and magnetite has leached out the silica, producing this high-grade hematite iron ore. (Photo courtesy of Dennis Cox, USGS.)
__Below:__ Botryoidal mass of hematite from Cumbria, England.

As is often the case, the hemimorphite crystals in these divergent aggregates display only one termination, obscuring their hemimorphic character.

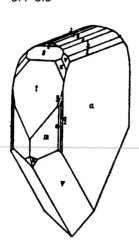

hemimorphite

Classification:
sorosilicate

Composition:
$Zn_4(Si_2O_7)(OH)_2 \cdot H_2O$
(hydrous zinc silicate)

Crystal System:
orthorhombic

Hardness:
4.5–5

Specific Gravity:
3.4–3.5

HEMIMORPHITE IS NAMED FOR THE CRYSTALLOGRAPHIC PROPERTY OF HEMIMOR-phism, of which it an excellent example. Its crystals typically display very different forms or combinations of forms at their opposing ends, where symmetrically related faces would normally be expected. This polar struc-ture is due to the silica tetrahedra in hemimorphite's Si_2O_7 groups all being in the same orientation, with bases facing the opposite direction from their points. Other species exhibiting hemimorphism include greenockite and tourmaline. In antiquity, hemimorphite was classed with other zinc minerals as calamine.

The distinctive crystals of this species consist of a prism flattened in one direction, terminated by a combination of domes and pedion faces at one end, and pyramidal faces at the other. Aggregates of divergent crystals are common, as are mammilary or granular masses. Hemimorphite displays one perfect cleavage, and is strongly pyroelectric and piezoelectric. The luster is vitreous and the color usually white, although green, blue, and yel-low hues are also common. Hemimorphite is heavier than similar-appear-ing aggregates of prehnite crystals, and unlike botryoidal smithsonite, does not effervesce in acid.

Hemimorphite occurs in the oxidized region of zinc-bearing sulphide deposits, in association with other secondary species such as anglesite, cerus-site, and smithsonite. Fine specimens are found in the zinc mines of Missouri, at Leadville, Colorado, in the Organ Mountains of New Mexico, and in the Elkhorn Mountains of Montana. Numerous Mexican sources include Mapimí, Durango and Santa Eualia, Chihuahua. Good specimens are also obtained from Cumberland and Derbyshire, England; Moresnet, Belgium; and locations in Germany, Sardinia, Romania, Algeria, and Namibia.

HETEROSITE AND PURPURITE ARE ALTERATION PRODUCTS OF THE MASSIVE BROWN phosphates triphylite and lithiophilite, respectively, differing from their parent minerals only in the absence of lithium. They are found in pegmatites along with a host of other, rarer secondary species. Both of these phosphates are conspicuous for their coloration, which is a deep rose red to purple—thus the name purpurite. The name heterosite is derived from the Greek word meaning "different."

Although small crystals are known, most material is either massive, or as anhedral grains displaying good cleavage. Both species are subtranslucent to opaque, with a dull to satiny luster and a reddish-purple streak. They are commonly coated with tertiary alteration products, in the form of brown or black iron and manganese oxides.

Heterosite and purpurite are found in most complex pegmatite districts, including the Black Hills of South Dakota; San Diego County, California; Yavapai County, Arizona; Kings Mountain, North Carolina; and Fairfield County, Connecticut. Significant European localities include Chanteloube, France; Varuträsk, Sweden; Mangualde, Portugal; and the pegmatites of Bavaria, Germany. Other occurrences are the Karibib District, Namibia; Namaqualand, South Africa; the Buranga pegmatite, Rwanda; the Pilbara District, Western Australia; and Afghanistan.

Classification:
phosphates

Composition:
heterosite: $(Fe^{+3}, Mn^{+3})PO_4$
purpurite: $(Mn^{+3}, Fe^{+3})PO_4$
(manganese iron phosphates)

Crystal System:
orthorhombic

Hardness:
4–4.5

Specific Gravity:
3.69

Anhedral fragment of heterosite, displaying cleavage, from Chanteloube en Razes, near Limoges, France.

heulandite

Classification:
tectosilicate, zeolite group

Composition:
$(Na,K,Ca,Sr,Ba)_5Al_9Si_{27}O_{72} \cdot 26OH$
(hydrous sodium calcium aluminum silicate)

Crystal System:
monoclinic

Hardness:
3.5–4

Specific Gravity:
2.1–2.2

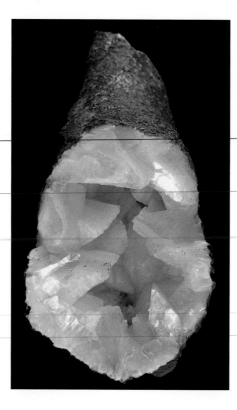

These heulandite crystals from Tiegarborn, Iceland grew inside a small gas cavity in a basaltic lava.

HEULANDITE IS ONE OF THE MOST OPEN-STRUCTURED OF THE ZEOLITE MINERALS, containing several sets of open channels which house a variety of large ions and water molecules. These channels dissect layers of six-membered $(Si,Al)O_4$ tetrahedra, which give heulandite its easily developed basal cleavage. This species is characterized by tabular, coffin-shaped crystals, often in warped, subparallel aggregates. Crystals are colorless, yellow, green, or reddish orange, and are transparent or translucent with a pearly luster and a white streak.

Heulandite crystallizes in cavities in basalts and other volcanic rocks, in association with calcite and other zeolites. It is sometimes found in contact metamorphic deposits, as well as in some sedimentary rocks and even sulfide veins. Heulandite is well-represented from the basalts of the Columbia River Plateau; Nova Scotia; Rio Grande do Sul, Brazil; India; the Faeroe Islands, and especially Iceland. Fine specimens are found in the diabase sills of the northern New Jersey; in the silver veins of Andreasberg, Germany; and in Kongsberg, Norway.

hornblende

Classification:
inosilicate, amphibole group

Composition:
$(Ca,Na,K)_{2-3}(Mg,Fe^{+2},Fe^{+3},Al)_5(Al,Si)_8O_{22}(OH)_2$
(complex potassium calcium iron-magnesium silicate)

Crystal System:
monoclinic

Hardness:
5–6

Specific Gravity:
3.0–3.4, increasing with iron

"HORNBLENDE" IS ACTUALLY A SOLID-SOLUTION SERIES BETWEEN THE TWO COMPOSITIONAL extremes ferrohornblende and magnesiohornblende, but most natural hornblendes contain both iron and magnesium. The intriguing name for this common amphibole is an ancient German miner's term for the mineral. *Horn,* meaning the same in English, probably refers to the shape or color of the crystals, while *blenden,* meaning "to blind or deceive," appears to be a petulant reference to its uselessness as an ore. Hornblende is one of the most important rock-forming minerals; the igneous rock type hornblendite and the metamorphic rock amphibolite may be composed almost entirely of hornblende.

Hornblende is abundant as small grains in rock, or as prismatic, stubby crystals, which may appear hexagonal in cross section. It also commonly forms acicular or fibrous aggregates in parallel orientation. Hornblende is brittle, with an uneven to subchonchoidal fracture and perfect prismatic cleavage at approximately 120°, which yields fragments of diamond-shaped cross section. Colors tend toward black, dark green, or brown, and crystals are opaque, translucent, or, very rarely, transparent, with a vitreous luster and a colorless streak. Hornblende is distinguished from tremolite and actinolite by its darker color, and from the pyroxenes by the wider angle between cleavages; similar-appearing black tourmaline lacks cleavage altogether. Hornblende pseudomorphs produced from the alteration of pyroxenes are known as *uralite.*

As noted, hornblende is an important component of many metamorphic rocks. In mica schists and gneisses, it is commonly associated with almandite garnet, biotite mica, and quartz; in greenschists, with albite feldspar and epidote. Hornblende is an important part of plutonic igneous rocks of intermediate composition, such as the diorites, and to a lesser extent of volcanic rocks like basalts and andesite. It is also found in association with aegirine and nepheline in nepheline syenites. Good crystals are found in the Grenville marbles of Canada, particularly along the Madawaska River in Lanark County, Ontario. Fine specimens are also found in marbles in New York state, and at Franklin, New Jersey. Interesting specimens are obtained from many localities worldwide. Many specimens in collections labeled "hornblende" may actually be the related amphiboles edenite, $NaCa_2(Mg,Fe^{+2})_5Si_7AlO_{22}(OH)_2$, or pargasite, $NaCa_2(Mg,Fe^{+2})_4AlSi_6Al_2O_{22}(OH)_2$.

Extraordinary black hornblende crystal, with white analcime, from Mont St. Hilare, Quebec.

HOWLITE IS EXTREMELY RARE IN CRYSTALLINE FORM, AND ALMOST ALWAYS OCCURS AS compact nodular masses which resemble heads of cauliflower sculpted in porcelain (although only clowns and ballerinas actually receive this honor). These are occasionally carved and polished as decorative objects. Howlite is always white in color, with a subvitreous luster, white streak, and conchoidal fracture. Datolite is similar in appearance but is harder, and unlike howlite does not dissolve in hydrochloric acid. The species is named for its discoverer, Nova Scotia geologist Henry How (b. 1828).

Howlite is a mineral of the continental evaporite association, typically occurring with other borate minerals in arid regions. At the original source near Windsor, Nova Scotia, howlite is found as nodules in anhydrite, associated with ulexite; it is also found in Newfoundland and New Brunswick. Most specimens of howlite are obtained from California, where it occurs as nodules, often very large, with colemanite and ulexite. Important sources include the Sterling Borax Mine in Tick Canyon, and deposits near Lang, Los Angeles County; Gower Gulch, Inyo County; and deposits near Daggett, San Bernardino County.

howlite

Classification:
borate

Composition:
$Ca_2B_5SiO_9(OH)_5$
(hydrated calcium silicon borate)

Crystal System:
monoclinic

Hardness:
3.5

Specific Gravity:
2.45

Nodular masses of howlite from Wentworth, Hant's County, Nova Scotia.

SOME OF THE MOST IMPORTANT SOURCES OF ECONOMICALLY VALUABLE MINERALS, AND of beautiful mineral specimens are the hydrothermal sulfide deposits. There are different types of hydrothermal orebodies, formed through a variety of processes; all share certain important characteristics, however. The term hydrothermal is derived from the words meaning *water* and *heat*, as these two elements are essential in the formation of all such deposits. In general, hot aqueous solutions derived from seawater, groundwater or magma circulate through cracks in the rocks. The circulation of these solutions is driven by heat provided by the magma. The solutions contain metal and other ions derived either from the magma itself or more likely by leaching of the rocks through which the hot solutions are circulating. As the solutions work their way up through the crust they cool, decompress and react further with their wall rocks. Due to these changes the solutions eventually become *supersaturated* in components of a certain mineral, at which point that mineral begins to precipitate. Many solutions carry sulfur, which combines with the dissolved metal ions to precipitate as sulfides.

Hydrothermal sulfide deposits have been mined for thousands of years, and many different classification schemes have been advanced since the systematic study of ore deposits began during the Renaissance. The dominant method of classification has long been one in which ore deposits are divided according of their supposed temperature of formation, which was thought to depend on depth. Classification schemes based on ore genesis—how a deposit actually formed—were generally flawed, since so little was really known about geological processes. In recent years, however, advances in geology, geochemistry, and geophysics have made the genetic classification of hydrothermal ore deposits attractive again.

Hot spring at Emerald Pool, Yellowstone National Park, Wyoming. When hydrothermal fluids reach the surface of the earth, their mineral load is precipitated in hot spring deposits. These relatively low temperature deposits are important sources of mercury, antimony, arsenic, and other elements.

Sulfide Veins Historically, the most important source of sulfide ores—and mineral crystals as well—have been the hydrothermal sulfide veins. Veins are fractures, faults, and other planes of weakness in country rock in which ore minerals, along with quartz and other gangue minerals, have precipitated from hydrothermal fluids. Vein deposits have been divided into a large number of types based on their mineralogy, which is determined by both the original composition of the hydrothermal fluids and the composition of the country rock. Veins typically exist in groups having approximately similar orientation, the orientation being determined by that of the original fracture network of the country rocks. They are found in specific localities because the sources of both heat and fluids at depth are themselves localized. For example, hydrothermal veins are common in the roof regions large plutons. Here hydrothermal activity may be particularly intense—in fact, instead of forming well-defined veins the fluids may permeate the rock and alter it completely. This is what happened in the cases of the hydrothermal porphyry copper deposits (see *Chalcopyrite*). In them the ore is disseminated and spread through vast tonnages of altered rock. The porphyry copper deposits have surpassed by far vein deposits in economic importance; however, they produce virtually no well-crystallized mineral specimens.

Because veins are usually associated with igneous intrusions, they are well represented in areas of mountain-building. This is especially true of the volcanic mountain ranges such as the Andes of South America, which are formed through the re-melting of oceanic crust as it is pushed (sub-

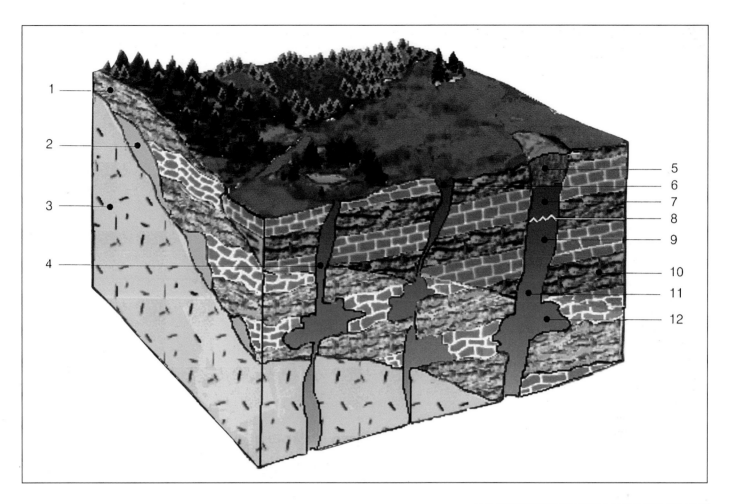

ducted) under the edge of a continent. It is thought that the metals concentrated in the oceanic crust by the hydrothermal processes described below end up in the new magmas under these mountain ranges. As the magmas rise and are emplaced in the crust, metal-bearing hydrothermal solutions are given off by the magmas as they crystallize. The varying behavior of the different metals in solution may determine the regional variations noted in the mineralogy of hydrothermal veins.

Submarine Sulfide Deposits In 1979, marine geologists discovered submarine hot springs flowing from vents on the oceanic spreading center called the East Pacific Rise, where basaltic magmas well up to form new sea floor. It has been determined that these springs result where sea water circulates through fractures in the sea floor, to be heated by hot rocks deep within the crust, and then ascend to the surface laden with metals leached from the surrounding rock. Where the hydrothermal solutions come into contact with the cold waters on the sea floor, large amounts of copper, zinc, iron, manganese, and lead sulfides are deposited. Similar springs have been discovered on spreading centers in other parts of the oceans, often associated with unusual communities of animals which depend on them for survival. In many regions where the large segments of the sea floor called ophiolites are exposed on land (see *Chromite*), rich sulfide deposits are found which were formed from submarine hot springs.

Hot Spring Deposits When hydrothermal solutions reach the surface on land, as opposed to under the sea, they form the familiar hot springs and geysers. Although these solutions may have traveled through a great distance of rock, and lost much of their original heat, they often contain metals in solution which can precipitate near the surface as ore minerals. Surface hydrothermal deposits are the primary commercial sources of antimony and mercury, and they often produce fine mineral specimens as well. Fossil hot

Diagram showing some of the features related to hydrothermal deposits.

1. *Metamorphic rocks*
2. *Skarn (contact metamorphic replacement deposit)*
3. *Igneous intrusion*
4. *Medium-temperature vein deposits*
5. *Gossan (leached zone)*
6. *Low-temperature vein deposits*
7. *Zone of oxidized enrichment*
8. *Water table*
9. *Zone of supergene enrichment*
10. *Sedimentary rocks*
11. *Primary sulfide ore*
12. *Hydrothermal replacement deposit*

Minerals of Hot Spring Deposits

anhydrite	gypsum
arsenic	mercury
barite	opal
calcite	orpiment
calomel	quartz
chalcedony	realgar
cinnabar	stibnite
dolomite	sulfur
fluorite	

Secondary Vein Minerals

adamite	enargite
anglesite	erythrite
antlerite	fluorite
atacamite	goethite
aurichalcite	gypsum
autunite	hemimorphite
azurite	libethenite
bornite	linarite
brochantite	malachite
caledonite	mimetite
chlorargyrite	mottramite
cerussite	olivenite
chalcanthite	phosgenite
chalcocite,	pyromorphite
chrysocolla	scorodite
copper	silver
coquimbite	smithsonite
covellite	torbernite
crocoite	vanadinite
cuprite	vivianite
descloizite	willemite
dioptase	wulfenite

spring deposits in California's Napa Valley, and at several locations in the Great Basin of Nevada, contain large low-grade deposits of finely disseminated gold. Such deposits are referred to as "bulk-minable," and are becoming one of the most important sources of gold.

Replacement Deposits Hydrothermal replacement deposits are the one type of sulfide deposit not obviously associated with igneous magmas, although there is evidence that very deep-seated heat sources may be involved. These deposits form through the replacement of carbonate rocks such as limestones and dolomites by sulfide minerals such as galena and sphalerite, at relatively low temperatures of less than 150°C. The process of hydrothermal replacement is also important in the formation of contact metamorphic skarn deposits (see *Metamorphic Rocks*).

Sulfide Vein Alteration The primary sulfides and other minerals which comprise all types of hydrothermal sulfide deposits undergo changes once they have been initially deposited, either due to chemical alteration by a second generation of hydrothermal fluids, including groundwater, or simply due to oxidation. The secondary mineral species thus formed may replace some or all of the primary vein minerals. The region of a vein or body of mineralized rock nearest the surface is known as the oxidized zone, and is topped by a mass or body of mineralized rock of porous limonite known as a *gossan*, or "iron hat," which formed through the leaching of primary pyrite and chalcopyrite. The part of the oxidized zone which lies within the area of water table fluctuation is called the zone of oxidized enrichment, and a wide range of colorful secondary minerals crystallize here. Below this is the zone of secondary enrichment, where the bulk of the metals leached from the oxidized zone are redeposited below the water table (see *Chalcocite*).

Secondary veins furnish some of the most interesting mineral specimens. The carbonates and sulfates are the most important sources of mineral specimens among the secondary minerals. In general, primary sulfide minerals are first converted into sulfates, which in turn react with primary vein or country rock carbonates (aragonite, calcite, and dolomite) to produce secondary carbonates. Secondary sulfides and sulfosalts may be important ore minerals in the enriched zone.

hydroxides

goethite
romanechite
diaspore
manganite
brucite

THE HYDROXIDES ARE CHARACTERIZED BY THE PRESENCE OF WATER (H_2O) molecules or hydroxyl (OH^-) ions. These groups have the property of forming weak atomic bonds and tend to be driven off by heating. Thus, the hydroxides are limited in distribution to low-temperature superficial deposits such as sedimentary rocks and the upper portions of hydrothermal veins.

Many of the hydroxides form as alteration products after other minerals, and as a result are poorly crystallized and porous. They tend to grow on the minerals they are replacing as radiating masses of minute crystals, or as pseudomorphs. Rust, composed of goethite, $FeOOH$, and other minerals, is a particularly widespread example of this group. Romanechite and manganite, along with other manganese hydroxides form the important manganese ore "wad," which is mined from large deposits of sedimentary origin. Similarly, diaspore, $AlOOH$, and related species form an aggregate called bauxite, which is the major source of aluminum.

HYDROXYLHERDERITE FORMS A SERIES WITH HERDERITE, WHICH DIFFERS ONLY IN THAT IT contains fluorine. Hydroxylherderite is fairly rare, but has been found as wonderful sharp, colorful crystals in many pegmatites around the world. The only verified specimen of herderite, however, is a single gem in the collection of the Smithsonian Institution. Some confusion arises from the fact that the shorter name is often used in place of tongue-twister hydroxylherderite.

Crystals are rare, stout prismatic to tabular in habit, and often of pseudo-orthorhombic symmetry; aggregates are typically botryoidal. Twinning is frequently observed, and there is one (poor) direction of cleavage. Hydroxylherderite ranges in color through yellow, light green, greenish blue, blue, and purple, and it is transparent to translucent with vitreous luster. Apatite is a very similar but much more common pegmatite species; it is difficult to distinguish massive material without chemical tests.

Hydroxylherderite forms as a late-stage hydrothermal mineral in granitic pegmatites. Magnificent hydroxylherderite crystals to 18 cm in length are found at Virgem da Lapa and the Golconda pegmatite in Minas Gerais, Brazil. Less dramatic but euhedral crystals are found at Newry, Hebron, Paris, Auburn, and Poland, Maine; the State Forest Mine, East Hampton, Connecticut; North Groton, New Hampshire; and Kings Mountain, North Carolina. European sources include Viitaneimi, Finland; Mursinsk in the Urals of Russia; and locations in Bavaria and Saxony, Germany.

hydroxylherderite

Classification:
phosphate

Composition:
$CaBe(PO_4)(OH)$
(hydrated calcium beryllium phosphate)

Crystal System:
monoclinic

Hardness:
5–5.5

Specific Gravity:
2.95–3.01

Hydroxylherderite with tourmaline and albite (variety cleavelandite) from the Xandra Mine, Virgem da Lapa, Brazil.

the igneous rocks

Igneous magmas which reach the earth's surface cool rapidly to form extrusive rocks, such as this fresh basaltic lava.

A THIN BUT WIDESPREAD VENEER OF SEDIMENTARY AND METAMORPHIC ROCKS serves to obscure the importance of the igneous rocks, which in fact comprise about 95% of the earth's crust. Heat and pressure can cause the localized melting of deep crust and mantle rocks within the earth, giving rise to bodies of molten rock called *magmas*. As a magma cools, minerals crystallize from it—but these are not always the same minerals present in the rocks from which the magma formed. The kind and proportion of different species present are determined both by the composition of the original melt, and by the changes it undergoes prior to cooling. For example, some of the chemical elements may be selectively crystallized as minerals, and the rest of the magma drawn off to crystallize elsewhere, in a process called *magmatic differentiation.*

Magmatic rocks are generally called igneous rocks (from the Indo-European root for "fire"), and divided into two main divisions: the *intrusive* and *extrusive* types. Intrusive rocks such as granite cool gradually at depth within the earth, and may form bodies of mountain-range proportions called batholiths or plutons; intrusive rocks are also called plutonic. Extrusive rocks, such as basalt, form when a magma erupts to cool rapidly at the earth's surface. An intrusive and an extrusive rock may form from the same magma and be identical in composition, but differ in texture due to different rates of cooling.

The igneous rocks are classified according to the nature of their constituent minerals, which reflect the composition of the magmas from which they solidified, and by their textural characteristics, which indicate the physical conditions under which they formed. Since virtually all igneous rocks are composed primarily of silicate minerals, a chemical classification scheme based on silica content is useful. Although the common igneous rocks contain from 40% to 75% SiO_2, the less silicic rocks often have their entire silica content tied up in dark silicate minerals, and contain no free quartz. The terms most often used to distinguish between silica-rich and silica-poor rocks today reflect the division of silicate minerals and the rocks they form into predominantly light- or dark-colored groups. Rocks composed primarily of light-colored minerals are referred to as *felsic*, a term derived from their dominant mineral groups, the feldspars and the silica polymorphs. Dark-colored rocks dominated by the pyroxenes, amphiboles, and olivines are termed *mafic*, because these minerals are rich in magnesium and/or ferrous iron.

The most felsic igneous rocks are *granite* and *granodiorite,* and their fine-grained volcanic counterparts *rhyolite* and *dacite.* Among the many rocks of intermediate composition are *monzonite* and *diorite,* whose volcanic equivalents are *latite* and *andesite.* At the mafic end of the spectrum are the *gabbros,* whose volcanic equivalents are the *basalts* (see *Basalt Cavities*). The felsic rocks do contain mafic minerals, typically in the form of biotite mica and amphiboles, but are predominantly composed of quartz (or its high-temperature polymorphs) and/or potassium feldspars. Rocks of intermediate composition tend to have little or no quartz, although they are sufficiently rich in silica to form alkali feldspar or sodic plagioclase. The mafic rocks such as gabbro contain calcic plagioclase, along with amphiboles, pyroxenes, and other dark minerals such as ilmenite and magnetite.

The *ultramafic* rocks, which comprise the earth's mantle, are the least silicic of all igneous rocks; *peridotite*, for instance, is composed almost exclusively of olivine and pyroxenes. Extrusive ultramafic rocks, known as *komatiites*, are very rare and formed mostly in Precambrian times. *Syenite* and its extrusive equivalent *trachyte* are sodium- and potassium-rich rocks which are poor in silica, but light-colored nonetheless (see *Feldspathoids*). Perhaps the most chemically eccentric igneous rocks are the *carbonatites* (see *Calcite*), which crystallize from magmas enriched in carbon dioxide. These rocks are composed primarily of calcium, magnesium, and sodium carbonates, and contain only minor silica.

The igneous rocks are classified independently of their composition, according to textural criteria. Since the size of individual mineral grains reflects the rate at which a magma cools, the intrusive rocks tend to be coarse-grained, and the extrusive rocks fine-grained. Most intrusive rocks cool slowly deep within the earth, their crystals generally forming homogenous textures of equant grains. However, very coarse-grained igneous rocks (see *Pegmatites*) form by crystallization of water-rich magmas.

Magmas which reach the surface of the earth form fine-grained volcanic rocks, which can be divided into two textural classes. The *pyroclastic* volcanic rocks include the *tuffs* and other rocks formed from fragments of crystals and glass. The other major textural class of volcanics is *lava*, such as the basalt or rhyolite, which flows from volcanoes or large fissures in the earth's crust. Basalts are usually entirely crystalline, though fine-grained, while the glassy variety of rhyolite called obsidian is completely noncrystalline. Many volcanic rocks display a *porphyritic* texture, containing euhedral crystalline grains called *phenocrysts* in a finer-grained or glassy groundmass. The illustrations of leucite and augite in this book are fine examples of this texture.

Left: *Granite.* **Right:** *Gabbro.*
Below: *Structures of intrusive and extrusive igneous rocks.*

1. *Basaltic lava plateau*
2. *Rhyolite dome*
3. *Obsidian flow*
4. *Maar*
5. *Lava flow*
6. *Basaltic volcano*
7. *Diatreme*
8. *Diabase sill*
9. *Metamorphic rocks*
10. *Pegmatite*
11. *Pluton*

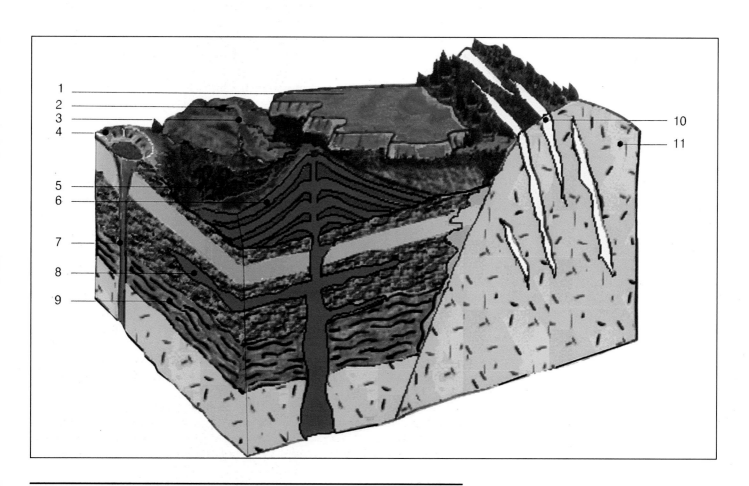

Ilmenite crystal from the eponymous locality near Orenburg, in the Ilmen Mountains of the Soviet Union.

ilmenite

Classification:
oxide

Composition:
$Fe^{+2}TiO_3$ (iron titanium oxide)

Crystal System:
hexagonal (rhombohedral)

Hardness:
5–6

Specific Gravity:
4.72

An engineer examines the components of a jet engine made with titanium alloy. Because of its great strength and resistance to heat and corrosion, titanium is ideal for many aerospace applications.

ILMENITE IS ONE OF THE PRIMARY ORES OF TITANIUM, A METAL ESSENTIAL TO THE aerospace and other industries because of its corrosion resistance, high melting point (1800°C), and especially its great strength. Ilmenite is also the principle source of titanium dioxide, the whitest of white paint pigments and by far the most important pigment used in paints. Rutile (TiO_2) is preferable for both of these uses because of its lack of iron, but ilmenite is by far the more abundant species. Ilmenite is also used as aggregate in heavyweight, high-stress concretes necessary for special purposes like bridges and dams. The name of this species comes from a locality in the Ilmen Mountains of the Soviet Union.

Ilmenite crystals are commonly thick tabular or acute rhombohedral, but most material occurs as lamellar or granular aggregates, and as disseminated grains in igneous rocks. Cleavage is lacking, but parting is observed, as is conchoidal fracture. The color is iron-black to brownish black, with a metallic to dull luster and a black streak. Ilmenite is distinguished from hematite by its black streak, and from the strongly magnetic iron oxide magnetite by its much weaker magnetism; rutile has a stronger luster and is not magnetic at all, while columbite–tantalite is heavier.

Ilmenite is a primary magmatic mineral in many igneous rocks, particularly in gabbros, and is frequently found intergrown with magnetite. Minable concentrations of ilmenite are formed in layered igneous complexes through magmatic segregation (the separation and concentration of one mineral species in molten rock). Ilmenite is concentrated in black sands with rutile, monazite, and zircon by wave action in coastal areas in many parts of the world; large amounts are recovered from beach deposits in Florida, Western Australia, and South Africa. Good crystals of ilmenite occur in the emery mines of Chester, Massachusetts; at Roseland, Virginia; with magnetite in dikes in gabbro at Iron Mountain, Wyoming; and with rutile, spinel, and biotite in gabbro at St. Urbain, Charleroix, Quebec.

THIS RARE AND UNUSUAL SPECIES IS NAMED AFTER THE ISLAND OF ELBA, FROM whence the first specimens were obtained. Ilvaite forms stout prismatic crystals with diamond-shaped cross sections and vertical striations on the prism faces, or radiating aggregates of acicular crystals. It is translucent with submetallic luster, and dark brown to almost black in color; the streak is black with a brownish or greenish cast. Lawsonite, $CaAl_2(Si_2O_7)(OH)_2 \cdot H_2O$, is a closely related sorosilicate found in metamorphic rocks of the blueschist facies, but rarely seen in collections.

Ilvaite is found in contact metamorphic deposits, or in sodalite syenites. Wonderful crystals to 8 cm long are found at the Laxey Mine, Owyhee County, Idaho; other North American occurrences include Colorado's North Pole Basin, the Dragoon Mountains of Arizona, and Balmat, New York. The original deposits at Rio Marina and Capo Calamita, Elba, still produce sharp crystals and fibrous, radiating aggregates associated with hedenbergite, magnetite, andradite, and pyrite. Other sources include Trepca, Yugoslavia; the island of Seriphos in the Greek Cyclades; Julianehåb, Greenland; and Japan and England.

ilvaite

Classification:
sorosilicate

Composition:
$CaFe^{2+}_2Fe^{3+}O(Si_2O_7)OH$
(hydrous calcium iron silicate)

Crystal System:
orthorhombic and monoclinic

Hardness:
5.5–6

Specific Gravity:
3.8–4.1

THE ORGANIC MATERIAL WHICH COMPRISES THE TEETH OF SEVERAL LARGE ENDANGERED animal species is called ivory. Most ornamental ivory comes from the elongated incisors, or tusks, of the African elephant, but much is also obtained from the smaller tusked Asian (or Indian) elephant. Other sources of ivory include the walrus, hippopotamus, and the narwhal and sperm whales. Ivory is composed of the very same substance as human teeth: the calcium phosphate apatite and calcium carbonate, in an organic framework of the proteinaceous material dentine. Because of its unique physical properties, ivory has been a popular ornamental material since ancient times. Although it is soft enough to be easily carved, its organic structure renders it tough and relatively flexible—perfect for wear in jewelry and use in decorative objects. The name ivory is of ancient Egyptian origin, via the Latin *ebur.*

Since mastodons and mammoths roamed the steppes of ice-age Europe and Asia, their fossil remains there are fairly widespread. In his *Natural History,* the Roman scholar Pliny recorded the prevalent belief that elephants buried their tusks, which doubtless arose from the discovery of such fossils. Ivory reached a pinnacle of popularity in the 13th century in both

ivory

Classification:
organic "gemstone"

Composition:
primarily calcium phosphate

Hardness:
approximately 2.5

Specific Gravity:
1.80

Europe and the Far East, with much of the supply coming from fossil sources in Siberia. Little distinction was made between fresh and fossil material, except that fossil ivory tends to be mottled or stained (see *Vivianite*). In the badlands of Inner Mongolia, the Chinese villagers still mine the remains of 15-million-year-old shovel-tusked proboscideans. These so called "dragon bones" are not used for ornamental purposes, but ground into powder and mixed with various herbs, minerals, and parts of modern animals to make traditional remedies.

Ivory has been used in many cultures as a symbol of wealth. The monarchs of Egypt and Mesopotamia cherished ivory, appointing their palaces with ivory thrones and fixtures. Elephant ivory was prized in the Middle Ages for its exotic origins, and became increasingly popular for small objects such as chessmen, sword hilts, and religious carvings. The long, twisted tusks of the arctic narwhal whale were objects of special wonder in medieval Europe, and were thought to be unicorn horns—relics from before the Flood.

The Victorian bourgeoisie demonstrated their status by treating this hard-won material from the Dark Continent with casual disregard, fashioning all sorts of mundane objects from ivory—including piano keys, umbrella handles, and billiard balls. At the same time, American whalers who hunted the sperm whale for its oil enlivened their long days at sea with the art of scrimshaw, carving miniature maritime scenes on the conical teeth of their quarry. Sperm whales are now protected by international treaty, but plenty of teeth still find their way into the hands of scrimshanders and collectors.

Genuine ivory is distinguished by its longitudinal grain, which is defined by variations in translucency, and which forms a subtle, curving, lace-like pattern on carved surfaces. Freshly killed ivory is a warm off-white color, but like human teeth ivory tends to yellow with age. Ivory may also crack as it ages and dries out, the cracks forming a distinctive pattern parallel to the grain. There are all kinds of excellent substitutes for ivory, including bone, several kinds of plastics, and the Tagua nut of the South American rain forest, also known as "vegetable ivory." Genuine ivory is higher in density than almost all of its imitations, and when burned, gives the distinctive smell of singed hair, while plastics yield an acrid, chemical odor.

Left: Tooth of a sperm whale. *Right:* Carving the tusk of an Indian elephant in Bali. Whole tusks are often carved in shallow relief so that they can be labeled as "artifacts," thereby circumventing bans on the importation of raw ivory.

Although its export and import are regulated, the enormous trade in illegal ivory is steadily decimating the remaining elephant population. Even the smallest ivory trinket requires the death of one of these magnificent, intelligent animals, which share the earth with us in ever-dwindling numbers. This lucrative trade has led to increased poaching in practically every country of sub-Saharan Africa, despite the valiant efforts of rangers and wardens to stop it.

Recently, a group of South African scientists devised a sleuthing tool which may help break the poaching and smuggling rings. This innovative technique uses analyses of the ratios between three sets of isotopes of naturally occurring elements in ivory (see *Atomic Structure*) to deduce where a piece of ivory originated. Specific carbon isotopes vary according to type of forage an elephant eats, while nitrogen isotopes reflect the drought stress it has experienced, and strontium or lead isotopes (which substitute for calcium in ivory) can reveal the age of the rocks underlying the animal's range. Using these three sets of data, the scientists have been able to pinpoint fairly closely the origin of contraband ivory. Hopefully, this information will allow game wardens to break the line of supply between the poachers and their markets.

JADEITE IS A RARE PYROXENE, WHICH IN ITS MASSIVE FORM PROVIDES THE MORE valuable of the two different minerals referred to as jade; the other being the massive variety of the amphiboles actinolite and tremolite known as nephrite. Although the two jades have in common the properties of extreme toughness and similar coloration, they are different chemically. Their structures differ as well, massive jadeite being a cryptocrystalline aggregate of equant grains, and nephrite a dense felted mass of short fibers. It is frequently difficult to distinguish one from the other, but a rather subtle distinction may be made on the basis of luster—nephrite generally appears oily, and jadeite vitreous.

Jade implements fashioned by primitive peoples have been found in numerous places in Asia, Europe, and the Americas. Jadeite was most highly prized by the pre-Conquest Mesoamerican cultures, beginning with the Olmec as early as 1500 BC. The role of jadeite in Mesoamerican cultures, while not the same as that of nephrite in Chinese culture, was of equal importance. It played an important part in the cosmology and social life of these peoples, carrying important spiritual meaning as well as being a vital trade commodity. Although the Maya might use jade to buy cocoa, for instance, they would also place a piece in the mouth of a departed relative to provide sustenance on the journey to the otherworld, Xibalba.

The Spanish conquerors of Mexico and Central America were puzzled by the high esteem in which the green stone—innocuous to them—was held. Not wanting such a large portion of their pillage to lose its value in translation, they followed the medieval practice of assigning curative powers to rare stones, and offered jade as a preventative for kidney failure—then as now a serious chronic disease. Thus, jade was named "piedra de ijada," Spanish for stone of the flank—the location of the kidneys. This was translated into French as *pierre de le ejade*, and when jadeite was first distinguished from nephrite by the French chemist Alexis Damour in 1863, the scientific name was coined from the original "trade name." The source of the jade used by pre-Columbian peoples was a mystery for over 450 years, until the ancient

jadeite

Classification:
nesosilicate, pyroxene group

Composition:
$NaAlSi_2O_6$ (sodium aluminum silicate)

Crystal System:
monoclinic

Hardness:
6.5–7

Specific Gravity:
3.3–3.5

Rough jadeite and a polished cabochon from the Uyu Chaung River, Sagaing, Burma.

Jadeite carving thought to represent the Mayan god of sacrifice by decapitation, from Rio Azul, Guatemala (350–500 AD).

quarries were discovered in the Motagua Valley of Guatemala. Although some Guatemalan jade is mined and worked for the tourist trade, almost all commercial jade is now produced from deposits in Burma.

Crystals of jadeite are extremely rare, although tiny ones are found in cavities in massive material. These crystals form elongated prisms or rectangular plates, and are usually striated and often twinned. The characteristic habit of this species is massive, as an aggregate of equant to bladed microscopic crystals. Massive jadeite has a splintery, uneven fracture, difficult to develop because of its extreme toughness; this durability causes jade to survive stream transport very well. Jadeite is translucent to opaque, with a vitreous to dull luster and a white streak. Among the many colors of this species are apple-green to emerald-green, white, pale lavender, bluish lavender, and reddish brown. The value of jade increases with its transparency, depth of color, and freedom from mottling and other imperfections. The most sought-after colors are the violets and emerald-green, the latter known as "Imperial Jade."

Many minerals have been used to imitate jade. The most common simulant is massive serpentine, which may have a very convincing color and luster but can be easily detected by its inferior hardness. More difficult to detect are harder silicates, such as the massive variety of vesuvianite called californite, massive diopside, and massive green grossularite garnet. The jade-workers of ancient Mesoamerica prized any hard, green stone with similar qualities to true jade, and for this reason even authentic artifacts cannot be assumed to be made of jadeite. An expert opinion is usually necessary to distinguish between jade and its many imitations.

Jadeite is intermediate in composition between the much more common sodium aluminum silicates nepheline and albite (plagioclase), and only forms in lieu of these species in very high-pressure metamorphic rocks. It is thus found in areas of continental collision, such as the California Coast Ranges and the Alps, typically in rocks of the blueschist facies, and in altered ultrabasic rocks such as serpentinites. In California, masses of jadeite are found in serpentinite from San Benito County northward into the San Francisco Bay area. Small pale-green crystals up to 0.6 cm in length occur with calcite in veins in glaucophane schist near Cloverdale, Sonoma County, California. The finest gem-quality jadeite, and virtually the entire world supply of gem material, comes from serpentines near Tawmaw, Upper Burma. Other deposits have been exploited in China's Hunan Province, Tibet, Guatemala, Japan, and New Zealand.

jamesonite and boulangerite

Classification:
sulfosalts

Composition:
jamesonite: $Pb_4FeSb_6S_{14}$
(lead iron antimony sulfide)
boulangerite: $Pb_5Sb_4S_{11}$
(lead antimony sulfide)

Crystal System:
jamesonite: monoclinic,
boulangerite: orthorhombic

Hardness:
2.5–3

Specific Gravity:
6.2–5.63

JAMESONITE AND BOULANGERITE ARE MINOR ORES OF LEAD, KNOWN AS "FEATHER ORE" in the miner's florid ergot because of their plumose aggregate habits. The official names honor the Scottish mineralogist Robert Jameson (b. 1774), and the French mining engineer Charles Louis Boulanger (b. 1810). Crystals of these species are prismatic, generally forming felted masses of long needles, sometimes arranged in a radiating (plumose) form. Their color is steel-gray to black, often with an iridescent tarnish; their luster is metallic and the streak grayish to black. The cleavage is good in one direction, and the fracture uneven. Stibnite can be very similar in appearance, but it is flexible whereas these are brittle.

Jamesonite and boulangerite form in hydrothermal sulfide veins in association with other sulfosalts and sulfides, carbonates, and quartz. They are found in many places throughout the United States, including the Coeur d'Alene and Wood River districts, Idaho; the Bingham and Park City districts, Utah; Silver City, South Dakota; Gunnison County, Colorado; and various locations in California, Nevada, and Washington. Classic specimens are found at the Mina Noche Buena near Mazapil, Zacatecas, Mexico. Other notable North American locations include British Columbia, New

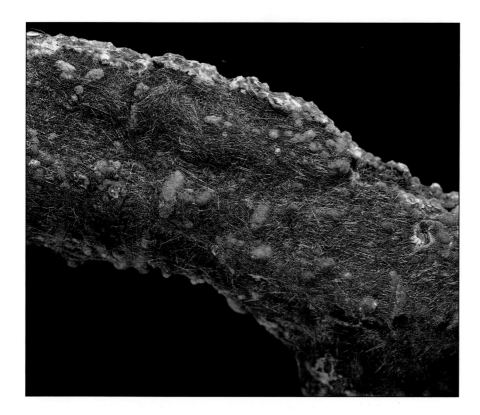

Felted mass of acicular boulangerite crystals from the Noche Buena Mine, Zacatecas, Mexico.

Brunswick, and Ontario, Canada. Among the important European sources are Moliéres, France; Pribram, Czechoslovakia; Felsobanya, Romania; and England, Germany, Yugoslavia, and Sardinia. Fine specimens have also been found in Algeria, Australia, China, Bolivia, and Argentina.

JET IS A VERY HARD AND DURABLE VARIETY OF COAL, WHICH IS HARD ENOUGH TO TAKE a high polish. It has been fashioned into ornamental objects such as beads and amulets for at least 3000 years, but the pinnacle of its popularity came during the Victorian era. Victorian matrons were enamored of its stern plainness, and found it especially suitable for funerals. Like the other Victorian gems, marcasite (actually pyrite) and garnet, jet is currently enjoying a renaissance.

Jet is derived from the compression of lignite, a soft brownish material formed from ancient driftwood fragments and other organic matter which are dispersed throughout some sedimentary rocks. The classic source of this material is the town of Whitby in Yorkshire, England, where jet has been mined and polished for generations. Jet from this deposit often retains the original shape of the fossil branches from which it formed. Jet is also found in many other parts of Europe, in Nova Scotia, and in the western United States.

Jet is inexpensive, but there are a number of imitations. Black tourmaline, chalcedony, obsidian, glass, and garnet are sometimes represented as jet, but all are much harder and cold to the touch. The plastic bakelite, and the dense rubber vulcanite both resemble jet, but give off an acrid odor when heated. Common anthracite coal is much more brittle than jet, and even if polished will not survive daily wear.

jet

Classification:
organic gemstone
Composition:
primarily carbon (C)
Hardness:
3–4
Specific Gravity:
1.30–1.35

Antique jet cabochons and ring, with raw material from Oles, Asturias, Spain.

kernite

Classification:
borate

Composition:
$Na_2B_4O_6(OH)_2 \cdot 3H_2O$
(hydrous sodium borate)

Crystal System:
monoclinic

Hardness:
2.5–3

Specific Gravity:
1.9

THIS BORATE MINERAL IS NAMED FOR KERN COUNTY IN CALIFORNIA'S MOJAVE DESERT, where it is mined as a source of commercial boron (see *Borax*) in the large open pit mine at Boron in the Kramer District. Although kernite is found in only one other location, in the Tincalayu Mine in Argentina's Salta Province, it is hardly a rare mineral. The deposit at Boron contains millions of tons of kernite; single crystals of kernite have been found measuring 1 x 3 m, and crystals 1 m in diameter are common. Accordingly, specimens of kernite are readily available to collectors.

The large crystals found at Boron are rarely euhedral, but usually form as large grains. Equant crystals are known, and these are commonly twinned. Kernite is very brittle, and has four easy, perfect cleavages which divide crystals into long lath-shaped fragments. Transparent and colorless when fresh, most specimens are white and opaque because kernite alters readily to tincalconite, like many other borates. The luster on fresh surfaces is vitreous to pearly, and the streak white. Kernite is distinguished from other borates by its rectilinear cleavage pattern; like many other evaporite minerals, it is soluble in cold water.

Kernite occurs primarily near the base of the thick evaporite sequence at Boron, buried beneath 300 m of Tertiary sediments. Because of this depth restriction and other features observed in the field, it is believed that kernite forms through the recrystallization of borax as the latter is subjected to the increased pressures and temperatures at depth. Other borates typically associated with kernite include borax, colemanite, and ulexite.

Transparent cleavage fragment of kernite from Kramer, Kern County, California.

Kyanite is one of the three major aluminosilicates, and is trimorphous with sillimanite and andalusite. These polymorphs are helpful for determining the degree of metamorphism the enclosing rocks have undergone. The presence of kyanite, for instance, implies that the rock formed under the influence of medium temperatures and relatively high pressure (see phase diagram, *Andalusite*). At lower pressures, the crystallization of one of the other two polymorphs will be favored. Like its polymorphs, kyanite is used in the manufacture of high-temperature porcelain products such as spark plugs, electrical insulators, and acid-resistant containers. Transparent material is sometimes faceted, but the easily developed cleavage makes kyanite a poor choice of gemstone. The name comes from the Greek *kyanos,* or "blue," in reference to its most common color.

Kyanite forms elongated, bladed crystals, often twinned or twisted in appearance, with perfect prismatic cleavage. It typically forms radiating or jumbled aggregates of bladed individuals. The color of kyanite is usually light blue, white, gray, or greenish, and it is transparent or translucent, with a vitreous to pearly luster and a colorless streak. Kyanite resembles no other species, and is easily identified by its peculiar strength properties—crystals are easily scratched by a knife blade parallel to their length, but remain unscathed in the perpendicular direction.

Kyanite forms in aluminum-rich regionally metamorphosed rocks, particularly mica schists and gneisses, in association with other aluminous silicates, such as staurolite and garnet, and occasionally corundum. It also forms, infrequently, as a primary igneous mineral in some granites and granitic pegmatites. Kyanite occurs in quantity in the emery deposits at Chesterfield, Massachusetts; throughout the metamorphic province of New England; and at many places in the southern Appalachians. Very large crystals are found in Minas Gerais, Brazil, and near Machakos, Kenya. In Europe, fine specimens are obtained from Pizzo Forno, Switzerland; Morbihan, France; and the Austrian Tyrol. Economically viable deposits are mined at Lapsa Buru, India, and in Kenya and Australia.

kyanite

Classification:
nesosilicate

Composition:
Al_2SiO_5 (aluminum silicate)

Crystal System:
triclinic

Hardness:
6–7.5 along cleavage planes
4–5 across cleavage planes

Specific Gravity:
3.53–3.67

Blue kyanite blades with staurolite in mica schist, from Pizzo Forno, Switzerland.

laumontite

Classification:
tectosilicate, zeolite group

Composition:
$CaAl_2Si_4O_{12} \cdot 4H_2O$
(hydrated calcium aluminum silicate)

Crystal System:
monoclinic

Hardness:
3.5–4

Specific Gravity:
2.2–2.4

LAUMONTITE IS NAMED FOR FRANCOIS NICHOLAS PIERRE GILLET DE LAUMONT (b. 1747), who discovered the first specimens in the cliffs of Brittany. Laumontite forms elongated, prismatic crystals with chisel-like terminations, and columnar, fibrous and radiating aggregates. It is usually white, though it may also be tinged yellow or pink, and is transparent with a vitreous to pearly luster. Laumontite crystals are extremely fragile, with two perfect cleavages, and great care must be taken in collecting and storing specimens. When exposed to the atmosphere, laumontite becomes opaque and begins to disintegrate due to dehydration; thus it is usually coated with a sealant or kept in an airtight container when collected.

Laumontite is one of the typical zeolite minerals of basalt cavities, and also forms in fissures and in many other types of igneous, sedimentary, and metamorphic rocks and in some low-temperature hydrothermal veins. Remarkable crystals, 30 cm in length, were recently discovered near Bishop, California, during a road-building project. Good specimens are also found in the French Pyrenees; New Zealand; northern Norway; and Patterson, New Jersey. Additional sources include the Alpine vugs near Ticino, Switzerland, and the Val d'Ossola, Italy.

Exceptional crystals of laumontite from Drain, Douglas County, Oregon.

LAZULITE AND SCORZALITE FORM A COMPLETE SOLID-SOLUTION SERIES, BUT SPECIMENS representing the lazulite end are far more abundant in nature. Lazulite is easily confused with lazurite, the main ingredient of lapis lazuli, often through wishful thinking. But even though lazulite and scorzalite are not gemstones, they are highly prized by mineral collectors, particularly specimens showing distinct crystal faces. The name lazulite is derived from the Persian *lazhuward,* meaning "blue"; scorzalite is named for the Brazilian mineralogist Evarista Pena Scorza (b. 1899).

Crystals take the form of simple dipyramids, are commonly twinned, and are rarely euhedral. They are very brittle, with good cleavage, and are almost impossible to remove from the surrounding matrix. They commonly appear as granular aggregates or disseminated grains. Both materials are deep blue to nearly black in color, transparent to opaque, and have a vitreous to dull luster and a white streak. Strongly pleochroic, they may appear dark blue, green-blue, or colorless depending on crystallographic orientation.

These species are found in quartzites and other quartz-rich metamorphic rocks, as well as in quartz veins and granitic pegmatites. Associated species include andalusite, kyanite, quartz, sillimanite, dumortierite, rutile, pyrophyllite, garnet, and mica. Deep-blue anhedral masses occur in the Champion Sparkplug Mine, in the White Mountains of California. Sharp, shattered, short dipyramidal crystals occur with kyanite and rutile on Graves Mountain, Lincoln County, Georgia. Good crystals embedded in quartz and calcite occur near Werfen, Austria, and crystals to 30 cm in length can be found near Horrsjoburg, Sweden. Specimens have also been obtained from the Blow River, Yukon Territory; the Burunda pegmatite in Rwanda, and several locations in Madagascar. Gem-quality crystals are found in the placers of Minas Gerais, Brazil.

lazulite series

Classification:
phosphates

Composition:
lazulite—$MgAl_2(PO_4)_2(OH)_2$
(magnesium-rich end member)
scorzalite—$FeAl_2(PO_4)_2(OH)_2$
(iron-rich end member) (magnesium-iron aluminum hydroxyl phosphates)

Crystal System:
monoclinic

Hardness:
5.5–6

Specific Gravity:
3.1–3.4

Dipyramidal lazulite crystal, still in its quartzite matrix but falling apart, from Graves Mountain, Lincoln County, Georgia.

lazurite

Classification:
tectosilicate, feldspathoid, sodalite group

Composition:
$(Na,Ca)_8(AlSiO_4)_6(SO_4,S,Cl)_2$
(sodium-calcium aluminosilicate, with sulfate, sulfur, and chlorine)

Crystal System:
isometric

Hardness:
5–5.5

Specific Gravity:
2.4–2.45

LAZURITE IS THE MAIN CONSTITUENT OF LAPIS LAZULI, AND LIKE LAZULITE, TAKES ITS name from the ancient Persian word *lazhuward.* Lapis, a natural composite of the minerals lazurite, calcite, and pyrite, has been prized as an ornamental stone for over 6000 years; the lapis lazuli mines high above the Kokeha Valley in northeastern Afghanistan were ancient even when visited by Marco Polo in 1271. Perhaps because deep-blue lapis with its flecks of brassy pyrite resembles an evening sky dotted with sparkling stars, it was long regarded as a cure for melancholy (the "blues"), and a talisman against the spirits of darkness. The cultures of ancient Mesopotamia traded lapis far and wide, regarding it at least as highly as gold. The Egyptians were equally fond of the stone, and nobles such as Tutankhamen were interred with great stores of lapis grave goods. Powdered lazurite is the basis for the pigment *ultramarine,* the deep blue color essential to artists' palettes. The production of synthetic ultramarine has fortunately alleviated the need to grind up natural lapis lazuli.

Crystals of lazurite are very rare, but crude dodecahedrons over 2 cm in diameter are occasionally found in Afghanistan. Lazurite is most commonly seen as granular aggregates contaminated with calcite, pyrite, and other silicate minerals, in the form of lapis lazuli. Pure lazurite is an intense deep blue, but the color of lapis lazuli is lightened by the presence of calcite. The luster is dull to greasy, and the streak light blue. Crystals are brittle, with an uneven fracture and poorly developed dodecahedral cleavage.

Lazurite is distinguished by its characteristic association with white calcite and tiny yellow pyrite crystals. Blue-dyed chalcedony or glass are sometimes offered as lapis lazuli, but are easily distinguished from it by their greater hardness, smooth conchoidal fracture and lack of "impurities." The synthetic gemstone manufacturer Pierre Gilson of Paris has developed an artificial lapis containing pyrite, but the relatively low cost of natural lapis has not encouraged the spread of this clever imitation. Lazurite resembles sodalite and the phosphate lazulite, but is generally much finer grained than these minerals.

Lazurite is formed through the contact metamorphism of marbles and is not widespread. Euhedral crystals are found only at the Firgamu mines in the Kokcha River Valley, Badakshan, Afghanistan. Very similar lazurite is produced from the Sayan Mountains, near Lake Baikal, in the Soviet Union. Very large masses of pale blue lapis, generally containing more calcite than the Asian material, are found in the Andes of Ovalle, Chile. Lazurite is also found in Italy near Mt. Vesuvius and in the Albani Mountains, and on Canada's Baffin Island. Very high-quality, dark-blue lapis has been found on Italian Mountain in the Sawatch Mountains of Colorado, and in the San Gabriel and San Bernardino Mountains of Southern California.

Above: *Pectoral ornament in the shape of a scarab beetle (a symbol of resurrection to the ancient Egyptians) from the tomb of the 18th Dynasty pharaoh Tutankhamen. Above the scarab is a carnelian sun, and below is a semicircular stone of blue-green amazonite.*
Opposite page: *Massive lazurite with calcite and pyrite (lapis lazuli) from the Firgamu mines, Kokcha River Valley, Badakshan, Afghanistan.*

lepidolite

Classification:
phyllosilicate, mica group

Composition:
$K(Li,Al)_{2-3}(Si,Al)_4O_{10}(F,OH)_2$
(hydrous potassium lithium aluminum silicate)

Crystal System:
monoclinic

Hardness:
2.5–4, softer on cleavage surfaces

Specific Gravity:
2.8–2.9

Large cleavage fragment, or "book" of lepidolite from Londonderry, Coolgardie, Western Australia.

THE GREEK WORD FOR "FISH SCALES," *LEPIDOS*, PROVIDES THE NAME OF THIS MICA, but only the most colorful tropical fish has the same flashing, vibrant color. Lepidolite gets its unusual pink to lilac hue from its lithium content; it also contains Na, Rb and Cs in substitution for K. It has been mined as an ore of this important element (the lightest metal), although most of the world's supply now comes from lithium brines. Lithium and its various artificial compounds are used in an amazing variety of applications, from atomic energy and metallurgy to the treatment of manic-depressive psychoses.

Sometimes lepidolite is found incrusting other minerals as distinct barrel-shaped or tabular crystals, but more commonly it forms massive aggregates of tiny flakes. Despite its softness, such massive material is carved into decorative objects to take advantage of its gaudy color and sparkle.

Lepidolite occurs in complex pegmatites with other lithium minerals like colored tourmaline and amblygonite. Major sources include the mines of the Pala District in San Diego County, California; the Harding Mine in Dixon, New Mexico; the pegmatite districts of New England; and the Black Hills of South Dakota. The pegmatites of Madagascar and Minas Gerais, Brazil, produce uncommonly large crystals. Other sources include Mozambique, Sweden, Japan—in short, everywhere complex pegmatites are found.

leucite

Classification:
tectosilicate

Composition:
$KAlSi_2O_6$ (potassium aluminum silicate)

Crystal System:
tetragonal

Hardness:
5.5–6

Specific Gravity:
2.4 –2.5

Leucite trapezohedra from Ariccia, near Rome, Italy. Notice how the volcanic rock pulled away from the large crystal as it contracted on cooling.

LEUCITE IS NOT ONE OF those minerals that spend hundreds of years gradually adding ion after ion in some quiet crevice. If you walk up to a fresh volcanic tuff, still steaming on the slopes of Mount Vesuvius in Italy, you will find perfect little trapezohedra of leucite resting fully formed in the otherwise glassy groundmass. The name comes from the Greek *leukois,* "white," in reference to its color.

Leucite forms euhedral, trapezohedral crystals, which are commonly twinned. The crystals are pseudoisometric, expressing a memory of their unstable high-temperature isometric symmetry. Leucite may be colorless and transparent; or translucent and colored white, gray, yellowish, or reddish, with a vitreous to dull luster and a white streak. The crystals have no cleavage to speak of, and are brittle with conchoidal fracture. Garnet has a similar crystal form, but is harder and usually darker in color; the zeolite analcime is also similar, but has a brighter luster.

This species forms in potassium-rich, silica-poor lavas. Good crystals have been found at Hamburg, New Jersey; Magnet Cove, Garland County,

Arkansas; the Bearpaw Mountains of Montana; the Leucite Hills and Absarokas of Wyoming; and along the shores of British Columbia's Vancouver Island. It is common in the lavas of Vesuvius and in the Alban Hills near Rome. Fine specimens are also found at Weisental, Czechoslovakia, and in France, Germany, Australia, Zaire, Uganda, and numerous other locations worldwide.

LIBETHENITE IS VERY SIMILAR TO THE RELATED COPPER PHOSPHATE OLIVENITE IN ITS physical characteristics and occurrence, and although its crystals rarely exceed 0.5 cm in length, it sometimes affords attractive specimens. Crystals are equant, acicular, bladed or short prismatic in habit, and typically form velvety mats or crusts on matrix. Two directions of prismatic cleavage may be observed. The colors include every shade of green, from pale yellowish green to nearly black, and the luster is vitreous to greasy.

Like olivenite, libethenite is usually found in the oxidation zone of copper deposits, associated with adamite, azurite, malachite, limonite, and other secondary minerals. The best specimens are the dark-green crystals on quartz from the original source near Libethen, Neusohl, Romania. North American localities include the Perkiomen Mine, Montgomery County, Pennsylvania; the Santa Rita district, New Mexico; Yerington, Nevada; and, in Arizona, Castle Dome in Gila County and the Coronado Mine, in the Morenci District. Specimens have also been recovered from glaucophane schist near Llanada, California. Other sources include Cornwall, England; Chuquicamata and Coquimbo, Chile; Mindouli, Congo; and Kitwe and Kabwe, Zambia.

libethenite

Classification:
phosphate

Composition:
$CU_2(PO_4)(OH)$
(copper hydroxyl phosphate)

Crystal System:
orthorhombic

Hardness:
4

Specific Gravity:
3.97

Crystals of libethenite from Tagilsk, in the Ural Mountains, Russia.

linarite

Classification:
sulfate

Composition:
PbCu(SO$_4$)(OH)$_2$ (lead copper sulfate)

Crystal System:
monoclinic

Hardness:
2.5

Specific Gravity:
5.3

Linarite is an uncommon, attractive secondary species that forms in the oxidized regions of lead- and copper-bearing sulfide veins. The name refers to a locality near Linares, in Spain's Jaen province. Crystals may take a thin, tabular form or an elongated prismatic one, and they often form clusters of randomly oriented prisms. Linarite is brittle, with conchoidal fracture and two directions of cleavage, one perfect and another poor. Its crystals are transparent to translucent, and deep azure-blue in color, with a vitreous to subadamantine luster and a pale-blue streak. This species is similar in appearance to azurite, but is softer, heavier, and fails to effervesce in dilute acid.

Linarite is commonly associated with malachite, cerussite, smithsonite, and brochantite in the oxidized enrichment zone of sulfide deposits. The finest specimens are the crystals to 10 cm in length from the Mammoth Mine in Pinal County, Arizona. Additional locations in the United States are the Coeur d'Alene District, Idaho; Butte, Montana; Park City and the Tintic District, Utah; and Cerro Gordo, Inyo County, California. Good specimens are found at Tsumeb, Namibia, and in many parts of Europe, including Red Gill, Cumberland, England; Lölling, Austria; and Sardinia.

Prismatic crystals of linarite from Red Gill, Caldbeck Fells, Cumbria.

THE TERM LUMINESCENCE COVERS ALL kinds of light emitted by minerals besides that resulting from incandescent or daylight. Most kinds of luminescence can only be seen under special types of lamps, or in the dark. The study of luminescence is not trivial, however, as it can be an effective means of identifying many minerals. Like the colors seen under white light, luminescence primarily results from the presence of transition element ions and various impurities, together referred to as "activators."

When the activator elements in a mineral become excited by exposure to ultraviolet light, x-rays or shower of electrons, it is said to be *fluorescent*. In this process the incident energy is absorbed by a specific electron, which is thereby elevated to a higher energy state. The excited electron spontaneously falls back to its more stable, lower energy state and emits an amount of energy equal to the energy difference between the two states. Luminescence is the emission of energy in the form of visible radiation. Sometimes this continues to occur after the incident source of radiation is turned off, and the mineral continues to luminesce for a fraction of a second, or even minutes. This type of behavior, which can be considered a type of fluorescence, is termed *phosphorescence*. Not all fluorescent minerals respond to the same wavelengths of ultraviolet radiation. Some fluoresce only under long-wave radiation, and others only under shortwave.

Because fluorescence may be due to element which is not intrinsic to a mineral's formula, not all specimens of the same species will display the same kind of fluorescence—if any at all. Scheelite for instance, only displays its characteristic blue fluorescence when there is substitution of molybdenum for tungsten; pure $CaWO_4$ does not fluoresce. Similarly, the commonly fluorescent species calcite and fluorite owe their luminescence entirely to extraneous elements. Nonetheless, the distinctive fluorescence of certain species can often be relied upon for practical purposes such as identification and ore separation. At the Bikita pegmatite in Zimbabwe, for example, the lithium aluminum silicate eucryptite is mined as an ore of lithium. Although it looks exactly like quartz in daylight, it can easily be recognized under ultraviolet light by its distinctive pink fluorescence.

Other kinds of luminescence are observable without the aid of special lamps or other equipment. When some minerals are heated, usually between the temperatures of 50° and 475° C, they become *thermoluminescent*. This type of luminescence is also due to the presence of activators, and is shown by the nonmetallic minerals apatite, calcite, fluorite, lepidolite and some feldspars. Minerals which emit light on being abraded or crushed are referred to as *triboluminescent*. This property was observed early on in dark mine tunnels, where massive fluorite and sphalerite would emit an eerie glow on being struck by a miner's pick. This property is best represented in nonmetallic minerals with good cleavage, including amblygonite, calcite, lepidolite and pectolite.

Willemite and calcite from Franklin, New Jersey, in white light **(above)**, *and under ultraviolet light* **(below)**. *Willemite from Franklin fluoresces green, and calcite red, but the activator in both cases is thought to be manganese.*

ALTHOUGH *LUSTER*, THE MANNER IN WHICH LIGHT IS REFLECTED FROM A MINERAL'S SUR-
face, is a rather subjective property, it is an extremely useful diagnostic
tool. Luster varies according to a mineral's refractive index. Thus, minerals
of low refractive index will appear dull on fresh surfaces, while those of
higher refractive index will be more reflective, or lustrous. The least reflective type of luster is termed *dull* or *earthy*, and refers to the granular surfaces of massive materials like limonite. *Waxy* luster is developed on the
more reflective surfaces of cryptocrystalline aggregates like chalcedony.
Slightly more reflective species are termed *greasy* or *oily*. Minerals like fluorite and quartz, which have a low refractive index but fairly bright luster,
are referred to as *vitreous*, which means "glass-like." A yet higher refractive
index yields a *resinous* luster, which is comparable to the appearance of a
varnished wood surface. Nonmetallic minerals with very high luster, like
diamond and zircon, are called *adamantine*, and the luster of species like
rutile, verging on the metallic, is termed *submetallic*. The highest possible
degree of reflection is displayed by minerals with a *metallic* luster, like
pyrite, which reflects virtually all of the light which strikes it.

m

magnesite

Classification:
carbonate

Composition:
$MgCO_3$ (magnesium carbonate)

Crystal System:
hexagonal (rhombohedral)

Hardness:
3.75–4.25

Specific Gravity:
3.0–3.1

MAGNESITE IS AN IMPORTANT SOURCE OF MAGNESIUM, WHICH IN THE FORM OF MAGNE-
sium oxide (magnesia) is familiar as the antacid and mild laxative in the
cobalt-blue bottle. Magnesium compounds are used to make the refractory
firebrick which line the furnaces used in steel-making, and have a wide
variety of other industrial uses as well. The name comes, by way of magnesium, from the cryptic Latin phrase *magnes carneus*, or "flesh magnet,"
possibly a reference to the use of magnesia and citrus as a cathartic.

Magnesite generally occurs as coarse to fine-grained, chalky or porcelaneous masses with conchoidal fracture. Very rarely, magnesite is found as
well-formed rhombohedral crystals, even more rarely as tabular, prismatic
or scalenohedral forms with perfect rhombohedral cleavage. Crystals are
transparent to translucent, white, yellow, or gray in color, with a vitreous
luster and a white streak. Impure material commonly displays blue or green
fluorescence under ultraviolet light. Magnesite forms a solid-solution series
with the iron carbonate siderite; intermediate, iron-rich magnesite is marked
by its brownish hue and strong luster. Magnesite can be distinguished from
calcite by its greater hardness, density, and failure to effervesce in cold
hydrochloric acid.

Magnesite is a widespread mineral which occurs in many different rock
types. The primary mode of formation is through the hydrothermal alteration of magnesium-rich rocks like peridotite by groundwater laden with
carbonate ions (carbonic acid). Gradual chemical processes may result in
the primary carbonates calcite or dolomite being altered to magnesite in
some metamorphic rocks. Magnesite also occurs in smaller amounts in
hydrothermal veins, and may form as a primary mineral in rare igneous
rocks such as carbonatites.

Large deposits of magnesite are mined in many parts of the world,
including Algeria, Austria, India, Korea, Manchuria, Poland, and the Soviet

Union. Good crystals are found in Austria, particularly the Zillertal area; at Snarum, Norway; in the Alpine clefts of St. Gotthard, Switzerland; and the Alto Adige, Italy. Extensive magnesite deposits occur in the western United States, particularly in the Coast Ranges of California and the Paradise Range of Nevada. Probably the finest specimens are those from the pegmatites of the Serra Das Eguas, Bahia, Brazil, where transparent, euhedral crystals to 5 cm on edge have been found.

Right: *Magnesite mine in hydrothermally altered rock, Gabbs, Nevada. Machine at left drills holes for explosives.*
Left: *Massive magnesite from Euboea, Greece.*

PEOPLE HAVE BEEN FASCINATED BY THE UNIQUE PROPERTIES OF MAGNETITE SINCE ancient times. All specimens of magnetite can be attracted by an artificial magnet, and the relatively rare variety known as lodestone is itself naturally magnetic. Lodestone was known to early Greek writers as the Heraclean Stone, and classified loosely with amber, which also appears to have the power of attraction because of its ability to store static electricity. All sorts of wonderful powers were ascribed to the lodestone, notably the ability to draw forth dreams and phantoms from the spirit world. Since a magnet can both attract and repel, lodestones were used both for love charms, and to detect marital infidelity. The name magnetite is derived from the ancient region of Magnesia in Asia Minor, now the environs of Manisa, Turkey.

By the 2nd century BC, the Chinese had discovered the use of magnetism to determine the north and south, and by the 12th century AD Arab traders had conveyed the concept of the compass to Europe. Magnetite is now of interest chiefly as an ore of iron rather than for its magnetic properties. Most of the artificial magnets used in industry today are based on iron alloys called *ferrites*, with other elements added according to the intended application.

Although several minerals containing iron, nickel, or cobalt display some magnetic properties, none are as responsive to an external field as magnetite. Magnetism is basically caused at the atomic level by the presence of unpaired, and thus unstable electrons. In most elements, the momenta of the spins of paired electrons cancel one another out, making their atoms magnetically neutral; some of the transition and rare-earth elements, however, are not magnetically neutral in their stable configuration. This results from the presence of unpaired electrons in their inner orbitals, which allow each atom to develop a net magnetic charge. When such atoms occur together in a crystal, their charges may become aligned, and their effects combined—resulting in the property of *ferromagnetism*. The magnetism of lodestone is due to this sort of special atomic arrangement.

Particles of magnetite and other iron-rich minerals deposited in sediments or in cooling igneous rocks (such as fresh volcanic lavas) tend to align their magnetic poles parallel to the earth's magnetic field, so that the geometry of the field is recorded in the hardened rock. Since the earth's magnetic field changes its orientation at random intervals, scientists have learned how to tell when a rock was formed by studying the orientation of the magnetic minerals it contains. In addition, comparing the alignment of

magnetite

Classification:
oxide, spinel group

Composition:
Fe_3O_4 (iron oxide)

Crystal System:
isometric

Hardness:
5.5–6.5

Specific Gravity:
5.2

magnetite particles in a rock to the expected alignment for a particular region can indicate how much a rock has moved since being formed. Paleomagnetism, as this fascinating science is called, is very valuable in dating rocks and fossils, and in tracking the paths of the drifting continents.

Magnetite crystals are opaque and iron-black, with a metallic to dull luster and a black streak. The most common crystal form is the octahedron, followed by the dodecahedron; these are often modified by other isometric forms. Striations and twinning are common. Magnetite has good parting, but no cleavage, and an uneven to subconchoidal fracture. Chromite and black spinel are similar in appearance, but the former has a brown streak and the latter a white one. Franklinite also has a brown streak, and ilmenite is less magnetic and differs in crystal morphology.

Magnetite is a late-crystallizing component of many mafic igneous rocks, widespread as small grains in volcanic rocks such as basalts, and in larger concentrations as strata in layered igneous intrusions. In metamorphic rocks, magnetite is formed from the breakdown of iron sulfides and silicates. It is a relatively durable mineral, and survives the weathering of its host rocks to form black sands, sometimes in minable quantities. Magnetite occurs in smaller concentrations than hematite, but is the richer of the two primary iron ores. The largest magnetite deposit in the world may be the Kiruna District in northern Sweden, where it is mined to supply the vigor-

Left: *Naturally magnetized magnetite "lodestone" from Andover, New Jersey.*
Right: *Magnetite octahedra from the Binnenthal, Valais, Switzerland.*

ous Swedish steel industry. Other major deposits include the Bushveld complex of South Africa; the Ural Mountains of Russia; and locations in New York, Utah, and Wyoming. Beautiful crystals are found in many parts of the world, including the Austrian and Italian Alps.

MALACHITE IS A UBIQUITOUS SECONDARY CARBONATE MINERAL, FORMING IN NEARLY ALL copper-bearing sulfide deposits, sometimes in great quantity. It is most commonly seen in its massive, banded form, which is used to advantage as a decorative stone. Malachite was mined by the ancient Egyptians in the Sinai, and malachite from the Ural Mountains was equally popular in Imperial Russia, appearing in every imaginable form, from tabletops to sarcophagi. In medieval times, malachite was thought to protect newborns, and talismans of the stone were placed in cradles. The name is derived from the Greek word for "mallow," a herbaceous plant, in allusion to its leaf-green color.

Malachite crystals are very rare and small, usually occurring as short prisms in radiating sprays. Crystals composed of malachite are almost

Classification:
carbonate

Composition:
$Cu_2CO_3(OH)_2$ (hydrous copper carbonate)

Crystal System:
monoclinic

Hardness:
3.5–4

Specific Gravity:
4.05

always pseudomorphs after the closely related species azurite. The classic habit of this species is fibrous aggregates in botryoidal or stalactitic form. Crystals are brittle, with perfect cleavage in one direction and subconchoidal to uneven fracture; massive material is fairly tough. Malachite is opaque to translucent, and light to dark green in color, with a light-green streak. Its luster ranges from vitreous to adamantine in crystalline material, and is silky or dull and earthy in massive material. Massive material displays concentric banding. Malachite can be confused with brochantite, but the latter rarely forms botryoidal masses, and the former rarely forms crystals.

Reniform malachite on azurite from Pinal County, Arizona.

Malachite is commonly associated with azurite and other secondary copper minerals in the upper, oxidized zone of hydrothermal sulfide veins. The classic sources are the Goumshevsk and Mednorudyansk mines in the Ural mountains of Russia, where masses as large as 50 tons have been mined. The copper mines of Arizona—notably those in Bisbee, Cochise County; Morenci, Greenlee County; and Globe, Gila County—produce fine specimens of massive malachite, and pseudomorphs of malachite after azurite. Today, ornamental malachite is produced primarily in Africa, where important sources include Tsumeb, Namibia; Katanga Province, Zaire; and Bwana Mkubwa, Zambia.

manganite

Classification:
oxide

Composition:
MnO(OH) (hydrated manganese oxide)

Crystal System:
monoclinic

Hardness:
4

Specific Gravity:
4.3

MANGANITE IS AN IMPORTANT SOURCE OF MANGANESE, AN EXTREMELY HARD METAL similar to iron but not magnetic, and useful in alloys such as manganese steel. Manganite crystals usually take the form of small, striated prisms with flat or wedge-shaped terminations and sharp edges. These are often clustered together in bundles of parallel rods, and may form either contact or penetration twins. Massive material is commonly fibrous and compact, forming concretions, stalactites, and fissure fillings. Crystals are brittle, with uneven fracture and three pronounced cleavages. Manganite is opaque, steel-gray to black in color, and displays a submetallic luster and red-brown streak.

Crystalline manganite is formed in low-temperature hydrothermal deposits with braunite, hausmannite, barite, calcite, and siderite. Massive lumps and crusts are formed in superficial deposits such as bogs and shallow water environments, in association with pyrolusite and goethite. Compact masses of manganite are mined from sedimentary manganese deposits in many parts of the world, including Nikopol in the Soviet Ukraine, and India, Brazil, and South Africa, but good crystallized specimens are rare. The finest specimens known are the crystalline aggregates on quartz, with barite and calcite, from Ilfeld in the Harz Mountains of Germany. North American localities include Picton County, Nova Scotia; Negaunee, Michigan; and numerous deposits in the state of Virginia.

Classic radiating clusters of rod-like manganite crystals from Ilfeld, Harz Mountains, Germany.

LIKE PYRITE AND A FEW OTHER SULFIDES, MARCASITE PRODUCES A SPARK WHEN STRUCK against quartz. In ancient times, this property was much appreciated by nomadic peoples such as the Arab bedouin, who would pause in their travels to make coffee-fires at the drop of a burnoose. The name marcasite is thus derived from the Arabic word *markaschatsa*, meaning "firestone," a term applied in olden times to all species with incendiary properties. The faceted "marcasite" of Victorian jewelry is actually pyrite; marcasite is much too delicate and unstable to withstand wear in jewelry. Like pyrite, marcasite is a major source of sulfuric acid for industry.

Marcasite rarely appears in simple, flattened prismatic crystals; it is more frequently twinned in the form of spear-shaped fivelings and the fanlike aggregates of stubby, twinned crystals known as "cockscombs." Radiating , nodular or stalactitic massive aggregates are also common. Marcasite is pale yellow with a slightly greenish tinge, bright metallic luster, and greenish-black streak. This fragile species oxidizes rapidly, altering to *melanterite* ($FeSO_4 \cdot 7H_2O$) unless coated with some protective substance. It is easily distinguished from pyrite by its unusual crystalline habits.

Marcasite is much less common than its polymorph pyrite, both because it is restricted to low-temperature environments, and because it is so easily altered. Some of the best specimens are found in low-temperature hydrothermal veins, particularly the so-called Mississippi Valley-type replacement deposits in limestone, in association with zinc and lead sulfides. Excellent specimens are found in the Tri-State mining districts and other lead-zinc deposits throughout the Mississippi Valley, and in cavities in dolomite at Mineral Point, Wisconsin. Fine specimens also originate in the sulfide deposits of Germany, Czechoslovakia, Romania, Bolivia, and elsewhere. Marcasite also crystallizes in all kinds of sediments under oxygen-poor conditions, forming spear-shaped or disc-shaped aggregates (the latter called "suns"). Excellent aggregates are found in the brick-clay deposits at Red Bank, New Jersey, and in the chalk cliffs around the English Channel.

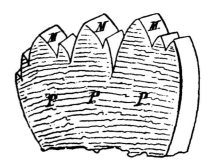

marcasite

Classification:
sulfide

Composition:
FeS_2 (iron sulfide)

Crystal System:
orthorhombic

Hardness:
6–6.5

Specific Gravity:
4.9

Spear-shaped twins of marcasite in chalk, from near Dover, Kent.

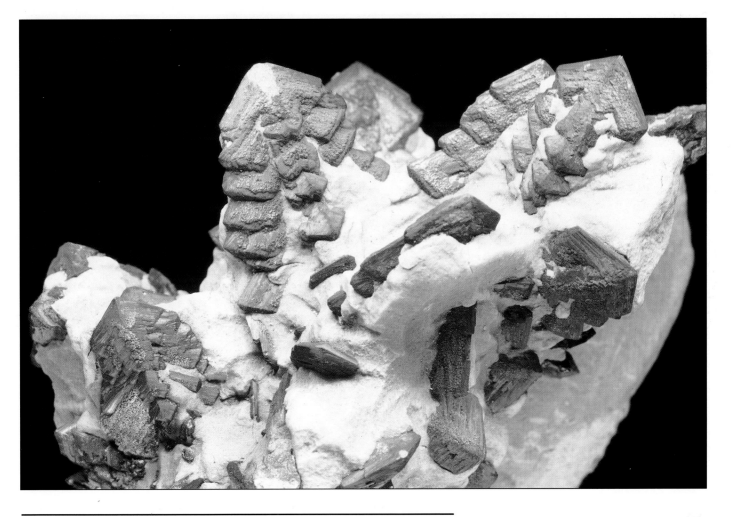

mesolite

Classification:
tectosilicate, zeolite group

Composition:
$Na_2Ca_2Al_6Si_9O_{30} \cdot 8H_2O$
(hydrous sodium, calcium, aluminum silicate)

Crystal System:
monoclinic

Hardness:
5

Specific Gravity:
2.25

THIS ZEOLITE TAKES ITS NAME FROM THE GREEK PHRASE MEANING "MIDDLE-STONE," since it was supposed to lie midway in composition and properties between natrolite and scolecite. Mesolite crystals are always twinned, and form very delicate acicular or fibrous divergent clusters, as well as compact masses. Cleavage is perfectly developed in two directions, and the fracture is uneven. Crystals are white or colorless, transparent to translucent, with a vitreous or silky luster and a colorless streak. Mesolite is distinguished from other zeolites by its fine, needlelike crystals, which are slightly coarser than those of natrolite.

Like all zeolites, mesolite forms in low-temperature hydrothermal environments such as basalt cavities, in association with datolite, prehnite, and other zeolites. Fine specimens are found in the basalts of the Columbia River Plateau in Oregon and Washington, the Bay of Fundy District, Nova Scotia, and in the traprock quarries of New Jersey. Other significant localities include Scotland, Ireland, Sicily, India, Australia, Greenland, and the Faeroes. Crystals 15 cm in length are found at Teigarhorn, Berufjord, Iceland.

Divergent, acicular tufts of mesolite from Neubauerberg, Czechoslovakia

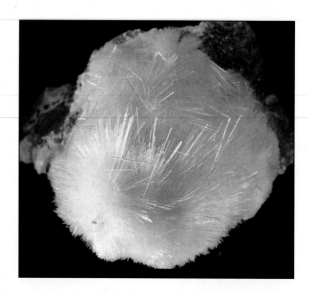

metamorphic rocks

Some Minerals in Regional Metamorphic Rocks

almandite	kyanite
anatase	muscovite
andalusite	plagioclase
biotite	pyrite
brookite	pyroxenes
chlorite	quartz
cordierite	rhodonite
corundum	rutile
epidote	sillimanite
graphite	staurolite
hornblende	talc

THE METAMORPHIC ROCKS ARE FORMED WHEN IGNEOUS, SEDIMENTARY, OR OTHER the metamorphic rocks are subjected to heat, pressure or deformation to the point that their original mineralogy and texture is altered (*metamorphosis* means "changed form" in Latin). Metamorphic rocks form under the broad range of conditions between the normal atmospheric pressures and temperature under which sedimentary rocks form, and the very high temperature conditions that give rise to igneous rocks. Unlike igneous rocks, however, which crystallize from magmas of variable composition, even those metamorphic rocks which recrystallized at extremely high temperatures generally retain their initial overall compostion. When significant amounts of new elements are introduced by hydrothermal fluids during metamorphism, the process is referred to as *metasomatism*. The metamorphic rocks are divided into the *regional* and *contact metamorphic* groups, based on the nature of the metamorphism.

Regional Metamorphism When areas of rock of hundreds or even thousands of square kilometers in extent are subjected to increased heat and pressure,

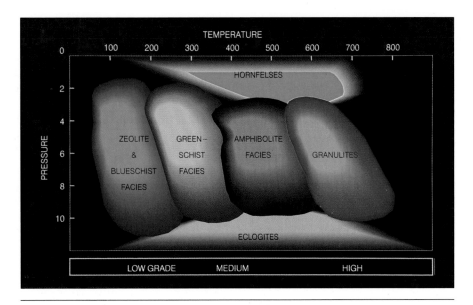

Diagram showing the general pressure and temperature conditions of the major metamorphic facies.

due to deep burial or tectonic pressures, regional metamorphism results. Most regional metamorphic rocks display a distinctive texture called *schistosity*, which results from the parallel alignment of platy minerals along planar surfaces. This texture is best exemplified by *slate*, which has such perfectly planar parting that it is suitable for use as roofing tile and blackboards. Slates are formed from the recrystallization of sedimentary shales at relatively low temperatures, and are thus so fine-grained that their individual crystals are indistinct. Perhaps the most abundant metamorphic rock are the *schists*, which form under a broad range of pressure–temperature conditions, and have a wide mineralogical range. Schists are typically named for their most abundant or conspicuous mineral component, e.g., mica schist, garnet schist, or staurolite schist. The *gneisses* are regional metamorphic rocks which have undergone a higher degree of metamorphism than the schists, and have recrystallized with a more equigranular texture. Gneisses usually display an indistinct foliation in the forms of parallel orientation of platy minerals or of compositional bands, composed of alternating layers of light and dark minerals.

Metamorphic Facies Regional metamorphic rocks can be classified on the basis of *metamorphic grade*, a subjective term which represents the relative intensity of the metamorphism. Slate, schist, and gneiss, for example, can be thought of as representing low, medium, and high grades of metamorphism, respectively. A more meaningful classification scheme is one based upon typical mineral assemblages (i.e., groups of minerals) called *facies*, which are understood to form under a particular set of physical conditions. The presence of a particular mineral assemblage indicates the metamorphic facies to which a rock belongs, and implies the conditions under which it formed. The assemblage albite, muscovite, the amphibole glaucophane, with or without jadeite is characteristic of the *blueschist facies*, for instance,

Some Minerals in Contact Metamorphic Rocks

actinolite	grossularite
andradite	hematite
anorthite	idocrase
apatite	ilmenite
aragonite	ilvaite
axinite	magnetite
biotite	phlogopite
brucite	quartz
calcite	rhodochrosite
chalcopyrite	rhodonite
chlorite	rutile
clinozoisite	spinel
corundum	tourmaline
diopside	titanite
dolomite	tremolite
epidote	wollastonite
fluorite	zircon
galena	zoisite
graphite	

which is known to form only in the very high-pressure and relatively low-temperature environments that exist where the earth's crustal plates are being subducted. A rock consisting of plagioclase, hypersthene, and garnet might belong to the *granulite facies*, and have undergone high-temperature metamorphism nearly to the melting point.

Contact Metamorphism Contact metamorphic rocks form concentric zones, or aureoles, around igneous intrusions. They form because the magma simply bakes the rock into which it intrudes. Although some contact metamorphic rocks display foliation, the vast majority have a granular texture. The contact metamorphism of shale, for instance, produces the equigranular and fine-grained rock *hornfels,* as opposed to the foliated regional metamorphic rock slate. Hydrothermal fluids from the intrusion, the country rock, or both are typically associated with contact metamorphism. These fluids are agents of *metasomatism,* introducing new chemical elements into the intruded rock. Metasomatic deposits formed where an magma has intruded carbonate rocks such as limestones or marbles are known as *skarn* deposits. Skarns are one of the few geological environments where there is an abundance of both silica and calcium, resulting in an interesting suites of calc-silicate minerals such as wollastonite and grossular garnet. Contact metasomatic skarns often form important orebodies, such as the zinc deposit at Franklin, New Jersey.

The *marbles* and *dolomites* are metamorphosed carbonate rocks composed primarily of calcite or dolomite, respectively, which can form through either regional or contact metamorphism. *Quartzite* is similarly

formed through either the regional or contact metamorphic alteration of relatively pure quartz sandstones.

Strongly folded schists in the Jacumba Mountains of Southern California, showing foliation and compositional zoning.

microcline

Classification:
tectosilicate, feldspar group

Composition:
$KAlSi_3O_8$ (potassium aluminum silicate)

Crystal System:
triclinic

Hardness:
6–6.5

Specific Gravity:
2.55–2.63

SOMETIMES DISPLAYING VIBRANT RED OR INTENSE BLUE-GREEN COLORATION, MICROCLINE is one of the more glamorous of the feldspars, a group not known for its dramatic specimens. The ancient Egyptians prized the blue-green variety *amazonite*, which compares favorably to turquoise in intensity of color. The potassium feldspars microcline and orthoclase (known as K-spar to the initiated) are polymorphs, with orthoclase crystallizing in the monoclinic system. The name microcline comes from the Greek phrase meaning "small inclination," in reference to the slight inclination of one crystallographic axis which gives this species triclinic symmetry. Despite this difference, the external morphology of both species is very similar, as are their physical properties. Microcline forms in relatively low-temperature igneous environments, while orthoclase is typical of higher-temperature rocks. An even higher temperature polymorph called sanidine occurs in some volcanic rocks.

Microcline is usually the dominant feldspar in pegmatites, sometimes forming crystals of enormous size—an entire feldspar quarry was operated within a single crystal in the Ural Mountains! Smaller crystals commonly grow freely into open cavities, which explains the abundance of euhedral specimens of this species. Microcline in pegmatites is not usually pure, but an intimate intergrowth with the plagioclase feldspar albite, as a composite called *perthite*. The two species initially crystallize as a single species at high temperatures, but as the magma begins to cool, the potassium and sodium feldspars draw apart (exsolve), and the plagioclase is confined into narrow strips called exsolution lamellae. In the final perthite crystal, these lamellae appear as parallel lines or an unmistakable fine plaid pattern. Another microcline hybrid with a distinctive texture is the rock type graphic granite, which is commonly associated with pegmatites. Graphic granite is a regular intergrowth of quartz and microcline, in which the quartz forms angular, cuneiform-like patterns in a feldspar matrix. These patterns arise from the concurrent growth of both phases, rather than from exsolution proper.

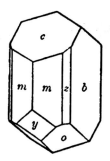

Microcline crystals are similar to those of orthoclase in habit, forming short prismatic to tabular blocky individuals. Twinning is very common, both polysynthetic and in several habits shared with orthoclase, including the Baveno, Carlsbad, and Manebach twin laws. Microcline has perfect cleavage in two directions, and four directions of parting, a feature which is distinctive even in massive material. White, gray, yellowish, flesh-red, and pink are the most common colors; the greenish or bluish-green variety amazonite is much more rare, and gains its coloration from trace amounts of lead. The luster is vit-

reous, or pearly on cleavages, and most crystals are translucent. Perthitic intergrowths are especially evident in red crystals and in amazonite, which show off the plaid-like pattern of white albite and are often capped with albite as well.

As noted, microcline is best represented in granitic pegmatites. It also occurs in other felsic igneous rocks, and in metamorphic rocks, though less abundantly than orthoclase. Good specimens can be obtained from virtually any of the world's many pegmatite districts, including those in Japan, Brazil, Madagascar, Norway, Sweden, Germany, Italy, Afghanistan, the Ural and Ilmen Mountains of the Soviet Union, and many parts of Africa. In North America, fine specimens come from the pegmatites of New England, the southern Appalachians, the Black Hills of South Dakota, and San Diego County and northern Baja California.

Amazonite is the most sought-after form of microcline, both for gemstones and mineral specimens, and its occurrence is much more restricted than that of microcline. The finest crystals are found in Colorado in the many small pegmatites cutting the Pikes Peak granite; particularly notable are the pegmatites of Crystal Peak, near Lake George in Teller County. The deeply colored amazonite crystals from Colorado are often capped by albite, and associated with very dark crystals of smoky quartz. Amazonite is also obtained from the pegmatites near Amelia Court House, Virginia; Renfrew County, Ontario; and various mines in Minas Gerais, Brazil.

Microcline, variety amazonite, from Pike's Peak, Colorado.

Octahedral crystals of pyrochlore in calcite from the Oka carbonatite, Deux-Montagnes County, Quebec.

microlite and pyrochlore

Classification:
oxides

Composition:
microlite: $(Na,Ca)_2Ta_2O_6(O,OH,F)$
pyrochlore:
$(Na,Ca,U)_2(Nb,Ta,Ti)_2O_6(OH,F)$
(hydrous sodium, calcium, tantalum, niobium oxides)

Crystal System:
isometric

Hardness:
5–5.5

Specific Gravity:
4.3–6.4

MICROLITE AND PYROCHLORE ARE THE TWO MOST COMMON MEMBERS OF A GROUP OF at least twenty distinct species (including betafite), known as the pyrochlore group. The minerals of this group are one of the main repositories of trace elements in pegmatite bodies; other members include ions of Ba, Bi, Ce, Cs, Pb, Sn, Y, and Zr, among others. These two minerals are the end members of a solid-solution series, but tend to be restricted to different geological environments: microlite occurs in granite pegmatites, while pyrochlore is usually found in carbonatites and nepheline-syenite pegmatites.

Microlite and pyrochlore form highly modified octahedral crystals, typically metamict due to the partial substitution of thorium and uranium. They usually occur in the form of disseminated subhedral grains, however. The color ranges from colorless to yellow, brown or reddish; microlite is sometimes emerald green. The streak is yellow to brown, and the luster vitreous to resinous.

Microlite is a primary mineral in granitic pegmatites, found in association with lepidolite, spodumene, and columbite-tantalite. Large, sharp crystals to 2 cm are obtained from Amelia Court House, Virginia; more modest specimens occur in the pegmatite districts of New England, New Mexico, Colorado, and the Black Hills of South Dakota. Excellent specimens occur in the Virgem da Lapa region, Minas Gerais, Brazil; Iveland, Norway; Verutrask, Sweden; Wodinga, Australia; and the Malagasy Republic. Fine crystals of pyrochlore are found at St. Peter's Dome and the Powderhorn District, Colorado; Hybla, Ontario; Oka, Quebec; Frederiksvarn, Norway; Laacher See and Kaiserstuhl, Germany; and in the carbonatites of several countries in Central and East Africa, particularly Mbeya, Tanzania.

Divergent sprays of acicular millerite crystals, from Antwerp, New York.

MILLERITE IS NAMED AFTER THE ENGLISH MINERALOGIST W. H. MILLER (B. 1801). Although sometimes found in abundance with other nickel minerals, it is not considered an important ore species. Crystals of millerite are greatly elongated and acicular, terminated by a rhombohedron, and typically form radiating sprays and matted aggregates. Crystals are brittle but elastic, with perfect cleavage. They are opaque and metallic yellow when freshly unearthed, but tarnish rapidly to a dingy green; the streak is greenish black.

Millerite is found in low-temperature hydrothermal environments, including limestones, serpentines, and carbonate replacement deposits, or as a secondary mineral in magmatic nickel deposits with pentlandite and niccolite. Fine specimens are found in geodes and in limestone cavities at various places in the Mississippi River Valley, and in the mercury mines of California. Unusually large crystalline masses are found at Timagami, Ontario; and at the Marbridge Mine in Quebec. Excellent specimens are obtained from Glamorgan, Wales; Siegen, Westphalia, Germany; Kladno-Rodna, and Joachimstal, Czechoslovakia; Kambalda, Australia; and in Finland, Bulgaria, and Namibia.

millerite

Classification:
sulfide

Composition:
NiS (nickel sulfide)

Crystal System:
hexagonal (rhombohedral)

Hardness:
3–3.5

Specific Gravity:
5.41–5.42

Divergent clusters of tapering, pseudohexagonal mimetite prisms, from Tsumeb, Grootfontein, Namibia.

mimetite

Classification:
arsenate

Composition:
$Pb_5(AsO_4)_3Cl$ (lead chloroarsenate)

Crystal System:
monoclinic (pseudohexagonal)

Hardness:
3.5–4

Specific Gravity:
7.28

MIMETITE IS THE ARSENATE END MEMBER OF A SOLID-SOLUTION SERIES, OF WHICH THE more common lead phosphate pyromorphite, $Pb_5(PO_4)_3Cl$, is the phosphatic end member. Both minerals are known for their well-developed and colorful crystals, but the two species are rarely well-represented in the same deposit. Mimetite is an incidental source of lead, and, because of its resemblance to pyromorphite, takes its name from the Greek word *mimetes*, meaning "imitator."

Mimetite crystals are usually acicular, and often take the form of pseudohexagonal prisms; most material is massive, as botryoidal, reniform, or incrusting aggregates. Crystals are brittle, with a subconchoidal to uneven fracture and no cleavage. Mimetite is usually transparent to translucent, and some shade of yellow, orange, or brown, with an adamantine to resinous luster and a white streak. The best means of distinguishing between the very similar species mimetite, pyromorphite, and vanadinite is on the basis of their very distinctive colors; in the case of ambiguous coloration, chemical tests are needed.

Mimetite is a secondary mineral formed in the oxidized portion of hydrothermal lead sulfide deposits, in association with anglesite, cerrusite, barite, galena, hemimorphite, wulfenite, mottramite, smithsonite, and vanadinite. The finest North American occurrences are in Mexico, at Santa Eulalia, Chihuahua; Mapimí, Durango; near Magdalena, Sonora; and at the Bilbao Mine, Ojo Caliente, Zacatecas. Among the numerous occurrences in the United States are the mines of Phoenixville, Pennsylvania, and the Banner District, Arizona. European localities include the Cornwall and Cumberland districts of England; Leadhills and Wanlockhead, Scotland; and mines in Sweden, France, and Germany. Excellent specimens have come from Tsumeb, Namibia; Broken Hill, New South Wales, Australia; and Algeria.

THE NAME OF THIS MINERAL IS DERIVED FROM THE GREEK WORD FOR "LEAD," *MOLYB-dos*. Molybdenite is the most important ore of molybdenum, which, in fact, is not at all like lead. Molybdenum has a very high melting point, and is used to make extremely durable and heat-resistant steels for high-speed tools, automobile parts, aerospace and other applications. Because of its resistance to heat and other forms of radiation, molybdenum metal is used in such appliances as electric furnaces and X-ray machines.

Rough, tabular, hexagonal crystals and barrel-shaped prisms are fairly common. The perfect basal cleavage of molybdenite results from its structure of interlayered sheets of Mo and S atoms; crystals are very delicate, sectile and flexible. Molybdenite also appears as foliated or granular masses and disseminated grains. Crystals are opaque, silver-gray in color, with a metallic luster and a greenish gray streak. The softness of molybdenite gives it a greasy feel, like graphite; but the latter has a black streak and much less dense.

The bulk of commercial molybdenite is disseminated in large porphyry-type deposits, but significant amounts also occur in quartz veins associated with greisenization (see *Cassiterite*), along with cassiterite and wolframite. Smaller quantities are found in contact metamorphic rocks, in granites and pegmatites, and in some carbonatites. At the vast porphyritic molybdenum deposit at Climax, Colorado, small grains of molybdenite are removed from the crushed rock via flotation. Molybdenite is found with beryl at the Urad Mine, Clear Creek County, Colorado; with quartz in Okanogan and Chelan Counties, Washington; and with scheelite, at Pine Creek, Inyo County, California. Euhedral crystals to 8 cm in diameter occur in contact deposits at Aldfield, Quebec; good crystals also come from La Trinidad, Sonora, and Guanajuato, Mexico. Commercial deposits are exploited in most industrial countries, including England, Germany, Norway, Sweden, Australia, China, Japan, and Korea.

molybdenite

Classification:
sulfide

Composition:
MoS_2 (molybdenum sulfide)

Crystal System:
hexagonal

Hardness:
1–1.5

Specific Gravity:
4.62–5.06

Left: Lustrous foliated plates of molybdenite, from Kingsgate, New South Wales, Australia. Compare with graphite. *Right:* A worker at the Xihuashan Tungsten Mine in China carries a load of molybdenite crystals, washed from the weathered rock that overlies the underground workings.

monazite

Classification:
phosphate

Composition:
(Ce,La,Y,Th)PO₄ (rare-earth phosphate)

Crystal System:
monoclinic

Hardness:
5–5.5

Specific Gravity:
4.6–5.4

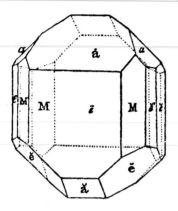

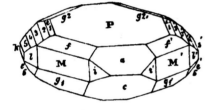

Massive monazite from Amelia Court House, Virginia.

THE NAME OF THIS RARE-EARTH PHOSPHATE MINERAL COMES FROM THE GREEK WORD *monazein*, meaning "to be alone," a reference to its habit of forming single isolated crystals as an accessory in igneous rocks. But like the great Garbo, monazite is not left alone—it is assiduously sought all over the world. It is the main source of the rare-earths cerium and lanthanum, and of thorium (up to 12% ThO₂), which can be used as a source of radiation. Because of the radioactivity of thorium, many monazite crystals are metamict, but most are sufficiently durable to survive stream transport and collect in placer deposits. The radioactivity of monazite makes it useful for determining, through radiometric dating techniques, the age of the rock in which it occurs (see *Radioactivity*). SiO₄ often substitutes for phosphorous in varying amounts.

Monazite is usually seen as crude grains or small, euhedral crystals, short prismatic to tabular, with wedge-shaped terminations. These may be twinned, or form subparallel aggregates. Crystal faces are often slightly curved, and commonly striated or etched. Good cleavage and uneven fracture is evident in those specimens where the crystal structure has not been damaged by radioactivity; metamict crystals tend to display good conchoidal fracture. Monazite is transparent to translucent, and yellow, brown, brownish red, greenish, pink, or nearly white in color, with a resinous, vitreous, or even subadamantine luster; the luster apparently increases with the degree of radioactivity .

Despite being a rare-earth mineral, monazite is a fairly common accessory in granites, syenites, gneisses, and vein deposits of various kinds. Euhedral crystals occur primarily in granitic pegmatites, in association with apatite, columbite, zircon, xenotime, fergusonite, samarskite and other species in feldspar matrix. Due to its high specific gravity, monazite is concentrated in large amounts in river and beach placer deposits with rutile and other heavy minerals. Extensive deposits of monazite sands are mined in Australia, Malaysia, Brazil, Sri Lanka, India, Nigeria, as well as along the southern Atlantic coast of the United States. Large crystals are found in the pegmatites of at Encampment, Wyoming; in the Petaca District of New Mexico, at Amelia Court House, Virginia; and Alexander County, North Carolina; and commercial quantities are produced from the Climax molybdenum deposit in Colorado. Excellent twinned crystals come from the tin mines at Callipampa, Bolivia. Good specimens are obtained from vein deposits throughout the Alps, and from pegmatites in Madagascar, Norway, and Finland.

PEGMATITES IN THE URAL MOUNTAINS ONCE SUPPLIED EUROPE WITH THIS MICA, which takes its name from *Muscovy*, an old name for the Moscow region of Russia. For centuries, large, translucent sheets of Muscovy glass were used for windows, until a method was found for making broad panes of glass. Mica continues to be used for windows in wood stoves, furnaces, and other places where glass would fracture or melt. Along with the other micas, muscovite finds its most important modern application in electrical and heat insulation. Muscovite is also used as a lubricant, and as an additive in the manufacture of porcelain, paper, paint, and rubber. Flexible, transparent sheets of muscovite captivated the imaginations of preindustrial peoples as well, and many cultures cut effigies and ornaments from mica traded over great distances.

Muscovite has several varieties. *Mariposite*, named for California's Mariposa County, is a blue-green chromium-rich variety which is often intimately associated with gold in the Mother Lode region; *fuchsite* is another chromian variety. *Sericite* is a fine-grained variety typically seen replacing aluminosilicate minerals as a pseudomorph. Rubidium-rich muscovite and the manganese variety *alurgite* are characterized by their red or pink colors.

Muscovite typically forms tabular crystals with pseudohexagonal or diamond-shaped outline, commonly intergrown as lamellar masses or radiating in plumose or stellate aggregates. Crystals are characterized by their perfect basal cleavage, which renders thin, flexible, elastic sheets. The characteristic coloration is silvery-white, greenish white, or yellow, but bright-green or deep-red variants are sometimes seen. Muscovite has a vitreous to pearly luster and a white streak.

Muscovite is one of the primary rock-forming minerals, comprising a large part of silica- and aluminum-rich plutonic rocks like granites and granitic pegmatites. Muscovite, along with the dark-colored mica biotite, is also a major component of the mica schists, widespread rocks derived from the regional metamorphism of aluminium and silica-rich sedimentary rocks. Remarkable specimens and economic concentrations are largely limited to the granitic pegmatites, however. Enormous crystals have been found in pegmatites in Africa, Brazil, Canada, Scandinavia, and the Soviet Union; a single crystal weighing 85 tons (76 metric tons) was extracted from a mine in Nelore, India. In the United States, muscovite is mined in New England, the Appalachian states, and throughout the West, particularly in the Black Hills of South Dakota. Fine specimens are found at many Alpine localities in Austria, Italy, and Switzerland.

muscovite

Classification:
phyllosilicate, mica group

Composition:
$KAl_2(AlSi_3O_{10})(OH,F)_2$
(hydrous potassium aluminum silicate)

Crystal System:
monoclinic

Hardness:
2.25 across cleavage;
4 parallel to cleavage

Specific Gravity:
2.77–2.88

Books of muscovite from the Indus Gorge near Chokpoing, in the Karakoram Range, India.

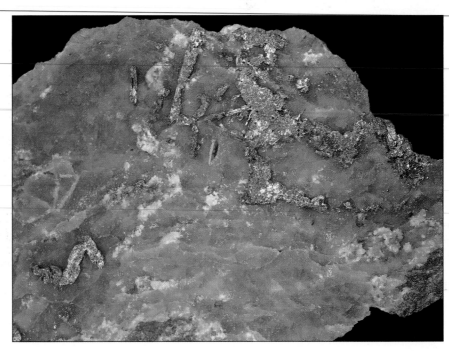

Left: Specimens of the semimetal tellurium, such as this one from the Graphic Mine, Boulder County, Colorado, are extremely rare. ***Right:*** Lead is extremely rare in its native form, occurring in abundance only at Langban, Sweden.

native elements

THIS MINERAL CLASS CONSISTS OF THE CHEMICAL ELEMENTS WHICH OCCUR IN NATURE in an uncombined state, and is divided into the *metals*, the *semimetals*, and the *nonmetals*. Although over twenty elements are found in their native state, only gold (Au), silver (Ag), copper (Cu), diamond (C), graphite (C), and sulfur (S) are commonly encountered. The rarity of uncombined chemical elements in nature reflects the fact that most elements readily combine with others to form compounds, i.e., the minerals of the other chemical classes.

The metals are heavy, soft, malleable, sectile, and metallic in luster when unaltered. They are prized for their rarity and for their excellent ability to conduct electricity. The characteristic malleability of gold (Au) and platinum (Pt) allows these metals to survive stream transport virtually intact after the erosion of their host rocks; this is why they are found in rounded lumps in the sedimentary deposits known as placers. The semimetals are heavy, soft, and metallic in appearance like the true metals, but their brittleness and generally good cleavage make them nonmalleable. Examples of this group are arsenic (As), antimony (Sb), bismuth (Bi), selenium (Se), and tellurium (Te). The nonmetals include the polymorphs of carbon (C)—diamond and graphite—and sulfur (S), the most common element found in an uncombined state.

Acicular crystals of natrolite from Neubauerberg, Bohemia, Czechoslovakia.

natrolite

Classification:
tectosilicate, zeolite group

Composition:
$Na_2Al_2Si_3O_{10} \cdot 2H_2O$
(hydrated sodium aluminum silicate)

Crystal System:
orthorhombic

Hardness:
5–5.5

Specific Gravity:
2.2

ALONG WITH SCOLECITE, MESOLITE, AND THOMPSONITE, NATROLITE IS ONE OF THE zeolite minerals which typically occur as tufts or sprays of acicular crystals, and are commonly confused with one another. The name is derived from the Greek *natron*, or "soda," in allusion to its sodium content. Although it sometimes occurs as discrete, slender, prismatic crystals with vertical striations, the typical habit is as divergent or globular aggregates of fibrous needles, or simply as loose felted masses. Crystals are colorless, white, pink, or yellowish, transparent with vitreous to pearly luster and a white streak. Some specimens fluoresce orange in ultraviolet light.

Natrolite is typically found lining cavities in basalts and other lavas, in association with calcite and other zeolites. It may also form as an alteration product of plagioclase feldspar in mafic igneous rocks. Veins of natrolite sometimes form in serpentinites, associated with chrysotile asbestos, as in San Benito County, California. Crystals as long as 1 m are found in the serpentinites of Asbestos, Quebec; very fine crystals come from nearby Mont St. Hilare and from the basalts of Nova Scotia and Ice Valley, British Columbia. Good specimens are also obtained from the basalts of the Columbia Plateau region in Oregon and Washington; northern New Jersey; Livingston, Montana; and Table Mountain, Colorado. Fine specimens of natrolite have also been found in the basalt fields of Ireland, Scotland, Germany, France, Greenland, Iceland, the Faeroe Islands, and many other places.

nepheline

Classification:
tectosilicate, feldspathoid group

Composition:
$(Na,K)AlSiO_4$
(sodium potassium aluminum silicate)

Crystal System:
hexagonal

Hardness:
5.5–6

Specific Gravity:
2.55–2.66

Blocky nepheline crystal in calcite, from Natural Bridge, New York.

NEPHELINE IS THE MOST ABUNDANT OF THE FELDSPATHOIDS, AND A MAJOR CONstituent of sodium-rich, silica-poor igneous rocks such as nepheline syenite. Nepheline forms from magmas in which the proportion of the alkaline elements (K, Na) to silica is too great to permit the crystallization of feldspars. Like the feldspars, nepheline is a workaday mineral, useful and geologically important but not known for dramatic specimens. Its industrial uses, in the manufacture of ceramics and glass, are similar to those of the feldspars. The Soviet Union, lacking access to large deposits of aluminum hydroxides, has used nepheline as an ore of aluminum. The name comes from the Greek *nephele*, "to cloud," because it becomes surrounded by a cloud of silica gel when placed in a bath of hydrochloric acid.

Crystals of nepheline are rare, forming simple hexagonal prisms with rough faces and pinacoidal terminations; nepheline is usually seen as granular aggregates or anhedral grains. The crystals are brittle, with two indistinct cleavages and subconchoidal fracture. Nepheline is transparent to opaque, with a vitreous to greasy luster, and displays a wide variety of colors, including white, yellow, gray, greenish, dark-green, brown, and red (the variety eleolite).

Nepheline is found in both intrusive and extrusive silica-poor igneous rocks, such as syenites, and in some schists and gneiss. Large masses are found in association with a number of interesting and valuable minerals in nepheline-syenite pegmatites. The largest body of nepheline-bearing rocks covers more than 600 square miles on the Kola Peninsula, in the far northwestern corner of the Soviet Union; other large formations occur in the Ural Mountains, Norway, Greenland, Burma, Korea, New Zealand, Cameroon, Zaire, Kenya, and South Africa. The only commercially viable deposit in North America is at Blue Mountain, Ontario, Canada, although other deposits are found in Montana, South Dakota, New England, and numerous other locations throughout the United States.

neptunite

Classification:
inosilicate

Composition:
$KNa_2Li(Fe^{+2},Mn)_2Ti_2O_2(Si_4O_{11})_2$
(potassium sodium lithium iron titanium silicate)

Crystal System:
monoclinic

Hardness:
5–6

Specific Gravity:
3.19–3.23

NEPTUNITE IS A RARE COMPLEX SILICATE, WHICH IS WELL-KNOWN FROM ITS ASSOCIATION with the even more rare and complex silicate benitoite in San Benito County, California. Because it was discovered in association with aegirine, named for the Norse god of the sea, neptunite was in turn named for the Roman sea god, Neptune.

Neptunite forms elongated, prismatic crystals, usually under 2 cm in length, square in cross section, with pointed terminations. It has perfect prismatic cleavage and conchoidal fracture. The color is black, with deep red-brown internal reflections. Neptunite is nearly opaque, with a very strong vitreous luster and a dark-red streak.

The finest neptunite crystals, some as long as 6 cm, have been found at the Dallas Gem Mine, San Benito County, California, in association with benitoite and natrolite in altered serpentine rocks. Other serpentine-hosted occurrences include Wood's Reef, New South Wales, Australia; and Mont St. Hilare, Quebec. Neptunite is found in the Soviet Union in nepheline syenites in the Kola Peninsula, and as fine specimens with many other rare species at Julianehåb, Greenland. Another notable locality is Point-of-Rocks, New Mexico.

Opposite page: Black neptunite crystals nestled in white natrolite from the Dallas Gem Mine, San Benito County, California.

niccolite (nickeline)

Classification:
arsenide

Composition:
NiAs (nickel arsenide)

Crystal System:
hexagonal

Hardness:
5–5.5

Specific Gravity:
7.78.

WHEN THE MINERS OF MEDIEVAL GERMANY ENCOUNTERED THIS COPPERY-RED metallic mineral in their mines, they expected to smelt some copper from it. After discovering that this was impossible, they called the mineral *kupfer nickel*, or "bewitched copper." The term nickel comes from the *nixes*, underground goblins that, like the *cobolds* (see *Cobaltite*) had their fun at the expense of the miners. Now that nickel is appreciated in its own right, niccolite is sought as an ore of this important metal, which is used in a variety of metallurgical, chemical, and decorative applications (see *Pentlandite*).

Crystals of niccolite are very rare and small, usually tabular or pyramidal, sometimes appear as fourling twins. Most material is massive, mixed with other nickel, silver, and cobalt minerals, or forms as reniform aggregates. The color is coppery-red, tarnishing to gray, with a metallic luster and a brownish-black streak. Niccolite lacks cleavage and is quite brittle, with an uneven fracture. This mineral commonly contains small amounts of iron, cobalt, and sulfur and, due to its arsenic content, and gives off a garlic odor when heated

Niccolite is found in hydrothermal sulfide veins, and in certain mafic igneous rocks with other nickel sulfides and arsenides, pyrrhotite, and chalcopyrite. This fairly rare species is found at a few locations in California and Colorado, and at the Franklin mines in Sussex County, New Jersey. The largest deposits are found in the Cobalt, Gowganda, Sudbury, and Thunder Bay districts of Ontario. Niccolite has also been found at several places in Germany, England, France, Austria, Czechoslovakia, Iran, the Soviet Union, South Australia, Morocco, Japan, and Mexico.

Massive niccolite from Talmessi, Anarak, Iran.

NICKEL-IRON IS THE MAIN CONSTITUENT OF THE SO-CALLED IRON METEORITES, FOUND on the earth as the debris from extraterrestrial impacts. The term nickel-iron includes the dark-colored low nickel (approximately 5.5% Ni) alloy *kamacite*, and the lighter, more nickel-rich (27%–65% Ni) alloy *taenite*. These two alloys crystallize as intergrowths parallel to octahedral crystallographic faces, forming a distinctive pattern which is evident on polished and etched meteorites. This distinctive texture is called the Widmanstätten pattern, after the Austrian mineralogist who discovered it. The iron meteorites probably formed as the core of planetary bodies that were subsequently fragmented by collisions with each other. In this respect they are probably analogous to the core of the earth, which is also essentially iron and formed as the early earth differentiated. (The earth's core, however, also must contain an unknown light element to satisfy the bulk properties of the earth.)

Nickel-iron would be a wonderful source of ore, but is far too rare. For centuries, the Inuit of Greenland made regular trips across the windswept ice to large meteorites they knew of, pounding off pieces for use as spear points and knives. Around the turn of the century the Inuit showed these meteorites to arctic explorers, who removed them to various museum collections where they can be seen today. Although iron is now produced in great quantities from hematite and goethite ores, the iron used by the first blacksmiths approximately 1600 years ago was obtained from meteorites. This is apparent from the high nickel content of early iron artifacts, and from the fact that many early chronicles refer to iron as a gift from the heavens.

Meteorites were apparently regarded as supernatural objects by many cultures. The Casa Grande meteorite was found carefully wrapped inside a temple in Mexico, and the most nickel-rich meteorite ever found (62% Ni) was exhumed from a Native American burial mound in Oktibbeha County, Mississippi. Indeed, it is thought that the Black Rock of Mecca—part of the jealously guarded Kaaba complex in Mecca, Saudi Arabia, and holy to all Islamic people— is a meteorite.

nickel-iron

Classification:
native elements
Composition:
(Fe,Ni) (iron and nickel)
Crystal System:
isometric
Hardness:
4–5
Specific Gravity:
7.88–8.22
(increases with the percentage of nickel)

Nickel-iron meteorite from Meteorite Crater, in Australia's Northern Territory. The polished surface displays the Widmanstätten pattern, while the rough surface shows the pitting acquired as the meteorite passed through the earth's upper atmosphere.

Nickel-iron occurs as rough pitted lumps, with a rusty exterior; only when cut and polished is its remarkable internal structure and metallic luster evident. Iron meteorites are strongly magnetic, very heavy, and malleable. Even more so than gold, meteorites are where you find them; since they fall from the sky, there is no geological control over their distribution. They may be concentrated on the earth's surface by the action of wind and water, however. Iron meteorites are found regularly in the stream gravels of Jackson and Josephine counties, Oregon; and in relative abundance on ancient expanses of windswept ice in Antarctica.

olivenite

Classification:
arsenate

Composition:
$Cu_2(AsO_4)(OH)$
(copper hydroxyl arsenate)

Crystal System:
monoclinic

Hardness:
3

Specific Gravity:
3.9–4.46

OLIVENITE FORMS A SOLID-SOLUTION SERIES WITH THE ZINC ARSENATE ADAMITE, AND A partial series with libethenite when phosphorous substitutes for arsenic. The name is derived from the descriptive German mining term *olivenerz*, or "olive" ore. Olivenite forms short prismatic or tabular crystals, diamond-shaped in cross section, or acicular, drusy clusters. Aggregates are fibrous and radiate in structure, forming globular or reniform masses; also earthy. Crystals are brittle, with conchoidal to irregular fracture. Most specimens are some shade of olive-green or greenish brown, but may also be yellow, gray, or white. Crystals are translucent to opaque, with a vitreous to adamantine luster and a colorless streak. Olivenite strongly resembles libethenite, and less so the iron phosphate ludlamite, which is brighter green.

Olivenite is a common secondary mineral in oxidized portions of hydrothermal sulfide veins, where it is typically associated with adamite, malachite, azurite, dioptase, goethite, and scorodite. Acicular druses occur in a number of mines in Coconino, Gila, and (especially) Pinal Counties, Arizona; in the Blackbird District, Idaho; and the Tintic District, Utah. Isolated euhedral crystals on rhyolite matrix are seen from the Myler Mine, Majuba Hill, Pershing County, Nevada; and excellent crystals to 2.5 cm are found at Tsumeb, Namibia. Superior specimens also come from, Gwinnear, Cornwall, England; Cap Garonne, France; and other localities in Chile, Germany, and Greece.

Cavity-filling druse of acicular olivenite crystals from Wheal Gorland, St. Day, Cornwall.

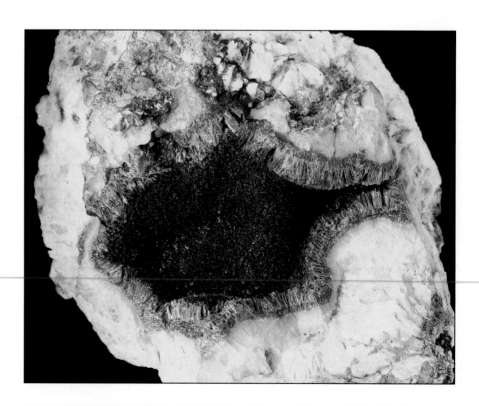

OLIVINE IS THE GENERAL NAME FOR THE SOLID-SOLUTION SERIES BETWEEN THE MAGNEsium-rich end member forsterite (named for the German naturalist Johann Forster), and the less common, iron-rich species fayalite (for the island of Fayal in the Azores, on which it occurs). The name olivine reflects the greenish hue of most specimens, although white, various shades of brown, and black are known. Peridot (possibly from the Arabic word for gem, *faridat*) is the name given to the most familiar form of olivine—the bright apple-green variety of forsterite from which gems are fashioned.

Peridot was also known to the ancients as *chrysolithos* (golden stone), and the modern derivative *chrysolite* has been in use until recently, despite its having been applied more appropriately to a variety of other gems. Perhaps because of its warm color, people have long associated peridot with the sun, and believed it capable of dispelling evil spirits and other nocturnal terrors.

Olivine crystals are usually thick and tabular, with vertical striations and wedge-shaped terminations. Disseminated grains and massive, granular aggregates are common; indeed, some types of peridotite are composed almost entirely of olivine. Crystals are brittle, with conchoidal fracture and cleavage in two directions. The olivines are distinguished by their distinctive color, strong vitreous to oily luster, and birefringence. Epidote is generally darker in color, and diopside lighter.

As the major constituent of peridotite, the rock type of which the earth's mantle is composed, olivine (and its high-pressure polymorphs) is appar-

---

Peridotite mantle xenolith, composed primarily of granular olivine and encased in basaltic scoria, from Mt. Franklin, Victoria, Australia.

olivine

Classification:
nesosilicate

Composition:
$(Mg,Fe)_2 SiO_4$ (magnesium iron silicate)

Crystal System:
orthorhombic

Hardness:
6.5–7

Specific Gravity:
3.27–4.32

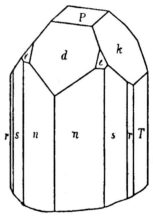

ently the earth's most abundant mineral by volume. On the surface, however, it is relatively inconspicuous. Although an important component of both continental and sea-floor silica-poor rocks (such as some basalts and gabbros), olivine weathers very rapidly to form the mineral serpentine. Serpentinized rocks include the kimberlites, in which diamonds are found, and the peridotites, gabbros, and basalts of ophiolite complexes, which contain deposits of chromite and other minerals. At Snarum, Norway, large pseudomorphs of serpentine after olivine are found which faithfully preserve the form of the original crystals.

Most gem-quality olivine (peridot) is taken from the small, basaltic volcanos and lava flows which convey fragments of peridotite from the deep mantle to the earth's surface. These cobblestone-size aggregates of bright-green, glassy olivine crystals and other mantle minerals, encased in dark basalt, are among our most important sources of information about the earth's interior. The Apache Indians of the San Carlos Reservation in Arizona mine peridot from deposits such as this.

Crystals of forsterite also form in marble in some contact metamorphic deposits, as at Crestmore, California, and Bolton, Massachusetts. The very large rounded crystals found in the gem gravels of Mogok, Burma, are thought to have been weathered from similar metamorphic rocks.

For over three thousand years peridot has been mined on barren and windswept St. John's Island in the Red Sea, which is also known by the gem's Arabic name, *Zebirgit*. Olivine occurs here in large, well-formed, light greenish yellow crystals in serpentinized peridotite, which has emerged from the actively rifting Red Sea floor. Since euhedral crystals of olivine are extremely rare, peridot from Zebirgit is usually more valuable in its natural form than cut into gems. In classical times, the island was known as Topazion, and peridot as *topazos* (topaz), a name currently applied to an entirely different mineral.

opal

Classification:
tectosilicate

Composition:
$SiO_2 \cdot n\,H_2O$ (silicon dioxide with variable amounts of water, usually 5%–9%, rarely as high as 20%)

Crystal System:
none, amorphous

Hardness:
5.5–6.5

Specific Gravity:
1.98–2.25, increases with water content

OPAL IS A WHIMSICAL STONE. THE PRECIOUS VARIETIES DELIGHT US WITH THEIR FLASHING display of spectral colors, and even the more common types are intriguing. A soft and brittle mineral, prone to dehydration and cracking because of its high water content, opal is a poor candidate for the pantheon of precious gems. Such shortcomings, however, are offset by its many unique properties, both real and imagined. Known during the middle ages as *opthalmus lapis*, opal has long been associated with the eyes in the popular imagination. The gem was thought to protect and improve the wearer's vision (especially at night), and to obscure that of unwanted observers: thus the traditional appellation "patron of thieves." Equally effective against supernatural scrutiny, opals were believed to render impotent the ubiquitous Evil Eye. The name comes to us from the Latin *opalus*, derived from either the ancient Sanskrit *upala* ("precious stone") or a common root.

Until recently, science was at a loss to explain the structure of opal: it is one of the few amorphous "mineraloids," which never occur in crystalline form. Studies using the electron microscope have finally revealed that opal is a sort of mineral gel, composed of hydrated silica spherules, instead of the ordered molecules that form symmetrical crystals. Opalescence, the play of colors characteristic of precious opal, results from randomly distributed rafts of these tiny spherules, each of which reflects a particular wavelength of light as the stone is turned. Opal is opaque to transparent, with a strong vitreous to waxy luster and a white streak. Some specimens fluoresce greenish or yellowish under fluorescent light.

Although some precious opals are clear, most contain fine-grained impurities which lend a white, black, or red background. White opals were the first to appear in Europe, and remain the most familiar variety; although the ancient mines in Czechoslovakia are exhausted, white opal often occurs where other types are found. Opals were discovered at a number of loca-

A seam of precious opal from the Baracoo River, Queensland, Australia, with a polished opal cabochon.

tions in Australia near the turn of the century, including Coober Pedy (from the Aborigine phrase *kupa pita,* or "white man in a hole"), where the miners both work and *live* underground to escape the blistering Outback sun. Rarest of all are the black opals, which are mined at Lightening Ridge in New South Wales and in the Virgin Valley of Nevada. The vast volcanic fields of Mexico produce fire opal, a red translucent variety which sometimes displays flashes of color.

Although a simple mineral containing only silicon, oxygen, and water, opal assumes many shapes through an amazing variety of natural processes. Precious and some common opal are deposited from silica-bearing waters in underground and cavities, or through the gradual impregnation of porous materials. The molds of trees buried by volcanic ash, and of fossil bones and shells in sedimentary rocks, provide some unusual sites for deposition. On the earth's surface, opal forms siliceous sinters around hot springs and geysers, like those in Yellowstone National Park.

Many of the microscopic plankton in the oceans secrete skeletons of opal. The remains of these complex and beautiful protists (diatoms and radiolarians), cover much of the ocean floor, and are exposed on land as sedimentary rocks. In California and elsewhere, diatomites are mined for use as abrasives (in toothpaste), filters (for beer and wine), and high-temperature insulation.

Opal is formed through less natural processes as well. Now that the secrets of its structure are known, several companies have begun to synthesize and distribute artificial opals which are virtually indistinguishable from their natural counterparts. Opal is most commonly confused with chalcedony, a fine-grained form of quartz, from which it differs in its lower hardness and density.

Reflection and refraction THE WONDER OF MINERALS, AND ESPECIALLY OF GEMSTONES, is largely visual; every mineral species has unique set of optical properties. When a light ray strikes the surface of a mineral, part is reflected from the surface, part is *absorbed* by the mineral, and part may be *refracted*—entering the crystal and passing out again. How these processes interact depends on the mineral's chemical composition, internal structure, and impurities. In metallic minerals, for example, a high proportion of the incident light is reflected, and much is absorbed, but none is refracted. In transparent minerals and gemstones, however, refraction is extremely important, while the reflection and absorption both vary according to the presence of the light-absorbing ions which cause color (below).

The ratio between the velocity of light in air and its velocity in a denser material such as a crystal is a constant number, unique for every substance, called the *refractive index*. Refractive index varies with the wavelength of light, and is less for the red end of the visible spectrum than for the violet. The difference between the refractive indices in red and violet light varies between minerals, and this phenomenon is called *dispersion* (of the refractive indices). The dispersion of diamond, for instance, is more than three times that of quartz, and is responsible for the characteristic "fire" of diamond gems.

The internal structure of a mineral can have a great affect on its optical properties. Minerals can be divided into two broad groups on the basis of their optical behavior. In minerals belonging to the isometric crystal system (and in noncrystalline substances such as glass), light moves with equal velocity in every direction, giving them a single refractive index and homogenous coloration from every angle. Such minerals are referred to as *isotropic*. In the minerals belonging to all other crystal systems, the velocity of light varies according to the direction in which it travels through the crystal, resulting in a range of refractive indices and colors. These minerals are referred to as *anisotropic*. The refracted light passing through an anisotropic crystal is *polarized* into two mutually-perpendicular waves, resulting in two different indices of refraction. The numerical difference between the two refractive indices is termed *birefringence*.

When the birefringence of an anisotropic mineral is very great, it may

Diagram illustrating the basic interaction of light with a crystal or gemstone.

INCIDENT RAY   REFLECTED RAY

REFRACTED RAY

produce the phenomenon of *double refraction,* in which the two refracted rays of light are evident even to the naked eye. The strong double refraction displayed by the calcite demonstrates how the atomic structure of a mineral can determine the path of the light which passes through it. If a cleavage fragments of calcite is placed over an image drawn on a piece of paper, two different images are seen, representing the two polarized rays of refracted light. Double refraction in calcite is observed when looking in the direction perpendicular to its rhombohedral cleavage planes, but not when looking down its long crystallographic axis.

Absorption and Color The color of a mineral is determined by the particular wavelengths of visible light the mineral absorbs, and the color perceived by the eye is a combination of those wavelengths which are *not* absorbed. As noted in *Atomic Structure,* the electrons in an atom occupy discrete orbitals, each of which represents a specific level of energy. The energy differences between electron orbitals is known as the *energy gap.* When a light ray with an energy level corresponding to that of the energy gap strikes an electron, it may push the electron out of its stable orbital and into a higher-energy one. In the process, the light energy is absorbed. If the electrons of a great many atoms in a crystal behave in this manner, particular wavelengths of light may be strongly absorbed, leaving the remaining wavelengths to be reflected as color.

Ions of the transition elements have partly filled inner orbitals which are easily excited by light within the visible part of the spectrum, making these elements particularly adept at imparting color to minerals. Iron is the most common of the transition elements, and is the most important coloring agent in nature, imparting green, red, and brown hues to hundreds of minerals. Other transition elements and their characteristic color signatures are titanium (blue), chromium (green or red), cobalt (pink or blue), copper (green or blue), manganese (pink and red), nickel (green), and vanadium (red). White or colorless minerals are those which lack elements capable of preferential absorption. The atoms in ionic compounds such as the halides have very stable electronic configurations, and since the energy required to dislodge their electrons is greater than that of visible light, their crystals are colorless unless colored by impurities.

The transition elements are usually an intrinsic part of the minerals they color, either as essential components or as substitutions. However, extraneous impurities such as particles of other minerals or organic matter can also impart color to minerals and gemstones. Tiny inclusions of hematite, for example, can cause calcite crystals to take on a bright-red coloration. Minerals colored by atoms which are essential to their composition are termed *idiochromatic,* while those colored by impurities are referred to as *allochromatic.*

Other minerals are colored by the absence of atoms. For example, when a fluorite crystal grows in a particularly calcium-rich environment, structural sites normally occupied by F^- ions may remain unoccupied, leaving holes. In order to preserve the electrical neutrality of the overall crystal structure, electrons may leap into these gaps, simultaneously absorbing light energy in the same way as the electrons of the transition elements. The commonly-seen deep purple fluorite crystals are colored in this way. Natural radiation can also color minerals, by driving off some of the electrons in their structures and leaving the remaining ones in an excited state. Smoky quartz is colored dark brown to black in this manner.

Light passing through an anisotropic crystal may be absorbed differently in different vibration directions. This phenomenon is called *dichroism* in hexagonal and tetragonal crystals, and *pleochroism* in all other crystals, although the latter term is commonly used for both groups. In some crystals more light is absorbed in one direction than in another, resulting in different intensity of color depending on the angle of observation. In other crystals, entirely different wavelengths of light are absorbed in different crystallographic directions, so that very different colors are observed.

Top: Double refraction seen through a rhombohedral cleavage fragment of calcite. ***Bottom:*** *The purple color of these fluorite crystals from the Lone Pine Prospect, New Mexico, is due to holes in their atomic structures. As electrons leap into the gap created by the absence of F^- ions, they absorb certain spectra of visible light, leaving only purple to be reflected to the eye.*

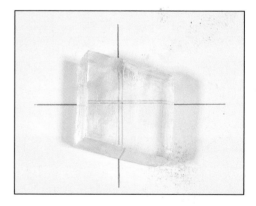

Exceptionally well-developed orpiment crystals from Quiruvilca, Santiago de Chuco, Peru.

orpiment

Classification:
sulfide

Composition:
As₂S₃ (arsenic sulfide)

Crystal System:
monoclinic

Hardness:
1.5–2

Specific Gravity:
3.49

ORPIMENT IS AN ORE OF ARSENIC, FOUND IN LEAD, SILVER, AND GOLD DEPOSITS WITH the closely related species realgar. Because the ancient Romans often used orpiment to paint their buildings and statuary a vivid golden yellow, this mineral acquired the Latin name *auri pimentum*, or "gold paint." Short prismatic crystals of orpiment are rare, and it usually occurs as foliated or granular masses, or earthy aggregates. Crystals display perfect cleavage in one direction, producing thin, flexible, sectile flakes. The color, so popular with the Romans, is a bright lemon-yellow, grading into orange and brown. Crystals are translucent to transparent, with a resinous luster (pearly on cleavages) and pale yellow streak. Sulfur resembles orpiment, but lacks its perfect cleavage.

Orpiment is found in low-temperature hydrothermal veins and hot spring deposits, commonly associated with cinnabar, realgar, and calcite. Specimens are obtained from hot spring deposits in several northern California counties, and as large platy crystals at Mercur, Tooele County, Utah. Fine specimens occur with realgar at several places in Nevada, including the Getchell Mine, near Golconda, Humboldt County; Steamboat Springs, Washoe County; and Manhattan, Nye County. Excellent crystals 3 cm in length are found at Pasto Bueno, Peru; and to 5 cm at Lukhumis, Soviet Georgia. There are many other occurrences throughout Europe, Turkey, China, and Japan.

ORTHOCLASE, ALONG WITH MICROCLINE AND SANIDINE, IS ONE OF THE POTASSIUM feldspar polymorphs. Orthoclase generally crystallizes at higher temperatures than microcline, but is more abundant overall, occurring in most intrusive and extrusive igneous rocks, including granites, syenites, and rhyolites; in metamorphic schists and gneisses; and even as a hydrothermal mineral in veins and sedimentary rocks. Since orthoclase has two prominent cleavages at right angles, it was named from a Greek phrase meaning "straight fracture."

Adularia is an orthoclase variant which generally forms in fissures in metamorphic rocks. It can be considered an *anti-perthite* (see *Feldspar Group,* and *Microcline*) to which microscopic lamellae of sodium feldspar lend a luminous, glowing appearance. Gemstones cut from adularia, called *moonstones,* are popular and inexpensive. Sanidine, a transparent feldspar found in volcanic rocks, is sometimes grouped with orthoclase as well.

Orthoclase crystals are short prismatic to tabular, rectangular or square on cross section, and very commonly twinned according to regular habits (or laws) such as the Baveno, Carlsbad, and Manebach laws. Crystal faces are generally rough, and anhedral cleavage masses, granular aggregates, and disseminated grains are most often seen. Orthoclase displays good cleavage in two directions at 90°, four directions of parting, and conchoidal to uneven fracture. It is transparent to translucent, and may be colorless or white, gray, yellowish, greenish, or brownish, with a vitreous luster and a white streak. Orthoclase can be distinguished from the sodium feldspars by its lack of polysynthetic twinning striations on cleavage surfaces, and from nepheline by its cleavage.

Good crystals of orthoclase occur as phenocrysts in volcanic rocks in many places around the world, including Sandia Mountain, above Albuquerque, New Mexico; and on Ragged Mountain, Gunnison County, Colorado, among many other locations. Excellent specimens of adularia are taken from many places in the Alps, particularly northern Italy and western Austria. A unique occurrence of transparent, greenish-yellow gem-quality orthoclase is found with diopside and zircon in a pegmatite at Itrongahy, in the Malagasy Republic. The faceted gems are offered for sale as "noble orthoclase."

orthoclase

Classification:
tectosilicate, feldspar group

Composition:
$KAlSi_3O_8$
(potassium aluminum silicate)

Crystal System:
monoclinic

Hardness:
6–6.5

Specific Gravity:
2.55–2.63

Blocky orthoclase crystals with quartz, from Baveno, Piemonte, Italy.

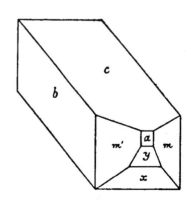

anatase
betafite
bixbyite
brookite
cassiterite
chromite
chrysoberyl
columbite–tantalite
corundum
cuprite
franklinite

hematite
ilmenite
magnetite
microlite and pyrochlore
perovskite
pyrolusite
rutile
spinel
uraninite
zincite

THIS HIGHLY VARIABLE MINERAL GROUP contains species as different as ice—the crystalline form of water, H_2O—and the extremely hard mineral corundum, familiar in its precious varieties ruby and sapphire. The most common of all oxides is quartz, SiO_2. The oxide silica readily combines with other oxides at high temperatures in magmas and metamorphic rocks to form silicate minerals, with free quartz itself representing the remaining unused silica. The result is that while the silicates are the most abundant minerals in the earth's crust, the oxides proper are relatively rare, and are usually restricted to silica-poor rock types. The silicates, and indeed all other chemical groups containing oxygen could be considered "oxides," but their further division into more narrowly defined chemical classes is useful.

The various oxide groups, including the hematite, rutile, and spinel groups, exhibit a variety of different structural types, which are generally characterized by strong ionic bonding. These groups can be divided into two main divisions. Most common are the simple oxides, which consist of one metal in combination with oxygen, in varying proportions. The multiple oxides, represented by the spinel group minerals, combine two metals with oxygen. The oxides are highly variable in their physical properties, but most are very hard minerals with high specific gravities. In addition to valuable gemstones like corundum and spinel, this group provides the most important ores of the metals chromium (chromite), iron (hematite and magnetite), and tin (cassiterite).

Above: Senarmontite, Sb_2O_3, is a rare oxide formed through the alteration of stibnite and other antimony minerals. These excellent octahedral crystals are from the Hamimad Mine, Ain Babouche, Algeria. *Below:* Tenorite, CuO, is ubiquitous in the oxidized portions of copper deposits. These divergent crystal sprays are from Italy's Mount Vesuvius. ***Opposite page:*** Minium, $Pb^{+2}Pb^{+4}O_4$, from Broken hill, New South Wales, Australia. Minium forms through the oxidation of lead minerals, and can even be found on old lead pipes and on bullets unearthed from old battlefields.

pearl

Classification:
organic gemstone

Composition:
CaCO₃
(Calcium carbonate, with organic matter)

Hardness:
2.5–4.5

Specific Gravity:
2.40–2.80

Large "baroque" freshwater pearl from Scotland.

THE MOST VALUABLE OF ALL ORGANIC GEMS, PEARLS HAVE BEEN PRIZED FOR THEIR delicate iridescence and unique forms for at least 6000 years. Pearls are among the only ornamental objects which humans are not compelled to re-work into a more pleasing form, and their origin was a cause for much speculation among the ancients. In his *Natural History*, Pliny the Elder recounts an ancient Indian myth suggesting that pearl oysters were drawn by the moon's rays to the surface of the sea, there to be fertilized by drops of dew. Not until Renaissance times was the theory advanced that pearls were merely an oyster's way of dealing with irritants.

Pearls are indeed formed when a foreign body such as a grain of sand or a parasite becomes trapped inside the shell of a mollusc. In self-defense, the shellfish gradually surrounds the intruder with the same material of which its shell is composed, rendering it less irritating. This substance is a composite material called nacre, which consists primarily of microscopic aragonite crystals held together by an organic binder called conchiolin. The nacre collects as thin, concentric layers, growing ever larger as the pearl and its host age. Although pearls are relatively soft, their concentric structure and organic binder give them great toughness. However, the organic nature of pearls makes them susceptible to dehydration and exfoliation, and pearls older than 100 years usually show some signs of disintegration.

Spherical pearls are the most commercially valuable, but asymmetrical "baroque" shapes are common in natural pearls. Hemispherical "blister pearls" grow on the inside surface of a shell whose occupant has successfully foiled the intrusion of a shell-boring predator. In color, luster, and texture pearls resemble the mother of pearl inside their host's shell. The distinctive rainbow-like iridescence of pearls is called the

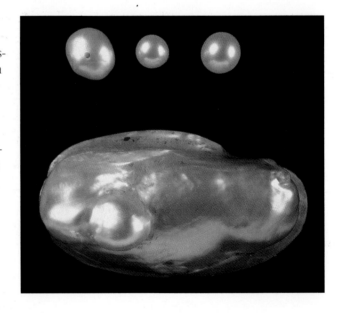

"orient," and derives from the dispersion of light by the thin, overlapping plates of aragonite in the nacre. Most pearls are white with a silvery or yellowish tint, but they may also be gray or nearly black. Pink pearls are extremely rare, and are usually formed by large marine snails.

The most important source of both natural and cultivated pearls are the different species of the genus *Pinetada*, especially *Pinetada martensi*. Pearls are also produced by some marine gastropods (snails), and many other species of bivalves in both fresh and salt water. Freshwater mussels were an important source of pearls in medieval Europe, before industrial pollution decimated the mussel population. Natural pearls have been harvested in the Persian Gulf and the Red Sea, in the waters between India and Sri Lanka, off the coasts of China, Japan, and the Philippines, and to a lesser extent in the Gulf of California and the Caribbean. Now, however, virtually all commercial pearls are cultivated. Although technically no different from natural pearls, cultivated pearls are artifacts of rigorously controlled mericulture.

The first attempts to cultivate pearls date from the 12th century A.D., when the Chinese learned to insert objects into a living oyster, returning to collect the irritant after some months or years. The large-scale production of cultured pearls began in Japan around the turn of this century. In the modern technique, a "seed" of nacre from a mussel shell is inserted into a small piece of flesh from a living oyster, which in turn is transplanted into the living tissue of the host oyster. These oysters are then set to work in cages in calm water. Shallow water is conducive to rapid growth, but deeper, cooler water improves the quality of the pearls; therefore, the cages are raised and lowered over the course of the year to achieve the best possible result. The pearls may be harvested as soon as five years after implantation, but longer periods of cultivation produce a finer product.

Despite all of this effort, the value of cultivated pearls is only a fraction of that of natural pearls. The only fool-proof way to distinguish between the two types is on the basis of their internal structure. Natural pearls usually have a very small nucleus surrounded by deep layers of nacre, while cultivated pearls have a relatively thin layer of nacre coating a substantial seed. X-ray examination is the preferred way to distinguish between the two types. Cheap imitation pearls of glass and plastic are common everywhere, but an excellent simulated pearl is also available, manufactured from opaque glass coated with guanine—a solution prepared from fish scales.

THE NAME OF THIS zeolite associate is derived from the Greek word for "compact," *pektos*—a reference to its typical compact, fibrous crystalline habit. Compact pectolite forms white to gray spherical aggregates, which are nearly as tough as nephrite jade. It also occurs as colorless acicular crystals, and rarely, as tabular individuals as large as 2 cm in diameter. Massive material displays a fibrous fracture, while crystals exhibit perfect cleavage in two directions. Crystalline pectolite is transparent to translucent, with a vitreous to silky luster and a white streak.

Pectolite is formed through hydrothermal processes in cavities in basaltic rocks, where it is typically associated with zeolite minerals, prehnite, calcite, and quartz. It also occurs as a minor constituent of some alkaline igneous rocks, mica-bearing peridotites, and contact metamorphic

pectolite

Classification:
inosilicate, pyroxenoid group

Composition:
$NaCa_2Si_3O_8(OH)$
(hydrous sodium calcium silicate)

Crystal System:
triclinic

Hardness:
4.5–5

Specific Gravity:
2.74–2.88

Radiating sprays of acicular pectolite crystals from Bergen Hill, Hudson County, New Jersey.

rocks, and as fracture fillings in serpentinites. Some of the finest specimens are found in New Jersey, as crystals in the marbles at Franklin and as mammillary masses in the basalts of the Paterson area. Good specimens also come from the mines at Thetford and Asbestos in Québec, and from Lake Nipigon in Ontario. Additional sources are the Kola Peninsula in the Soviet Union, and locations in Czechoslovakia, Japan, Greenland, Scotland, Sweden, Italy, Morocco, and the island of Los, off the coast of Guinea.

pegmatites

Pegmatite Minerals

albite	microlite
allanite	molybdenite
almandite garnet	monazite
amblygonite	muscovite
andalusite	orthoclase
apatite	phenakite
beryl	purpurite
betafite	pyrochlore
biotite	quartz
bismuth	rutile
brazilianite	samarskite
cassiterite	scheelite
chrysoberyl	spessartite garnet
columbite-tantalite	spodumene
euxenite	stilbite
fergusonite	strengite
fluorite	thorite
gadolinite	titanite
goethite	topaz
heterosite	tourmaline
hydroxylherderite	triphylite
kaolinite	uraninite
laumontite	wolframite
lepidolite	xenotime
lithiophilite	zircon
microcline	

PEGMATITES ARE BODIES OF COARSE-GRAINED ROCK WHICH ARE GENERALLY ANALOGOUS in composition to ordinary finer grained igneous rocks such as granites and nepheline syenites. The composition of pegmatites may differ from these rocks by an increased concentration of such volatile constituents as water and the halogen elements, and rare metallic elements such as beryllium, bismuth, lithium, niobium, tantalum, tin, tungsten, uranium, and the rare earths. These elements comprise a great variety of interesting and unusual minerals, many of which are found exclusively in the pegmatite environment. Besides being of great interest to scientists and collectors, many of these minerals are economically important as sources of rare metals, industrial crystals, and gemstones. In addition, many common species such as feldspars, quartz, micas, and clay minerals occur in larger and purer concentrations in pegmatites, where they form deposits of commercial value.

Although there are several general pegmatite types, those of granitic composition are by far the most abundant. In addition to the characteristic suite of silicates found in granites (quartz, micas, and sodium and potassium feldspars), these pegmatites often include unusual minerals such as beryl, tourmaline, topaz, and columbite–tantalite, and more rarely lithium-bearing species such as amblygonite, spodumene, and lepidolite mica. Much less common are pegmatites of mafic (silica-poor, iron- and magnesium-rich) composition, which form in bodies of gabbro and diorite. These are composed primarily of plagioclase feldspar and contain few unusual minerals. The syenite and nepheline-syenite pegmatites are locally abundant in regions where these alkali feldspar- and feldspathoid-rich rock types are dominant. Although usually not as enriched in rare elements as their granitic cousins, these pegmatites may contain concentrations of unusual rare-earth, niobium, and uranium minerals.

While pegmatites are sometimes found in larger bodies of igneous rock which apparently crystallized from the same magma, most are intruded into unrelated metamorphic or igneous rocks along zones of weakness, such as faults and fractures. Pegmatites of similar composition usually occur in clusters, presumably emanating from the same deeply buried stock, although each individual dike seems to have a unique mineralogical signature. Pegmatite bodies range in size from stringers of a few centimeters in thickness to enormous intrusions of a kilometer or more. Their shapes are highly variable, ranging from simple pods, lenses, or pipes to large elaborately branching bodies.

The most commonly encountered morphology, however, is the dike: a sheet-like body of a more or less planar geometry. The Himalaya pegmatite in the the Mesa Grande District of San Diego County, California, is a classic example of this two-dimensional form; although it has produced hundreds of tons of gem tourmaline, beryl, and other valuable minerals over the years, it averages only 1.5 m in thickness. Dikes are analogous to veins—planar hydrothermal bodies which are composed primarily of quartz, calcite, or other hydrothermal minerals. Veins are often found in close proxim-

ity to pegmatites, since both rely on igneous heat sources and exploit fissures and faults.

The origin of pegmatites has intrigued geologists for years, and the debate has been contentious at times. One extreme position held that pegmatites are purely magmatic intrusions, like basalt dikes. On the other extreme, many miners familiar with the textural similarities between hydrothermal veins and pegmatites held that the latter crystallized gradually from aqueous solutions. Not surprisingly, it appears that pegmatites owe their origin to a combination of these two processes, forming from "igneous" melts charged with high-temperature aqueous fluids.

Geologist relaxing in the Alto Amancio pegmatite, Minas Gerais, Brazil. The feldspar in this pegmatite has largely altered to white clay, which has eroded to expose the large, subhedral quartz crystals (under hammer) originally intergrown with the feldspar.

The necessary conditions for pegmatite formation can apparently be achieved through either igneous or metamorphic processes. Igneous pegmatites appear to form from the last liquid portion of a crystallizing igneous magma—the part most enriched in silica, water, halogens, and other volatile constituents, as well as high concentrations of rare elements in some cases. If this mixture crystallizes slowly in place, a pegmatite will form which grades into the surrounding rock with gradually decreasing coarseness of crystal size. If it is forced outward under pressure, it can intrude into adjacent rocks to crystallize as a pegmatite with sharp boundaries and a "quenched" outer zone of relatively small crystal grains.

Other pegmatites appear to have formed through metamorphic processes, in rocks with considerable interstitial water that were subjected to high temperatures. In this environment, silica and the other materials mentioned above are leached out of the country rock, either replacing the original rock and reprecipitating as pegmatite in place, or migrating through the rock under pressure to invade fissures and other areas of weakness. Such processes would account for the commonly-seen pegmatites which form isolated lenses surrounded by metamorphic rock, with no apparent conduit for igneous emplacement, as well as the very large, "regional" pegmatites found in the metamorphic shields of Canada, Scandinavia, and central Africa.

On the basis of mineralogy, pegmatites can be broadly divided into *simple* and *complex*, with the simple kind being by far the more abundant. Simple granitic pegmatites are composed primarily of quartz, feldspars, and mica, with black tourmaline and some columbite–tantalite or allanite present. Complex mineralogy is signaled by the presence of lithium minerals, often accompanied by phosphates and other rare species. While some pegmatites display a fairly homogenous texture, most are texturally and mineralogically zoned to some degree. The simplest textural zonation consists of a fairly pure quartz core surrounded by a coarse-grained mixture of quartz, feldspars, and micas. In more chemically complex pegmatites, zones dominated by spodumene, lepidolite, phosphates, and other species may occur. The more unusual mineral species tend to be concentrated near the core region, and cavities containing euhedral crystals of quartz, gem minerals, and other minerals are usually confined to this region as well. In most cases, the zonation of complex pegmatites appears to reflect one or more stages of secondary hydrothermal activity. The textures in these rocks seem to indicate that some of the original material has been dissolved, and replaced by a different suite of minerals.

pentlandite

Classification:
sulfide

Composition:
$(Fe,Ni)_9S_8$ (iron nickel sulfide)

Crystal System:
isometric

Hardness:
3.5–4

Specific Gravity:
4.6–5

PENTLANDITE, NAMED FOR THE IRISH NATURALIST JOSEPH BARCLAY PENTLAND (b. 1797), is one of the primary ores of nickel. Like chromium, nickel is widely used as a protective and ornamental coating for steel and other metals, because of its great resistance to corrosion and its ability to take a high polish. Often, the two metals are used together, a thin veneer of the brighter but less durable chrome overlying a thicker base of nickel. Its main use, however, is in a variety of alloys including stainless and other types of steel, nickel bronze, "German" silver, and nichrome. Nickel is alloyed with copper to make coins such as the United States 5-cent piece, and as a catalyst in various chemical reactions. Over the past decade, large, low-grade residual deposits called nickel laterites have begun to replace the pentlandite ores in gabbroic igneous rocks as the main source of nickel. The nickel in lateritic deposits is contained as impurities in iron oxides, and in the unassuming nickeliferous phyllosilicate garnierite.

Oddly, pentlandite occurs only in a granular massive form—never as discrete crystals. It is often intimately associated with pyrrhotite as exsolution intergrowths; even when pure, the two minerals are almost indistinguishable but for pentlandite's lack of magnetism. Masses of pentlandite display an uneven to conchoidal fracture and distinctive octahedral parting. It is opaque and light bronze-yellow in color, with a metallic luster and a bronze-colored streak.

Pentlandite differs from other nickel minerals such as millerite and niccolite, which are commonly found in hydrothermal veins, in that it is an igneous mineral. It forms in mafic igneous rocks, particularly in layered igneous intrusions, as a product of magmatic segregation. Associated species commonly include cubanite, chalcopyrite, and other nickel sulfides and arsenides, in addition to pyrrhotite. Pentlandite is mined from the layered igneous intrusions at Sudbury, Ontario, and Lynn Lake, Manitoba; large single-crystal grains several centimeters across are found in the Yale District of British Columbia. Other notable occurrences include the Key West Mine in Nye County, Nevada; Yakobi Island, Alaska; and Kimbalda, Western Australia. An enormous layered intrusion in the Transvaal region of South Africa, known as the Bushveld Complex, is another important source of pentlandite.

THIS INTERESTING TITANIUM OXIDE has cerium- and niobium-rich varieties, which result from the partial substitution of these elements for titanium and typically display pseudo-octahedral symmetry; "pure" crystals are usually pseudocubic and striated parallel to the "cube" edges. All are often highly modified by other isometric forms, with penetration twinning being common. They are usually seen in massive form as lamellar and reniform crystalline aggregates. Perovskite is black, brown, yellow, or amber in color, and translucent with adamantine to submetallic luster and a pale yellow streak. Varieties rich in niobium, cerium, and rare-earth elements are sometimes exploited as ore minerals.

Perovskite crystallizes in silica-poor igneous rocks such as syenites and carbonatites, in the metamorphic rocks derived from them, and in some contact metamorphic marbles. Small crystals are found in the Crestmore Quarries, Riverside County and the Diablo Range, San Benito County, California; and in the Bearpaw Mountains of Montana. Crystals of niobium-rich perovskite to 2 cm are found in skarns at Magnet Cove, Arkansas, and in Quebec's Oka carbonatite. Crystals are also found in Sweden, Switzerland, and in the Ural Mountains of Russia.

perovskite

Classification:
oxide

Composition:
$CaTiO_3$ (calcium titanium oxide)

Crystal System:
orthorhombic

Hardness:
5.5

Specific Gravity:
4

Pseudocubic perovskite crystals in calcite, from Achmatovsk, in the Ural Mountains of Russia.

THE NAME OF THIS UNUSUAL PEGMATITE MINERAL IS DERIVED FROM THE GREEK WORD for "leaf," *petalon*— an allusion to its conspicuous, easily developed cleavage. Although petalite is a potential source of lithium (see *Lepidolite*), it is far more important as the raw material for the new synthetic materials called "crystallized glass ceramics." These super-glasses have enormous strength and extremely low thermal expansion relative to normal glass, rendering them suitable for cooking utensils and specialized applications such as telescope mirrors.

Petalite is seldom seen in euhedral form as small, tabular, or columnar crystals. It more commonly occurs as blocky masses in matrix displaying perfect basal cleavage (plus a second, less well-developed cleavage) and, often, polysynthetic twinning striations. Petalite is colorless or white, and transparent to translucent with a vitreous to pearly luster. The distinctive cleavage of petalite results from its sheet-like structure, which is characterized by broad layers of Si_4O_{10} groups linked by AlO_4 tetrahedra, with lithium distributed throughout in tetrahedral coordination with oxygen. An interesting characteristic of petalite is its emission of blue phosphorescence when gently heated. It is distinguished from spodumene by its lower specific gravity and cleavage; like spodumene, petalite is sometimes faceted into gemstones despite its tricky cleavage.

Petalite is associated with lepidolite, spodumene, and tourmaline in some lithium-bearing pegmatites. Petalite was considered very rare until the large deposits were discovered at the Verutrask pegmatite on the island of Uto, Sweden. This source is largely depleted, and petalite is now produced mainly from the large deposit at Bikita, Zimbabwe, and from smaller deposits in the Karibib District of Namibia and at Londonderry, Western Australia. Excellent euhedral crystals to 20 cm in length were found in the past near Norwich, Massachusetts. Petalite is also found in the pegmatites of San Diego County, California; Oxford County, Maine; Bernic Lake, Manitoba; Finland; and on the Italian island of Elba.

petalite

Classification:
tectosilicate

Composition:
$LiAlSi_4O_{10}$ (lithium aluminum silicate)

Crystal System:
monoclinic

Hardness:
6–6.5

Specific Gravity:
2.5

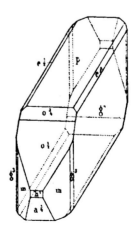

Classification:
nesosilicate

Composition:
Be₂SiO₄ (beryllium silicate)

Crystal System:
hexagonal (rhombohedral)

Hardness:
7.5–8

Specific Gravity:
3

PHENAKITE GETS ITS NAME FROM the Greek *phenakos*, or "deceiver," because it resembles quartz and topaz. It is considerably harder than quartz, however, and has vertical rather than horizontal striations, and very different twin habits. For its part, topaz is distinguished from phenakite by its well-developed basal cleavage. Crystals of this species are often quite complex, ranging from equant forms to long prismatic or even acicular crystals terminated by rhombohedral faces. They may be white, colorless, honey-yellow, pinkish, or brown, with a white streak, and are transparent with a very bright vitreous luster. Transparent crystals are sometimes faceted as gemstones.

Phenakite is found in pegmatites—associated with quartz, chrysoberyl, beryl, apatite, and topaz—and in greisens (see *Cassiterite*). It also forms in hydrothermal veins and Alpine-type vugs in mica schists. Phenakite is widely distributed in small amounts in the North American pegmatite districts from Pala, San Diego County, California, to Oxford County, Maine. Among the many notable localities are Amelia County, Virginia; Bald Face Mountain, New Hampshire; Rib Mountain, Wisconsin; and the Mt. Antero and Crystal Peak regions of Colorado. Very large crystals have been taken from São Miguel di Piracicaba, Minas Gerais, Brazil; and Kragero, Norway. While most specimens occur in pegmatites, fine crystals have also been found in the emerald- and chrysoberyl-bearing mica schists along the Takowaja River in the Urals of the Soviet Union. Specimens are also obtained from Austria, Czechoslovakia, France, Switzerland, Poland, Namibia, and Tanzania.

Phenakite crystals from São Miguel de Piracicaba, Minas Gerais, Brazil.

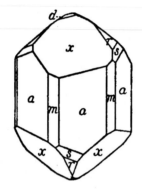

THE PHOSPHATES, ARSENATES AND VANADATES ARE DISCUSSED TOGETHER DUE TO THE similarities of their anion complexes: $(PO_4)^{-3}$, $(AsO_4)^{-3}$, and $(VO_4)^{-3}$. These basic structural units form tetrahedra, which easily substitute for one another when there is an opportunity. For instance, the phosphate pyromorphite, $Pb_5(PO_4)_3Cl$, the arsenate mimetite, $Pb_5(AsO_4)_3Cl$, and the vanadate vanadinite, $Pb_5(VO_4)_3Cl$, share the same crystal structure, and form a three-way solid-solution series.

All of the species in these classes are nonmetallic, and most are soft, brittle, and easily dissolved in acids. The phosphates and arsenates are either anhydrous or contain water, hydroxyl, and/or a halogen ion like chlorine or fluorine. The anhydrous phosphates are mostly magmatic in origin. Although there are a great many species in these classes, few are commonly encountered. The most important and abundant is apatite, which is the chief inorganic repository of the vital nutrient phosphorous. Other important phosphates include the gem mineral turquois and the rare-earth ore mineral monazite. Many of the arsenates and vanadates are important secondary ores, and often form colorful crystals as well.

Opposite page: *Brazilianite, $NaAl_3(PO_4)_2(OH)_4$ from the Galilea Mine, near Governador Valadores, Minas Gerais, Brazil. This rare phosphate was discovered in Brazil in 1944, and is found only in pegmatites.*
Inset: *The rare phosphate ludlamite, $Fe_3(PO_4)_2 \cdot 4H_2O$, was discovered at Wheal Jane, near Truro, Cornwall.*

plagioclase series

Classification:
tectosilicates, feldspar group

Composition:
albite: $NaAlSi_3O_8$
anorthite: $CaAl_2Si_2O_8$
(sodium-calcium aluminum silicates)

Crystal System:
triclinic

Hardness:
6–6.5

Specific Gravity:
2.62 (albite)–2.76 (anorthite)

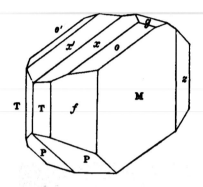

Top: Labradorite from Sweden displaying the striking iridescence known as the schiller effect. This phenomenon results from the the scattering of light by extremely fine, planar zones of compositional variation called exsolution lamellae. ***Bottom:*** Cluster of albite crystals from Zermatt, Valais, Switzerland.

THE PLAGIOCLASE SERIES INCLUDES ALL OF THE SODIUM AND CALCIUM-RICH FELDSPARS. Albite is the sodium-rich end member; the other species, in order of increasing calcium content, are oligoclase, andesine, labradorite, bytownite, and anorthite—the latter being the calcium-rich end member. The name of the group comes from the Greek phrase meaning "oblique fracture," because of the angle between the two prominent cleavages. The name albite is derived from the Latin *albus*, or "white," in allusion to its color; oligoclase takes its name from the Greek phrase for "little cleavage," because it was thought to have less perfect cleavage than albite; andesine is named for its occurrence in the Andes; labradorite from the locality in Labrador; bytownite comes from the "Bytown" locality, now Ottawa, Ontario, Canada; and anorthite comes from the Greek phrase meaning "not upright," in allusion to its oblique crystals.

Most euhedral crystals belong to the albite-oligoclase end of the series, while the others usually occur only as anhedral grains in rock. Crystals are typically less blocky than those of the microcline or orthoclase; the variety of albite found in pegmatites, known as clevelandite, forms rosettes of bladed crystals. Nearly every plagioclase exhibits polysynthetic twinning, which is indicated by fine striations on cleavage planes. Twinning according the Carlsbad, Baveno, or Manebach laws also occurs frequently, as in the potassium feldspars. The plagioclases are brittle, with an uneven to conchoidal fracture and two prominent cleavages.

The plagioclases in general are transparent to translucent, with a vitreous to pearly luster and a white streak. Albite and andesine are usually white or colorless, and oligoclase is similarly colored but sometimes appears slightly greenish. Both albite and oligoclase may display opalescence, and such stones are marketed as "moonstone." Golden, iridescent oligoclase which contains tiny plates of hematite is called "sunstone," and is a sometimes used as a gem as well. Labradorite, bytownite, and anorthite are commonly grayish, but may be nearly black due to the presence of inclusions; some labradorite is pale yellow. Some specimens of andesine and labradorite are known for their flashing display of colors,

play of colors, not unlike that of opal; these are sometimes used as ornamental materials.

The plagioclases are easily distinguished from the potassium feldspars by the delicate twinning striations evident on cleavage surfaces. In pegmatites, the distinctive bladed crystals of clevelandite further serve to distinguish this variety from similar associated species. The end members of the series can be distinguished by the difference in their specific gravities, and by their solubility in hydrochloric acid: anorthite and the other calcium-bearing plagioclases are soluble, while albite is not.

Albite can be classed with microcline and orthoclase as an alkali feldspar, and like those species occurs in silica-rich igneous rocks, both plutonic and volcanic. The bladed variety, cleavelandite, often replaces primary microcline in pegmatite dikes. Excellent specimens of clevelandite occur in the granitic pegmatites of Amelia Court House, Virginia, and in New England, California, Brazil, and numerous other sites. Oligoclase is common in monzonites and granodiorites, but is found in granitic pegmatites as well, particularly at Kragero, Norway. Bytownite and labradorite are typical of basalts, gabbros, and anorthosites, the last of which may be composed exclusively of labradorite. Exceptional ornamental labradorite occurs in the anorthosites of eastern Labrador, and at Lammenpaa, Finland. Andesine occurs primarily in andesites and diorites, and anorthite in contact metamorphosed limestones.

LIKE GOLD, SILVER, AND COPPER, PLATINUM IS FOUND IN NATURE IN ITS NATIVE STATE, but since it occurs as small, inconspicuous flakes, it never attracted the

attention of ancient peoples as did the other precious metals. Since its melting point is so high (1755°C), early metallurgists would probably have been unable to work with it anyway. When first discovered in the placers of the Rio Pinto in New Granada (modern Colombia) in 1741, platinum was actually considered a nuisance. It was soon discovered that the "worthless" platinum could be added to gold without reducing its specific gravity (19.3) as other metals did, making the adulteration undetectable. To protect the integrity of the gold supply from the New World, the King of Spain sent his soldiers shut down the platinum workings on the Rio Pinto. The name of this metal comes from *"platina del Pinto,"* platina being the diminutive of *plata*, the Spanish word for "silver," and Pinto a reference to its first source.

Ironically, platinum is now more valuable than gold, due to both its great rarity and its intrinsic value in industry. The many industrial uses of platinum take advantage of its extremely high melting point, its resistance to chemical corrosion, and its great hardness (for a metal); platinum alloys are widely used in medical equipment, electronics, and dentistry. Platinum is one of the most effective catalysts for all kinds of chemical reactions, and its largest single application is in automobile catalytic converters, which break down harmful exhaust emissions. Large quantities are also used as catalysts in petroleum refining, and the production of nitric and sulfuric acid. In jewelry, platinum makes a *very* expensive setting for precious stones.

Platinum occurs in nature as malleable, lustrous, blue-gray lumps, or very occasionally as tiny, malformed cubic or octahedral crystals. It is

Composition:
Pt (native platinum, naturally alloyed with other metals)

Crystal System:
isometric

Hardness:
4–4.5

Specific Gravity:
14–19 (21.46 when pure)

Rough nugget of platinum from the placers of Nizhni-Tagilsk, Perm, Russia.

nearly always alloyed with iron, which renders it slightly magnetic, and often with copper, gold, and nickel as well. Platinum is usually alloyed with other metals of the platinum group, of which platinum itself is by far the most abundant. The other members of this group include iridium, osmium palladium, rhodium, and ruthenium. These elements all share the properties of extremely high specific gravities and melting points, and great resistance to corrosion. They each have unique properties as well, which make them suitable for diverse applications from ink pen nibs to search-light reflectors to electronics.

The placer deposits of Colombia remained the only source of platinum until 1822, when prospectors searching for gold found native platinum in the placers of the Upper Tura River, on the eastern slope of the Ural Mountains in Russia. The platinum was eventually traced back to its source in an area of serpentinized dunite, but the concentrations were so small that it was unattractive to mine. It remained more profitable to wash it from the stream beds where it had been naturally concentrating over the millennia. Russia now produces much of the world's supply of palladium.

The most important source of platinum is South Africa, where it is mined from the Bushveld Complex, a sheet-like body of gigantic size, covering an area of roughly 90,000 km². This formation is a layered igneous intrusion, so called because it consists of layers of igneous rocks, varying in composition from peridotite to diorite which formed through the segregation of successive generations of crystals from a single magma. One layer, called the Merensky Reef, is the richest source of platinum in the Bushveld Complex, although it is generally less than a meter in thickness. In addition to the native metal, platinum occurs here in a number of unusual minerals, including the platinum arsenide sperrylite.

Platinum is also obtained from the layered igneous intrusion at Sudbury, Ontario, which is also a source of copper and nickel. A platinum-bearing layered intrusion similar to the Merensky reef has recently been discovered in the Rocky Mountains of Montana. This deposit, called the Stillwater Complex, is providing the United States with a more stable supply of this vital element. Smaller quantities of platinum are found with gold in placer deposits in many parts of the world, including California, Alaska, North Carolina, Australia, Borneo, Brazil, Ireland, Finland, Germany, Haiti, Honduras, and New Zealand.

polybasite

Classification:
sulfosalt

Composition:
$(Ag,Cu)_{16}Sb_2S_{11}$
(silver copper sulfosalt)

Crystal System:
monoclinic

Hardness:
2–3

Specific Gravity:
6.30

Tabular crystals of polybasite from Las Chispas mine, Arizpe, Sonora, Mexico.

POLYBASITE IS A DARK, soft, heavy, and rare ore of silver, prized for its sometimes attractive crystals. Its name is derived from the Greek phrase meaning "many bases," because it contains a number of base metals—that is, metals that are not gold. Crystals are usually tabular, either pseudo-hexagonal or pseudo-dorhombohedral, and rare. They are commonly twinned, and typically display triangular growth marks. Polybasite is brittle, with one imperfect cleavage and an uneven fracture. It is opaque and iron-black in color, but appears deep ruby-red in thin fragments; the luster is metallic and the streak black. Polybasite is softer and denser than hematite, and is distinguished from proustite and pyrargyrite by its black streak. Stephanite is a closely related silver sulfosalt which is nearly identical to polybasite in its physical properties and occurrence.

Polybasite is found in low- to medium-temperature hydrothermal sulfide veins, in association with argentite, native silver, galena, proustite, pyrargyrite, tetrahedrite, and other species. Excellent specimens are found in Mexico at Arizpe and Las Chiapas, Sonora, as well as in the famous silver mines of Guanajuato. Fine specimens are found in Europe at Pribram, Czechoslovakia, and at Andreasberg and Freiberg, Germany. Polybasite crystals have also been recovered from silver deposits in Colorado, Idaho, Montana, Nevada, Chile, Bolivia, Peru, Sardinia, and Australia.

polymorphism

MINERALS ARE FORMED UNDER WIDELY VARYING PHYSICAL CONDITIONS, FROM environments of intense heat and pressure deep within the crust, to cool damp caverns near the earth's surface. Since most elements are widely distributed in the earth's crust, it should come as no surprise that chemically similar compounds form in very different physical environments. Thus, the same compound may assume two or more very different internal structures, each of which is stable under differing conditions. Such minerals with a common composition and distinct crystal structures are called *polymorphs*, meaning "several forms." If a compound has two polymorphs, these are called dimorphs, if three, trimorphs.

A classic example is carbon in its two main forms: diamond and graphite. Diamond forms incredibly hard crystals with a compact atomic arrangement at high temperatures and pressures deep within the earth, while graphite forms soft, loosely bonded crystals at relatively low temperatures and pressures. Although diamond is not the stable form of carbon at the earth's surface, there is no need to worry about your diamond ring turning into graphite: temperatures above 1000°C are necessary to break its existing atomic bonds.

There are three major mechanisms by which one polymorph can alter into another. *Displacive* polymorphs are very common and not at all dramatic, as the structural differences between such polymorphs are not usually apparent in the crystals' external shapes. In displacive polymorphs, the transition from one structure to another occurs without the breaking of atomic bonds; the transformation from high to low quartz is of this type.

More dramatic are *reconstructive* polymorphs, in which the the two structures are very different. The change from one form to another in this

Structures of the two main polymorphs of carbon, diamond and graphite. Each carbon atom in a diamond crystal (left) enjoys strong covalent bonding to four immediate neighbors. In graphite (right), each carbon atom is covalently bonded to only three other atoms, while weak van der Waals' forces (represented here by lines) hold the structural layers together.

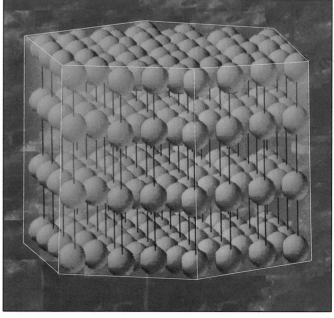

case requires the wholesale destruction of the original structure, and recrystallization "from scratch"—a process which usually requires an outside source of energy. The relatively unstable silica polymorphs cristobalite and tridymite, for example, will not undergo reconstructive conversion to the more stable form of quartz without the application of heat or pressure.

The third form of polymorphism is the *order-disorder* type, in which one polymorph will have a more random distribution of components than the other. This distinction separates the disordered, high-temperature potassium feldspar sanidine from its ordered counterpart microcline.

Polymorphs are extremely valuable in petrography because they allow one to make accurate estimates of the pressure and temperature at which a particular rock was formed. The aluminosilicate (Al_2SiO_5) polymorphs andalusite, kyanite, and sillimanite, for instance, have a well-known stability field (see *Andalusite*), and their presence singly or in combination in any rock indicates the conditions of its formation.

prehnite

Classification:
phyllosilicate

Composition:
$Ca_2Al(AlSi_3O_{10})(OH)_2$
(hydrous calcium aluminum silicate)

Crystal System:
orthorhombic

Hardness:
6–6.5

Specific Gravity:
2.90–2.95

THIS SPECIES IS NAMED FOR HENDRIK VON PREHN (B. 1733), A DUTCH MILITARY OFFIcer who enlivened his duties in South Africa by collecting minerals. Although it scarcely resembles most other sheet silicates, prehnite is classified as such because of its structure, which consists of parallel layers of silica and aluminum tetrahedra. Compact material is sometimes fashioned into decorative objects and gemstones because of its pleasing greenish coloration.

Prehnite is very rarely seen as discrete crystals of tabular or pyramidal morphology. It more often forms barrel-shaped aggregates, and especially radiating fibrous or lamellar aggregates with mammillary morphology. Its perfect basal cleavage reflects its sheet structure. Most material is translucent, and pale to dark green, gray, white, or colorless, with a vitreous luster and a white streak. Prehnite may resemble hemimorphite, but has a much lower specific gravity.

Crystalline aggregates of prehnite from West Paterson, New Jersey. Note the reflections from the multitude of tiny crystal terminations on the surface of each aggregate.

Prehnite is a typical mineral of cavities in basaltic rocks, where it is associated with calcite, datolite, pectolite, quartz, and zeolites. It is also found in low-temperature hydrothermal deposits in fissures in igneous and metamorphic rocks, and in limestones. Fine masses are found with native copper in Keweenaw County, Michigan, and in the basalts and diabases of northern New Jersey; Westfield, Massachusetts; Farmington, Connecticut; Fairfax County, Virginia; and North Carolina. Good specimens are also obtained from Mt. Sneffels, Colorado, and the Crestmore Quarries in California. Excellent crystalline specimens are found near Dauphine, France, and in Scotland, Switzerland, India, South Africa, New Zealand, and other locations worldwide.

THESE SECONDARY SULFIDE MINERALS ARE ISOSTRUCTURAL WITH ONE ANOTHER, BUT do not form an isomorphous series, as little substitution occurs between antimony and arsenic. The two species are usually found together in low-temperature hydrothermal sulfide veins, where they form as alteration products of argentite and silver-bearing galena. Pyrargyrite is more common and darker in color than proustite, although it is rarely as well-crystallized. Its deep ruby-red color earned it the miner's name "dark ruby silver;" the proper name, pyrargyrite, is equally poetic if less euphonious, meaning "fire silver" in Greek. Proustite is named for the French chemist Joseph Louis Proust (b. 1754).

Although they usually occur in massive form, these species are best known for their dramatic crystals. Those of proustite are usually rhombohedral or scalenohedral, often striated, distorted, and twinned. Pyrargyrite crystals typically form roughly hexagonal prisms with blunt hemimorphic terminations. Both species are fragile, with good rhombohedral cleavage. Recently excavated crystals of proustite are blood-red, and translucent with

proustite and pyrargyrite

Classification:
sulfosalts

Composition:
proustite: Ag_3AsS_3
(silver arsenic sulfosalt)
pyrargyrite: Ag_3SbS_3
(silver antimony sulfosalt)

Crystal System:
hexagonal (rhombohedral)

Hardness:
2.5

Specific Gravity:
proustite: 5.65;
pyrargyrite: 5.85

Rude hexagonal prisms of pyrargyrite from the Mina la Luz, Guanajuato, Mexico.

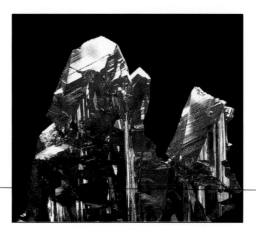

Highly modified scalenohedral crystals of proustite from the classic locality at Chanarcillo, Copiapo, Chile.

an adamantine luster and a scarlet streak, but exposure to the atmosphere can render them opaque, with submetallic luster and a gray streak. Pyrargyrite is deep ruby-red, or black with dark-red internal reflections, and has a dark-red streak.

Proustite and pyrargyrite are found with native silver, other sulfides, calcite, dolomite, and quartz in low-temperature hydrothermal veins. The best specimens of these species are obtained from the Andean sulfide veins in Bolivia, Chile, and Peru, particularly the excellent proustite crystals of 15 cm in length from the silver mines of Chanarcillo, Chile. Fine specimens are also found in Batopilas, Chihuahua; Guanajuato and Zacatecas, Mexico; and at Cobalt, Ontario. Important European sources include the German regions of Freiberg, Saxony, and Andreasberg in the Harz Mountains; Pribram, Czechoslovakia; Spain; and Sardinia. Proustite and pyrargyrite are widespread in silver deposits of the western United States, but are rarely found as exceptional specimens.

pseudomorphs

Original Crystal	New Crystal
galena	anglesite
aragonite, celestite	calcite
feldspars, tourmaline, beryl, spodumene	clay minerals
cuprite, azurite, aragonite	copper
anhydrite, aragonite	gypsum
magnetite	hematite
cuprite, azurite	malachite
tourmaline, spodumene	muscovite
glauberite	opal
pyrite, siderite, magnetite, chalcopyrite, sphalerite	goethite
manganite	pyrolusite
calcite, aragonite, fluorite, serpentine	quartz
olivine, pyroxenes	serpentine
quartz; pyroxenes	talc

This pseudomorph of malachite after azurite from Tsumeb, Namibia is an uncommonly fine example of a very common pseudomorphic relationship.

WHEN THE ORIGINAL CRYSTAL FORM OF ONE MINERAL IS OCCUPIED BY ANOTHER, chemically or structurally different species, the resulting specimen is referred to as a *pseudomorph* (from the Greek "false form"). This situation can arise through three different processes: gradual chemical change, structural change, and wholesale replacement. Most common is the gradual alteration of chemical composition due to changes in the physical environment. This usually occurs through the loss or gain of volatile elements or compounds, such as water. The alteration of gypsum to anhydrite, or borax to tincalconite, through dehydration are typical examples. Primary species are also replaced through the gradual in-place reorganization of their constituent elements, leaving in their place new species roughly similar in composition, but otherwise unrelated. This is what occurs when feldspar or spodumene crystals alter into chemically analogous clay minerals, or when the aluminosilicate andalusite alters to mica.

Minerals can be altered in the solid state without undergoing any chemical change at all. Changes in the pressure or temperature can initiate *paramorphism*, in which crystal structure is altered while chemical elements are preserved in the original proportions. Examples of paramorphic changes in which the internal structure of a mineral changes without affecting its outward crystal form include the conversion of aragonite to calcite, ($CaCO_3$), or rutile to brookite (TiO_2). Some minerals which are only stable

at high temperatures, such as cristobalite and tridymite (SiO_2), change their internal structure as they cool in fresh igneous rock, while retaining the external form of the high-temperature polymorph.

Perhaps the most remarkable kind of pseudomorphs are those in which one species is replaced by another completely unrelated species. This can occur when crystals embedded in rock or encrusted by other minerals are dissolved, leaving a cast or mold, which is later filled by a secondary species which mimics the form of the original. Strange specimens of quartz in the cubic shape of fluorite crystals have formed in this way.

THE NAME PYRITE MEANS "FIRESTONE" IN GREEK, REFLECTING ITS EARLY USE AS A source of sparks for starting fires. It was believed that the pyrite actually contained fire, which was knocked out when the stone was struck. In antiquity, the term *pyrite* was used collectively for all minerals that produced sparks, including chalcopyrite and marcasite. Pyrite is mainly used today in the production of sulfuric acid, which has many applications in manufacturing and refining. The acid is rendered from pyrite through oxidation, as the mineral is cooked in the presence of air. The resulting iron residue is used as a red pigment and as iron ore—nothing is wasted. Pyrite often contains commercially exploitable quantities of gold as well, in the form of discrete, microscopic grains; nickel may also substitute for iron. The stern ladies of the Victorian era adorned themselves with jewelry set with dark, metallic, faceted pyrites. These stones were and still are marketed as marcasite, but this polymorph of pyrite is itself much too delicate for wear in jewelry.

Pyrite forms some of the finest specimens of all the sulfides, and is often found as large euhedral crystals. Although the crystals may display a complex array of isometric forms, pyrite is most often found in cubes, octahedra, or pyritohedrons (twelve-faced forms with each face a pentagon). The faces of cubes and pyritohedrons are nearly always striated, due to competition for expression between these two forms. Penetration twins are fairly common; those involving pyritohedrons are called "iron crosses." Typical aggregate habits include massive granular, reniform, and stalactitic. Pyrite is opaque, metallic, and a distinctive, brassy yellowish-white, unless coated with a rusty film of goethite. Pseudomorphs of goethite or limonite after pyrite are very common, as the sulfide breaks down fairly easily in the presence of oxygen and hydroxyl. Pyrite is distinguished by its sharp, striated crystals, and it is harder than other iron-bearing sulfides. Although sometimes called "fool's gold," pyrite bears little resemblance to the real thing: it is brittle rather than malleable, and light yellow-white rather than gold in color.

pyrite

Classification:
sulfide

Composition:
FeS_2 (iron sulfide)

Crystal System:
isometric

Hardness:
6–6.5

Specific Gravity:
5

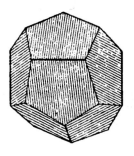

A cluster of cubic pyrite crystals from the Greek island of Irisses, in the Sporades.

Pyrite is the most abundant and widespread of all sulfides, occurring in all rock types of all ages, throughout the world. Perhaps the best crystals are those formed in hydrothermal sulfide deposits; however, excellent specimens are also recovered from cavities in sedimentary and metamorphic rocks, and from contact metamorphic deposits. It also occurs in primary magmatic rocks from layered intrusions to pegmatites, usually due to the decay of other sulfides such as pyrrhotite. Pyrite crystals are often the main iron component of limestones, coal deposits, shales, and even some regional metamorphic rocks such as slates. Fine specimens are found in numerous locations in the United States, including the American Mine and Park City in Utah; Chester County, Pennsylvania; and Sparta, Illinois. Important European deposits include Rio Marina, on the Isle of Elba, Italy; Cassandra on the Khalkidhikí Peninsula, Greece; Rio Tinto, Huelva Province, Spain; Alemtejo Province, Portugal; Falun, Sweden; Sulitjelma, Norway; and Rammelsberg, Germany.

pyrolusite

Classification:
oxide

Composition:
MnO_2 (manganese oxide)

Crystal System:
tetragonal

Hardness:
6–6.5

Specific Gravity:
5.06

THIS RATHER UNIMPRESSIVE-LOOKING MINERAL IS THE MAJOR ORE OF THE METAL MANganese (see *Manganite*). Pyrolusite is particularly familiar for the delicate patterns it leaves in all kinds of rock, most notably the variety of cryptocrystalline quartz called moss agate. As manganese-bearing mineral grains in any rock are dissolved, the manganese is commonly reprecipitated in fissures and crevices as lacy, dendritic stains of pyrolusite. The name is derived from the Greek phrase meaning "fire-wash," because it was added to glass to remove through oxidation the greenish color imparted by reduced iron impurities.

Crystals of this species are rare, and are referred to by the varietal name polianite. They are typically equant to long prismatic, occurring as radiating aggregates. The usual habits of pyrolusite are reniform, concretionary, or stalactitic aggregates, or noncrystalline earthy masses associated with other manganese oxides (referred to as "wad"). Crystals are brittle, with one perfect cleavage; massive material fractures with earthy or fibrous surfaces. Pyrolusite is opaque; iron-black or gray with submetallic to metallic luster in crystals, and flat black and dull in massive form; the streak is blue-black. Earthy varieties are very soft and greasy, leaving their streak on everything. Pyrolusite commonly forms pseudomorphs after primary manganese minerals, especially manganite.

Pyrolusite forms from the alteration of primary manganese minerals such as manganite or rhodonite, as coatings, crusts, and crystals, and as an interstitial mineral in soils and rocks in association with psilomelane, goethite, and limonite. Sedimentary pyrolusite forms as a chemical precipitate in both shallow bodies of water and the deep ocean, as the primary mineral in sedimentary manganese deposits. Good crystalline specimens are found in very few locations, including Cornwall, England, and Czechoslovakia. The large sedimentary manganese deposits which contain massive pyrolusite occur in Brazil, Soviet Georgia, India, Ghana, and South Africa.

Tufts of acicular pyrolusite crystals from Teny Capel, Hant's County, Nova Scotia.

PYROMORPHITE TAKES ITS NAME FROM A GREEK PHRASE MEANING "FIRE-FORMED," since it was observed early on that after being melted, this mineral would reassume its crystalline form upon cooling. Pyromorphite is the phosphatic end member of a solid-solution series with the arsenic-rich end member mimetite, $Pb_5(AsO_4)_3Cl$. A minor ore of lead, pyromorphite is prized for its interesting and colorful crystals. These typically form barrel-shaped hexagonal prisms, which are often hollow; they are commonly clustered in arcuate, subparallel aggregates, which taper to a fine point. Other crystalline habits are equant, tabular, or pyramidal; aggregate habits include granular, fibrous, botryoidal, or globular.

Pyromorphite crystals are generally translucent, and their typical coloration is some shade of green, although yellows or browns are common and orange, colorless, or white crystals are also known. Like many other lead-bearing minerals, pyromorphite has a very high index of refraction, giving it an adamantine luster; the streak is white. The best means of distinguishing between the very similar arsenates mimetite, pyromorphite, and vanadinite is on the basis of color; in the case of ambiguous coloration, chemical tests are needed.

Pyromorphite is a secondary mineral formed in the oxidized portion of hydrothermal lead sulfide deposits, in association with anglesite, cerrusite, barite, galena, hemimorphite, wulfenite, mottramite, smithsonite, and vanadinite. Fine specimens have been recovered from the Wheatly mines, Chester County, and the Ecton and Perkiomen mines, Montgomery County, Pennsylvania; Galena and Carbonate, Lawrence County, South Dakota; the Coeur d'Alene District in Idaho; and many other deposits in the western states. Some of the world's finest specimens have come from the Society Girl Mine, at Moyie, British Columbia. There are many fine sources of pyromorphite in Germany, including Bad Ems in the Rheinland; Johanngeorgenstadt, Saxony; and Kantenbach, Mosel. Other European sources include Cumberland, England; Leadhills, Scotland; Pribram, Czechoslovakia; Beresovsk, in the Ural Mountains of Russia; and Brittany. Good specimens are also found at Broken Hill, New South Wales, Australia, and in a number of other countries including Mexico, Algeria, Burma, and Zaire.

Hexagonal prisms of pyromorphite from Bad Ems, Koblenz District, Rhineland-Pfaltz, Germany. Note the parallel prisms forming a single crystal.

pyromorphite

Classification:
phosphate, apatite group

Composition:
$Pb_5(PO_4)_3Cl$

Crystal System:
hexagonal

Hardness:
3.5–4

Specific Gravity:
7

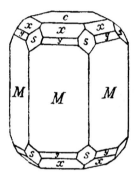

Stellate aggregate of pyrophyllite crystals from Tres Cerritos, Mariposa County, California.

pyrophyllite

Classification:
phyllosilicate

Composition:
$Al_2Si_4O_{10}(OH)_2$
(hydrous aluminum silicate)

Crystal System:
monoclinic, triclinic

Hardness:
1–2

Specific Gravity:
2.65–2.90

THOUGH NOT A PARTICULARLY ATTRACTIVE SPECIES, PYROPHYLLITE HAS GREAT INTRINSIC value. It is very soft, and like most sheet silicates, mechanically weak, readily splitting apart between its structural layers. When heated, it exfoliates as the water is driven off, and it is from this behavior that its Greek name, "fireleaf," is derived. Beyond that change, however, pyrophyllite is extremely stable thermally, withstanding temperatures of 800°C before beginning to decompose further. For this reason it is widely used in refractories. Other important uses are as a carrier (inert ingredient) in insecticides, and a filler for paint and other products. An unusual, black-colored massive variety found in the Transvaal province of South Africa can be molded into a variety of elaborate shapes for use in special high-temperature applications, and is known commercially as "South African Wonderstone."

Crystals of pyrophyllite are rare, tabular, and usually subhedral, and distorted; this species usually forms foliated, fibrous, radiating, lamellar, or compact masses. Crystals have perfect micaceous cleavage in one direction, with resulting laminae that are flexible but not elastic. Pyrophyllite is translucent to opaque, and may be colored white, gray, yellow, light green, pale blue, or brownish, with a pearly to dull luster and a white streak. It has a distinctive greasy feel, but strongly resembles talc and other fine-grained phyllosilicates; chemical tests are usually required for certain identification.

Pyrophyllite is a metamorphic mineral, occurring as an accessory in schists with andalusite, kyanite, sillimanite, lazulite, and muscovite; and in large replacement deposits formed through the wholesale alteration of volcanic rocks. Interesting star-shaped crystal groups up to 2.5 cm in diameter are found in Randolph County, North Carolina; extensive bedded deposits are mined in Guilford and Orange Counties. Other deposits in the Appalachian region include Chesterfield County, South Carolina and Graves Mountain, Lincoln County, Georgia. Pyrophyllite deposits are exploited throughout California and in Arizona as well. Pyrophyllite is also mined in Belgium, Switzerland, Sweden, the Soviet Union, Mexico, Brazil, Korea, and Japan.

THE PYROXENES ARE A GROUP OF DARK, ROCK-FORMING SILICATE MINERALS, WHICH constitute a common constituent of most major igneous rock types. They are closely related in crystal form and composition and have the general formula $ABSi_2O_6$, where

A = Ca, Na, Mg, or Fe^{+2}; and
B = Mg, Fe^{+2}, Fe^{+3}, Fe, Cr, Mn, or Al, with silicon sometimes replaced in part by aluminum.

The structure is based upon a a single chain of silica tetrahedra aligned parallel to the central crystallographic axis. Pyroxenes may crystallize in the orthorhombic or monoclinic systems, and are referred to as orthopyroxenes or clinopyroxenes, respectively. They typically form short, stout prismatic crystals ranging in color from white to dark green or black. The name comes from the Greek words *pyro*, meaning "fire," and *xenos*, meaning "stranger," reflecting the incorrect belief that the pyroxenes were included in lavas and other igneous rocks by accident, as contaminants. This is probably because some species form isolated euhedral phenocrysts in the otherwise noncrystalline groundmass of volcanic rocks.

The pyroxenes are analogous in chemical composition to the amphiboles, except that the pyroxenes lack hydroxyl (OH⁻). The generally dark glassy crystals of the two groups can easily be confused, except for their characteristic cleavage patterns. Both display good prismatic cleavage in two directions, but pyroxene cleavages intersect at nearly 90° (actually 87° and 93°), producing distinctive blocky fragments, while amphibole cleavages intersect at angles of about 56° and 124°.

MANY MINERAL SPECIES HAVE VARIABLE COMPOSITION, BUT PYRRHOTITE VARIES IN AN unusual way, through the omission of one of its essential ions. Pyrrhotite is usually deficient in iron, with many of the iron sites in its crystal structure simply unoccupied. Its composition approaches that of the very rare, simple iron sulfide troilite (FeS), which is found primarily in meteorites. Pyrrhotite is the only mineral beside magnetite that is strongly magnetic, although it is still the less magnetic of the two. Its magnetism varies along with its iron content, the iron-depleted material being the more strongly magnetic. The name is from the Greek term for redness, *pyrrhotes*, in allusion to its typical rosy-bronze tarnish.

Pyrrhotite is usually found in massive granular form, mixed with pyrite, pentlandite, and other sulfides. Crystals are rare but interesting, usually forming thin, tabular or dipyramidal, horizontally striated forms of hexagonal outline, often twinned. Pyrrhotite lacks cleavage but displays basal parting; the fracture is uneven to subconchoidal. The material is opaque and yellow-bronze in color, often with a rosy iridescence and bright metallic luster. It is best distinguished from pyrite by its magnetism and tarnish.

Pyrrhotite occurs as a minor accessory mineral in mafic and ultramafic igneous rocks; in layered igneous intrusions it may be associated with pentlandite, chalcopyrite, and other sulfides. It is also found in some high-grade metamorphic rocks, and in high-temperature hydrothermal sulfide veins with other sulfides and oxides. Rarely, small crystals are found in granitic pegmatites, and in sedimentary deposits associated with siderite.

Large concentrations of pyrrhotite are found in association with nickel sulfides and chalcopyrite in the layered igneous orebody at Sudbury, Ontario, in the Bushveld Complex of South Africa, the Stillwater Complex of Montana, and in other layered intrusions. The finest specimens, however, such as the euhedral hexagonal crystals from the Bluebell Mine, British Columbia, occur in hydrothermal sulfide deposits. Other notable North American localities include Standish, Maine; Lancaster County, Pennsylvania; and Ducktown, Tennessee. Crystals as large as 10 cm in diameter are found at Trepca, Yugoslavia; other European locations include Kisbanya, Romania; Leoben, Austria; Trentino, Italy; and Schneeburg, Andreasberg, Bodenmas, and Freiberg, Germany. The tin mines of Llallagua, Bolivia, have produced extremely large, if rough, crystals; finer specimens come from the Morro Velho Mine, near Ouro Preto, Minas Gerais, Brazil. Pyrrhotite is also found in meteorites.

Twinned pseudohexagonal prisms of pyrrhotite from Santa Eulalia, Chihuahua, Mexico.

IN ADDITION TO BEING ONE OF THE MOST ABUNDANT MINERALS IN THE EARTH'S CRUST, quartz is also one of the most familiar and most useful. Both the crystalline and massive varieties were humankind's main source of tool-making materials over the million years or so that passed between the advent of tool-making and the invention of metallurgy. As technology has advanced, this remarkable material has been adapted to ever more sophisticated uses; the United States' space shuttles, for example, are protected from the cold of outer space and the heat of re-entry by blankets of sintered quartz tiles.

Quartz occurs as euhedral crystals more frequently than any other mineral, and it has attracted the attention of human beings from earliest times to the present. Many theories have been offered to explain these perfectly clear, hard symmetrical objects found in such abundance—including that they were fragments of the nearer stars, fallen to earth. The dominant notion until the time of the Renaissance was that quartz was a special form of ice, so compacted that it was impervious to melting, and which formed, as Pliny maintained, "only where the winter snow brings the most cold." The hexagonal shape of the quartz prism was thought to result from its having been compacted in the high snowfields like the cells of a honeycomb. The Greeks called quartz *krystallos,* or "ice," and the derivative term *crystal* was applied exclusively to quartz until 1669, when Nicholas Steno illustrated that all minerals form regular crystalline shapes with constant interfacial angles.

The main use of quartz has historically been as a gemstone and ornamental material. The many colorful crystalline varieties such as amethyst and citrine are cut into faceted stones for use in jewelry, and both the crystalline and cryptocrystalline varieties (such as agate) have been carved into an endless variety of decorative and devotional objects. Unworked quartz crystals have been objects of reverence in nearly every culture, even before the Roman emperor Augustus consecrated a giant specimen in the Capitol. Small quartz crystals were important parts of the "medicine bundles" used by Native American shamans. Many people in contemporary societies still ascribe vague supernatural powers to quartz crystals, making the sale of "magic" or "healing" crystals a thriving industry.

Most commercial quartz, however, finds more mundane use in heavy industry and technological applications. Quartz sand, the most abundant and easily exploited source of quartz, is the primary raw material for the glass used in containers and windows. It also finds use in fluxes, as an abrasive, and in the manufacture of porcelain. Ever since the Roman physicians first cauterized wounds by focusing the sun's rays through quartz lenses, quartz has been prized for its optical uses. Its transparency to both infrared and ultraviolet light makes it important in a variety of specialized optical applications, as does its ability to manipulate light rays, so that white light can be broken down into its monochromatic components.

The most important technological uses of quartz depend on its *piezoelectricity,* the ability to develop an electric charge when subjected to external pressure. During World War I it was discovered that submarines could be detected by the piezoelectric current generated when their sound waves struck a quartz plate; quartz (and tourmaline) gauges are still used to detect

quartz

Classification:
tectosilicate

Composition:
SiO_2 (silicon dioxide)

Crystal System:
hexagonal (rhombohedral)

Hardness:
7

Specific Gravity:
2.65

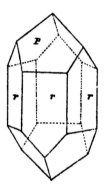

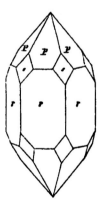

Quartz crystals twinned at right angles according to the Japan Law, from Kurasawa, Kai Province, Japan.

changes in pressure. In the 1920s, quartz plates were first used to control radio frequencies. The quartz plate in a "quartz" watch controls the rate at which the watch records time by vibrating at a set frequency as it receives electricity from a battery. These vibrations in turn control a circuit which sends out pulses at one-second intervals.

The structure of quartz is based on a network of simple of silica tetrahedra. There are several other polymorphs of SiO_2, of which only cristobalite and tridymite are are abundant. The other polymorphs are either synthetic or, like *coesite* and *stishovite*, formed only under restricted conditions such as the extreme pressures associated with a meteorite impact. Quartz itself has two polymorphs, known as *high quartz* and *low quartz*. High quartz forms at temperatures above 573°C and has hexagonal symmetry; upon cooling, it converts to trigonal low quartz. This transformation causes the original, hexagonal atomic structure of high quartz to break down into alternating, mirror-image trigonal units. This results in Dauphine twinning, which is difficult to detect except on sawed or etched cross sections.

Crystalline quartz forms short to long six-sided prisms, with prism faces usually horizontally striated. The terminations consist of six sloping rhombohedral faces; these may develop equally to form hexagonal pyramids, or one set may develop at the expense of the other so that three large faces alternate with three small ones. Crystals are *enantiomorphic*, meaning that they develop either as right- or left-handed forms. Crystalline quartz is brittle, although the cryptocrystalline varieties are often tough enough for use as mortars and pestles. The fracture is perfectly conchoidal and the cleavage indistinct, although crystals tend to fracture parallel to rhombohedral faces.

RHODONITE IS NAMED FROM THE GREEK WORD *RHODON*, OR "ROSE," IN ALLUSION TO its pink color. Along with pectolite and wollastonite, rhodonite belongs to the pyroxenoid group of inosilicates. As in the pyroxenes, the pyroxenoid structure is based upon single chains of SiO_3 groups; in the latter, however, the chains are "kinked" rather than straight, resulting in a triclinic rather than monoclinic crystal symmetry. The formula at right is misleading, as rhodonite is never pure. It always contains some calcium, and both iron and zinc often replace manganese; the zinc-rich variety is known as fowlerite. Massive rhodonite has a delightful pink color, and is usually dissected by a network of black veins of manganese oxides. This material has long been fashioned into cabochons, beads, and other ornamental objects. It was particularly fashionable in 18th-century Russia, where it vied with malachite as the stone of choice for the decorative excesses of the Imperial Court, and was used in a range of objects including tabletops, balustrades, and sarcophagi.

Rhodonite primarily occurs as tough, compact granular masses, cut by the characteristic veins of black manganese oxides. In rare instances it can be found as tabular or prismatic crystals, sometimes with rounded edges, and usually imbedded in matrix. The color is a rich pink, and crystals are transparent to translucent, with a vitreous luster. It is distinguished from the similarly colored carbonate rhodochrosite by its hardness, insolubility, and perfect prismatic cleavage.

Rhodonite forms during the metamorphism of limestones rich in manganese and silica, usually in contact metamorphic settings. It also forms as sedimentary manganese ore bodies that have been subjected to metamorphism. The czars obtained their rhodonite from large bodies in the Ural Mountains near Sverdlovsk; similar deposits are found at Langban and Pajsberg, Sweden; Simsio, Finland; and at Broken Hill, Australia. There are important deposits in California, Colorado, Massachusetts, Maine, and

Classification:
inosilicate, pyroxenoid

Composition:
$MnSiO_3$
(manganese iron magnesium silicate)

Crystal System:
triclinic

Hardness:
5.5–6.5

Specific Gravity:
3.57–3.76

Massive rhodonite from Ompanihy, Southern Madagascar.

Montana, and good crystals of the zinc-rich variety fowlerite can be found in the marbles of Franklin, New Jersey. Deposits of rhodonite also occur in Brazil, South Africa, Japan, Madagascar, and New Zealand.

romanèchite (psilomelane)

Classification:
oxide

Composition:
$(Ba,H_2O)(Mn^{+4},Mn^{+3})_5O_{10}$
(hydrous barium manganese oxide)

Crystal System:
monoclinic

Hardness:
5–6

Specific Gravity:
3.7–4.7

Botryoidal romanèchite with manganocalcite (intermediate in composition between calcite and rhodochrosite) from Ironwood, Michigan.

THE NAME *PSILOMELANE* AT ONE TIME REFERRED TO BARIUM-BEARING MANGANESE oxides as well as undifferentiated manganese oxides. The name romanè-chite (derived from an occurrence at Romanèche, France) has since been applied to the barium species, and psilomelane reserved for the group. Not everyone agrees on this distinction, and psilomelane continues to be used as a species name—largely because the only way to tell one fine-grained manganese oxide from another is by chemical analysis. It is agreed that romanèchite is an important ore of manganese, however (see *Manganite* and *Pyrolusite*).

Never seen in crystals, romanèchite forms botryoidal aggregates or sta-lactitic aggregates with concentric banding, or earthy masses. These are black and opaque, with submetallic luster and a brownish-black to black shiny streak. Romanèchite forms as a primary mineral in residual sedimen-tary deposits with psilome-lane, or as a secondary min-eral through the weathering of primary manganese silicates and carbonates. Large deposits occur at Chiatura, Soviet Georgia, and Nikopol, in the Ukraine, as well as in the United States, Belgium, France, Germany, Scotland, Sweden, and India.

rutile

Classification:
oxide

Composition:
TiO_2 (titanium oxide)

Crystal System:
tetragonal

Hardness:
6–6.5

Specific Gravity:
4.2–4.25.

Stubby prism of rutile from Brazil.

NOT ONLY DOES RUTILE PROVIDE interesting crystals for the col-lector but it is an important ore mineral as well, and has even been used as a gem-stone. There are three poly-morphs of TiO_2: rutile, anatase, and brookite. Of these, rutile is by far the most common, apparently because its structure is stable over a wider range of temperature and pressure conditions. The rutile structure is also shared by the manganese oxide pyro-lusite and the tin oxide cassi-terite. The name is from the Latin, *rutilus*, meaning "golden-red."

Along with ilmenite, rutile is an important ore of titanium, the wonder metal of the rocket age. Titanium metal, or alloys of other metals with tita-nium, are extremely light and strong, and so find extensive use in the air-craft, aerospace, and defense industries. Titanium is also used in various compounds for everything from skywriting to water-proofing to converting electrical current into sound. Because it is so highly reflective, rutile itself is ground up and added to cosmetics such as lipstick and eye shadow, to add that glamorous sheen. The primary use of rutile, however, is in the coating of welding rods.

Transparent synthetic rutile, produced like corundum through the Verneuil process, has extremely high dispersion and was a popular diamond substitute in the 1940s and 1950s before being overshadowed by other, more durable imitations. It is still on the market, however, under trade names such as Titania, Miridis, and Kenya Gem. Although dark in color and rarely transparent, natural rutile is cut as a gemstone for collectors because of its high index of refraction.

Rutile forms elongated or stubby, commonly striated prismatic crystals. Cyclically twinned "belt" crystals may form closed rings; elbow and heart-shaped contact twins are also common. Reticulated aggregates intersecting at 60° angles are known as sagenite. The extremely fine acicular crystals which often occur as inclusions in quartz or other minerals are known as "maiden hair." Rutile is usually opaque or translucent, colored a rich red-brown, dark brown, or black (usually with a reddish tint); the streak is light brown to colorless. Varieties containing iron, niobium, or tantalum may be nearly black, and the fine maidenhair inclusions are typically yellow to orange. Some transparent specimens display dichroism, appearing dark red or nearly black depending upon the crystal direction. Rutile can be distinguished from cassiterite by its lower specific gravity and distinctive crystal forms; the strong adamantine to submetallic luster of rutile is especially distinctive.

Rutile commonly forms an alteration product after primary titanium minerals such as titanite and ilmenite. It is fairly widespread as small grains in many rock types, particularly granites, gneisses, mica schists, and marbles. Since these grains prove very durable after weathering from their host rock, they tend to accumulate as a constituent of heavy placer sands, where they are mined for their titanium content. The most important deposits of rutile sands are exploited in New South Wales and Queensland, Australia.

Euhedral rutile specimens are usually found in contact metamorphic rocks, in pegmatites, and in cavities in quartz veins. Very large, generally simple crystals to 12 cm are found in quartzite and pyrophyllite at Graves Mountain, in Lincoln County, Georgia; similar but smaller specimens are found in pyrophyllite at the Champion Sparkplug Mine in Inyo County, California. Excellent black crystals occur at Magnet Cove, Hot Springs County, Arkansas, including cyclic belt twins and pseudomorphs after brookite. Reticulated sagenite is found in the pegmatites of North Carolina, particularly from near Hiddenite, Alexander County. Beautiful twinned crystals are found at Cerrado Frio, in Minas Gerais, Brazil; and extraordinary examples of maidenhair rutile in quartz are found in the iron deposit at Itibiara, Bahia, Brazil. Fine specimens come from Yrieix, France, Kragero, Norway; and from numerous localities in the Austrian, Italian, and Swiss Alps.

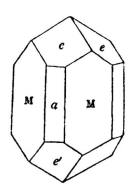

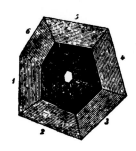

Rutile has many uses, but the most important is as a coating for welding rods.

scheelite

Classification:
tungstate

Composition:
$CaWO_4$ (calcium tungstate)

Crystal System:
tetragonal

Hardness:
4.5–5

Specific Gravity:
6.10

Dipyramidal crystals of scheelite from Saxony, Germany.

SHEELITE IS NAMED FOR THE 18TH-CENTURY SWEDISH CHEMIST KARL WILHELM Scheele, who discovered the metal tungsten (known in Europe as wolfram). Tungsten is an interesting metal. One of the heaviest, it also has the highest melting point of any metal and finds use in strong, heat-resistant alloys and fine filaments for lamps. Among the important tungsten compounds are tungsten carbide, used in high-speed tools and, like diamond, in drill bits; sodium tungstates are used in fireproofing and dying. The minerals of the wolframite series are the most important ores of tungsten. Molybdenum commonly substitutes for tungsten in scheelite, and a solid-solution series exists between scheelite and the calcium–molybdenum tungstate powellite.

Scheelite usually forms dipyramidal crystals resembling truncated octahedra, with faces that are sharp to crude, and often striated or etched. Crystals also occur as penetration or contact twins. Scheelite usually forms massive aggregates, and is commonly found in placer deposits as disseminated grains. Crystals are brittle, with one good and two indistinct cleavages, and a subconchoidal to uneven fracture. Scheelite is transparent to translucent, and may be colorless, white, gray, yellowish, reddish, brownish, or greenish, with a vitreous to adamantine luster and a white streak. It often fluoresces bright blue to white under short-wave ultraviolet light, becoming yellowish with increasing molybdenum content. Scheelite has an unmistakable combination of distinctive characteristics, including its dipyramidal crystals, great density, strong luster, and fluorescence.

Sheelite is found in hydrothermal veins and pegmatites in association with cassiterite, wolframite, topaz, fluorite, tourmaline, and mica; and in placer deposits with other dense species. However, most commercial sheelite concentrations occur in a carbonate-rich contact metamorphic environments called tactite (formed by the intrusion of granites into carbonate rocks), which also contain axinite, garnet, epidote, diopside, tremolite, and wollastonite.

Excellent crystals are obtained from a number of mining regions in the western United States, including the Owens Valley and the Greenhorn Mountains of

California; the Hualpai and Cabezas Mountains of Arizona; Utah's Mineral Mountains; and Mill City, Nevada. Excellent specimens come from Mina Perdida, Huancaya, Peru; and various localities in Bolivia, Brazil, and Mexico. Fine euhedral crystals are found at Caldbeck Fells, Cumberland, England; Traversella, in the Italian Piedmont; at various places in the Swiss Alps; Saxony, Germany; at Zinnwald, Czechoslovakia; and in the Andalucia province of Spain. The largest crystals of scheelite are those from Taehwa, Korea, which may exceed 12 cm in length. Good specimens are also found in Burma, Japan, Malaysia, and Australia.

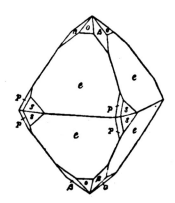

THE NAME IS DERIVED FROM THE GREEK *SKOLEX*, OR "WORM," AN ALLUSION TO ITS habit of curling into worm-like shapes when heated. Scolecite is very similar in appearance and properties to the zeolites natrolite and mesolite, sharing their general structure of parallel chains of AlO_4 and SiO_4 tetrahedra. This structure is reflected in the perfect prismatic cleavage of scolecite, and in its very slender, prismatic, vertically striated crystals. These are usually clustered in radiating groups, and are colorless or white, with a vitreous to silky luster.

Scolecite is found in basalt cavities and in contact metamorphic environments such as the Crestmore Quarry in California. Good specimens are found in most of the major zeolite occurrences, including those in northern New Jersey; the Columbia Plateau of Oregon and Washington; Table Mountain, Colorado; the Bay of Fundy District, Nova Scotia; Iceland; the Faeroe Islands; northern Scotland; Poona, India; and Rio Grande do Sul, Brazil.

scolecite

Classification:
tectosilicate, zeolite group

Composition:
$CaAl_2Si_3O_{10} \cdot 3H_2O$
(hydrated calcium aluminum silicate)

Crystal System:
monoclinic

Hardness:
5–5.5

Specific Gravity:
2.27

A radiating spray of acicular scolecite crystals in basalt, from Ostero, Faeroe Islands.

ALTHOUGH THE SEDIMENTARY ROCKS ACCOUNT FOR ONLY A SMALL FRACTION OF THE earth's crust, they cover nearly 80% of the surface. Some sedimentary rocks are derived from other rock types through the process of weathering. Chemical weathering decomposes the actual minerals in the rocks, converting feldspars to clays, for instance, while mechanical weathering physically dismantles the rock to create sediments. Once weathered from their parent rock, sediments are collected in a variety of depositional environments, from desert dunes to riverbeds to ocean basins; and unless they are reworked by erosion, the process of lithification turns them into sedimentary rock. Sedimentary rocks formed through the decomposition of other rocks are called *detrital* rocks, from the word detritus.

Other sedimentary rocks are formed through the strictly chemical processes. Elements and compounds derived from the chemical weathering of rocks, such as carbonates, silica, salt, and phosphorous, are transported in solution to oceans and lakes. If these bodies of water become saturated with respect to a particular chemical, it may precipitate as solid grains and collect in sediment form. Organisms which use dissolved chemicals to build their skeletons also contribute to chemical sedimentation. The two main groups of sedimentary rocks, detrital and chemical, are described below.

The currents of water and wind which carry detrital sediments to their final resting places sort the mineral grains by size and mass; stronger currents carry larger and heavier rock or mineral grains. Detrital sedimentary rocks are generally divided into categories on the basis of grain size. Conglomerates are composed of coarse, rounded rock or mineral fragments of boulder to gravel size, usually suspended in a finer-grained matrix; breccias are rocks containing equally coarse-grained, but more angular particles. Such rocks are said to be poorly sorted, because they contain a variety of different grain sizes. The sandstones are composed of medium-sized, rounded or angular grains, usually of quartz. Pure quartz sandstones result from the chemical elimination of feldspars and other less resistant mineral grains. Graywackes are dark sandstones that contain considerable feldspar and small fragments of metamorphic or volcanic rocks. Rocks composed primarily of clay and silt-sized particles are generally referred to as mudstones. Shale is a variety of mudstone which contains an abundance of clay or mica particles in parallel orientation, giving it a roughly planar cleavage called fissility.

The chemical sedimentary rocks are divided on the basis of their mineralogy, which of course reflects the chemical or biological processes of their formation. The most important chemical rocks are those composed of the carbonate minerals calcite and dolomite. Calcite and aragonite are extracted from sea water by planktonic animals, coral and molluscs, which use these minerals to form their skeletons. Aragonite may precipitate directly from seawater, without biological mediation; it eventually alters to the more stable form of calcite. Rocks composed of calcium carbonate are called *limestones*. Magnesium-rich limestones may in time alter to the magnesium carbonate dolomite.

The second major class of chemical sediments are the *evaporites*, which form through the precipitation of

Top: *Detrital sedimentary rocks. From left, conglomerate, shale, and sandstone.*
Bottom: *Limestone coquina composed of marine mollusc shells.*

large quantities of anhydrite, gypsum, halite and other minerals from over-saturated bodies of water (see *Borates, Evaporites, Halite).* Cherts and diatomites are siliceous chemical sediments composed of quartz and opal, respectively. They form in much the same way as limestone, except that the microscopic animal skeletons of which they are composed are made of SiO_2 rather than $CaCO_3$. The *banded iron formations* are an ancient form of chemical sedimentary rock, consisting of hematite, ankerite and siderite (see *Hematite).* Phosphorites are sedimentary rocks containing a mixture of detrital sediments and phosphate minerals (see *Apatite).*

serpentine

Classification:
phyllosilicate

Composition:
$(Mg,Fe^{+2})_3Si_2O_5(OH)_4$
(magnesium-iron hydroxyl silicate)

Crystal System:
monoclinic and orthorhombic

Hardness:
approximately 2–5

Specific Gravity:
approximately 2.5–2.6

SERPENTINE CAN BE CONSIDERED A SINGLE SPECIES WITH HIGHLY VARIABLE PHYSICAL properties, or a mineral group containing three polymorphs. Serpentine is very abundant as the main constituent of serpentinite, which forms through the *in situ* alteration of silica-poor igneous rocks such as peridotite, dunite, and even kimberlite. As such, serpentine itself can be thought of as a product of the decomposition of olivine and pyroxenes, with water added. Relict igneous textures, such as pseudomorphs of serpentine after olivine and pyroxene crystals, are commonly observed in serpentinites. The name is in reference to the sinuous snake-like markings visible in carved and polished material.

The two main subdivisions of serpentine are based on structure. Antigorite and lizardite are types of serpentine which form minute mica-ceous crystals which compose the groundmass of most serpentinites. Another form is the fibrous, or asbestiform, variety called chrysotile, from the Greek words meaning "golden fiber." Chrysotile forms as semi-crys-talline tubes, composed of sheets of $Mg_3Si_2O_5(OH)_4$ rolled around a hollow core like a parchment scroll. The length of these tubes may be as much as 10,000 times their width, and they form as parallel aggregates of extremely tough fibers.

Serpentine has two main uses, both of which have ambiguous merit. Serpentine in its massive, translucent green form has long been used as a substitute for jade (see *Jadeite* and *Actinolite–Tremolite).* While ornamental serpentine, sometimes called bowenite or *verde antique,* makes very attractive carvings and building materials, much of it is fashioned into bangles and other jewelry and sold as jade. The unfortunate buyer of such pieces soon discovers that serpentine, with a hardness of 2–5 on the Mohs Scale and much lower tenacity than either form of jade, does not wear very well in jewelry.

The other use of serpentine is in the form of chrysotile asbestos, the most important of the two main forms of asbestos (the other is crocidolite, the asbestiform variety of the amphibole riebeckite). Asbestos, from the Greek word meaning "incombustible," is a wonderful substance in some ways. It was discovered that its long, strong fibers were heat-resistant and flexible, and could thus be shredded, spun, and woven like cotton and made into useful articles like gloves that were impervious to heat. Asbestos was also used as fireproofing and insulation in buildings, electrical insulation, pipes, gaskets, paper, and especially, brake linings for automobiles. As a wonder mineral, asbestos had few equals, until it was found that the tiny fibers liberated by the mining, milling, and use of asbestos products are potent carcinogens, causing three types of lung disease, including lung cancer. Since the amphibole variety of asbestos is apparently more dangerous than chrysotile, the asbestos industry is cham-

Chrysotile, the fibrous variety of serpentine, is the most important type of asbestos. Its incombustible fibers are essential to many products, but long-term exposure to them can result in lung cancer and other diseases.

Massive serpentine from the Aosta Valley in the Italian Piedmont.

pioning the latter as "safe" asbestos, but the future of asbestos use remains in limbo as the government considers further regulations. No satisfactory substitutes for asbestos have been found.

Serpentine is quite distinctive, usually forming large bodies of green, waxy-looking rock with patches of white alteration. Massive granular material has an uneven to fibrous fracture, while the fibers of chrysotile asbestos can be dislodged by rubbing—although this is not recommended, for obvious reasons. The color of the massive varieties ranges from dark blackish-green through olive-green, blue-green, and yellowish-green, and they are translucent to opaque, with a waxy or greasy luster and a colorless streak. Chrysotile asbestos is golden yellow in color, with a silky luster. Serpentine feels greasy when rubbed, and is harder than talc (soapstone) and softer than nephrite jade.

In addition to forming through the alteration of basic igneous rocks, serpentine forms in smaller quantities in calcareous metamorphic rocks such as marble, and in some schists. Common associates include chromite, brucite, chlorite, magnesite, and magnetite. Pure masses of antigorite have been found at the eponymous deposit in Val Antigorio, in the Italian Piedmont, and lizardite at The Lizard in Cornwall, but more ambiguous material is common and widespread. Serpentinized peridotites are exposed on land where sections of the oceanic crust, called ophiolites (see *Chromite*), have been thrust onto the continent through tectonic processes. Notable ophiolite exposures are found in the California Coast Ranges, in the Mediterranean region, and in the Indo-Pacific area. Chrysotile asbestos was long mined in southeastern Quebec, at the 2-km-wide, 900-m-deep Jeffrey Mine.

siderite

Classification:
carbonate

Composition:
$FeCO_3$ (iron carbonate)

Crystal System:
hexagonal (rhombohedral)

Hardness:
3.5–4.

Specific Gravity:
3.8–3.9

TRANSPARENT OR TRANSLUCENT AND RELATIVELY LIGHT IN COLOR, SIDERITE MAKES AN improbable source of iron, which is usually found in opaque metallic sulfides or black silicates. But its high iron content (about 48%) makes siderite a plausible ore of this metal. The name comes from the Greek word for iron, *sideros.* Siderite is an excellent example of how the chemical properties of isomorphic minerals can affect their physical properties: although both calcite ($CaCO_3$) and siderite have the same crystalline form and cleavage pattern, siderite is much heavier and darker than calcite, and unlike its isomorph, does not dissolve easily in acid. Manganese, magnesium, calcium, and cobalt commonly substitute for iron in siderite, and solid-solution series exist between siderite and both rhodochrosite ($MnCO_3$) and magnesite ($MgCO_3$). Sideroplesite is the name given to the intermediate magnesium-rich variety.

Euhedral crystals of siderite are uncommon, but simple small rhombohedra may form druses lining fissures in hydrothermal deposits. The classic habit of siderite, however, is a warped, or saddle-shaped rhombohedron, formed by the aggregation of several offset individuals. It is commonly massive, either as botryoidal aggregates, oolites, or concretions. Siderite is

Siderite crystals from the Virtuous Lady Mine, Buckland Monachorum, Tavistock, Devon.

brittle, with an uneven to conchoidal fracture and perfect rhombohedral cleavage. Most specimens are translucent and some shade of brown, with a vitreous luster and a white streak. Color variations include colorless, honey-colored, gray, or greenish; manganese-rich material may be nearly black. Siderite may be coated by iridescent film, or partially altered to the iron hydroxide goethite.

Siderite is distinguished from its isomorphs and solid-solution relatives by its brown color and unusual warped composite crystals. Although it may superficially resemble sphalerite, it is easily distinguished by its cleavage. Unlike calcite, siderite does not effervesce in cold hydrochloric acid.

Siderite commonly forms fissure-fillings and bedded deposits in sedimentary rocks, but the best crystals are generally found in hydrothermal sulfide veins, associated with fluorite, barite, galena, sphalerite, and other minerals. Siderite also occurs in some metamorphic rocks and pegmatites, and in cavities in basaltic rocks. At Mont St. Hilaire, Quebec, excellent siderite crystals are found in cavities in a carbonatite formation. An unusual but important source of siderite is the cryolite-bearing pegmatite at Ivigtut, on Arsuk Fjord in Greenland, where it forms cleavages 30 cm on a side. Very large cleavage rhombs are also obtained from near Roxbury, Litchfield County, Connecticut. Interesting spherical aggregates are obtained from basalt cavities in several areas of Washington State. Colorado produces very good specimens from a number of deposits, including the mines of the Gilman District, and the pegmatites of the Crystal Peak region. Siderite is an important constituent of the Homestake iron deposit in South Dakota; good specimens are obtained from many other deposits throughout the western United States. Wonderful crystals are found at several localities in Cornwall, England, particularly Redruth and St. Austell. Among the many German sources are the mines of Saxony, Lintorf, Hannover; and Neudorf, in the Harz. Alpine locations include Erzberg, Austria; and Traversella, in the Italian Piedmont. Extraordinary specimens of siderite with pyrite are found at Colavi, Bolivia; and siderite with quartz can be found at the Morro Velho gold mine, in the state of Minas Gerais, Brazil.

THE SILICATES COMPRISE BY FAR THE LARGEST AND MOST DIVERSE OF THE MINERAL classes. Silicates make up over 90% of the earth's crust and include 25% of all known mineral species, reflecting the fact that oxygen and silicon are the most abundant elements in the crust (62% and 21%, respectively). The silicates are major components of virtually every of igneous and metamorphic rock type, and since they are relatively hard and insoluble, they survive physical and chemical weathering to contribute to sedimentary rocks as well.

The structure of all silicates is based on the silica tetrahedron, composed of one Si^{+4} cation surrounded by four O^{-2} anions. The bond that holds the silica tetrahedron together is half ionic and half covalent, arising both from the attraction of oppositely charged ions, and the sharing of electrons between silicon and oxygen. It's no overstatement to say that this bond is the glue which holds the earth itself together.

Since each oxygen in a silica tetrahedron has only half of its bonding energy satisfied, any oxygen atom is available to form a bond with another silicon atom. Only one oxygen may be shared between any two tetrahedra, but one, two, three, or all four oxygen can combine with other tetrahedra. The linkage of silica tetrahedra results in the wide range of structures which characterize the different silicate groups described below.

Aluminum is the third most abundant element in the earth's crust after oxygen and silicon, and plays a very important role in the chemistry of the silicates. Since the atomic radius of the Al^{+3} ion is similar to that of Si^{+4}, aluminum and oxygen form tetrahedra of approximately the same size as silica tetrahedra, and the two frequently occur in combination. Aluminium may also combine with six oxygen molecules in octahedral groups, which are also important in the structure of many silicates. Mg, Fe^{+2}, Fe^{+3}, Mn^{+2}, and Ti^{+4} are also found in octahedral groups in the silicates, and these ions are frequently involved in solid solution. Larger cations such as Ca^{+2} and Na^{+1} are typically surrounded by eight oxygen atoms. Hydroxyl (OH) is also present in many species, as is water.

Silicates containing isolated tetrahedra are called *nesosilicates*. Ionic bonds bind these isolated tetrahedra together with interstitial cations; the structures and physical properties of the nesosilicates are largely controlled by the size and charge of these same cations. The dense structure of the nesosilicates gives them high density and hardness, while their relatively homogeneous structure gives them equant crystal habits and poor cleavage (kyanite and sillimanite are conspicuous exceptions). Nesosilicates are abundant in high-temperature igneous and metamorphic rocks. Olivine is an extremely important nesosilicate in mafic igneous rocks, while the garnets and the aluminum silicates andalusite, kyanite, and sillimanite are essential components of regional metamorphic rocks.

Nesosilicate tetrahedron, $(SiO_4)^{-4}$

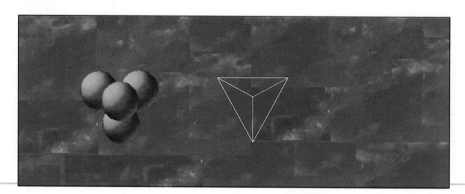

A simple elaboration of the nesosilicate tetrahedron produces the basic unit of the *sorosilicate* structure, an $(Si_2O_7)^{-6}$ group, or two tetrahedra sharing one oxygen. As in the above group, the physical properties of the nesosilicates are largely controlled by the nature of the other ions present. Although over 70 sorosilicate species have been described, only a few are geologically important, including allanite, epidote, hemimorphite, and vesuvianite.

The structures of the *cyclosilicates* are characterized by interconnected rings of silica tetrahedra. Three basic ring geometries exist, all preserving a

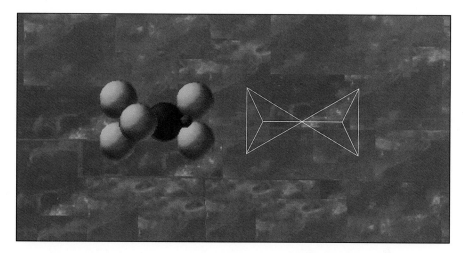

Sorosilicate group, $(Si_2O_7)^{-6}$

silicon to oxygen ratio of 1:3. The simplest is the triangular Si_3O_9 ring, found only in benitoite and two closely allied species. Nearly as rare is the square Si_4O_{12} ring, which occurs in the complex triclinic cyclosilicate axinite. The structures of the most important cyclosilicates are based upon neatly stacked Si_6O_{18} rings. In beryl and cordierite, these rings are stacked in layers, their central openings forming channels which can accommodate a variety of interstitial ions. The structure of tourmaline is somewhat more complex, and gives rise to hemimorphic crystals.

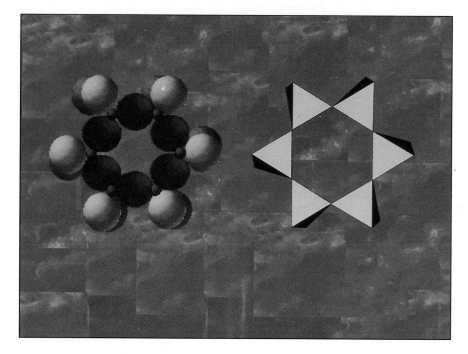

Cyclosilicate ring, $(Si_6O_{18})^{-12}$

In the *inosilicates*, silica tetrahedra are linked to form long single chains, or ribbon-like double chains, held together by interstitial metal cations. The single-chain inosilicates of the pyroxene group and the double-chain members of the amphibole group are among the most important rock-forming minerals. The amphiboles generally form at lower temperatures than the pyroxenes, and contain hydroxyl, which the pyroxenes do not. Members of both groups are otherwise similar in composition and appearance, although they can be distinguished by the differing angles between cleavages—a result of the differing width of their structural chains. Most inosilicates display one or more good prismatic cleavages, with poor cleavage or none in other directions, because bonds are strong within chains and relatively weak in between. The chain structure is also expressed in the external morphology of inosilicate crystals, which are typically prismatic, acicular or fibrous.

Inosilicate single chain

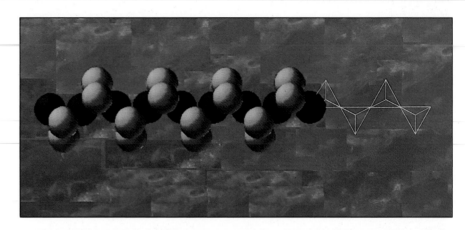

Inosilicate double chain

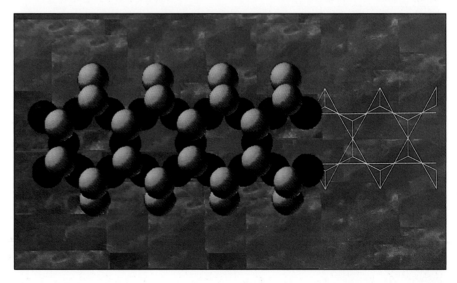

The silica tetrahedra in the *phyllosilicates* are arranged in two-dimensional sheets, in which each tetrahedron shares three oxygens with its neighbors. These tetrahedral sheets are held together by positive interstitial ions, all of which are stacked in either two- or three-layer sequences. Two-layer species such as kaolinite (see *Clay Minerals*) and serpentine contain alternating sheets of silica tetrahedra and of octahedra composed of Al or Mg ions, coordinated with both the oxygen of the silica tetrahedra and hydroxyl. In the three-layer phyllosilicates, such as talc, the octahedral sheets are sandwiched in between *two* layers of silica tetrahedra, their apices of pointing toward one another. Because these sheets are held together by weak van der Waal's forces, the phyllosilicates are generally soft and display perfect cleavage between sheets, resulting in flexible (and sometimes elastic) cleavage lamellae. The phyllosilicates are important rock-forming minerals. Micas are important in igneous rocks and are the dominant component of the metamorphic schists. The clays, chlorites, and serpentines are often the stable products of weathering , and thus form a major part of many metamorphic and sedimentary rocks.

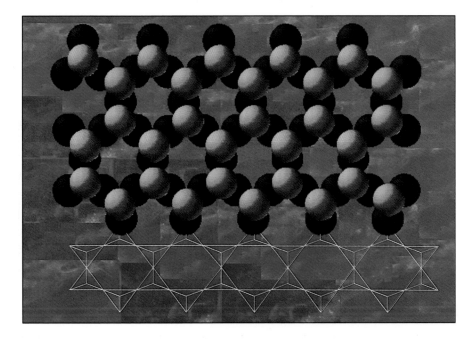

Phyllosilicate sheet structure

In the *tectosilicates*, all four oxygens in each silica tetrahedron are bound to other tetrahedra, resulting in relatively open three-dimensional frameworks. The large interstices thus formed can accommodate large ions such as Ba^{+2}, Ca^{+2}, K^{+1}, Na^{+1} and even H_2O. The simplest tectosilicates are the silica polymorphs, including quartz, cristobalite, and tridymite, all of which are pure SiO_2. The most abundant tectosilicates, and indeed the most abundant of all minerals, are the feldspars. These minerals are formed where Al is able to substitute for Si in the silica framework, producing a net negative charge and necessitating the presence of positively charged ions of K^{+1}, Ca^{+2} and Na^{+1}. Other important tectosilicate groups include the feldspathoids and zeolites.

Tectosilicate framework (cristobalite), SiO_2

sillimanite

Classification:
nesosilicate

Composition:
Al_2SiO_5 (aluminum silicate)

Crystal System:
orthorhombic

Hardness:
6–7

Specific Gravity:
3.23–3.27

Fibrous parallel crystals of sillimanite from Le Clion, Valpelline, Piemonte, Italy. The sillimanite defines the foliation in this rock, which was subjected to metamorphic compression perpendicular to the orientation of the crystals.

ALONG WITH ANDALUSITE AND KYANITE, SILLIMANITE IS ONE OF THE THREE ALUMINUM silicate polymorphs, each of which is stable over a different range of pressures and temperatures. The dominant polymorph indicates the metamorphic grade of the enclosing rock; sillimanite is found in rocks subjected to the highest temperatures, above the stability range of either andalusite or kyanite (see diagram in *Andalusite*). Like its cousins, it is used in the manufacture of refractory brick, tile, and high-temperature crucibles. Some transparent specimens, and others which display chatoyancy, are cut into gemstones. This species is named for Benjamin Silliman (b. 1779), a professor of chemistry and geology at Harvard.

Sillimanite crystals usually take the form of long slender prisms or wisps, drawn out parallel to the grain of the host rock; these are squarish in cross section and generally lack distinct terminations. Radiating crystalline aggregates and granular masses are common; parallel, fibrous aggregates are referred to as fibrolite. The crystals display perfect prismatic cleavage and uneven fracture. Sillimanite is transparent to translucent, with a vitreous to silky luster and a colorless streak. Characteristic colors include colorless, white, gray, yellowish, brownish, greenish, and bluish. Sillimanite sometimes occurs as acicular inclusions in other silicate minerals.

Sillimanite is a very widespread and important constituent of high-temperature regional metamorphic rocks such as schists and gneisses. It also occurs in the innermost zone of some contact metamorphic deposits, and as a minor constituent in some granites and pegmatites. It is common in the metamorphic rocks of New England and the related groups in Northern Europe, in the Appalachian Mountains, and in the Alps. Well-formed crystal groups are found in Czechoslovakia, Italy, and Germany. Large deposits of industrial sillimanite are mined in India, and transparent blue crystals are recovered from the gem gravels of Burma.

silver

Classification:
native element

Composition:
Ag (elemental silver)

Crystal System:
isometric

Hardness:
2.5–3

Specific Gravity:
10.5

BECAUSE NATIVE SILVER IS MORE CHEMICALLY REACTIVE THAN GOLD, IT IS FOUND LESS often in its native form, and is usually deeply tarnished and not easily recognized. Even though silver is actually the more abundant metal, many ancient cultures valued it more highly than gold because of the difficulty of obtaining it (for the same reason, copper was valued more highly than gold by some early peoples). Today, however, the value of silver is only a fraction of that of gold. Many ancient cultures associated silver with the moon in their cosmology and rituals.

Since pure silver is too soft for silverware and jewelry, it is usually alloyed with copper. Silver alloys are marked with their silver content in parts per thousand; "sterling" silver has a content of 925 parts of pure silver and 75 parts of copper. Native silver usually contains small amounts of gold, mercury, arsenic, or antimony. Other than in jewelry and silverware, its main uses are in the electronics industry, in plating technology, and as a catalyst in chemical processing. Large quantities of silver, in the form of synthetic silver halides, are used to make light-sensitive photographic emulsions.

Crystals of silver are rarely distinct, and commonly occur as anhedral masses, thin wires, sheets, and plates. Crystals are mostly crude cubes, but also form octahedrons and dodecahedrons. The typical aggregate habit consists of twinned, arborescent parallel growths called "herringbones," and dendrites. Silver is highly malleable, ductile, and sectile, and displays a hackly fracture. When naturally alloyed with gold, the specific gravity of silver increases to about 11 and falls to about 10 when alloyed with other metals. Silver is opaque, and brilliant white on fresh surfaces, although most specimens are tarnished gray to black due to alteration in surface layers. The streak is shiny white and the luster metallic. Silver can usually be distinguished by its malleability, high specific gravity, and black tarnish.

Native silver occurs in hydrothermal sulfide veins and in some basaltic rocks. When hydrothermal deposits containing silver are subjected to weathering at the earth's surface, chemical reactions may produce an enriched zone of secondary silver minerals (see *Chlorargyrite*), and sometimes, native silver. In only a few of its widespread occurrences has native silver been an important ore. Native silver has been mined continuously for over three hundred years at Kongsberg, Norway, where it occurs as a primary mineral in extensive low-temperature veins, associated with calcite, quartz, sulfides, and zeolites. Large masses of pure silver, some weighing hundreds of kilograms have come from this source, as have delicate silver crystals and wires that are probably the finest specimens known.

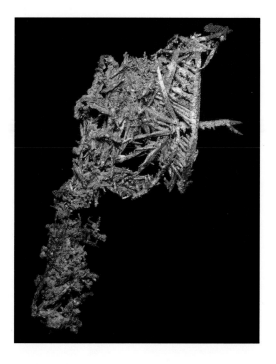

Silver has been mined even longer from the Erzgebirge, or "ore mountains," which lie between the Saxony region of Germany and the Bohemia region of Czechoslovakia, and from Freiberg, where it is found in veins associated with arsenides and sulfides of cobalt and nickel and with native bismuth. The Dominican scholar Albertus Magnus (b. 1193) noted in his *Book of Minerals* that the silver at Freiberg was found as "columns standing up under the earth and extending through the earth like strings."

Exceptional specimens have been obtained from copper deposits of the Keweenaw Peninsula, the silver being intimately associated with copper in cavities in basalt, associated with prehnite, calcite, analcime, stilbite, and other zeolites. Small crystals of silver occur within earthy chalcocite at Bisbee, Cochise County, Arizona, where wire silver in gossans can also be found. In Canada, large sheets, slabs, and irregular masses of silver are found with silver and nickel sulfides at Cobalt, Gowganda, and O'Brien, Ontario. Interesting specimens of silver embedded in dolomite occur on Silver Islet, Thunder Bay District; dendritic masses in pitchblende deposits occur in the Great Bear Lake District, Northwest Territories; and wires with calcite, pyrite, and sphalerite, can be found at Beaver Dell, British Columbia. Excellent wire and arborescent silver comes from Batopilas, Chihuahua, Mexico, and from numerous localities in the states of Sonora, Durango, and Zacatecas. Good wire specimens come from Broken Hill, New South Wales, Australia; and small sheets and wires with bornite and chalcocite from Tsumeb, Namibia.

Left: Reticulated aggregate of silver crystals from Copiapo, Chile. *Right:* Cerro Rico ("Rich Hill") looms over Potosí, Bolivia, center of the world's richest silver mining district. The silver veins of Cerro Rico have produced over 2.5 billion ounces of silver since the mines were opened in 1544.

skutterudite

Classification:
arsenide

Composition:
$(Co,Ni)As_3$ (cobalt nickel arsenide)

Crystal System:
isometric

Hardness:
6

Specific Gravity:
6.1–6.9

SKUTTERUDITE AND ITS ARSENIC-POOR RELATIVE SMALTITE, $(Co, Ni)As_{3-x}$ (x = 0.5-1), are important ores of cobalt, nickel, and arsenic. A nickel-rich variety is called nickel–skutterudite, and it also has an arsenic-deficient analog called chloanthite. Skutterudite has a unique structure, based on a group of four arsenic atoms arranged in a perfect square. Its crystals form cubes, octahedra, dodecahedra, and various combinations of these shapes; and are fragile, with two directions of cleavage. The color is tin-white, with iridescent tarnish, metallic luster, and a black streak.

Skutterudite is named for the occurrence of fine crystals at Skutterud, Norway. It is found in medium- to high-temperature hydrothermal veins, associated with cobalt and nickel sulfides, arsenopyrite, native silver, bismuth, and calcite. Other occurrences include Cobalt, Ontario; Bou Azzer, Morocco; the Anarak District of Iran; Schneeberg and elsewhere in Saxony, Germany; and a few scattered locations in the western United States, including the Elk Mountains of Colorado, and Graham County, Arizona.

Complex crystal of skutterudite from Skutterud, Modum, Norway, showing a variety of isometric forms.

The English chemist and mineralogist James Smithson (b. 1754), known for having left his fortune as an endowment to establish the Smithsonian Institution in Washington, D.C., was honored by having this lovely mineral named after him. Previously, smithsonite fell under the general term calamine, as all the zinc ores that could be used for the production of brass (alloyed zinc and copper) were collectively known. Smithsonite and the similar-appearing zinc silicate known as hemimorphite were considered together under this rubric. Smithsonite is isostructural with calcite, and appears to form a solid-solution series with rhodochrosite ($MnCO_3$). Still used as an ore of zinc, smithsonite also finds favor as an ornamental stone in its more colorful massive forms.

Smithsonite rarely occurs as distinct rhombohedral or scalenohedral crystals; aggregates of fine radiating crystals are the rule. Its typical aggregate habits include botryoidal, reniform, and stalactitic; miners called the characteristic open honeycomb masses "dry-bone ore." Smithsonite would be white if pure, but it seldom is; common impurities include cadmium, cobalt, copper, iron, and manganese. Colors include a copper-influenced blue-green, violet from cobalt or manganese, and brown due to iron oxides; the yellow cadmium-rich variety of smithsonite is called "turkey-fat ore." The streak is always white, however.

Smithsonite is formed at the expense of primary zinc minerals such as sphalerite, when intermediate zinc sulfates react with carbonate minerals, as in Mississippi Valley-type hydrothermal replacement deposits. Common

smithsonite

Classification:
carbonate

Composition:
$ZnCO_3$ (zinc carbonate)

Crystal System:
hexagonal (rhombohedral)

Hardness:
4–4.5

Specific Gravity:
4.4

Left: *Large scalenohedral crystals of smithsonite from the Broken Hill mines, Zambia.*
Right: *Botryoidal aggregates of blue smithsonite from the Kelley Mine, Magdalena, New Mexico.*

associates include anglesite, cerrusite, hemimorphite, malachite, and pyromorphite. Some of the classic sources for smithsonite specimens are the Kelley Mine, Magdalena, New Mexico; Laurium, Greece, and Chihuahua, Mexico. Euhedral crystals as large as 1 cm, either colorless or pink, green, or white, are found at Tsumeb, Namibia, and Broken Hill, Zambia. Extensive stalactitic deposits of turkey-fat ore occur in Sardinia and in the lead mines at Yellville, Arkansas.

sodalite

Classification:
tectosilicate, feldspathoid

Composition:
$Na_8(AlSiO_4)_6Cl_2$
(sodium aluminum silicate with chlorine)

Crystal System:
isometric

Hardness:
5.5–6

Specific Gravity:
2.14–2.4

MASSIVE BLUE SODALITE IS EASILY CONFUSED WITH THE RELATED MINERAL LAZURITE, IN the form of lapis lazuli, and with lazulite. However, sodalite is usually more translucent than either of these species (if not transparent) and has a distinctive violet cast; unlike lazurite, it is not typically associated with pyrite and calcite. Like lapis lazuli, sodalite has been used as a decorative stone, but it is neither as rare nor as highly valued. One drawback to its use as an ornamental stone is that the lovely violet-blue color displayed by sodalite in natural light is often replaced by a nearly black color under artificial light.

Sodalite almost always occurs as granular masses, disseminated grains, or nodular aggregates; dodecahedral crystals are sometimes encountered, however. It is transparent to translucent, and colored blue, gray, yellowish, white, colorless, green, or pink, with a vitreous to greasy luster and a colorless streak. It may fluoresce under ultraviolet light, particularly the pink variety known as hackmanite. Sodalite is brittle, with one poor cleavage and uneven to conchoidal fracture.

Sodalite forms as a primary mineral in nepheline syenites and related rocks (including nepheline-syenite pegmatites), as well as in certain calcareous contact metamorphic deposits. An unusual occurrence is in the lavas of Vesuvius in Italy, which have undergone mixing with carbonate country rocks. Sodalite is found in Montana's Bearpaw Mountains, at Cripple Creek, Colorado; at Magnet Cove, Arkansas; at Beemerville, New Jersey; and at several sites around New England. Ornamental sodalite has been quarried in Hastings and Renfrew Counties, Ontario. Specimens of massive sodalite are obtained from Kicking Horse Pass and Ice River, British Columbia; and Mont St. Hilaire, Quebec. Other sources include Angola, Bolivia, Brazil, Burma, Greenland, Korea, Romania, Norway, Italy, Germany, Scotland, and Zambia.

Massive sodalite from Dungannon, Hastings County, Ontario.

IN THE SAME WAY THAT "SOLID ROCK" SYMBOLIZES PERMANENCE AND STABILITY, gemstones and mineral crystals represent purity in the popular imagination. But just as earthquakes and drifting continents point up the fallacy of geologic permanence, so the principle of *solid solution* challenges the notion of crystal "purity." The term solid solution reflects the fact that the chemical behavior of crystalline solids can be analogous to that of chemical compounds in liquid solutions, which fluctuate between compositional extremes in response to temperature changes and other factors. The systematic compositional variation exhibited by many minerals can provide vital clues about the conditions of rock formation and the origin of ores.

The most important mechanism of solid solution is *substitution*. Each ion in a crystal occupies a particular position because of its valence state and ionic radius, and ions with similar properties may substitute for one another in various structural sites. Substitution occurs most easily between ions whose ionic radii differ by less than 15%; as the size difference becomes greater, substitution becomes less likely. Simple ionic substitution can involve either cations or anions.

The need to maintain electrical neutrality in a crystal structure is as important a factor in substitution as ionic size. Although substitution typically takes place between ions of the same charge, such as Fe^{+2} and Mg^{+2}, other ions involved in solid solution have differing charges. In such cases, an anion and a cation must be replaced in tandem in order to preserve the electrical neutrality, in the process known as *coupled substitution*. An important example of coupled substitution is the solid solution between the plagioclase feldspars albite ($NaAlSi_3O_8$) and anorthite ($CaAl_2Si_2O_8$), in which substitution occurs between monovalent Na^+ ions and divalent Ca^{+2} ions. For every Ca^{+2} ion replaced by Na^+, for example, one Si^{+4} ion in the silica tetrahedra framework must be replaced by an Al^{+3} ion in order to maintain electrical neutrality (see *Silicates*).

The compositional variation which exists between the sodium and calcium plagioclases is an example of a complete *solid-solution series*. In such series there is a complete range of minerals with compositions intermediate between two ideal *end members* (in this case, albite and anorthite). In the case of the plagioclases, species of intermediate composition are given individual names (see *Plagioclase*), but in most cases of complete solid solution only the end members are recognized. An important example is the olivine solid solution series, in which Fe^{+2} replaces Mg^{+2} between the end members forsterite (Mg_2SiO_4) and fayalite (Fe_2SiO_4). In most solid-solution

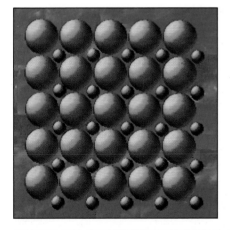 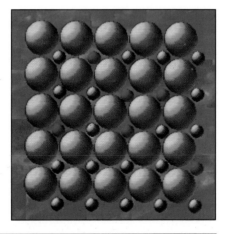 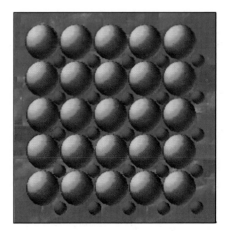

Simple illustration depicting the principle of solid solution. The two pure end members (left and right) have one type of ion in common, and each contains one other, different type of ion as well. If the ions unique to each end member have similar atomic radii and charges, a minerals of intermediate composition (center) are possible.

series, pure end members (completely lacking ionic substitution) are very rare; thus, most mineral formulae are only approximations.

More common in nature than complete solid-solution is *limited solid solution*, in which the substituting ions are less perfectly analogous and can only substitute for one another to a limited degree without disrupting the crystal structure. An example of this is the narrow range of solid solution which exists between anhydrite, $CaSO_4$, and barite, $BaSO_4$. Since Ba^{+2} is significantly larger than Ca^{+2}, only a small percentage of barium can replace the calcium in anhydrite, and a similarly small amount of calcium can be accommodated by barite; thus, most specimens of either species are relatively pure.

Limited solid solution is greatly influenced by the temperature at which a mineral has formed. At higher temperatures, the ions in a crystal are more disordered, and its structure "looser" and more accommodating of imperfectly fit ions. For this reason, minerals that have crystallized at high temperatures tend to exhibit a greater degree of substitution than those formed at lower temperatures. For example, at low temperatures there is almost no solid solution between the sodium-rich plagioclase feldspar albite and the potassium-feldspar microcline (see *Feldspar Group*). Sanidine, however—the high-temperature polymorph of microcline—commonly accommodates sodium in place of potassium in its structure.

specific gravity

ONE OF THE MOST CONSPICUOUS ASPECTS OF MINERALS IS THE STRIKING DIFFERENCES in weight between similar-sized specimens of different species. For example, a white lump of massive barite may *look* identical to a piece of gypsum, but it will be nearly twice as heavy. This is due to their differing densities. The density of a mineral is determined by its composition and by the manner in which its atoms are packed within its crystal structure. Minerals containing iron, uranium, and other elements with high atomic weights will have high densities; minerals that are covalently bonded tend to have more open structures, and thus lower densities. Native metals such as gold and copper, for example, tend to have closely packed atomic structures and thus high densities. Density is among the factors controlling the transmission of light and heat through minerals, and the transmission of seismic waves from earthquakes through the earth. Density usually is related to conditions of a mineral's formation, as is reflected by some polymorphs.

Density is calculated as the ratio of a substance's mass to its volume, and is expressed in grams per cubic centimeter. Since variations in density aid in identification, a method has been devised to measure the relative, or comparative, density of minerals. The standard measure of the relative density of minerals is *specific gravity*. The specific gravity of a material is calculated by dividing its density (in grams per cubic centimeter) by the density of water at 4°C, which is 1 g/cm^3. Thus, the specific gravity of a material is its density relative to the density of water at 4°C. The terms density and specific gravity are used interchangeably, although the former refers to a material's mass relative to its volume, and is expressed in units of measure; and the latter compares a material's density with a common standard, and is a unitless, or dimensionless, number.

Iron-rich, "blackjack" sphalerite from Nenthead, Alston, Cumbria.

SPHALERITE IS THE MAIN ORE OF ZINC, A METAL WHICH WAS UNKNOWN AS SUCH prior to the 16th century. Zinc literally escaped notice because it vaporizes at normal smelting temperatures; because sphalerite failed to render any metal despite its metallic appearance, it was named from the Greek word *sphaleros*, meaning "treacherous." Eventually, it was discovered that the encrustations on the walls of a furnace in which sphalerite ores had been smelted could be resmelted with copper, "transmuting" the latter into brass. These encrustations, known as tuchia or "tutty," were actually zinc oxide that had sublimated from the zinc vapors.

Brass is composed primarily of copper, with variable proportions of zinc added depending upon the properties desired to suit its intended application. In general, brass is stronger and more resistant to corrosion than pure copper, and finds use in bullet cartridges, and in plumbing and lighting fixtures and other hardware. Zinc is used in a number of other alloys as well, but its primary importance is in the galvanizing of iron and other chemically reactive metals and alloys. In this process, iron is given a thin coating of zinc either through electroplating or dipping it in molten zinc, which protects it from rusting. The elements cadmium, gallium, germanium, and indium exist in solid solution in sphalerite and are primarily obtained as by-products of its smelting; these rare metals also find use in various protective coatings and electronic applications.

Sphalerite almost always contains a variable amount of iron as well, sometimes as much as 50%, depending on both the amount of iron available and the temperature of crystallization. If there is mineralogical evidence for an excess of iron in the precipitating solutions (usually the pres-

sphalerite

Classification:
sulfide

Composition:
ZnS (zinc sulfide)

Crystal System:
isometric

Hardness:
3.5–4

Specific Gravity:
3.9–4.1

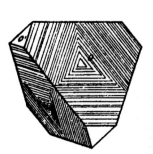

243

ence of pyrrhotite), the iron concentration in sphalerite serves as a recording thermometer of the temperature of precipitation, since the iron content varies with temperature.

Sphalerite crystals take the form of tetrahedra, dodecahedra, or pseudo-octahedral twins with striated faces, and typically display rounded edges. They are commonly seen as aggregates of distorted crystals, botryoidal masses, or stalactites. Crystals are quite fragile, with perfect cleavage and conchoidal fracture. The color ranges from white (cleiophane) through yellow, red ("ruby zinc"), and reddish brown, to black (the iron-rich variety marmatite, or "blackjack"). Sphalerite is usually translucent, with a distinctive adamantine or resinous luster; the marmatite variety is opaque with a submetallic luster. The streak may be pale brown, yellow, or colorless. Specimens deficient in iron commonly fluoresce under ultraviolet light or X-rays. The mineral wurtzite is a rare, high-temperature hexagonal polymorph of sphalerite.

Sphalerite is fairly widespread in its distribution, and good specimens are found in most deposits of economic importance. The favored environment is the low-temperature hydrothermal lead-zinc sulfide deposit (generally hosted by limestones or dolomites), in which sphalerite is associated with galena, greenockite, chalcopyrite, barite, fluorite, and other species. It is also found on occasion in pegmatites, contact metamorphic deposits, and even meteorites. Perhaps the finest sphalerite specimens in the world are obtained from the Tri-State mining district, straddling the borders of Missouri, Kansas, and Oklahoma. Important European sources include Alston Moor, England; Trepca, Yugoslavia (marmatite); Kapnik, Hungary; Pribram, Czechoslovakia; Bleiberg, Austria; Sardinia; and Santander, Spain. Excellent transparent crystals occur in the dolomites of the Swiss Binnental, and in the famous Carrara marble of Tuscany, Italy. Fine specimens are also found at Sullivan, Canada; Broken Hill, New South Wales, Australia; Tsumeb, Namibia; and many other places worldwide.

spinel

Classification:
oxide, spinel group

Composition:
$MgAl_2O_4$ (magnesium aluminum oxide)

Crystal System:
isometric

Hardness:
8

Specific Gravity:
3.58

SPINEL IS A MEMBER OF THE SPINEL GROUP OF OXIDES, WHICH ALSO INCLUDES chromite, franklinite, and magnetite. The arrangement of the atoms in the spinel structure is extremely efficient and compact (see illustration), and it is among the most intensely studied of all crystal structures. Members of the Spinel Group are able to form in very high pressure and temperature geological environments (it is thought that olivine, a mineral which may compose up to 90% of the earth's mantle, adopts the structure of spinel at about 350 km below the earth's surface, based on studies of how seismic waves travel through the earth). Spinel is one end member in four-way solid-solution series, with hercynite, an iron-aluminum oxide; gahnite, a zinc-aluminum oxide; and galaxite, a manganese-aluminum oxide. Substitutions involving the metals named, and also chromium, take place extensively. Several varieties of spinel are known, and the transparent varieties of various colors are collectively called gem spinels. The name is apparently derived from the Latin *spinella*, or "little thorn," in allusion to its dipyramidal crystals.

Spinel is one of the loveliest of gemstones, but it has had the misfortune to be mistaken for corundum and other gems throughout history.

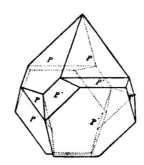

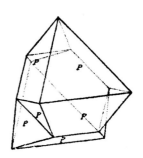

Since antiquity, brilliant red spinels from Afghanistan, India, and Southeast Asia were widely traded as "Balas rubies"; an example is the particularly fine 5-cm wide spinel in the British Imperial crown, still called the "Black Prince's Ruby." It was not until 1783 that spinel was identified as a distinct mineral species. Natural spinel is also mistaken for sapphire, amethyst and zircon. To complicate matters further, spinel synthesized using the Verneuil process (see *Corundum*) is available in an even wider variety of colors than its natural counterpart. Synthetic spinel is used to imitate diamond, aquamarine, emerald, peridot, and chrysoberyl, in addition to the above gems. As with other stones manufactured by the Verneuil process, however, magnification usually reveals the presence of tiny gas bubbles.

Most spinel crystals are simple octahedra, but dodecahedral modifications are sometimes seen. Crystal faces may be sharp and smooth, or rounded, etched, or skeletal. Twinning is common, according to the spinel twin law, which yields interpenetrating octahedra. Aggregates of rounded grains are also commonly encountered. Spinel lacks cleavage, and has an indistinct parting and conchoidal fracture. Crystals are transparent to opaque, and display a wide range of colors including black, pink, red, orange, dark green, blue, purple, yellow, and brown. The luster is vitreous, and the streak may be colorless, pale gray, green, or brown. Spinel can be distinguished from magnetite by its white streak and lack of magnetism.

Spinel forms in various high-temperature environments, including contact metamorphic rocks, granulites, and some ultramafic rocks, and as an accessory mineral in other igneous rocks. The best crystals are formed in marbles affected by contact metamorphism. Since it is so durable, spinel is common in many alluvial and marine placers. Sharp octahedrons have been found in marble near the zinc deposits of Franklin and elsewhere in New Jersey; in schist near Rowe, Massachusetts; in St. Lawrence County, New York, and at various locations in the Appalachian and western states. Fine specimens are found in Canada, in the marbles of Renfrew and Leeds counties, Ontario; and Ottawa County, Quebec. In Europe, excellent crystals come from Aker, Helsingland, Sweden; from Slatoust in the Ural Mountains; and in ejected marble blocks at Monte Somma, Vesuvius, Naples, Italy. Sharp octahedra are found in the gem gravels of Burma and Sri Lanka, and excellent black crystals are obtained at Antanimora and Ambatomainty, Madagascar, associated with diopside, tourmaline, phlogopite, and tremolite.

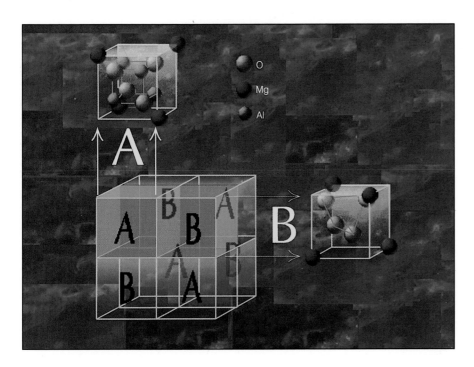

Spinel and the other members of the spinel group are mixed oxides, containing two different types of metal cations, one in tetrahedral coordination with four oxygen atoms, and the other in octahedral coordination with six. The resulting structure is very stable under high-pressure conditions. **Opposite page:** *Gem spinel from Ceylon, with a penetration twin (note reentrant angle girdling crystal) from Mogok, Burma.*

spodumene

Classification:
inosilicate, pyroxene group

Composition:
LiAlSi$_2$O$_6$ (lithium aluminum silicate)

Crystal System:
monoclinic

Hardness:
6.5–7.5

Specific Gravity:
3.0–3.2

AMONG THE MANY DRAB, WORKADAY ROCK-BUILDERS OF THE PYROXENE GROUP, SPOdumene is a real show-stopper. While sometimes found as delicate, colorful, gem-quality crystals, it also occurs as enormous laths 15 m in length and weighing several tons—which are mined as a source of lithium. Lithium is the lightest metal, important in a variety of metallurgical uses, and its various compounds are vital to industry and medicine. Lithium carbonate, for instance, is used in the glass and ceramic industries and as a treatment for manic-depressive psychosis (see *Lepidolite*). The name spodumene is derived from the Greek phrase meaning "reduced to ashes," in reference either to its common ashen color or to its behavior when subjected to the blowpipe test.

There are two strikingly colored gem varieties of spodumene—the emerald-green hiddenite and the lilac kunzite. Both gems are relatively new on the scene. Hiddenite was discovered in 1879 when a farmer plowed up some "green bolts" on his farm near what was then called Salem Church, North Carolina. Those bolts were emeralds, but frantic digging soon turned up the more abundant, emerald-green hiddenite crystals, along with aquamarine, topaz, apatite, and rutile in a series of atypical, decomposed pegmatites. An entrepreneur named William Hidden quickly bought the land and formed a mining company, and the town changed its name to Hiddenite, shifting its economic base from packing chewing tobacco to mining. Hiddenite is still found in Hiddenite and nowhere else, although paler green stones from various locations have been marketed under its name.

Kunzite was discovered in the pegmatites of the Pala District in San Diego County, California, in 1901. Like hiddenite, its identity was a mystery at first. It was the famous gemologist George F. Kunz of Tiffany's in New York who finally identified the strange lilac crystals, declaring that their beauty was "unrivaled by any other mineral in North America." Since then, kunzite has been discovered in many places from Brazil to Afghanistan.

Spodumene forms prismatic crystals, usually etched, with indistinct terminations and deep vertical striations. It is also common as massive cleavable aggregates. Its easily developed, perfect prismatic cleavage and two parting directions sometimes present problems in cutting and wearing spodumene gemstones—one sharp tap and a gem may break cleanly in two. Common spodumene is whitish, gray, yellowish, or greenish, and translucent to opaque, with a vitreous to dull luster. Transparent gem varieties may be colorless, yellow, light green, emerald-green (hiddenite), or violet (kunzite). Spodumene is trichroic, and the

Left: *Crystal of spodumene of the variety hiddenite, measuring 7 cm, from Hiddenite, North Carolina. Note preferential etching along the sides of the crystal, delineating a cleavage plane.* **Right:** *Prismatic spodumene (variety kunzite) crystal from Mawi, Nuristan Province, Afghanistan, with a cut stone from Pala, San Diego County, California.*

depth of color in transparent crystals differs according to the angle at which it is viewed; for this reason, spodumene is sometimes called triphane, meaning "three aspects." Some specimens are fluorescent.

Spodumene occurs in complex pegmatites, with quartz, feldspars, columbite–tantalite, lepidolite, beryl, and tourmaline. Crystals often alter into mica, albite, and various clay minerals, while keeping their external form. Spodumene is found in virtually all pegmatite districts around the world. The huge spodumene crystals mentioned above are mined at the Etta and Tin Mountain mines in the Black Hills of South Dakota, at Bernic Lake in Manitoba, and in the Ural Mountains of Russia. Gem-quality kunzite is found at Pala, California, and the Laghman Province of Afghanistan. Hiddenite is found in Alexander and Cleveland Counties, North Carolina. Both gem varieties are mined in the Malagasy Republic and in Minas Gerais, Brazil.

THE DISTINCTIVE CROSS SHAPE COMMON TO STAUROLITE CRYSTALS HAS GIVEN THEM A special place in the hearts of Christian peoples everywhere. These cruciform twins take the form of either the classic Greek cross, with a reentrant angle of 90° between members, or a St. Andrew's cross, with angles of 60° and 120°. Traditionally, Christians have imbued this species with supernatural significance, using the twinned crystals in baptisms and other rituals, and wearing them as religious jewelry. It is reported that Teddy Roosevelt was never without a staurolite cross, which he wore on his watch-chain. Petrologists also find staurolite meaningful, and use it to gauge the grade of regional metamorphic rocks. Above a certain temperature and pressure (800°C and 3000 atm), staurolite breaks down into sillimanite and a form of spinel. The name is derived from the Greek word for "cross," *staruros*.

Staurolite forms short prismatic crystals with rough faces and flat terminations, which may or may not be twinned. It also occurs as disseminated grains, massive aggregates, and parallel intergrowths with kyanite. It is reddish brown to brownish black, translucent to opaque, with a vitreous to resinous luster and a gray or colorless streak. Since there are not enough staurolite crosses to go around, imitations are frequently carved from fine-grained stone, dyed, and sold to the faithful.

Staurolite is restricted to medium-temperature regional metamorphic rocks (schists and gneisses), where it is associated with garnet, quartz, muscovite, and kyanite. Crystals are commonly found lying about loose after having been weathered from their host rock. Its relative durability

staurolite

Classification:
nesosilicate

Composition:
$Fe_2Al_9O_6(SiO_4)_4(O,OH)_2$
(hydrous iron magnesium aluminum silicate)

Crystal System:
monoclinic (pseudo-orthorhombic)

Hardness:
7–7.5

Specific Gravity:
3.65–3.83

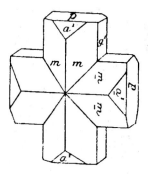

Staurolite "Saint Andrew's cross" from Governador Valadores, Minas Gerais, Brazil.

makes staurolite disproportionately well-represented in clastic sedimentary deposits. Cruciform twins are collected in Fannin County, Georgia; North Carolina; Patric County, Virginia; Windham, Maine, and elsewhere in New England; Rio Arriba County, New Mexico; Coconino and Yavapai Counties, Arizona; Snohomish and Chelan Counties, Washington; the Black Hills of South Dakota; and Montana. European occurrences include Ireland; Scotland; France; Aschaffenberg, Germany; and Monte Campione and Pizzo Forno, Ticino, Switzerland, where excellent crystals are found in association with kyanite and paragonite. Fine crystals are also found in Canada, Brazil, Greenland, Australia, and West Africa.

stephanite

Classification:
sulfosalt

Composition:
Ag_5SbS_4 (silver sulfosalt)

Crystal System:
orthorhombic

Hardness:
2–2.5

Specific Gravity:
6.25

STEPHANITE IS AN INCIDENTAL ORE OF SILVER, NAMED FOR VICTOR STEPHAN (B. 1817), Archduke of Austria. Although it usually occurs in massive form, the rare prismatic to tabular crystals of stephanite are highly prized by collectors. Crystals often take the form of pseudohexagonal twins, and display horizontal striations on the prism faces. Cleavage is poorly developed in two directions, and the fracture is uneven to subconchoidal. The color is iron-black, and the material is opaque with a metallic luster and an iron-black streak. Polybasite is a closely related silver sulfosalt which is nearly identical to stephanite in its physical properties and occurrence.

Stephanite is common in low-temperature hydrothermal silver veins, where it occurs in association with native silver, tetrahedrite, and other sulfides like polybasite, acanthite, and proustite. Stephanite was once extensively mined for silver from the Comstock Lode, Virginia City, Nevada; and is presently exploited at Cobalt, Ontario. Excellent specimens have come from Andreasberg and Freiberg in Germany; Pribram, Czechoslovakia; and from the states of Zacatecas and Sonora in Mexico.

Pseudohexagonal twins of stephanite from Freiberg, Germany.

STIBNITE IS A REMARKABLE MINERAL, FORMING ELEGANT METALLIC CRYSTALS WHICH CAN be bent with the fingers or melted over a match flame. The Egyptians, Greeks, and Romans all used powdered stibnite as makeup and as a medicine for eye ailments. Medieval alchemists coveted stibnite for use in making *antimony glass*, which was thought to have curative powers, and especially for their efforts to refine gold. By the 15th century it was known that stibnite could be used to part gold from silver, by fusing the stibnite together with the adulterated gold in a crucible. In this process, the sulfur from the stibnite combines with the silver to form black argentite, while the metallic arsenic and freed gold collect as a metallic button. On heating, the arsenic could be driven off to render pure gold. Stibnite is now the most important source of antimony, which is used to harden the lead used for shot and for metal type. It is also used in the paint and ceramics industries, as a fireproofing material for textiles, and as a component of rubber. The name comes from the Greek name for this mineral, *stimmi*, via the Latin *stibium*—also the source of antimony's chemical symbol, Sb.

stibnite

Classification:
sulfide

Composition:
Sb_2S_3 (antimony sulfide)

Crystal System:
orthorhombic

Hardness:
2

Specific Gravity:
4.63–4.66

Stibnite crystals from the classic locality at Mt. Kosang, Shikoku Island, Japan.

Stibnite crystals typically occur as divergent sprays of deeply striated, metallic-gray prismatic or acicular crystals. These display perfect prismatic cleavage, with distinctive crosshatching on cleavage surfaces. The prismatic form of stibnite crystals reflect its atomic structure, which is characterized by parallel chains of covalently bonded antimony and sulfur atoms; the cleavage occurs between these chains. The much rarer sulfide bismuthinite (Bi_2S_3) is isostructural with stibnite, and very similar except in its specific gravity (6.78); otherwise, stibnite is unique in its softness, fusibility, and habit.

Stibnite is formed in low-temperature hydrothermal veins in association with lead, mercury, and silver minerals, and in hot-spring deposits with cinnabar, orpiment, and realgar. The world's finest stibnite specimens are the complex crystals as large as 60 cm in length which were collected in the 1880s from the Ichinokawa Mine on the Japanese island of Shikoku. The most important deposits are now those of the Hunan and Guangdong Provinces, China, where stibnite occurs in association with cinnabar. Other important deposits are worked in France, Romania, Peru, Mexico, Bolivia, and Borneo.

stilbite

Classification:
tectosilicate, zeolite group

Composition:
$NaCa_4(Si_{27}Al_9)O_{72} \cdot 30H_2O$
(hydrous calcium, sodium, aluminum silicate)

Crystal System:
monoclinic

Hardness:
3.5–4

Specific Gravity:
2.09–2.20

STILBITE IS ONE OF THE MOST INTERESTING ZEOLITE MINERALS, DUE TO ITS UNUSUAL and distinctive crystalline habit. The name is derived from the Greek *stilbein*, meaning "to shine," a reference to the strong pearly luster on its cleavage faces. Single, tabular crystals are very rare. Stilbite almost always forms bladed, cruciform twins which simulate orthorhombic symmetry; these, in turn, are grouped into subparallel aggregates which are pinched in the middle, and thus resemble tied sheaves of wheat. Other aggregate habits include divergent, radial, globular, and massive. Crystals display perfect cleavage in one direction, with an uneven fracture. Stilbite is transparent to translucent, with a colorless streak; common colors include white, gray, yellowish, reddish, pink, and brown. Its distinctive wheat-sheaf aggregates are sufficient to distinguish it from other zeolites and associated species.

Stilbite is a typical mineral of cavities in basalts, andesites, and other volcanic rocks, where it is associated with other zeolite minerals and calcite. It also occurs in fissures in plutonic and metamorphic rocks, and as a late-stage species in cavities in some pegmatites. Good specimens are found in all the major continental basalt fields, including the Deccan Traps of India; Rio Grande do Sul, Brazil; and the Columbia River Plateau of Washington and Oregon. Excellent specimens are found in the basalts of Nova Scotia, Iceland, the Faeroe Islands, Scotland, Ireland, and many places on the European Continent.

"Wheat-sheave" aggregates of stilbite from Teigarhorn, Iceland.

THE COLOR OF THE POWDER trail produced as a mineral specimen is dragged across an unglazed porcelain plate is known as its *streak*. Even though a particular mineral species may vary in color, its color in powdered form is usually constant, making the streak a very important diagnostic tool. Since the hardness of the plate is around 7 on the Mohs scale, only minerals softer than this can be tested.

Some minerals, such as cinnabar and azurite, produce a streak that is nearly identical to their actual color, as might be expected. Many others, however, leave surprisingly different colors on the streak plate. Fluorite, for example, always has a white streak, although its crystals may be purple, blue, yellow, or green. Metallic minerals also have unexpected streaks: brassy pyrite crystals leave a black streak, and black hematite a striking red one.

ALONG WITH THE STRONTIUM SULFATE CELESTITE, STRONTIANITE IS AN IMPORTANT ORE of strontium, which is used in glass-making and sugar refining, and to produce the essential "rocket's red glare" in fireworks. Strontianite is named for the classic locality at Strontian, Argyllshire, Scotland.

Although strontianite rarely forms euhedral crystals, it is sometimes seen as bladed prismatic crystals with good prismatic cleavage. The occurrence of pseudohexagonal sixling twins point out the fact that strontianite is isostructural with aragonite. More commonly seen, however, are bundles of acicular crystals and granular or fibrous masses. Strontianite is typically colorless or white, yellowish, pinkish, or gray, and transparent or translucent, with a vitreous to resinous luster and a white streak. It sometimes fluoresces blue under ultraviolet light. Strontianite can be distinguished from celestite by its poorer cleavage and lack of effervescence in dilute hydrochloric acid.

Strontianite is found in low-temperature hydrothermal veins, with barite, calcite, celestite, and sulfides. It also forms concretionary masses in carbonate sedimentary rocks. Economic deposits are found in the Strontium Hills of California; other notable North American localities include Schoharie, New York; Winfield, Pennsylvania; Cave-in-Rock, Illinois; and Woodville, Ohio, where sixling twins are found in dolomite. European sources include the Austrian Tyrol, Switzerland, Italy, and Westphalia, Germany.

strontianite

Classification:
carbonate, aragonite group
Composition:
$SrCO_3$ (strontium carbonate)
Crystal System:
orthorhombic
Hardness:
3.5–4
Specific Gravity:
3.78

Left: *Plumose aggregate of strontianite crystals from Strontian, Strathclyde Region, Scotland.* **Right:** *The "rockets' red glare" in fireworks is due to strontium nitrate.*

251

THE HUNDREDS OF SULFATE SPECIES CAN BE DIVIDED INTO THE ANHYDROUS SULFATES, the hydrated sulfates, and those containing the hydroxyl (OH) ion or one of the halogen elements such as chlorine. The so-called compound sulfates contain both carbonate and sulfate groups. Many of the sulfates containing hydroxyl are soft and unstable. Gypsum, the most common hydrated sulfate, contain alternating sheets of water molecules and sulfate-calcium groups, which give it a well-defined, perfect cleavage. Members of the barite group (barite, celestite, and anglesite) are quite durable in comparison. The majority of sulfates are white or colorless or only slightly colored, and are very soft and relatively fragile.

The chromates, molybdates, and tungstates are classed with the sulfates because of the similarities between their anion complexes, in which either one sulfur, chromium, molybdenum, or tungsten atom is surrounded by four oxygen atoms in a tetrahedral arrangement, similar to the silica tetrahedra of the silicate minerals. These classes enjoy a commercial popularity entirely out of proportion to their abundance. The sole chromate of importance is crocoite, $PbCrO_4$; similarly, the only molybdate seen to any extent is the ubiquitous lead molybdate wulfenite, $PbMoO_4$. Scheelite, $CaWO_4$, and the wolframite group minerals are the most commonly seen tungstates, and provide an important source of tungsten.

Coquimbite, $Fe_2^{+3}(SO_4)_3 \cdot 9H_2O$, from the Concepción Mine, Zalamea, in the Heulva Province of Spain. A hydrous sulfate, coquimbite loses water rapidly on being unearthed, and must be protected to keep it from disintegrating.

sulfides and sulfosalts

THE SULFIDES AND SULFOSALTS ARE DISTINCT CHEMICAL CLASSES WHICH SHARE MANY important properties and usually occur in similar environments. Generally classified with the sulfides are the structurally similar sulfarsenides, arsenides, and tellurides. Among the many species in these classes are the major ores of the industrial metals, including copper, lead, mercury, nickel, silver, and zinc. While many sulfides and some species of the other classes occur in a wide variety of geological environments, the greatest number of species and the largest economic concentrations of ore minerals are found in sulfide veins, and massive and disseminated sulfide deposits (see *Hydrothermal Deposits*).

In the sulfides proper, one or more types of metal and/or semi-metal cations occur in combination with anions of sulfur. In sulfarsenides such as cobaltite and arsenopyrite, arsenic shares anionic positions with sulfur, and in arsenides such as skutterudite, sulfur is absent altogether. The tellurides, including calaverite, $AuTe_2$, and hessite, $AgTe_2$, are rare minerals in which tellurium occupies the anion position.

Opposite page: Löllingite, $FeAs_2$ (an arsenide), from Temearne Cliff, Cornwall.

Left: *Stannite, Cu₂FeSnS₄, from Wheal Kitty, Cornwall. This rare sulfide is a minor ore of tin.* **Right:** *Bravoite crystals, (Ni,Fe)S₂, from Mill Close Mine, Darley Dale, Derbyshire, with calcite containing sulfide inclusions.*

The sulfosalts differ from the above groups in that the semimetals arsenic and antimony occupy positions like those of the metals, rather than that of sulfur. In the sulfide arsenopyrite (FeAsS), for example, arsenic occupies a structural position like that of sulfur, while in the sulfosalt enargite (Cu_3AsS_4), arsenic acts like a metal ion, coordinated with four sulfur ions. Other important sulfosalts include proustite, pyrargyrite, tetrahedrite, tennantite, jamesonite, and bournonite.

The minerals of these classes all have relatively high densities, and most are brittle, although some are sectile—meaning that shavings can be pared from them with a knife blade. Most are opaque and dark in color, and typically tarnished on the surface due to oxidation. Unaltered specimens are usually strongly metallic in luster, while even the translucent species such as sphalerite and cinnabar display strong submetallic to adamantine lusters.

sulfur

Classification:
native element

Composition:
S (elemental sulfur)

Crystal System:
orthorhombic

Hardness:
1.5–2.5

Specific Gravity:
2.05

Sulfur seems not to be made for this world. It is so delicate that it cracks in the heat of one's palm, and erupts into blue flames when placed in the fire. The ancients recognized the special properties of sulfur, attributing special healing powers to it and using the acrid fumes of burning sulfur to dispel disease, mosquitos, and malevolent spirits. These fumes are composed of sulfur dioxide, which is presently being pumped into the earth's atmosphere by the thousands of tons per day by factories, coal-burning power plants, and smelters. Sulfur dioxide combines with water vapor to form sulfuric acid, or acid rain, which then returns to earth, poisoning lakes and waterways and devastating vegetation.

The most obvious occurrence of sulfur in nature is around the volcanic vents, or solfataras, where it crystallizes from vapors in vibrant yellow crusts. Such volcanic occurrences undoubtedly reinforced the ancients' notion of "brimstone" as an element from the underworld. Sulfur is important in many industries, including the production of rubber, insecticides, fungicides, fibers, and explosives. Its primary industrial application, however, is the intentional production of sulfuric acid, which, ironically, is vital to the fertilizer industry.

Sulfur forms well-developed bipyramidal crystals, granular masses, and powdery crusts of a characteristic yellow color. Its notorious instability is due to its structure, which consists of rings of eight-membered sulfur atoms very loosely bonded together by van der Waals' forces. Impurities may lend sulfur a brownish, greenish or gray cast, and its high refractive index gives it a greasy to adamantine luster. At high temperatures, sulfur crystallizes in a monoclinic form known as beta-sulfur, which is the type that forms around solfataras.

Sulfur is mined from a handful of volcanic deposits in Indonesia, Japan, Mexico, and at Ollague, Chile—situated at an elevation of 6 km in the Andes. The most important sulfur deposits are of sedimentary origin, however. In these deposits, gypsum and anhydrite are decomposed by anaerobic bacteria, which produce calcium sulfide. Groundwater containing carbon dioxide then converts the calcium sulfide to elemental sulfur and calcium carbonate, in the form of calcite and aragonite. The marvelous crystals of sulfur and aragonite from Agrigento and other locations in Sicily apparently formed in this manner.

Sulfur has been mined in Sicily since the Middle Ages, in a very primitive and destructive manner. Workers would dump baskets of sulfur from the mines into a pit, where it would be ignited. The heat derived from the burning of most of the sulfur would melt the remainder, which would then be cast into convenient shapes for transport. The sulfur dioxide fumes produced by this process killed all plant life for miles around the mines, and undoubtedly did little to improve the health of the Sicilians.

At the turn of the 20th century, however, enormous reserves of sulfur, geologically similar to the Sicilian deposits, were found beneath the Gulf Coast during oil exploration. They remained inaccessible for some time, due to their great depth and the instability of the surrounding rock. Eventually, a chemist named Herman Frasch developed a process in which superheated water could be pumped into a drillhole, melting the sulfur at depth so that it can be pumped to the surface in liquid form. This efficient process quickly supplanted all other sources of sulfur, and did wonders for the landscape of Sicily. Now, the production of sulfur as a by-product of petroleum refining has overtaken the Frasch Process as the most important source of sulfur.

sylvite

Classification:
halide

Composition:
KCl (potassium chloride)

Crystal System:
isometric

Hardness:
2

Specific Gravity:
1.99

POTASSIUM IS AN EXTREMELY REACTIVE ELEMENT WHICH NEVER OCCURS IN ITS NATIVE metallic form, but always in natural or artificial compounds. One of these compounds was a digestive salt proffered by the Dutch chemist and physician Francois Sylvius de le Boe (b. 1614), and called *sal digestivus Sylvii*. Before this nostrum became available, however, potassium was hard-won through the leaching of wood or kelp ashes to obtain potash, or potassium carbonate. The element potassium derives its name (via potash) from this process, which was undertaken in iron pots. Potash was first used mainly in tanning and the manufacture of lye soap and gunpowder, but the most important use of potassium compounds today is as an essential fertilizer in agriculture.

Sylvite and the more abundant halite or salt (NaCl) share many similarities, including their atomic structure. There is little solid solution between the two, however, since potassium has a much greater atomic radius than sodium. Like salt, sylvite often forms colorless to white cubic crystals with a well-developed cubic cleavage, although sylvite crystals tend to be pinkish, and modified by octahedral faces. Sylvite has a salty taste, but unlike salt it has an unpleasant, bitter edge.

Like halite, sylvite is present in the oceans in solution, although it is much less abundant. It is also more soluble, and thus does not precipitate until the brines become extremely concentrated. So, while halite can precipitate gradually from over-saturated bodies of water like the Mediterranean to form thick deposits over many thousands of years, the presence of bedded sylvite implies that an inland sea virtually dried up.

Large evaporite deposits containing sylvite were first discovered during the 19th century at Strassfurt, Germany, and Kaluszyn, Poland. These deposits provided the bulk of the world's potash until the political upheavals of this century made further prospecting necessary. Extensive but deeply buried deposits of a sylvite–halite mixture called sylvinite were eventually found near Carlsbad, New Mexico, and adjacent parts of Texas, and these now supply the bulk of the United States potassium requirements. Extensive reserves of sylvite are also located in Saskatchewan, Canada, covering a vast area at depths of 1000 m. Similar deposits exist in the Soviet Union, and smaller ones in France, Israel, Jordan, Spain, and the United Kingdom.

Sylvite cubes, modified by octahedral faces, from Stassfurt, Magdeburg, Germany.

TALC IS THE SOFTEST MINERAL KNOWN. ALTHOUGH IT DOES NOT OFTEN PROVIDE dramatic specimens for the collector, it is a very familiar mineral and has been used by humans for millennia. In its powdered form, talc can be found in almost every bathroom cabinet, where, as Ogden Nash observed, "A little talcum is always walcum." Early cultures fashioned the soft but relatively strong massive variety known as steatite, or soapstone, into figurines and cooking vessels. Since talc is a poor conductor of heat and thus a great thermal insulator, these vessels were not used over the cooking fire; rather, heated stones were placed inside them to warm the victuals from within. Soapstone is still carved into decorative objects by the Inuit and other Native Americans, and massive quantities are used in the cosmetics, paint, paper, rubber, and textile industries. The name is derived from the Arabic *talq*, meaning "talc."

In addition to its softness, talc is distinguished by its greasy feel and appearance and by its white streak. It is almost never seen in distinct crystals, but occurs as greenish-white foliated masses, sometimes showing stellate aggregates on fracture surfaces of massive material. Steatite is grayish and has a distinctive felted texture.

Talc is derived from the alteration of various magnesium silicates during the metamorphism of silica-poor igneous rocks, or from the alteration of "dirty" dolostones containing silicate grains. Massive talc deposits are mined in many parts of the world, and virtually every industrial country exploits deposits within its borders. In the United States, talc is produced in New York, Vermont, California, and several other states. The purest talc is mined in Italy, and is exported for use in the cosmetics industry.

talc

Classification:
phyllosilicate

Composition:
$Mg_3Si_4O_{10}(OH)_2$
(hydrous magnesium silicate)

Crystal System:
triclinic

Hardness:
1

Specific Gravity:
2.7

Left: Translucent talc on serpentine from Stubachthal, Ober-Pinzgau, Salzburg, Austria.
Above: The massive fine-grained variety of talc called steatite or "soapstone" is soft enough to be easily carved, yet tough enough that many cultures used it to make durable wares. This North American Indian beaver-motif pipe bowl undoubtedly furnished many a contented smoke.

Tetrahedrite tetrahedra modified by other isometric forms, from Musen, Nordrhein-Westfalen, Germany.

tetrahedrite series

Classification:
sulfosalts

Composition:
$Cu_{12}Sb_4S_{13}$ (tetrahedrite)
$(Cu,Fe)_{12}As_4S_{13}$ (tennantite)

Crystal System:
isometric

Hardness:
3–4.5

Specific Gravity:
4.6–5.1 (tetrahedrite)
4.59–4.75 (tennantite)

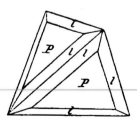

THE TETRAHEDRITE SOLID-SOLUTION SERIES CONSISTS OF THE ANTIMONY-RICH END member tetrahedrite, the most abundant of the sulfosalts, and the less-common arsenic-rich end member tennantite. Iron, zinc, silver, and even mercury substitute for copper in each, and bismuth sometimes substitutes for arsenic in tennantite. Tetrahedrite is named for its characteristic crystal form, the tetrahedron; tennantite is named after the English chemist Smithson Tennant (b. 1761).

Both species commonly occur as good crystals, tetrahedrite generally forming larger and sharper tetrahedral crystals than tennantite. Other forms include cubes, tritetrahedra and dodecahedra, and the characteristic tetrahedron of both species is often modified by one or more of these forms. Crystal faces are usually smooth, but may also be covered by overgrowths of tiny chalcopyrite crystals. Contact and penetration twins are common; the latter type is characterized by the sharp corners of one crystal protruding from the faces of the other. Crystalline druses and granular aggregates are typical; no cleavage, but subconchoidal to uneven fracture is displayed. Crystals are opaque, steel gray to black, with metallic or splendent luster and a black, brown, or dark-red streak. The characteristic crystal form is distinctive, as is the lack of cleavage; otherwise, both species resemble a host of other sulfides and sulfosalts.

Tetrahedrite and tennantite are abundant in many low- to medium-temperature hydrothermal sulfide veins, in association with calcite, dolomite, siderite, barite, fluorite, quartz, and other sulfides. They also occur with galena and bornite in carbonatites; and sometimes in contact metamorphic deposits. Excellent, large and lustrous tetrahedrite crystals occur at Bingham, Utah; and smaller crystals are found at Butte, Montana, and in the Sunshine Mine, Kellogg, Idaho. Fine tetrahedrite crystals also come from Mina Bonanza, Concepcíon del Oro, Zacatecas, Mexico, and the Windermere District, British Columbia. Tennantite specimens are found near Idaho Springs, Colorado; in Buckingham County, Virginia; in Barrie Township, Ontario; and in the Lillooet District, British Columbia. Tetrahedrite and tennantite also occur in the Andes of Bolivia, Chile, and Peru, and in Algeria, Australia, and Tsumeb, Namibia. Classic European sources include the mines of Pribram, Czechoslovakia; Cornwall, England; and Freiberg and the Harz, Germany.

UNLIKE MANY OF THE ZEOLITE MINERALS, THOMSONITE RARELY FORMS DISTINCT CRYS-tals, but is usually seen as radiating clusters or lamellar aggregates. They are usually colorless, white, yellowish, pink, or greenish, and transparent to translucent with a vitreous to pearly luster and a colorless streak. Sometimes the crystalline aggregates form tough, translucent, chatoyant masses known as lintonite, which can be fashioned into cabochons. Thomsonite is named for the Scottish chemist Thomas Thomson (b. 1773), who was the first to analyze the mineral.

Thomsonite forms in cavities in basalts and other igneous rocks, in association with calcite, prehnite, and other zeolites, and occasionally in schists or contact metamorphic rocks. The gem material lintonite is found on the shores of Lake Superior in Cook County, Minnesota. Attractive rosettes on prehnite, as large as 5 cm in diameter, are found in the basalt cavities of northern New Jersey; and long, slender radiating clusters are found at Peters Point, Nova Scotia. Excellent specimens have been recovered from the basalts of Table Mountain, Colorado, and at numerous sites in Oregon. European sources include Czechoslovakia, Scotland, and Germany.

thomsonite

Classification:
tectosilicate, zeolite group

Composition:
$NaCa_2Al_5Si_5O_{20} \cdot 6H_2O$
(hydrated sodium calcium aluminum silicate)

Crystal System:
orthorhombic

Hardness:
5–5.5

Specific Gravity:
2.25–2.40

Divergent sprays of acicular thomsonite crystals from Old Kilpatrick, Strathclyde, Scotland.

A druse of wedge-shaped titanite crystals from Capelinha, Minas Gerais, Brazil.

titanite (sphene)

Classification:
nesosilicate

Composition:
$CaTiO(SiO_4)$ (calcium titanium silicate)

Crystal System:
monoclinic

Hardness:
5–5.5

Specific Gravity:
3.4–3.55

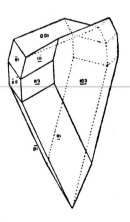

THE OFFICIAL NAME TITANITE IS A RATHER PROSAIC REFLECTION OF THIS SPECIES' TITANium content. However, most earth scientists still refer to it as sphene, a name derived from the Greek *sphen,* or "wedge." This old name reflects its most striking feature—its sharp, wedge-shaped crystal form. Other habits include tabular or platy crystal clusters and massive aggregates. Titanite commonly forms contact or penetration twins; the latter are particularly common in the Alpine deposits. Mineral collectors who prize its interesting crystals must compete with lapidaries, who covet titanite for the lovely and valuable gemstones that can be cut from it. Titanite is usually yellow to greenish yellow, more rarely pink, brown, or black, and has an adamantine luster. It is sometimes trichroic, meaning that three different shades of color can be observed in different crystal directions. Axinite crystals may be similar in appearace to those of titanite.

Titanite is formed in a wide variety of environments. It is a common accessory mineral in granites and other silica-rich igneous rocks, and accordingly is sometimes found as well-developed crystals in pegmatites, as in northern Baja California and Brazil. Some of the finest specimens have been found in dolomites, in association with apatite, calcite, and scapolite. At Renfrew, Ontario, such deposits have produced single crystals as large as 50 kg; similar deposits extend from Québec into New York, and are also found in the Swiss Binnental. Elsewhere in the Swiss and Italian Alps, titanite is found in vugs in metamorphic rocks, often discolored by inclusions of chlorite. It is actually mined as an ore of titanium at the unusually massive Khibina deposit on the Soviet Union's Kola Peninsula, where it occurs with apatite in a nepheline-syenite body.

The name topaz is thought to be derived from *TOPAZION*, an old name for the island of Zebergit in the Red Sea. Zebergit, or St. John's Island, is a famous source of peridot (olivine), so the name was probably applied to peridot originally. Topaz occurs in several different colors, and this has given rise to a great deal of confusion over the centuries. The rarest and most valuable kind of topaz is the golden-yellow, hydroxyl-rich variety called "imperial topaz." However, citrine quartz and yellow sapphire are so often substituted for imperial topaz that it is assumed to be more common than it is. In fact, the most common topaz is the fluorine-rich, colorless to aquamarine-blue variety. Blue topaz is becoming more popular, not so much on its own merits but because it is seen as an inexpensive substitute for the increasingly fashionable aquamarine variety of beryl.

Well-developed crystals of topaz are common, ranging in size from very small to hundreds of kilograms in weight. Crystals are typically stubby to elongated prisms with wedge-shaped terminations and diamond-shaped cross sections; the warm-colored hydroxyl-rich topaz typically forms elongate prismatic crystals, while the colorless or blue fluorine-rich crystals tend to adopt squat, equant shapes. Granular masses and columnar aggregates are less common. Topaz is susceptible to corrosion, and pitted masses are commonly found with no trace of their original faces. Etching and corrosion often affect the separate faces of a crystal differently, effacing some while leaving adjacent faces perfectly smooth. Gas and liquid inclusions are also common. Topaz displays conchoidal fracture and perfect, easily developed basal cleavage, which deleteriously affects its durability as a gemstone. The most common colors are colorless to light blue, grading into aquamarine-blue; various shades of yellow to rich wine-yellow or brownish orange are less common; and green, pink, and reddish stones, though rare, may also be encountered. Most crystals display distinct pleochroism; yellow crystals range from light to deep yellow, and blue crystals range from colorless to deep blue. Crystals are transparent to translucent, with a vitreous luster and a colorless streak.

The best topaz crystals are obtained from cavities in granitic pegmatites, although fine specimens have also been found in hydrothermal veins and in cavities in the volcanic rock rhyolite. In New England, topaz is found in the pegmatites of Oxford and Sagadahoc counties, Maine; Carroll County, New Hampshire; and Fairchild County, Connecticut. The granites of Mason County, Texas, have produced many fine topaz crystals, some to 10 cm long. Pegmatites in Teller, Douglas, Park, and El Paso counties, Colorado, have also produced excellent topaz crystals. Small perfect crystals are found with quartz, hematite, bixbyite, garnet, and red beryl in cavities in rhyolite on Thomas Mountain, Juab County, Utah. Excellent blue topaz crystals are found in the Ramona District, and on Aguanga Mountain in San Diego County, California.

topaz

Classification:
nesosilicate

Composition:
$Al_2SiO_4(F,OH)_2$
(aluminum hydroxyl fluorine silicate)

Crystal System:
orthorhombic

Hardness:
8

Specific Gravity:
3.49–3.57

Topaz gem and crystal from near Mursinsk, in the Ural Mountains of the Soviet Union.

A unique deposit near Ouro Preto, Minas Gerais, Brazil, produces most of the world's imperial topaz, which occurs as fine crystals in a matrix of kaolinite. Other localities in Minas Gerais and elsewhere in Brazil produce topaz crystals of all colors. The largest Brazilian crystals exceed 200 kg in weight. Classic topaz specimens once came from the pegmatites near Mursinsk in the Ural Mountains, and fine Chilon crystals are still found in the Adun-Chilon and Ilmen mountains, in the Soviet Union. Other important European localities include Schneckenstein; Saxony; the Mourne Mountains of County Down, Ireland, and the Cairn Gorm Mountains of Scotland. Fine crystals are found in Omi and Mino provinces, Japan; and Pine Creek, Northern Territories, and Flinders Island, Victoria, Australia.

torbernite

Classification:
phosphate

Composition:
$Cu(UO_2)_2(PO_4)_2 \cdot 10H_2O$
(hydrated copper uranium phosphate)

Crystal System:
tetragonal

Hardness:
2–2.5

Specific Gravity:
3.3

TORBERNITE IS NAMED FOR THE SWEDISH MINERALOGIST TORBERN OLAF BERGMAN (b. 1735). Though it resembles a mica in overall morphology, it is not a member of this group. The two-dimensional layers of uranium phosphate in torbernite are loosely connected, mimicking the crystal lattice of a phyllosilicate (mica) and giving torbernite a micaceous cleavage. The crystals form flat tabular plates, scaly aggregates, and crusts. Crystals are a brilliant emerald-green, or lighter yellowish green, with a vitreous to pearly luster. Unlike most secondary uranium minerals, torbernite is not fluorescent under the ultraviolet light; it is radioactive, however. Torbernite is isostructural with autunite, which it closely resembles and with which it is often found in association.

Torbernite is an oxidation product of primary uranium minerals such as uraninite, and occurs in pegmatites, hydrothermal veins, and sedimentary uranium deposits. Beautiful specimens are found at Redruth, Cornwall, and Weardale, Durham, England; the Puy-du-Dome District of France; Katanga District, Zaire; Mounana, Gabon; Mount Painter, Australia; and in Germany, the Congo, Mexico, and Chalk Mountain in North Carolina.

Opposite page: Tabular plates of torbernite from Weardale, County Durham, England.

Classification:
cyclosilicates

Composition:
$(Ca,K,Na)(Al,Fe^{+2},Fe^{+3},Li,Mg,Mn^{+2})_3$
$(Al,Cr^{+3},Fe^{+3},V^{+3})_6$
$(BO_3)_3Si_6O_{18}(O,OH,F)_4$
(general formula, complex borosilicate)

Crystal System:
hexagonal

Hardness:
7

Specific Gravity:
3.10–3.25

"Watermelon" tourmaline gemstone from Minas Gerais, Brazil, with a tricolor, doubly terminated crystal perched on quartz from Mesa Grande, San Diego County, California.

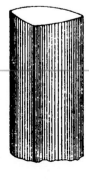

ONE GLANCE AT THE GENERAL FORMULA FOR THE TOURMALINE GROUP SHOWS WHY the Victorian scholar John Ruskin said it was "more like a medieval doctor's prescription than the making of a respectable mineral." Tourmaline has a structural site for virtually any kind of ion available in a given geological environment; while the constituents are highly variable, the basic structure always remains the same. Its name comes from the appropriately ambiguous Singhalese term *turamali*, which was applied in general to the odd mixture of unidentifiable gem pebbles from the alluvial deposits of Ceylon (now Sri Lanka). The tourmaline group is divided into several species on the basis of composition, but it must be kept in mind that there is considerable substitution between species. Indeed, single crystals often change composition as they grow, due to variation in the supply of specific ions. The most common tourmaline is the black, iron-rich variety *schorl*. The brown magnesium-rich tourmalines found in marbles are *dravite* and *uvite*, while *elbaite* and *liddicoatite* are the lithium-rich tourmalines which provide colored gemstones. The different color variations of elbaite are given their own names: pink or red, *rubellite*; colorless, *achroite*; and blue, *indicolite*.

The tourmaline structure consists of planar BO_3 groups in combination with rings of silica tetrahedra. Unlike the rings in other cyclosilicates such as beryl, the silica rings in tourmaline are all oriented with the tetrahedral points in one direction. This gives rise to the marked polarity in both the hemimorphic crystal structure of tourmaline and its distinctive electrical properties. Tourmaline displays *pyroelectricity* and *piezoelectricity*, acquiring an electric charge through rubbing or otherwise warming, or through the application of pressure. Like quartz, which is also piezoelectric, tourmaline finds use as a frequency stabilizer and in gauges that measure changes in pressure.

The pyroelectricity of tourmaline was appreciated by the Dutch traders who brought the first tourmalines to Europe from the East Indies in the early 18th century. They called tourmaline *aschentrekker* ("ash remover"), because the static electricity generated by warming a tourmaline crystal was handy for removing ashes from their pipes. This same property causes tourmaline specimens stored in warm display cabinets to collect dust at a surprising rate. Although tourmaline got a late start as a gemstone, its popularity has steadily increased as an ever-greater variety of rich colors continues to appear from deposits around the world. The many colors of gem tourmaline (elbaite) have lead to its being confused with virtually every other type of colored stone.

Tourmaline is very commonly seen as fine crystals, which are usually short to long prismatic with either a hexagonal or roughly triangular cross section, and terminated by low to steep pyramidal faces. Deep vertical striations are a very distinctive feature of this species; striated crystals are triangular in cross section and the prism faces bow outward. Doubly terminated crystals usually show hemimorphic development at their terminations, where one end will be terminated by lower pyramids than the other. Tourmaline has no cleavage, and its fracture is conchoidal to uneven. Parallel inclusions often give rise to a chatoyant, "cat's eye" effect. Schorl, as a common rock-forming species, is often seen as divergent sprays in granite and other rocks, and as granular or fibrous massive aggregates.

Tourmaline is seen in every color of the rainbow, although black tourmaline is by far the most common variety. Lithia tourmaline is often zoned, with colors blending into each other along the length of the crystal, or arranged concentrically. A typical variation is watermelon tourmaline, which has a pink or red core surrounded by a green exterior. Tourmaline ranges from transparent to opaque, but even the blackest shorl crystals may be translucent on thin edges; tourmaline has a vitreous luster and a colorless streak. Pleochroism is distinct to strong, the color being most intense when the crystal is viewed end-on. Tourmaline is harder than apatite, and further distinguished from apatite and beryl by its striations.

Schorl can be distinguished from hornblende by its typical triangular cross section.

Shorl is a relatively common rock-forming species, and occurs as an accessory mineral in schists and gneisses, greisens (see *Cassiterite*), high-temperature hydrothermal veins, and granites and other felsic igneous rocks. Crystals of schorl in granitic pegmatites may reach several meters in length. Dravite and the closely related species uvite are found primarily in calcareous metamorphic rocks such as contact metamorphic marbles, but also in some pegmatites. The colorful lithium tourmaline elbaite is restricted to complex granitic pegmatites, where it is found with quartz, beryl, lepidolite, columbite, and tantalite. Several pegmatite districts in North America produce fine specimens. In New England, elbaite is found in Middlesex County, Connecticut, and at several mines in southwestern Maine. Elbaite is also found in the pegmatites of Colorado and the Black Hills of South Dakota. The best North American specimens by far are found in San Diego County, California, in the Pala, Mesa Grande, Ramona, and Rincon districts. Excellent elbaite has also been found in the pegmatites of northern Baja California. Most commercial gem tourmaline now comes from Minas Gerais and several other states in Brazil, where crystals of virtually every color are found in decomposed pegmatites.

Although tourmaline localities are not well-represented in Europe, the lithium variety elbaite does take its name from the important deposit at San Piero in Campo, on the Island of Elba, off the coast of Tuscany. The pegmatites of the Soviet Union produce fine specimens of elbaite as well, from a number of locations including Mursinka, in the Ural Mountains, and Nertschinsk and Transbaikal. Fine shorlite crystals occur near Kragero, Norway, and excellent dravite crystals are found near Dobrava, Austria.

Stubby prismatic crystals of the common black tourmaline schorlite, from New York.

Crystal of the calcium- and sodium-rich tourmaline uvite in marble, from Goveneur, New York.

Excellent tourmaline specimens are found in the pegmatites of Laghman Province in Afghanistan, and recently, from Pakistan's Northwest Frontier province.

There are many important sources of colored tourmaline in Africa, including Usakos and Karibib, Namibia; Zimbabwe; Alto Ligonha, Mozambique; Tanzania; and many places in Madagascar. Near Antsirabe on Madagascar hexagonal prisms of liddicoatite as much as 1 m in length occur in weathered soils. These crystals display remarkable triangular color zonation, such that thin slices display as many as thirty sharp triangles or hexagons of various colors in concentric arrangement. Enormous dravite crystals are found at Yinnietharra, and green elbaite near Spargoville, in Western Australia; elbaite crystals are also found on Kangaroo Island, South Australia.

tridymite

Classification:
tectosilicate, silica group

Composition:
SiO₂ (silicon oxide)

Crystal System:
monoclinic

Hardness:
7

Specific Gravity:
2.26

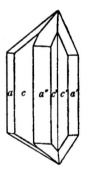

TRIDYMITE IS ONE OF SEVERAL POLYMORPHS OF SiO_2, AND IS COMMONLY ASSOCIATED with the higher temperature form cristobalite in siliceous volcanic rocks. It first forms as hexagonal *beta-tridymite*, which is stable only at very high temperatures. Cooling brings about a solid-state conversion to *alpha-tridymite*, which conceals its monoclinic structure within the hexagonal shell of its predecessor. Even this form of tridymite is unstable, however, and eventually converts to quartz. Synthetic tridymite is used in heat-resistant ceramics and glazes.

Tridymite crystals are very small, pseudohexagonal individuals, spherules, or rosettes. The original beta-tridymite crystals commonly form twins of various habits; trilling twins (composed of three individuals) give tridymite its name. It is very brittle, colorless or white, and transparent or translucent with a vitreous luster. It is nearly impossible to distinguish from cristobalite without special tests.

Tridymite is typically associated with quartz, cristobalite, fayalite, hematite, hornblende, and augite, in cavities in felsic volcanic rocks. It also forms *phenocrysts*, or euhedral crystal grains enclosed in massive volcanic rock. Originally noted in the andesites of Cerro San Cristobal, Pachuca, Mexico, tridymite is found in volcanic rocks throughout Latin America and the western United States. Euhedral pseudomorphs of quartz after tridymite over 1 cm long are found in the Euganean Hills of Italy. Other localities include the Siebengebirge region of the German Rhineland, and Puy de Dome, France.

Tridymite crystals on rhyolite from Cerro San Cristobal, Pachuca, Mexico.

TRIPHYLITE AND LITHIOPHILITE ARE BOTH LITHIUM, IRON-MANGANESE PHOSPHATES, forming a continuous series between end members enriched in either iron or manganese. Triphylite takes its name from a Greek phrase meaning "family of three," in honor of its three cations; lithiophilite is derived from an equally cozy phrase meaning "lover of lithium." They occur together in granitic pegmatites, usually as large anhedral grains but sometimes displaying rough, curved crystal faces. Both display three directions of cleavage and subconchoidal to uneven fracture. Triphylite is greenish or bluish gray in color, and lithiophilite is reddish, yellowish brown, or pinkish; however, both are commonly blackened by secondary manganese oxides. Sometimes there is nothing left of the original mineral but a black stain.

Like blue cheese, these two minerals are famous for going bad with style. In pegmatites infiltrated by groundwater, large grains riddled with cavities and porous sections display an interesting and colorful suite of alteration products, including dark-red sicklerite; pinkish hureaulite; yellowish salmonsite; bright-yellow stewartite; dark-blue vivianite; and blue, red, and purple strengite, purpurite, and heterosite. Another suite of alteration products is associated with triphylite and lithiophilite in pegmatites which have been affected by late-stage hydrothermal fluids. Among the typical minerals in this suite are eosphorite, reddingite, fairfieldite, dickinsonite, phosphoferrite, wolfeite, triploidite, and fillowite. The former collection of alteration products is typical of the pegmatites in the Pala District of San Diego County, California; the latter is well represented at Branchville, Fairfield County, Connecticut. Significant European localities include Verutrask, Sweden; Mangualde, Portugal; and the pegmatites of Bavaria, Germany. Other localities worldwide include the Karibib District, Namibia; Namaqualand, South Africa; the Buranga pegmatite, Rwanda; and the Pilbara District, Western Australia.

triphylite and lithiophilite

Classification:
phosphates

Composition:
triphylite—Li(Fe,Mn)(PO$_4$)
(lithium iron-manganese phosphate)
lithiophilite—Li(Mn,Fe)(PO$_4$)
(lithium manganese-iron phosphate)

Crystal System:
orthorhombic

Hardness:
4–5

Specific Gravity:
3.34

Large unaltered cleavage fragment of triphylite from the Dan Patch Mine, Keystone, South Dakota.

Turquoise in matrix from Chuquicamata, Chile, with a cabochon from Esmeralda

turquoise

Classification:
phosphate

Composition:
$CuAl_6(PO_4)_4(OH)_8 \cdot 4H_2O$
(hydrous copper aluminum phosphate)

Crystal System:
triclinic

Hardness:
5–6

Specific Gravity:
2.6–2.84

IMAGINE HOLDING IN YOUR PALM A FRAGMENT OF PERFECT SUMMER SKY, EVEN IN THE gray depths of winter. No other stone has the unmistakable robin's-egg blue color of high-quality turquoise. Prized for millennia, it has been sought by miners and traders in some of the most remote corners of the world. Turquoise is a phosphate of aluminum and copper, which contains a significant amount of water in its structure. The copper content is responsible for its color, which ranges from powder blue through blue-green to flat green. The name turquoise, which means "Turkish" in French, was given to this mineral for the same reason that turkeys are called turkeys—both were first introduced to Europe via Turkey.

Turquoise was discovered at a very early date, probably because it is a secondary mineral which forms near the earth's surface, often in the area of copper deposits. The most ancient turquoise mines known are those at Sarabit el Khadem on the Sinai Peninsula, which appear to have been established over 5000 years ago. The beduin still mine turquoise there to some extent, but the heyday of the mining operations was in the time of the Egyptian dynasties. Extensive underground workings reflect two thousand years of slave labor in the service of the pharaohs.

Turquoise was also very important to the Native Americans. Large quantities of turquoise beads, pendants, and other objects have been found in Anasazi and Hohokam sites in Arizona, New Mexico, and Colorado. The Zuñi and other groups still make offerings of turquoise to their deities, and their jewelry and other turquoise artifacts are in much demand. One of the many turquoise deposits worked by the Native Americans in the Southwest is in the Los Cerillos Mountains in New Mexico. This ancient mine consists of an open cut, 50 m deep and 100 m wide, excavated entirely by hand; surrounding it are tons of tillings, from which the precious turquoise was cobbed by hand. Following their conquest of the region, the Spaniards continued to exploit the mines with Indian labor.

Turquoise almost always occurs as a fine-grained aggregate, usually as nodules or thin seams encased in rock. Crystals are extremely rare, and only of microscopic size. The color ranges from sky-blue through bluish green to apple-green; iron (Fe^{+2}) accounts for the green color. Turquoise is translucent to opaque, its luster waxy to dull, and its streak white to pale green. Gem-quality turquoise ranges in color from pale blue to bright blue, with clear, unmottled material being the most valuable. "Spiderweb" turquoise, which displays a netlike pattern of dark lines, is slightly less valuable. Chrysocolla is softer than turquoise, but variscite is more difficult

to distinguish, although it never displays the characteristic sky-blue color of some turquoise. Turquoise is relatively porous, and will change color as it absorbs liquids, grease, or perspiration. Jewelers take advantage of this fact to impregnate dull-colored material with plastics and dyes; in fact, most commercial turquoise has been treated in some way.

Turquoise is a secondary mineral which forms near the Earth's surface, in phosphatic rocks rich in copper and aluminum and saturated with groundwater. These conditions are met in some igneous and pelitic sedimentary rocks, and rarely in pegmatites, as at Hagendorf, Bavaria. The most famous turquoise deposits are in the trachytes of the Ali-Mirsa-Kuh Mountains, near Nishapur, Khurasan, Iran. These mines, though probably over 2000 years old, are still active. The most important modern deposits are those in the southwestern United States. Very large nodular masses of fine-quality turquoise have been mined at Battle Mountain, Lander County, Nevada; smaller deposits are intermittently worked at several locations in Arizona, California, and Colorado. Several deposits are still being worked in the Cerillos Mountains of New Mexico. Microscopic crystals of turquoise are found in small copper prospects in Virginia, one at Kelly Bank Mine, Rockbridge County, and the other near Lynch Station, Campbell County. Turquoise is also found at Chucicamata, Chile; in Australia, and in England and France.

The Navajo of Arizona and New Mexico learned of turquoise from their Pueblo Indian neighbors, and the art of silversmithing from the Spanish. They combined the two media into a distinctive art form, here displayed by a Navajo woman in her finest turquoise jewelry.

twinning

MINERALS OFTEN DEVELOP NOT AS SINGLE CRYSTALS, BUT IN COMPOSITES OF TWO OR more crystals known as twins. Twins are regular intergrowths whose component crystals have a definite relationship to one another, determined by shared crystallographic information. They should not be confused with crystal aggregates. Crystal twins start growing in much the same way as do animal twins, except that the raw materials are inorganic ions rather than cells. When a crystal is still composed only of a very few ions, a single ion may take a position that is almost, but not quite perfectly aligned with the original structure. This ion then attracts more ions at the same rate as its neighbors, but the crystal it forms grows at a different angle than the original. The misalignment of twin seed ions is controlled by the same regular forces that shape the structure of single crystals, so twins tend to grow at consistent angles. Many minerals occur more commonly as twins than as single crystals, and can be identified on this basis.

Twins are composed of two or more individual crystals, or *members*, and come into contact along a surface known as a *composition plane*. The three general types of twins are contact twins, penetration twins, and repeated twins, although a vast array of variations are covered under these headings. In *contact twins*, two crystals are united by a composition plane to produce mirror images of each other; well-known examples are the nearly right-angled Japan Law twins of quartz, fish-tail twins of calcite and gypsum, and Manebach twins of orthoclase feldspar.

Penetration twins result from two identical members growing into each other in a consistent, symmetrical fashion, with the corners of each protruding from the faces of the other. Fluorite, tetrahedrite, and the Carlsbad twins of orthoclase are good examples of this habit. *Repeated twins* take two major forms: *lamellar* or *polysynthetic* twins, and *cyclic* twins. Polysynthetic twins are composed of multiple members sandwiched together in a parallel series. In the plagioclase feldspars, the reentrant sutures between members are indicated by exceedingly fine parallel striations, which are evident on cleavage surfaces, and serve to identify feldspars of this series even as small grains. Cyclic repeat twins consist of several crystals arranged like the spokes of a wheel or rays of a star; rutile and chrysoberyl are characteristic examples of cyclic twinning.

Twinning can be an aid to mineral identification, and is usually not difficult to detect; most habits are characterized by sharp depressions, called *reentrants*, marking the location of the composition plane. In other instances, twinning is harder to detect. Polysynthetic twins of sphalerite, for example, often resemble a single crystal; the individual members are only apparent from alternating bands of differing luster which encircle the "crystal."

Types of twinning. **Top:** *Contact twinning in rutile (left) and calcite (right).* **Middle:** *Penetration twinning in arsenopyrite (left) and orthoclase (right).* **Bottom:** *Polysynthetic twinning in plagioclase and cyclic twinning in chrysoberyl.*

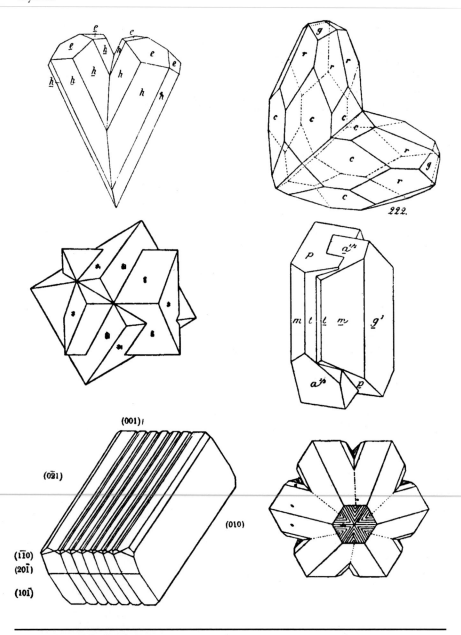

ULEXITE, NAMED FOR ITS DISCOVERER, THE GERMAN CHEMIST GEORGE LUDWIG ULEX (b. 1811), was once the most important source of borax (see *Borates* and *Borax*). Before the discovery of minable deposits of colemanite in the mountains above Death Valley in 1882, gangs of Chinese immigrants labored at picking loose ulexite efflorescences called "cotton balls" from the dry lake beds on the valley floor.

Ulexite very rarely forms distinct individual crystals, more often occurring as the rounded masses of loose acicular crystals mentioned above. It also forms vein-filling aggregates of extremely elongated, parallel crystals with a silky, chatoyant luster. This latter habit gives rise to a fiber-optic effect, capable of transmitting an image from one end of the aggregate to the other, even over many centimeters. Ulexite is sometimes called the "television stone" for this reason. Another distinctive property of ulexite is its solubility in hot water.

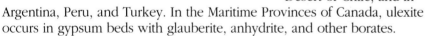

Ulexite is found with other borates in the evaporite deposits of the inland ephemeral lakes. Individual crystals are found at Boron, California, and large massive deposits occur elsewhere throughout the Mojave Desert. It is also found in the Atacama Desert of Chile, and in Argentina, Peru, and Turkey. In the Maritime Provinces of Canada, ulexite occurs in gypsum beds with glauberite, anhydrite, and other borates.

THIS HIGHLY RADIOACTIVE MINERAL IS NAMED FOR THE ELEMENT URANIUM, OF WHICH it is one of the most important sources. The slow process of radioactive decay, which turns uranium into lead, causes uraninite to be metamict, and its physical properties may vary with age. The composition of uraninite is highly variable, and radium, thorium, cerium, and yttrium commonly substitute for uranium. When uraninite is heated, it gives off a gas composed primarily of helium, since helium is produced by the radioactive decay of uranium. It is from a sample of uraninite from Czechoslovakia that helium, polonium, and radium were first identified by the Curies in 1898. In addition to providing uranium for the nuclear industry, uranium compounds provide pigments used in photography and other applications. Uraninite provides the bulk of the world's radium, despite the fact that hundreds of tons of uraninite must be processed to obtain one gram of radium salts.

Uraninite most commonly occurs as black, banded cryptocrystalline aggregates known as pitchblende. Crystals usually take the form of cubes, octahedra or dodecahedra, or cubes slightly modified by the latter forms. These are black and opaque, with a submetallic luster and black streak. The rock surrounding uraninite is commonly discolored with yellow, orange, or green secondary uranium minerals, referred to by the general name gummite, but consisting of several distinct species.

Uraninite, especially the pitchblende variety, is commonly found in metalliferous medium- and high-temperature hydrothermal veins. Large quantities also occur in sedimentary deposits in the Colorado Plateau region of the United States and elsewhere (see *Carnotite*). Detrital uraninite grains are also mined, along with gold, from ancient placer deposits formed over 2 billion years ago, before the earth's atmosphere became oxygenated. The largest of these unusual deposits are in Witwatersrand, South Africa, and Blind River, Saskatchewan.

The best crystallized specimens of uraninite are found in pegmatites, however. Uraninite crystals several centimeters in diameter have been found in the pegmatites of Bancroft District, Ontario, in association with apatite and fluorite. Good crystals are also found at Elvestad, Norway; in the Uluguru Mountains of Tanzania, and in pegmatite deposits throughout the United States. Huge masses of pitchblende are mined in Canada's Blind River and Great Bear Lake regions. In the hydrothermal veins of Shinkolobwe, Katanga, Zaire, both pitchblende and uraninite crystals are found in association with gold, cobalt, copper, molybdenum, tungsten, and platinum minerals. Other notable sources include Rum Jungle, Australia, and Germany, Portugal, and France.

Botryoidal uraninite from Schneeberg, Germany.

VANADINITE IS NAMED AFTER THE ELEMENT VANADIUM, OF WHICH IT IS AN ORE. Vanadium is used as an alloy in steel, as a catalyst, and as a mordant, or permanent dye. This species has a variable composition, with arsenic and phosphate ions substituting for the vanadium group, and calcium, copper and/or zinc occupying the lead positions. A solid-solution series exists between vanadinite and mimetite, with an intermediate variety called *endlichite*. Along with pyromorphite, these species are isostructural with apatite; however, there is no confusing vanadinite with other species, as its vibrant red color is unmistakable.

Vanadinite usually forms sharp small crystals in the shape of hexagonal prisms, which are often skeletal or hollow. It also occurs in radial aggregates and encrustations. Crystals are typically orange-red, yellow, or brown, with an adamantine to resinous luster and yellowish white streak.

Vanadinite is a secondary mineral native to the oxidation zones of lead deposits, where it occurs in association with pyromorphite, mimetite, cerrusite, anglesite, limonite, and wulfenite. Very large crystals have been found at Grootfontien in South Africa, and at Mibladen and Taouz, Morocco. Several mines in the Southwest produce fine specimens, including the Apache Mine in Gila County, and the Old Yuma Mine in Pima County, Arizona. The yellow, arsenic-rich variety known as *endlichite* is known from several New Mexican deposits, and from Santa Eulalia and Los Lamentos in Old Mexico as well.

vanadinite

Classification:
vanadate

Composition:
$Pb_5(VO_4)_3Cl$ (lead vanadate)

Crystal System:
hexagonal

Hardness:
2.75–3

Specific Gravity:
6.9

Parallel growth in tabular vanadinite, from Mibladen, Ksar es Souk, Morocco.

VARISCITE IS WELL-KNOWN IN ITS MASSIVE FORM AS POLISHED SECTIONS OF APPLE-green nodules, or cut into cabochon gemstones. Strengite is less well known but more widespread, forming as a common alteration product of other iron-bearing phosphates. Variscite takes its name from Variscia, an archaic name for the Vogtland District of Germany where it was first discovered. Strengite is named for the German mineralogist J. A. Streng (b. 1830).

Variscite crystals are quite rare and of microscopic size; their morphology is pseudo-octahedral. Variscite is much more commonly seen as cryp-

tocrystalline aggregates, forming nodules, and as veinlets enclosed in matrix. Strengite crystals may also be pseudo-octahedral, though they appear as tabular or stout prismatic as well; they commonly form druses of radiating acicular individuals.

Both species have two directions of cleavage, although the size of the crystals makes this hard to see; massive variscite is tough, and has a splintery to good conchoidal fracture. Crystals of both species are transparent with a vitreous luster; variscite is translucent to opaque with a waxy to dull luster when massive. Variscite ranges in color from deep green through yellow-green, to nearly white in more porous material. Strengite is red, violet, or colorless; both species have a white streak. Variscite nodules may resemble greenish turquoise.

Variscite forms through the action of low-temperature hydrothermal fluids on aluminum and phosphate-rich rocks. Common associates include wavellite, apatite, chalcedony, and goethite. The classic variscite specimens are nodules to 25 cm in diameter from the brecciated sedimentary rocks of Clay Canyon, near Fairfield, Utah County, Utah. Other Utah localities include Lucin, in Box Elder County; and the Stansbury Mountains, Tooele County. Variscite is also found in Nevada at several localities in Esmeralda County and Mineral County. Microscopic crystals occur in Garland and Mongomery counties, Arkansas.

Strengite is a secondary mineral which forms through alteration of iron-rich phosphates such as triphylite in granitic pegmatites, or from phosphates associated with iron ores. Deep purple crystals of strengite occur in small cavities in the pegmatites of Bavaria, Germany; Mangualde, Portugal; Blatun, Belgium; Buranga, Rwanda; and Pala, San Diego County, California.

Top: *Polished nodule of massive variscite from Fairfield, Utah.* **Bottom:** *Strengite crystals from Pleystein, Bavaria, Germany.* **Opposite page:** *Tiny crystals of variscite in a limestone breccia, from the de Linde Mine, Garland County, Arkansas.*

variscite and strengite

Classification:
phosphates

Composition:
variscite: $AlPO_4 \cdot 2H_2O$
(hydrous aluminum phosphate)
strengite: $FePO_4 \cdot 2H_2O$
(hydrous iron phosphate)

Crystal System:
orthorhombic

Hardness:
3.5–4.5

Specific Gravity:
2.57 (variscite)
2.87 (strengite)

vesuvianite (idocrase)

Classification:
sorosilicate

Composition:
$Ca_{19}Fe(Mg,Al)_8Al_4(SiO_4)_{10}(Si_2O_7)_4(OH)_{10}$
(calcium, magnesium, aluminum silicate)

Crystal System:
tetragonal

Hardness:
6–7

Specific Gravity:
3.33–3.45

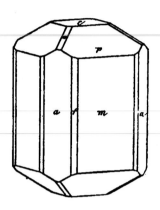

Stout prismatic crystal of vesuvianite from Yakutsk, Siberia.

THE VOLCANO VESUVIUS, NEAR NAPLES, ITALY, IS HOME TO MANY INTERESTING MINERALS, including this species, named for the volcano. The lava of which Vesuvius is composed crystallized from magmas with an interesting history. As the molten rock percolated beneath the volcano, it incorporated a certain amount of the limestone country rock. The silicate melt of the magma absorbed the carbonates of the limestone, producing a hybrid suite of calc-silicate minerals, one of which is vesuvianite. An alternate name for vesuvianite, idocrase, comes from the Greek phrase meaning "mixture of forms," reflecting the complex shape of some vesuvianite crystals. Vesuvianite has two gem varieties. One is a compact massive form commonly referred to as californite, in honor of its occurrences in northern California. Californite is tough, translucent, and resembles jade in color. Transparent vesuvianite, in shades of yellow, green, blue violet, or brown, is also fashioned into gemstones, which are often very bright and beautiful.

Crystals are pyramidal, or more commonly, short prisms with pyramidal terminations and square cross section. They may also be columnar, granular, and cryptocrystalline (californite). Vesuvianite has three indistinct cleavages, and an uneven to conchoidal fracture. Colors include brown, green, yellow, white, red, violet, or blue; the blue variety is known as cyprine. Crystals are transparent to translucent, with a vitreous to resinous luster and a white streak. Californite can be difficult to distinguish from jadeite and nephrite, a fact which is sometimes exploited by unscrupulous dealers. Zircon crystals have a morphology similar to that of vesuvianite crystals, but rarely achieve similar size.

Despite its occurrence in the lavas of Vesuvius, this species is more characteristic of contact metamorphic settings, where it is associated with grossular garnet, wollastonite, diopside, and epidote in impure marbles. It also occurs as a magmatic mineral in carbonatites, pegmatites, and nepheline syenites, and as a hydrothermal mineral in fissures in ultrabasic rocks. Cyprine is found at Franklin, Sussex County, New Jersey. Fine crystals are found in Lyon County, Nevada; at Scratch Gravel, near Helena, Montana; and in the Crestmore Quarry near Riverside, California. Californite is mined in Butte County, and near Happy Camp, Siskiyou County, California. Transparent crystals are found in pegmatites cutting marble in Laurel Argenteuil County, Quebec; and yellow prismatic crystals are found in skarns at Xalostoc, Morelos, and Lake Jaco, Chihuahua, Mexico. Good specimens are also obtained from Czechoslovakia, Finland, France, Italy, Norway, Russia, Pakistan, Japan, Korea, Taiwan, Kenya, and Australia.

VIVIANITE IS NAMED FOR ITS DISCOVERER, THE ENGLISH MINERALOGIST J. G. VIVIAN. IT is commonly associated with fossil bones and teeth, deriving phosphate from the bones (see *Apatite*) and iron from the ground water. Mammoth and mastodon tusks and other fossil ivory that has been stained blue by vivianite is called odontolite, or "bone turquoise," and has been used as a gemstone for millennia. This species is not particular about where it precipitates, as long as the chemistry is right. Recently, a 14,000-year-old frozen long-horned bison was unearthed from the permafrost in Alaska, its skin turned blue, not from the cold but from vivianite. Of course, it was dubbed "Babe," after Paul Bunyan's mythical blue ox. When found in large concentrations, vivianite is sometimes used as a pigment.

Freshly unearthed crystals are colorless to white, but they have the peculiar property of turning green, blue, or black with exposure to air, due to the oxidation of the iron component. The streak is also colorless or white, changing rapidly to blue or brown. Vivianite forms as elongated, prismatic crystals, or massive, fibrous, or bladed rosettes. Perfect cleavage parallel to the prism face is easily developed, breaking crystals into thin flexible flakes. Continued abuse will result in a fibrous fracture. Its extreme softness, excellent cleavage, and tendency to change color are sufficient to distinguish vivianite from other species.

Vivianite is widespread, typically forming as a secondary mineral in sulfide deposits, generally in the absence of oxygen. It is the product of the interaction between hydrothermal fluids containing phosphoric acid, and iron minerals like pyrite and siderite. It is also formed in pegmatites through the hydration of primary iron phosphates. Fine specimens are found throughout the United States, most notably in Utah. Large crystals are found in the pegmatites of Galilea, in Minas Gerais, Brazil, in association with amblygonite. Good specimens of vivianite come from the tin deposits of Cornwall, England, and Poopo and Llallagua, Bolivia. Star-shaped aggregates of vivianite, and enormous single crystals over 1 m in length have been found in the clay deposits near N'gaoundere, Cameroon.

vivianite

Classification:
phosphate

Composition:
$Fe_3^{+2}(PO_4)_2 \cdot 8H_2O$
(hydrated iron phosphate)

Crystal System:
monoclinic

Hardness:
1.5–2

Specific Gravity:
2.58–2.68

Prismatic crystals of vivianite from the Blackbird Mine, Lemhi County, Idaho.

wavellite

Classification:
phosphate

Composition:
$Al_3(PO_4)_2(OH,F)_3 \cdot 5H_2O$
(hydrous aluminum phosphate)

Crystal System:
orthorhombic

Hardness:
3.5–4

Specific Gravity:
2.36

Opposite page: Wavellite from Trenice, Czechoslovakia. Most of these originally globular aggregates have been broken off, showing the points at the center of their bases from which the fibrous crystals began to radiate outward.

THIS PHOSPHATE IS NAMED FOR ITS DISCOVERER, THE ENGLISH PHYSICIAN WILLIAM Wavell (b. 1829). Isolated crystals of wavellite are very small, stout to long prismatic and are quite rare. The characteristic habit is radiating fibrous aggregates in the form of globular hemispheres, clustered on rock matrix like so many puffballs. It also forms stalactitic and botryoidal crusts that resemble chalcedony. Wavellite displays three directions of cleavage, one perfect, and an uneven to subconchoidal fracture. It is transparent to translucent, and colored green, yellow, white, gray, or brown; black, blue, or colorless crystals are encountered, but rarely. The luster is vitreous to pearly and the streak white. It is unmistakable in its characteristic habit of radiating, spherical aggregates.

Wavellite forms as a secondary mineral in hydrothermal veins, in some aluminous and contact metamorphic rocks, and in phosphorites. Excellent specimens are found in Garland, Hot Springs, and Montgomery counties, Arkansas. Good specimens are also obtained from Chester and Cumberland counties, Pennsylvania; St. Clair County, Alabama; Marion County, Florida; the King turquoise mine, Saguache County, Colorado; and Slate Mountain, California. Numerous localities exist worldwide, though notable deposits are found in England, Ireland, France, Portugal, Germany, and the Balkans.

willemite

Classification:
nesosilicate

Composition:
Zn_2SiO_4 (zinc silicate)

Crystal System:
hexagonal (rhombohedral)

Hardness:
5.5

Specific Gravity:
3.89–4.19

Willemite crystals in calcite, from the Taylor Mine, Franklin Furnace, New Jersey.

THIS VERY RARE AND UNUSUAL SPECIES IS NAMED AFTER WILLEM I, KING OF THE Netherlands (b. 1772). It is abundant only in the peculiar contact metamorphic zinc deposits at Franklin and Ogdensburg, Sussex County, New Jersey, where it has actually been exploited as an ore of zinc. Willemite forms hexagonal crystals with rhombohedral terminations, which range from short and stout to long and thin prismatic. These display two poor cleavages and an uneven to conchoidal fracture. Material is commonly granular or fibrous, or present as disseminated grains. Crystals are transparent to translucent, and are colored yellow, green, red, brown, white, colorless, or gray, with a vitreous to resinous luster and a white streak. Willemite fluoresces a vibrant yellow-green under ultraviolet light, probably due to the presence of manganese impurities. This was accidentally discovered by a miner in the New Jersey locality when a lamp malfunctioned, and was quickly taken advantage of as a means of sorting the otherwise homogenous-looking zinc ore.

The finest specimens of willemite are those

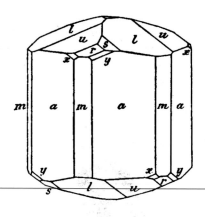

from the unusual, marble-hosted zinc orebody at Franklin and Ogdensburg, Sussex County, New Jersey, where they are associated with calcite, black franklinite, red zincite, and garnet. Elsewhere, willemite is found in more normal hydrothermal zinc-bearing sulfide deposits. Pale blue crusts of willemite occur with wulfenite, vanadinite, and mimetite in the Mammoth–St. Anthony Mine, Tiger, and the Apache Mine, Globe, Arizona. Willemite is also found at the Cerro Gordo and Ygnacio mines, Inyo County, California; Beaver County, Utah , and in various places in Canada and Mexico. Small amounts are also found at Altenberg, Belgium; Langban, Norway; and in Greece, Russia, Algeria, Zaire, Zambia, Iran, and Namibia.

witherite

Classification:
carbonate, aragonite group

Composition:
$BaCO_3$ (barium carbonate)

Crystal System:
orthorhombic

Hardness:
3–3.75

Specific Gravity:
4.29

Classic pseudohexagonal dipyramids of witherite from the Fallowfield Mine, Hexham, Northumberland.

ALTHOUGH MUCH LESS COMMON THAN THE BARIUM SULFATE BARITE, WITHERITE IS ALSO mined as an ore of barium when found in sufficiently large concentrations. Witherite and barite are very similar in massive form; however, witherite dissolves easily with effervescence in dilute hydrochloric acid, while barite is insoluble. Witherite crystals are very distinctive, usually forming horizontally striated, pseudohexagonal dipyramids composed of three individuals, or parallel growths of such twins resulting in pseudohexagonal prisms with curved terminations and stepped sides. Scepter-shaped or globular aggregates, and crusts are also common. Witherite displays two indistinct cleavages and an uneven fracture. Crystals are transparent to translucent, and colorless or white, with a vitreous to resinous luster and a white streak. Bluish phosphorescence and fluorescence are observed under ultraviolet light.

Witherite typically occurs in low-temperature hydrothermal veins, associated with barite, galena, and sometimes fluorite. The finest specimens have come from the lead mines of England, including Alston Moor, Cumberland; Hexham, Northumberland; and the Morrison Mine, Durham. The outstanding United States source is the Minerva No. 1 Mine, at Rosiclaire, Illinois, where excellent witherite crystals as large as 3 inches on edge are found in association with fluorite.

HUEBNERITE, WOLFRAMITE, AND FERBERITE ARE, RESPECTIVELY, THE MANGANESE, intermediate, and iron members of an isomorphous series. Wolframite is an arbitrary designation, but since most specimens are indeed intermediate between the two end members, it is the field name of choice. All three are important ores of tungsten. Tungsten has the highest melting point of any metal, and is used in strong heat-resistant alloys and fine filaments for lamps. Among the important tungsten compounds are tungsten carbide, used in high-speed tools and, as is diamond, in drill bits; and sodium tungstates, used in fireproofing and dying. Huebnerite was named for the German metallurgist Adolph Huebner, and ferberite for a fellow German, Adolph Ferber. Wolframite was named for the German word for tungsten, *wolfram*, which is thought to come from the German phrase meaning "wolf cream," probably a reference to the scum that formed atop the melt during the smelting of tungsten ores.

Huebnerite commonly forms long, lath-like striated crystals with wedge-shaped terminations; wolframite forms short prismatic or tabular, similarly striated crystals; and ferberite grows in elongated striated prisms. Contact twins are common in each, sometimes with one member rotated 180° like the Carlsbad twins of orthoclase. Crystals are often arranged in parallel aggregates or divergent sprays, and are also commonly found as granular, or bladed material. They are brittle, with perfect prismatic cleavage and uneven to conchoidal fracture. Crystals may appear to "peel" along easily developed parting planes parallel to the crystal faces.

Color and streak generally grow darker with increasing iron, that is, toward ferberite; huebnerite is transparent to translucent and ferberite nearly opaque. Huebnerite is yellowish to reddish brown, ferberite reddish brown to black; lusters are submetallic to resinous. Ferberite is slightly magnetic. Members of this series are heavier and softer than goethite, and distinguished from cassiterite and columbite–tantalite by their cleavage, parting, and morphology.

The wolframite series is best represented in hydrothermal quartz veins and pegmatites related to granitic plutons. Typical associates include quartz, feldspar, cassiterite, arsenopyrite, hematite, scheelite, tourmaline, topaz, and fluorite. Wolframite is also found in some sulfide veins. Excellent specimens occur in Boulder, Gunnison, San Juan, and Park counties, Colorado; and numerous other locations in the western United States. The classic European localities are at Zinnwald and Schlaggenwald, Bohemia, Czechoslovakia. Fine specimens are found in the tin veins of Llallagua, Bolivia; Pasto Bueno, Peru, and elsewhere in the Andes. China is the world's largest producer of commercial wolframite.

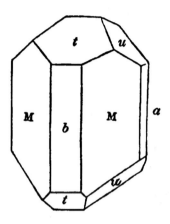

wolframite series

Classification:
tungstates

Composition:
$MnWO_4$ (huebnerite)
$(Fe,Mn)WO_4$ (wolframite)
$FeWO_4$ (ferberite)

Crystal System:
monoclinic

Hardness:
4–4.5

Specific Gravity:
7.1 (huebnerite) to 7.5 (ferberite)

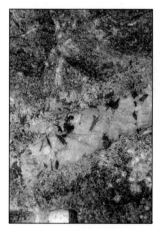

Left: *Wolframite crystals from the Panasqueira Mine, Serra da Estrella, Portugal.* ***Right:*** *A quartz vein containing black wolframite and molybdenite in the Xihuashan tungsten mine in China. The granite surrounding this hydrothermal vein has been altered through greisenization. (Photo courtesy Dennis Cox, USGS.)*

wollastonite

Classification:
inosilicate

Composition:
$CaSiO_3$ (calcium silicate)

Crystal System:
triclinic

Hardness:
4.5–5

Specific Gravity:
2.87–3.09

WOLLASTONITE IS ONE OF THE CALCIUM SILICATES CHARACTERISTIC OF THE CONTACT metamorphic deposits, or *skarns*, that result when a limestone or marble is intruded by igneous rocks. It was named for the English mineralogist William Wollaston (b. 1766), and finds use in the manufacture of refractory ceramics. Discrete, tabular crystals of wollastonite are rare. The most common aggregate habits are fibrous, acicular or radiating, or granular. A delicate mineral, wollastonite has one perfect and two good cleavages, and a splintery fracture. It is transparent to translucent and colored white, gray, pale green, or colorless, with vitreous to pearly luster, or silky when fibrous. Stilbite, cummingtonite, sillimanite, and other similar-appearing species are not found in the same contact metamorphic association.

In addition to its occurrence in skarns, minor amounts of wollastonite form in calcareous regional metamorphic rocks. Large deposits are found in the Black Forest of Germany, in Brittany, and at Willsboro, New York, where wollastonite is mined for use in ceramics. Interesting specimens are found in Chiapas, Mexico; Csiklowa, Romania; Pargas, Finland; and in Colorado, California, Ontario, Quebec, Norway, Italy, Greece, and China.

wulfenite

Classification:
molybdate

Composition:
$PbMoO_4$ (lead molybdate)

Crystal System:
tetragonal

Hardness:
3

Specific Gravity:
6.8

WULFENITE IS NAMED FOR FRANZ XAVER VON WULFEN (B. 1727), AN AUSTRIAN JESUIT priest whose interest in the many aspects of Creation resulted in his becoming an authority on lead ores. Wulfenite is isostructural with scheelite, and commonly contains some calcium and tungsten in the lead and molybdenum sites, respectively. Although not nearly as important an ore as molybdenite (MoS_2), wulfenite is exploited for its molybdenum content.

Wulfenite is one of the most attractive mineral species: since it often forms clusters of thin tabular crystals set on edge at odd angles to one another, many matrix specimens resemble nothing so much as a cluster of brightly colored tropical butterflies, frozen in stone. Other habits include stubby pyramids and compact aggregates and crusts. Wulfenite is brittle and weak, with greasy cleavage. It is commonly an intense yellow, orange, or red color, with an adamantine luster and a white streak.

Top: Thin tabular crystals of wulfenite from the 79 Mine, Banner District, Gila County, Arizona. *Bottom:* One of the classic specimens of wulfenite collected from the Red Cloud Mine in the Trigo Mountains of Arizona in the late 1930s.

Wulfenite is a secondary mineral which forms in the oxidation zones of hydrothermal lead sulfide deposits containing molybdenum, of which it is a minor ore. Typical associated minerals include descloizite, pyromorphite, vanadinite, mimetite, cerrusite, limonite, calcite, and hemimorphite. Classic wulfenite specimens include the sharp, colorless, blue or yellow crystals from Tsumeb, Namibia; the gray wedges from Pribram, Czechoslovakia; and the yellow, pseudocubic crystals on white dolomite from the Sierra de los Lamentos, Chihuahua, Mexico. Legendary bright orange-red specimens on limonite matrix were found at the abandoned Red Cloud Mine in Yuma County, Arizona.

wurtzite

Classification:
sulfide

Composition:
(Zn,Fe)S (zinc–iron sulfide)

Crystal System:
hexagonal

Hardness:
3.5–4

Specific Gravity:
3.98

THIS RARE ZINC MINERAL, NAMED FOR THE FRENCH CHEMIST ADOLPHE WURTZ, IS A polymorph of both the common zinc ore sphalerite and the much rarer species *matraite*. Wurtzite has the densest structure possible for a hexagonal crystal, while sphalerite has an equally dense but isomeric atomic structure similar to that of diamond. Wurtzite is the higher temperature polymorph, stable at temperatures in excess of 1020°C at normal pressure.

Wurtzite forms small isolated tabular or hemimorphic crystals, with one of its terminations being a hexagonal pyramid with horizontally striated faces, and the other smooth and flat. Wurtzite is brittle, with two directions of cleavage and an even to conchoidal fracture. Crystals are translucent, with a resinous luster and brown streak. The typical color is brownish black to orange, and orange fluorescence is observed under longwave ultraviolet light.

Wurtzite is found in hydrothermal sulfide deposits with sphalerite, and more rarely in concretions in sedimentary rocks, as in Ohio and Pennsylvania. Good specimens to 2.5 cm are found at Oruro and Llallagua, Bolivia. Wurtzite is found in numerous locations throughout the western United States, Peru, England, Romania, Czechoslovakia, and Namibia.

Drusy wurtzite from Montserrat, Poopo, Bolivia.

XENOTIME IS A RELATIVELY RARE BUT WIDESPREAD ACCESSORY MINERAL, OCCURRING AS small crystals in granitic pegmatites, granites, and placer deposits. Because of its relative obscurity, xenotime was named from the Greek expression meaning "a stranger to honor." This is perhaps a reference to the more abundant rare-earth phosphate monazite, with which xenotime is often found in placer deposits. Like its more assertive cousin, xenotime is exploited for several of the useful elements which typically substitute for yttrium, including erbium, cerium, and other rare earths, as well as thorium, uranium, beryllium, and zirconium.

Xenotime is isostructural with zircon, which is to say that they share a similar crystal structure, but are not isomorphic. Xenotime is not as hard as zircon and can also be distinguished by its perfect cleavage. Crystals are prismatic, pyramidal, or equant, sometimes form rosettes, and rarely exceeding 2 cm in size. The pegmatites of Setesdal, Iveland, and other places in Norway produce well-formed crystals, as do the pegmatites of Brazil and Madagascar. In the United States, xenotime is found in California, Colorado, New York, and the southern Appalachian states.

xenotime

Classification:
phosphate
Composition:
$Y(PO_4)$ (yttrium phosphate)
Crystal System:
tetragonal
Hardness:
4–5
Specific Gravity:
4.4–5.1

zeolite group

THE NAME OF THIS INTERESTING GROUP COMES FROM THE GREEK PHRASE MEANING "boiling stone," reflecting the fact that the zeolites bubble as water is driven off in a flame. Indeed, many zeolites desiccate spontaneously when removed from the ground, crumbling into powder unless preserved with a sealant. Approximately thirty zeolite species are known, but only a few are commonly encountered, most notably analcime, chabazite, heulandite, harmotome, laumontite, natrolite, and stilbite. The zeolites are usually colorless, white, or very slightly colored, forming brittle crystals with good cleavage. The zeolites have three basic structural types, which are usually apparent in their external morphology. The fibrous zeolites have a chain structure, the platy ones a sheet structure, and the equant zeolites a framework structure.

Beyond these differences, all zeolites share an open tectosilicate framework in which various large cations like sodium and potassium balance the negative charges of the silica tetrahedra. Substitution between these loosely-held cations is easily achieved; the water component is also easily

Zeolites

chabazite	natrolite
harmotome	scolecite
heulandite	stilbite
laumontite	thomsonite

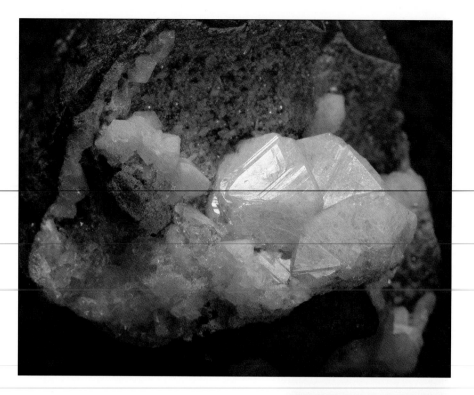

Top: These crystals of gmelinite, $(Na_2Ca)Al_2Si_4O_{12} \cdot 6H_2O$, on basalt from Flinders Island, Australia exemplify the typical appearance of many zeolites.

Bottom: The zeolite minerals have very open atomic structures, with large gaps in their framework of silica tetrahedra which can accommodate alkali ions and water molecules. The chain-like structure pictured is characteristic of the fibrous zeolites like natrolite and mesolite.

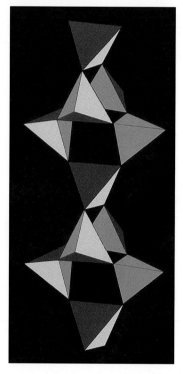

lost and regained. When a zeolite is heated and its interstitial water driven off, capacious channels remain in the undisturbed crystal structure. These channels have specific diameters depending upon the species, and can be used to filter gasses and liquids on the molecular level. Such zeolites are termed "molecular sieves," and are used to purify compounds such as liquid ammonia and mercury vapor.

The peculiar ion-exchanging abilities of zeolite have made them popular as water softening agents. When so-called "hard water" containing calcium ions in solution is routed through a zeolite filter, the calcium is exchanged for sodium and/or potassium from the zeolites. The calcium ions remain in the filter, and the sodium-rich "soft water" is passed on to the consumer.

The zeolites are very widespread in low-temperature hydrothermal environments, particularly in cavities and fissures in basalt and diabase in association with apophyllite, calcite, datolite, pectolite, prehnite, and quartz. Zeolites occur in smaller quantities in sulfide veins, granitic pegmatite pockets, and sedimentary rocks, typically as some of the last minerals to crystallize. Recently, large commercially important deposits of massive zeolites have been discovered in the western United States and in Tanzania, the result of the in-place alteration of beds of volcanic ash.

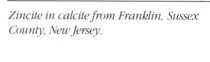

Zincite in calcite from Franklin, Sussex County, New Jersey.

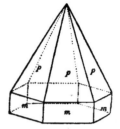

THIS EXTREMELY RARE MINERAL HAS ACTUALLY BEEN EXPLOITED AS AN ORE OF ZINC AT Franklin Furnace, New Jersey, the one locality where it occurs in abundance. The hemimorphic crystals of zincite are as strange as they are rare, consisting of a hexagonal pyramid which sits squarely atop a simple pedion. Zincite ranges in color from deep yellow to orange to dark red, and is translucent with subadamantine luster and orange-yellow streak.

Zincite is found very sparingly in particular zinc deposits, except at the unique contact metamorphic deposits at Franklin and Sterling Hill, Sussex County, New Jersey. Here zincite is found in 10-cm thick veins, in massive aggregates with white or pink calcite, green willemite, gray tephroite, and black franklinite, in rough crystals of 3 cm in size. Zincite has also been found at the Dick Weber Mine, Saguache County, Colorado; the Bottino Mine, Tuscany, Italy; at Tsumeb, Namibia; and in Poland, Spain, and Tasmania.

zincite

Classification:
oxide

Composition:
ZnO (zinc oxide)

Crystal System:
hexagonal

Hardness:
4

Specific Gravity:
5.68

ZIRCON IS THE MAIN SOURCE OF THE METAL ZIRCONIUM, AND IS AN ORE OF HAFNIUM as well, which may substitute for a large proportion of the zirconium content. Zircon compounds are valued for their refractory properties; zirconium oxide crucibles are so refractory that they can be used to melt platinum (melting point 1755°C). Because of its heat and corrosion resistance, zircon metal is used to coat the fuel rods in nuclear reactors. Ironically, natural zircon crystals illustrate the destructive potential of radiation. Since zircon usually contains some thorium and uranium, alpha particle radiation renders many specimens metamict. The terms high, intermediate, and low zircon are used to indicate the degree of radioactive decay a specimen exhibits. High zircon is unaffected by radioactivity and is the source of most gem material, while low zircon is so metamict that its internal structure has become completely amorphous.

Zircon is a common constituent of many igneous rock types, and is especially well-suited for use in the radiometric dating of ancient rocks;

zircon

Classification:
nesosilicate

Composition:
$ZrSiO_4$ (zirconium silicate)

Crystal System:
tetragonal

Hardness:
7.5

Specific Gravity:
4.6–4.7

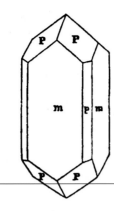

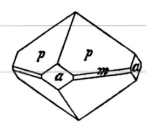

Zircon crystals from the Ilmen Mountains, near Orenburg, Russia.

crystals separated from rocks in Greenland have yielded the oldest dates yet measured on earth. Some varieties are used as gemstones, since the refractive index and dispersion of zircon gems approach that of diamond. Zircon has had its image sullied by its use as a diamond imitation, thus establishing it as a "cheap simulant," when in fact it is an interesting and beautiful gem in its own right. Most natural gems are reddish brown, but heating produces yellow, colorless, and blue stones—the latter often sold as "starlite." Slightly metamict intermediate zircon is also fashioned into gems, which are usually greenish and slightly cloudy. The name comes from the Persian phrase *zar gun*, or "gold colored."

Zircon typically forms short to long prismatic crystals, with square cross sections and pyramidal terminations, or simply dipyramidal crystals. Crystals usually occur as isolated individuals, sometimes quite sharp, suspended in rock matrix; they are also common as anhedral grains. Aggregates are sheaflike or radiating; metamict specimens often form curved, subparallel aggregates. Zircon has two poorly developed cleavages and an uneven fracture (conchoidal in metamict specimens). It is commonly some shade of brown or reddish brown, though it may also be grayish, greenish, violet-gray, or colorless. Crystals are transparent to translucent with a vitreous to adamantine luster; metamict specimens, however, are usually opaque and vitreous to greasy in luster.

Zircon is a widespread accessory mineral in nearly all kinds of igneous rocks, especially gran-ites and syenites and their pegmatites, and in the metamorphic rocks derived from them. Because of its density and durability, zircon is concentrated in placer deposits in the form of small grains; these are recovered from beach placers in Australia, Brazil, Florida, and the Carolinas. Very large crystals of zircon are found in marbles of Dungannon Township, Hastings County, and in Sebastopol Township, Renfrew County, Ontario. Fine specimens are also found nearby in Buckingham Township, Ottawa County; and at Grenville, Argenteuil County, Québec. Other North American zircon

localities include Custer County, South Dakota; the Ouachita Mountains of Oklahoma; the pegmatites of St. Peter's Dome, El Paso County, Colorado; Llano County, Texas; and Litchfield, Maine. Large crystals occur in the Langesundfjord district, Norway, and elsewhere in that country and in Sweden. Lustrous brown crystals are common from deposits near Miask, in the Ilmen Mountains of Russia; the Harts Range, Northern Territories, and in the New England District, New South Wales, Australia. Fine crystals to 10 cm occur at Mount Ampanobe, Madagascar. Water-worn crystals are abundant in the gem gravels of Mogok, Burma, and in Sri Lanka, Thailand, and elsewhere in Southeast Asia.

ZOISITE IS AN UNCOMMON MINERAL FOUND PRIMARILY IN METAMORPHIC ROCKS. IT IS dimorphous with the more common, monoclinic epidote relative clinozoisite. Zoisite was primarily known to collectors in its pink variety thulite, until the discovery of a new gem variety in 1966. That year, a tailor and itinerant prospector found a deep blue gem mineral in the schists of the Usumburu Mountains, near Mt. Kilimanjaro in northern Tanzania. Despite its intense, almost purple color, this stone was at first taken for sapphire (corundum); however, chemical analysis soon showed it to be a new variety of zoisite. The Merelani Mine was established, and the striking new stone was soon being sold as tanzanite by Tiffany and Company. Tanzanite is quite unlike any other gem species, and as the deposit at Merelani is apparently becoming depleted, it may join benitoite as one of the rarest gems in existence. Massive blue-green zoisite enclosing blebs of red ruby is another recent Tanzanian discovery, fast becoming popular as an ornamental material.

Zoisite is usually seen as long prismatic crystals with deep vertical striations, or as fibrous to granular aggregates. Crystals display perfect prismatic cleavage, which along with its relative softness gives cause for caution when wearing cut stones; the fracture is uneven to conchoidal. Zoisite is transparent to translucent, and the most common shades are gray, greenish, or yellowish brown; it has a vitreous to pearly luster and a colorless streak. The pink variety thulite usually fluoresces under ultraviolet light. Pink tourmaline (rubellite) resembles thulite, but the former lacks cleavage and does not fluoresce. Zoisite is named for the Czechoslovakian Baron S. Zois van Edelstein (b. 1747), and the variety thulite for Thule, an archaic name for Norway.

Zoisite is found in a wide variety of geological environments. It forms in contact metamorphic marbles and dolomites in association with grossular garnet, tremolite, and wollastonite; and in calcareous schists in association with almandite garnet and hornblende. Magmatic occurrences include some basic igneous rocks and pegmatites. Brown zoisite crystals occur in zinc ore at Ducktown, Polk County, Tennessee; and large, gray crystals (to 15 cm in length) in glaucophane schists of Mendocino County, California. Thulite is found in Okanogan County, Washington; Mitchell and Yancey Counties, North Carolina; Gila County, Arizona; Tulare County, California; at many places in Nevada; and in the Black Hills of South Dakota. Good zoisite crystals are found at the Jeffry Mine, Asbestos, Quebec; and northern Baja California, Mexico. Fine specimens of thulite are still found at the classic locality at Telemark, and elsewhere in Norway. Good thulite specimens are also obtained from the Aar Massif of Switzerland, and from locations in Germany, Italy, Scotland, Finland, the Soviet Union, Greenland, and Japan. So far, tanzanite has been found only at the Merelani deposit in Tanzania.

zoisite

Classification:
sorosilicate

Composition:
$Ca_2Al_3(Si_2O_7)(SiO_4)(OH)_2$
(calcium aluminum silicate)

Crystal System:
orthorhombic

Hardness:
6–6.5

Specific Gravity:
3.3

Zoisite (variety tanzanite) gem and crystal, from near Arusha, Tanzania.

Contents

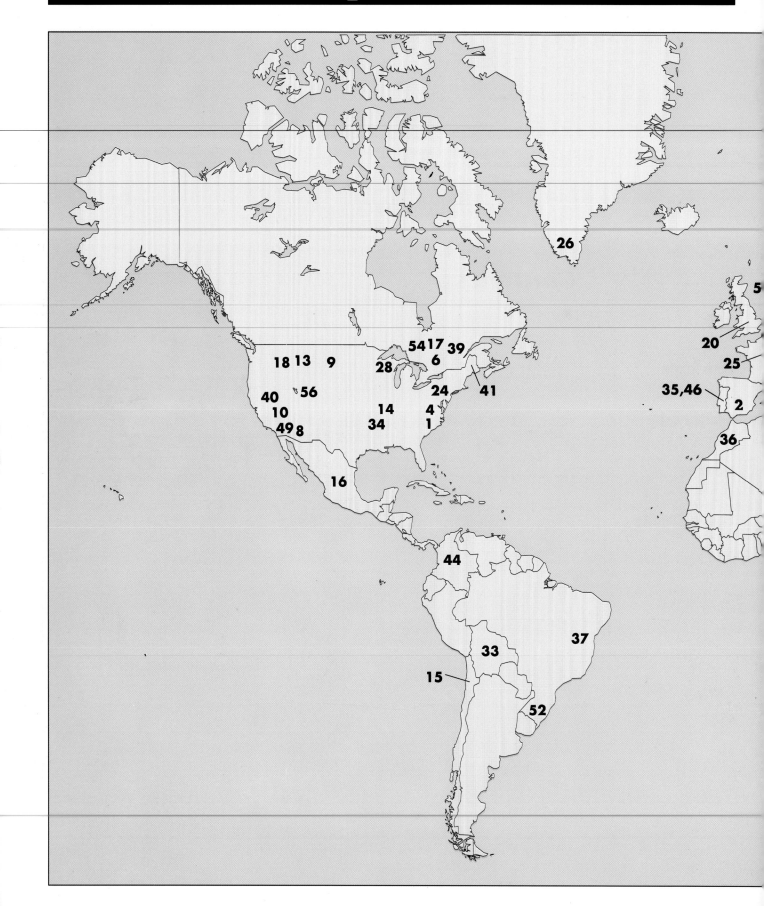

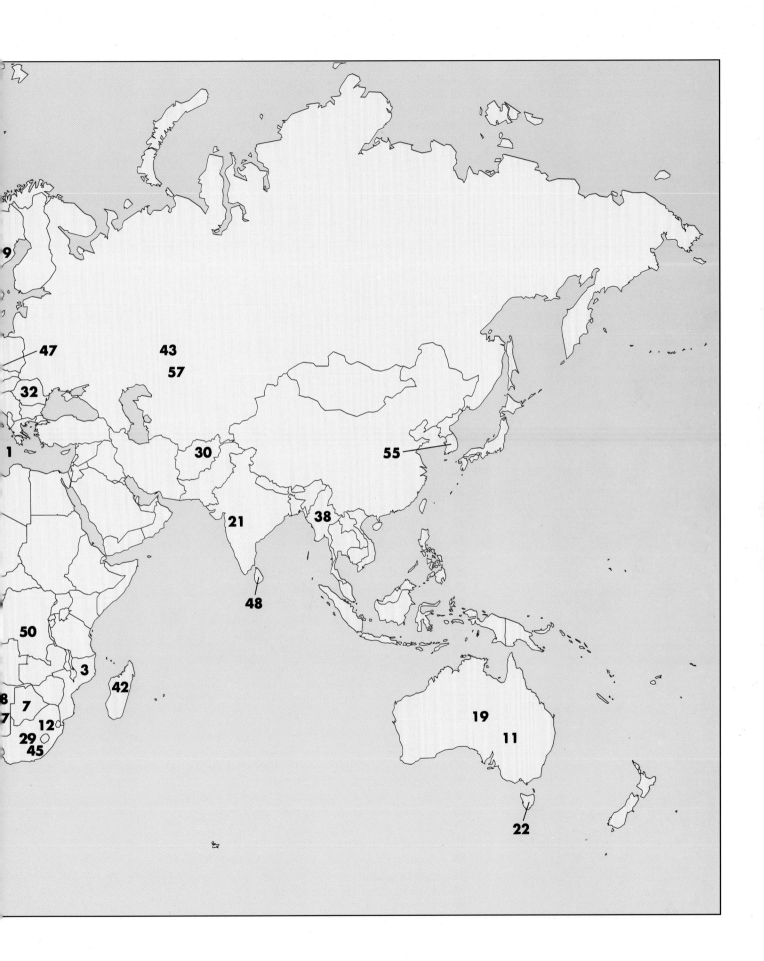

9

47
43
57
32
1
30
55
21
38
48
50
3
42
8
7
7
12
19
29
11
45
22

Key

1. Alexander County emerald and hiddenite veins, North Carolina
2. Almaden mercury mine, Rio Tinto District, Huelva Province, Spain
3. Alto Lingonha region pegmatites, Mozambique
4. Amelia Court House pegmatites, Virginia
5. Arendal and Kongsberg, Norway
6. Bancroft, Ontario
7. Bikita pegmatite, Zimbabwe
8. Bisbee, Tiger, Morenci, Ajo sulfide deposits, Arizona
9. Black Hills pegmatites, South Dakota
10. Boron, Death Valley, Searles Lake evaporites, California
11. Broken Hill, N.S.W.; Bendigo and Ballarat, Victoria, Australia
12. Bushveld complex, South Africa
13. Butte, Montana
14. Cave-in-Rock, Illinois; Joplin/Sweetwater districts, Missouri
15. Chanarcillo, Chuquicamata, and Copiapo, Chile
16. Chihuahua, Durango, San Luis Potosi, and Zacatecas sulfide veins, Mexico
17. Cobalt district, Ontario
18. Coeur d'Alene District, Idaho
19. Coober Pedy, Australia
20. Cornwall, Cumberland, Derbyshire, Devonshire, Durham mining areas, United Kingdom
21. Deccan basalt quarries, Poona, India
22. Dundas, Tasmania
23. Falun, Kiruna, and Långban, Sweden
24. Franklin and Sterling Hill, New Jersey
25. Harz Mountains and Saxony, Germany
26. Ivigtut pegmatite, Kalaallit Nunaat, Greenland
27. Karibib District pegmatites, Namibia
28. Keeweenaw Peninsula copper deposits, Michigan
29. Kimberly/Cullinan diamond mines, South Africa
30. Laghman Province pegmatites, Afghanistan
31. Laurium, Greece
32. Libethen, Felsobanya, and Nagyag, Romania
33. Llallagua and Potosi, Bolivia
34. Magnet Cove, Arkansas
35. Mangualde pegmatites, Portugal
36. Mibladen, Bou Azzer, Morocco
37. Minas Gerais pegmatites, Brazil
38. Mogok gem mines and Upper Burma jadite deposits, Burma
39. Mont St. Hilare, Jeffry Mines, Quebec, Canada
40. Mother Lode gold-quartz veins, California
41. Mt. Apatite, Mt. Mica, and other Maine pegmatites
42. Mt. Bity and Anjanabonoina pegmatite districts, Malagasy Republic
43. Mursinka and Nurchinsk pegmatites, U.S.S.R.
44. Muzo and Chivor, Colombia
45. Palabora carbonatite, South Africa
46. Panasquiera, Portugal
47. Pribram, Schemnitz, Zinnwald mining districts, Czechoslovakia
48. Ratnapura gem mines, Sri Lanka
49. San Diego County pegmatite districts, California
50. Shinkolobwe, Katanga province, Zaire
51. Sicilian sulfur mines, Italy
52. Soledade, Rio Grande do Sul, Brazil
53. Strontian, Leadhills and Wanlocklhead, Scotland
54. Sudbury, Ontario
55. Taewha tungsten mines, Korea
56. Tintic district, Utah
57. Tokovaya Mines, Sverdlovsk, U.S.S.R.
58. Tsumeb and Grootfontien, Otavi District, Namibia
59. Ytterby and Varutrask pegmatites, Sweden

			Million years ago
CENOZOIC	QUA-TERNARY	RECENT	
		PLEISTOCENE	0.01
		PLIOCENE	2
	TERTIARY	MIOCENE	7
		OLIGOCENE	26
		EOCENE	37
		PALEOCENE	53
			65
MESOZOIC		CRETACEOUS	136
		JURASSIC	190
		TRIASSIC	225
PALEOZOIC		PERMIAN	280
		CARBONIFEROUS	345
		DEVONIAN	395
		SILURIAN	430
		ORDOVICIAN	500
		CAMBRIAN	570
PRECAMBRIAN		PROTEROZOIC	2300
			2800
		ARCHEOZOIC	4600
			4700

TIME PERIODS

Bibliography

Gemstones

Arem, Joel E. *Color Encyclopedia of Gemstones*, Second Edition. New York, NY: Van Nostrand Reinhold, 1987. The best comprehensive guide to gems.

Bruton, Eric. *Diamonds*. Second Edition. Radnor, PA: Chilton, 1978. The last word on diamonds.

Desautels, Paul. *The Jade Kingdom*. New York, NY: Van Nostrand Reinhold, 1986. The complete story of jade in both the Far East and Mesoamerica.

Dietrich, R.V. *The Tourmaline Group*. New York, NY: Van Nostrand Reinhold, 1985. Excellent overview of this complex and fascinating mineral family.

Liddicoat, Richard T. *Handbook of Gem Identification*. Santa Monica, CA: Gemological Institute of America. An indispensable guide for the serious gem collector.

Sinkankas, John. *Gemstones of North America*, Volumes I and II. New York, NY: Van Nostrand Reinhold, 1959, 1976. Exhaustive study of virtually every occurrence of every kind of gem species on the continent.

Sinkankas, John. *Emerald and Other Beryls*. Radnor, PA: Chilton, 1981. All you ever wanted to know about the mineralogy, gemology, geology and lore of the beryls. The *magnum opus* of this prolific and dedicated author.

Mineralogy

Deer, W.A., Howie, R. A., and Zussman, J. *An Introduction to the Rock-Forming Minerals*. Harlow, Essex: Longman, 1966. Condensed version of the classic technical work covering all of the most geologically-important minerals.

Hurlbut, Cornelius S., Jr., and Klein, Cornelius. *Manual of Mineralogy*. 20th Edition. New York, NY: Wiley, 1977. The most well-written and comprehensive of all general textbooks on mineralogy, updated and expanded from James Dana's classic *System of Mineralogy*.

Roberts, W.L., Campbell, T. J., and Rapp, G. R., Jr. *Encyclopedia of Minerals*. New York: Van Nostrand Reinhold, 1990. The most comprehensive compendium of mineral data available, with entries covering over 3200 mineral species.

Sinkankas, John. *Mineralogy for Amateurs*. New York: Van Nostrand Reinhold, 1964. A classic, very accessible and well-illustrated introduction to the study of minerals.

Sorrell, Charles A. *Rocks and Minerals*. New York: Golden Press, 1973. An excellent introduction to minerals, especially for young people, with colorful and accurate illustrations by George Sandström.

Geology

Best, Myron G. *Igneous and Metamorphic Petrology*. W.H. Freeman and Company, 1982. Best general textbook on the origins and relationships of igneous and metamorphic rocks.

Press, Frank, and Siever, Raymond. *Earth*. Fourth Edition. New York: W.H. Freeman and Company, 1986. Excellent, accessible introduction to all aspects of geology, widely used in introductory geology courses.

Parker, Sybil P., Editor. *McGraw-Hill Encyclopedia of the Geological Sciences*. Second Edition. New York: McGraw-Hill Book Company, 1988. Excellent desk reference on all aspects of geology.

History and Lore

Bancroft, Peter. *Gem and Crystal Treasures.* Tucson, AZ: Western Enterprises/Mineralogical Record, 1984. A unique worldwide guide to famous mines and mineral deposits, chock full of historical anecdotes and other trivia.

Kunz, George F. The Curious Lore of Precious Stones. New York, NY: Dover, 1971 (Originally published in 1913). An erudite and often humorous treatment of the religious, symbolic and therapeutic uses of gemstones down the ages.

Magnus, Albertus. *Book of Minerals* (translated by Dorothy Wyckoff). Oxford: Oxford University Press, 1967. A fascinating compendium of medieval mineral and gemstone lore and superstition.

Mineral Uses

Hurlbut, Cornelius S., Jr. *Minerals and Man.* New York: Random House, 1969. Interesting popular treatment of minerals and their place in human culture.

Desautels, Paul. *The Mineral Kingdom.* New York: Grosset and Dunlap, 1968. Like the above, a popular study of the culturally-important minerals.

Cotterill, Rodney. *The Cambridge Guide to the Material World.* Cambridge University Press: Cambridge, 1985. A fascinating, rambling account of the origins and uses of metals, glasses, cements and nearly everything else.

Guidebooks

Chesterman, Charles W. *The Audubon Society Field Guide to North American Rocks and Minerals.* New York: Alfred A. Knopf, 1979. Handy, well-organized guide, useful for other continents as well.

Pough, Frederick H. *A Field Guide to Rocks and Minerals.* Fourth Edition. Boston: Houghton Mifflin Company, 1988. The classic field guide to minerals, hardcover.

Periodicals

The American Mineralogist. Mineralogical Society of America, 1707 L St., NW. Washington, D.C. 20036. Technical journal for professional mineralogists and deadly-serious amateurs.

Mineralogical Record. Post Office Box 783, Bowie, Maryland, 20715. Intelligent, well-illustrated journal bridging the gap between professional mineralogists and hobbyists.

Lapidary Journal. Post Office Box 2369, San Diego, California, 92138. The best of many periodicals for amateur lapidaries and mineral collectors.

Index

Figure Credits